Outing
Goethe
&
His Age

Outing Goethe
&
His Age

Edited by Alice A. Kuzniar

Stanford University Press, Stanford, California 1996

Stanford University Press, Stanford, California
© 1996 by the Board of Trustees of the Leland Stanford Junior University
Printed in the United States of America

CIP data are at the end of the book.

Stanford University Press publications are distributed exclusively by
Stanford University Press within the United States, Canada, Mexico,
and Central America; they are distributed exclusively by
Cambridge University Press throughout the rest of the world.

Acknowledgments

This collection, from its incipience, has been a rewarding joint effort. For their generous, constant advice and encouragement, I want to thank in particular Roman Graf, Simon Richter, Stephan Schindler, and Bob Tobin — the four speakers at the 1992 MLA session that gave rise to this volume. In every way — from the assembling of contributors to lengthy, invaluable comments on my introduction — they have made my task a pleasurable one and the very existence of this book possible. I also want to thank Liliane Weissberg, who urged me to turn the MLA panel into a book, as well as David Clark, Jonathan Hess, Isabel Hull, and Dan Wilson, for their contributions to the introduction. Rosemary Hoag charitably offered her time to compile the final list of works cited, and both she and Margaret Polo have been generous in sharing computer facilities with me. I am extremely grateful for the comments from the anonymous reader at Stanford University Press and to the humanities editor, Helen Tartar, for her enthusiastic, speedy reception of this volume.

Contents

Contributors

ROMAN GRAF is Assistant Professor of German at Middlebury College. He is completing a book-length gay reading of Jakob Michael Reinhold Lenz and has investigated the queerness of Kaspar Hauser and Stifter's *Brigitta*.

SUSAN E. GUSTAFSON is Associate Professor of German and Comparative Literature at the University of Rochester. She is the author of *Absent Mothers and Orphaned Fathers: Narcissism and Abjection in Lessing's Aesthetic and Dramatic Production* (Wayne State University Press, 1995).

MARTHA B. HELFER is Assistant Professor of German at the University of Utah. Her forthcoming book from SUNY Press is entitled *The Retreat of Representation: The Concept of "Darstellung" in German Critical Discourse.*

SUSANNE T. KORD is Assistant Professor of German at Georgetown University and author of *Ein Blick hinter die Kulissen: Deutschsprachige Dramatikerinnen im 18. und 19. Jahrhundert* (1992). Current projects include a book on women's anonymity and authorship between 1700 and 1900.

ALICE A. KUZNIAR is Associate Professor of German and Comparative Literature at the University of North Carolina, Chapel Hill. Her book *Delayed Endings: Nonclosure in Novalis and Hölderlin* (University of Georgia Press, 1987) won the South Atlantic Modern Language Association Award.

CATRIONA MACLEOD is Assistant Professor of German at Yale University and author of the forthcoming book from Wayne State University Press *Embodying Ambiguity: Androgyny and Aesthetics from Winckelmann to Keller.*

JOACHIM PFEIFFER teaches at the Universität Eichstätt in Germany, where he is completing his *Habilitationsschrift*, entitled *Der Tod in der literarischen Moderne*. His publications include *Die zerbrochenen Bilder. Gestörte Ordnungen im Werk Heinrich von Kleists, Literaturpsychologie 1945–1987. Eine systematische und annotierte Bibliographie*, and an essay on AIDS in German literature.

SIMON RICHTER, Assistant Professor at the University of Maryland, has written *Laocoon's Body and the Aesthetics of Pain: Winckelmann, Lessing, Herder, Moritz, Goethe* (Wayne State University Press, 1992) in addition to numerous articles on erotics from Winckelmann to Eichendorff.

LAURENCE A. RICKELS, who holds graduate degrees in Clinical Psychology and German Literature and teaches at the University of California, Santa Barbara, is author of *Aberrations of Mourning: Writing on German Crypts, Der unbetrauerbare Tod*, and *The Case of California*, and editor of *Looking After Nietzsche* and Gottfried Keller's *Jugenddramen*. Two new books, *Nazi Psychoanalysis* and *The Vampire Letters*, are forthcoming.

STEPHAN K. SCHINDLER is Assistant Professor of German at Washington University, St. Louis. His publications include *Das Subjekt als Kind. Die Erfindung der Kindheit im Roman des 18. Jahrhunderts* (1994) and articles on postmodernism, cultural anthropology, and GDR literature.

ROBERT D. TOBIN, Associate Professor of German at Whitman College in Walla Walla, Washington, has written a number of essays on sexuality and medicine in the writings of Goethe and Thomas Mann. He has just completed *Doctor's Orders: Medicine in Goethe's 'Wilhelm Meister'* and is currently working on a series of queer readings of German writers, beginning with Lichtenberg and Jean Paul.

W. DANIEL WILSON is Professor of German at the University of California at Berkeley. He has published several books, most recently *Geheimräte gegen Geheimbünde. Ein unbekanntes Kapitel der klassisch-romantischen Geschichte Weimars* (1991) and *Impure Reason: Dialectic of Enlightenment in Germany* (edited with Robert C. Holub, 1993).

Abbreviations

Outing
Goethe
&
His Age

Alice A. Kuzniar

Introduction

Nowadays the terms "to out" and "to come out" are fighting words used to defy a straight culture that would curb alternative sexualities to its perceived norm. Outing a celebrity, revealing his or her homosexuality to the media, flagrantly exhibits not only details about an individual's personal life but also the societal assumptions about sexual preference that have allowed and abetted idolization: outing takes sardonic revenge on the sexual status quo. Similarly, when gays and lesbians come out of the closet to claim entry into society, they force it to challenge its presuppositions regarding gender.

But working against the agonistic, dualistic premise that governs current gay usage of the word "out" is the performative, transitional, processual aspect to outing and coming out or, as Shane Phelan puts it, "becoming out." She writes: "That stability [of what it means to be lesbian or gay] is not given by discovery of deep truth; one realizes one is lesbian or gay by participating in particular historical communities and discourses. Coming out is partially a process of revealing something kept hidden, but it is more than that. It is a process of fashioning a self—a lesbian or gay self—that did not exist before coming out began" (774). The dichotomies in/out, straight/gay, and heterosexual/homosexual, as Eve Sedgwick has shown in *Epistemology of the Closet*, operate on the premise that we know what the opposite terms signify in relation to each other; their very duality lends them a deceptive clarity. But if the boundary dividing these terms blurs, if coming out is seen to be a continual process, an ongoing discussion with one's family and ever changing circle of friends, acquaintances, and colleagues, then the finality and certainty of what it means to be "out" dissipates. In a reverse process, the outed movie actor continues to perform his straight (screen) act, which for his fans must rather queerly merge with what they consider to be reality. Gendered identities, in other words, cling to the past while evolving in the present; constantly developing, they repeatedly negotiate the gap between one's self-perception and one's self as others see it. They are not just situationally but also historically contingent. Gender affiliations and sexual desires are therefore never totally predictable and never really fathomable to oneself, let alone to others. One cannot definitively map out the trajectory they (will) follow.

The finality or resolution that the word "out" suggests (outcome, school's out) can thus be countered by another signification: that of going beyond the limits and scope of conventional positions (a reaching out, a branching out). It is this resonance to the word "out" that the present volume explores. In "outing" certain authors of the "Age of Goethe" we do not pretend to outdo Goethe scholarship by claiming suddenly to know something previously hidden but now exposed and conclusive. In fact, by calling into question binary sexual oppositions, homosexuality disrupts the place from which we speak and know. This investigation of late-eighteenth- and early-nineteenth-century same-sex relationships instead is intended to bring out and into circulation gender-transitive readings of canonical texts as well as texts by marginalized authors. Like "becoming out," this endeavor is conceived as a processual, negotiated one. We want to raise rather than resolve certain questions, following Sedgwick's admonition that "no one *can* know *in advance* where the limits of a gay-centered inquiry are to be drawn, or where a gay theorizing of and through even the hegemonic high culture of the Euro-American tradition may need or be able to lead" (*Epistemology* 53).

Among the questions to be addressed are: How does one read (for) homosexuality in an age of increasing gender polarity — specifically, at a time when the bourgeois marriage contract promises individual fulfillment through love and emotional attachment? In this new societal context, what does it mean to fall in love with someone of one's own sex? What codes and genres does the often hidden discourse of same-sex attraction assume? What does the censoring of homosexuality reveal about the hegemonic discourses on sexuality and nature? In its blurring of the line between the genders, does homosexuality destabilize normal sexuality or does it serve as the nonnormative by which heterosexuality defines itself? As the contributors to this volume show, homosexuality forms a division around which eighteenth- and early-nineteenth-century culture organizes itself. The topic informs the larger issues of pedagogy, the cult of friendship, the socialization of the subject, the regulation of sexuality in the bourgeois family, and the subjugation and representation of the body and its pleasures. Having been exhaustively examined in light of heterosexual desire as well as exposed to desexualized readings, such canonical texts as Goethe's *Faust*, Schlegel's *Lucinde*, and Kleist's letters beg to be read for their queerness or oddity of passion, which often involves not just a faint but an arduous homoeroticism that merges with the sexual.

Given the provocative title of this collection, however, we need briefly to ventriloquize and ask what it would mean to out Goethe — in other words, to know or assume that he were gay. What would it mean if he had sexual intercourse with men or if he fantasized about same-sex relations? Or if, for the most part, he repressed these fantasies? Would we then conclude that Goethe was bisexual? Would certain biographically "revelatory" poems from the *Roman Elegies* (*Römische Elegien*) constitute evidence or proof (see Gilman, "Goethe's Touch")? How would his sexuality change the appraisal of his works? Apart from the anachronism of applying such terms as "gay," "homosexual," "bisexual," or "out" to the late eighteenth century (see following discussion) and the bracketing of the metaphoricity of literature from consideration, the egregious error in such questioning lies with its pseudo-psychologizing and presumptiveness. To declare someone as "gay," especially when he is not "out," endows the speaker with the self-congratulatory privilege of knowing what this other person is presumed to be repressing or what a third party can't see or isn't privy to.

The contributions to this volume, I believe, refrain from indulging in such superciliousness, either toward the authors being discussed or toward other critics. Their claim is not to expose the sexual secret of certain authors and then to flaunt it. They do not pretend to benefit from — and here I'm being ironic — belonging to a later, more enlightened culture that would presume to know what homosexuality really is. If anything, these essays bring a certain modesty and respect to bear on sexualities necessarily different from our own, a spectrum that cannot be easily mapped onto contemporary categories.

If coming out involves a constant dialogue that entails a sustained reading of the situation, of how to (re)present oneself, then in our examination of homosexuality around 1800 the burden lies with the reader: decoding for desire is a constant process in which we must repeatedly question gender assumptions. In other words, the various homosexualities the essays in this volume explore help defamiliarize and denaturalize the present from which we speak. Rather than current notions of sexuality informing our reading of these earlier texts, the inverse occurs. If we do not recognize ourselves in the homosexuality available to writers around 1800, then perhaps our potentially straitjacketing notions regarding gay identity might be unsettled and we can begin to conceptualize alternative forms of masculine or feminine self-identification, following Foucault's injunction that we use (homo)sexuality to imagine diverse interpersonal affiliations:

We must be aware of . . . the tendency to reduce being gay to the questions: "Who am I?" and "What is the secret of my desire?" Might it not be better if we asked ourselves what sort of relationships we can set up, invent, multiply or modify through our homosexuality? The problem is not trying to find out the truth of one's sexuality within oneself, but rather, nowadays, trying to use our sexuality to achieve a variety of different types of relationships. (Quoted in Cohen 88)

I

Terminological or taxonomic correctness is nonetheless a major concern of this volume, precisely because, as Foucault points out, sexualities evolve over time.[1] As has been repeatedly emphasized in historical studies of same-sex relations, the term "homosexuality" itself was coined at the late date of 1871 in Carl Westphal's "Contrary Sexual Feeling" ("Die conträre Sexualempfindung") (other sources cite an 1869 publication by the physician and writer Karoly Maria Kertbeny-Benkert). What has not so emphatically been noted is that the discourse on homosexuality arose and continued for twenty years exclusively in a German context (which leads one to speculate about the cultural legacy enabling this discourse), for the term was then popularized by the sexologists Karl Heinrich Ulrichs, Johann Ludwig Casper, Richard von Krafft-Ebing, Albert Moll, and Magnus Hirschfeld and not imported into the English language until the translation in the 1890s of Krafft-Ebing's *Psychopathia Sexualis*. It is noteworthy that only after the word "homosexuality" was coined did the expression "heterosexuality" enter psychological/ psychoanalytic discourse. Like its sister labels "autoeroticism" and "nymphomania," also coined in the late nineteenth century, the concept of homosexuality arose to signify a pathology, a medical association that explains the gay community's abandonment of the term for self-designation.

In a frequently cited passage from the *History of Sexuality*, Foucault explains the epistemological break signaled by the neologism, contrasting it with the term "sodomy":

As defined by the ancient civil or canonical codes, sodomy was a category of forbidden acts; their perpetrator was nothing more than the juridical subject of them. The nineteenth-century homosexual became a personage, a past, a case history, and a childhood, in addition to being a type of lie, a life form, and a morphology, with an indiscreet anatomy and possibly a mysterious physiology. . . . Homosexuality appeared as one of the forms of sexuality when it was transposed from the practice of sodomy onto a kind of interior androgyny, a hermaphrodism of the soul. The sodomite had been a temporary aberration; the homosexual was now a species. (1:43)

According to Foucault, homosexuality presupposes sexuality, that is to say, a realm that infuses and informs the identity of a person — his or her childhood, emotions, innate disposition, personality, as well as biology and physiology. (Homo)sexuality as a dimension around which an entire life is organized and as a distinguishing mark between individuals did not exist per se prior to the end of the nineteenth century. In fact, as Jeffrey Weeks has pointed out with regard to premodern Western culture, "It seems likely that homosexuality was regarded not as a particular attribute of a certain type of person but as a potential in all sensual creatures" (*Sex* 99).

In recent years much work has been devoted to laying out how all-male or all-female sexual relations were circumscribed, categorized, accepted, or stigmatized prior to 1870. What these studies share is the recognition, as Weeks puts it, that "sexual meanings and identities are historical constructs. A human identity is not a given in any particular historical situation but is the product of different social interactions, of the play of power, and sometimes of random choices. The homosexual orientation may be strong, but its significance depends on a host of factors that change over time" ("Inverts" 128). In this essay I shall concentrate on the scholarship regarding same-sex relations in the eighteenth century, using the term "homosexuality" guardedly to refer to these relations, mindful of the historic difference, and hoping that it is at least less anachronistically provocative and hence jarring than the word "gay." More important, I want to argue that Foucault's choice of "sodomy" to characterize pre-1870 same-sex relations is far too limiting, with the result that the very label has restricted not only the nature of texts he and others have chosen to investigate but also what they have discerned in them.

Around 1700 the terms "sodomy" and "buggery" did not designate only sexual offenses between men but also referred to diverse forms of anatomical penetration between women and beasts. Among the multitude of activities covered by this "crime against nature" was another fact of nonprocreative sex, namely, birth control. The category indeed encompassed a broad range of sins: " 'Sodomite' was an extreme and opprobrious form of condemnation designating religious blasphemy, political sedition, and even satanic activities including demonism, shamanism, and witchcraft" (G. S. Rousseau, "Pursuit" 136). Over the course of the eighteenth century, however, the definition narrowed: the "sodomite became an individual interested exclusively in his own gender" (Trumbach, "Sodomitical Subcultures" 118).

Trumbach attributes this major shift in signification to a reorganization of gender identity. Previously a debauchee or libertine might be called effeminate because of spending excessive time in the company of women. He could indiscriminately seek out boys as well, but this difference did not influence the application of the word "effeminate" to signify profligacy. As the eighteenth century progressed, however, sexual interest, whether in women or other men, became a marker for gender difference: "Most men conceived first of all that they were male, because they felt attraction to women, and to women alone. Gender differences were presumed therefore to be founded on an ineradicable difference of experience: men did not know what it was like to desire men, and women did not desire women. . . . A man interested in women never risked becoming effeminate as he had once done, since there was never a chance that he might passively submit to another male" ("Sodomitical Subcultures" 118). Trumbach's conclusion is extremely suggestive in its implications for how masculinity constructs itself in contradistinction to its implied opposite and, specifically, for how the changing definition of sodomy founds modern gender distinctions that adhere to this day.

I shall return to this epistemic shift in gender definition shortly, but the question that Trumbach does not address and yet concerns us here is whether homosexual practice at the close of the eighteenth century is sufficiently subsumed under the category of the sodomite as a man who engages in forbidden sexual acts with other men but who is not perceived to have a distinctive gender identity built around sexual preference. In other words, if being a man who desires women became a means of defining one's masculinity, did homosexual orientation likewise begin to define one's gendered or sexualized state of being? To answer this question we need to address how during this period in Germany the category of the sodomitical intersects with a barrage of other concepts — the pederastic, homoerotic, homosocial, homoplatonic, and so on. The interfacing of these categories might then permit one to discern the makings of a combined personal and social identity that is affiliated with sexual orientation.

Sodomiterey was not the only word current in eighteenth-century Germany to refer to sexual activity between men. As Paul Derks has so amply noted in his compilation of references to male homosexuality in German literature between 1750 and 1850, other terms include *florenzen* (like sodomy, associated with a foreign city), *Päderastie* (which encompassed all male homosexuality, not just intercourse with boys), and Socratic or Greek love. Platonic love did not have the exclusive meaning of asexual love, as it does today, but was also, like Socratic love, a code word for homosexuality, an ambivalence on which Heinrich Heine plays in his famous poem about tea-party chitchat:

> Love must be strictly Platonic,
> The emaciated Councilor cried.
> His spouse smiled slightly ironic,
> And murmured, Oh dear me! and sighed.

Die Liebe muss sein platonisch,
Der dürre Hofrat sprach.
Die Hofrätin lächelt ironisch,
Und dennoch seufzet sie: Ach! (6–7)

A uniquely German expression for homosexuals still current today is *warme Brüder* (warm brothers), references to which Derks
uncovers in writings from Hamann and Herder to Heine. He conjectures that its source lay in Berlin homosexual circles that presumably
sprung up during the urban growth the city witnessed in the late
eighteenth century. The association of this phrase with such clubs is
recorded in the *Letters on the Gallantries of Berlin* (*Briefe über die
Galanterien von Berlin*, 1782), an anonymously composed piece
now attributed to Johann Friedel, "an author and Jacobin social
critic of some note" (Steakley 169). In these letters a visitor to a
Berlin gathering queries his host about the unusual displays of tenderness he sees between men and receives the following response:

"Oh, you mustn't be surprised. These seven gentlemen are warm brothers."
— Warm brothers? What's that? — "You don't know anything about that,
and already four months in Berlin, that surprises me! I'll have to give you a
small description of it. You must have read something about Socratic love?"
(Quoted in Steakley 169)

This passage seems to indicate that homosexual practices must
have been prevalent enough in Berlin that one could not escape
noticing them. For the sake of reclaiming a gay past, it would be
tempting to regard this text as evidence of an active subculture and
the liberality of the reign of Frederick the Great, himself deemed to
have directed his erotic impulses toward men (Steakley 165–68).
Steakley in fact sees "the emergence of a visible homosexual minor-
ity in Berlin" (170), signaled in these letters, as leading up to changes
in the penal code: sodomy laws had relaxed to the extent that the
1532 Carolinian law demanding the death penalty was revoked in
1794 in Prussia (1787 in Austria), following three decades of debate
regarding whether vices should be criminally prosecuted (see Derks
140–73). Apart from seduction of minors and public display, sodomy laws were then abolished under Napoleonic rule. Still, it would
be wrong to read these positive signs as tokens of a flourishing,
permitted homosexual culture in Germany, even in Berlin. Unlike
Steakley, Derks doubts the documentary veracity of the *Letters*,

reading them instead as a literary farce. He also warns us of the actual difficulty one had in finding a pickup or partner in Germany around 1800, when homosexuality was not discursively encoded by immediately identifiable gestures, code words, or meeting places. Trial and error, he suggests, was likely the only way of approaching someone (106). There may have been an underground culture where male prostitutes were available; it was still unthinkable, however, that a homosexually inclined man could encounter a like-minded social equal, even in the more tolerant intellectual circles that discussed Socratic love. Derks (107) illustrates his point with reference to the poet August von Platen (vilified by Heine for his sexual preferences), who probably never got to know another homosexual outside of his experiences in the very different culture of Italy.

It was Italy, though, that was the adopted home for an important luminary of the eighteenth century and one essential to the writing of a gay archaeology, Johann Joachim Winckelmann. In his essay "The Pursuit of Homosexuality in the Eighteenth Century: 'Utterly Confused Category' and/or Rich Repository?" G. S. Rousseau tries to sort out the confusion surrounding the catchall term "sodomy" by sketching six categories that he hopes will help organize and focus future research.[2] One of these groupings is "the Teutonic tradition and its creation of a German myth based on the physical superiority and extraordinary self-sufficiency of the white-skinned, blue-eyed, blond-haired, Aryan male" (139), a category that encompasses German writers from Johann Winckelmann to Thomas Mann. However helpful Rousseau's essay might be in opening new terrains for investigation, this one category is, to my mind, irresponsible for its implication of numerous homosexual German writers as forerunners of Nazism. For the wrong reasons Rousseau is right, though, in starting with Winckelmann, for it is with him that eighteenth-century homosexuality begins decisively to accrue meaning beyond that which Foucault ascribes to it and which he capsulates in the term "sodomy," only to find it not surprisingly an "utterly confused category" (*History* 1:101).

II

Born into abject poverty in the city of Stendal in northern Germany, Winckelmann rose to illustrious heights as the papal prefect of antiquities, librarian to the art-collecting Cardinal Albani, and author of the extraordinarily influential *Reflections Concerning the Imitation of the Greeks* (*Gedancken über die Nachahmung der Griechischen Werke*, 1755) and *History of Ancient Art* (*Geschichte der Kunst des Alterthums*, 1763). He met a bloody, possibly sexually motivated death in Trieste, murdered by a cook by the name of Arcangeli under circumstances that have never been clarified. Winckelmann's attraction to handsome young men (among whom, incidentally, the 38-year-old pockmarked Arcangeli cannot be counted) has been variously documented. In his *Winckelmann and His Century* (*Winckelmann und sein Jahrhundert*), for instance, Goethe wrote: "Thus we often find Winckelmann together with beautiful youths, and never does he appear more animated and gracious than in such, often merely fleeting, moments" (*WA* 46:30). Indeed, as revealed in passionate letters, Winckelmann maintained long-lasting friendships with his protégés, most notably Peter Friedrich Wilhelm Lamprecht and Friedrich Reinhold von Berg (see Sweet 151–54; Richter and McGrath). That this interest was not solely pedagogical has been suggested by Giacomo Casanova, who, in memoirs published after Winckelmann's death, mentions having once walked unannounced into Winckelmann's room, only to catch him with a handsome young man in the act (197–98).

One can debate the factual truth of Casanova's report as well as question whether Goethe's observation harbored a similar intent to air, albeit more indirectly, Winckelmann's penchant for boys. But of interest is not so much what Winckelmann did in his private quarters or whether one can call him "homosexual," but that his contemporaries recognized and accepted his inclinations — to the extent that Goethe tacitly mentions this attraction without stigmatizing it.[3] Indeed, if in any way Winckelmann's sexual propensities effeminized him in the mind of his contemporaries or robbed him of his masculinity (as would have occurred if Winckelmann had lived 100 years later), Goethe certainly would not have written in 1805 that Winckelmann "lived as a man and departed from the world a perfect man [*als vollständiger Mann*]" (*WA* 46:69). It is thus less Winckelmann's life and sexual preference that concern us here than his reception by his contemporaries, who, far from ignoring or whitewashing the homoeroticism of his writings, openly alluded to it. Herder, for instance, compares Winckelmann's rapture over the

Apollo Belvedere to Petrarch's gazing into the eyes of his beloved Laura, thereby mapping heterosexual onto homosexual captivation in a reconfiguration that seems to put them on par with each other (1:56). It is even conceivable that the reverence and awe Winckelmann and his work commanded from the intellectuals of his day stem in part from the respect they had for someone who was not ashamed of his adulation of male youth — whether expressed in personal letters and published writings or even, if we are to believe Casanova, when he is caught having sex with an anonymous young man. Moreover, as Derks points out (192), his initial admirers — to a single one — did not try to distinguish between his life and work, an effort that would have marked the attempt to closet his sexuality and disassociate it from his aesthetics.

Winckelmann's vibrant descriptions of ancient art betray the sensual impact it left on him, as with this painting of a naked sixteen-year-old Ganymede: "I find nothing that can compare with this face; so much voluptuousness [*Wohllust*] blossoms forth from it that his whole life seems to be solely one kiss" (*SW* 5:138).[4] It is tempting to read Winckelmann with camp sensibility, so overt and clinically detailed are his depictions of eroticized body parts, from the full, feminine buttocks of a Bacchus to the contours of the nipples (see Parker 530) on a male torso. It was, however, the immediacy of these descriptions that Winckelmann's contemporaries lauded, for it allowed them to imagine bridging the centuries-wide span between the ancients' past and their present. Testifying to his personal involvement, Winckelmann himself said that one must be as familiar with these works of art as with a friend (*Kleine Schriften* 30). The arousal or communication of a sense of intimacy was contagious enough for Herder to confess that he devoured Winckelmann's writings like letters from a distant bride (8:441). Denis Sweet summarizes Winckelmann's unique power thus: "The man . . . was not an antiquarian in the usual eighteenth-century sense of a master of arcana, but someone who communicated to his European contemporaries an immediacy of art and a vision of antiquity. . . . There was no one else writing like this in Europe at the time" (158).

Hans Mayer, though, has detected a melancholic tinge to Winckelmann's love of the past: the historian of ancient art must have regretted that the social norms of ancient Greece were more accepting of male-male sexual relations than eighteenth-century Europe, a difference that forced him to stylize and idealize the Greeks. His work, according to Mayer, thus reproduced the divisions of a closeted way of life. The problem with this admittedly ingenious argument lies in its limiting or, as Sedgwick would say, minoritizing view of homosexuality, which strictly separates genital practice from homoeroticism or homoaesthetics and thus plays down the way in which sensuousness is by no means concealed but rather is exalted in Winckelmann's writings.[5] For it is precisely the infusion of homoeroticism into aesthetics that marks the moment in which Winckelmann is writing as significant, foreshadowing and perhaps even enabling the later articulation of an aestheticized gay identity in the work of Wilde or Mapplethorpe. Winckelmann inaugurated a cultured, hence permissible voicing of same-sex attraction. Even more strikingly, he facilitated, if you will, "The Birth of Aesthetics out of the Spirit of Homoeroticism" (see in this volume Richter and MacLeod).

The next chapter in this "Gay Geisteswissenschaft" calls for pushing the debate further and arguing in light of Winckelmann's work for a queer — in the sense not only of gay but also of unusual — reading of an Idealist philosophy of history. One of Kaja Silverman's psychoanalytic models of homosexuality here presents itself as a framework in which to reassess how the writers of this period inscribed themselves into the history of time and thereby carved a modern identity for themselves; again the issue Mayer broaches of Winckelmann's historicized consciousness of his relationship to the ancients resurfaces. Among Silverman's three Freudian paradigms of male homosexuality that reconfigurate the Oedipal triangle, it is the second, the "Greek" model, that applies here. At the base of this model is Freud's view, subsequently historically corroborated by Foucault and Halperin, that in ancient Greek society the boy, treated as a passive erotic object like the woman, would later graduate as a free citizen to being the desiring subject. Silverman outlines this model: "In youth one plays out one's feminine identification, and in maturity one's masculine identification. The adult subject might thus be said, in loving the youth, to love a femininity which was once his own, but which has become 'encrypted' or sealed up, to borrow a metaphor from Nicolas Abraham and Marie Torok." Further, "he not only looks to the boy for the image of what he once was, but for the image of what he presently is. He also loves the boy, in other words, for the masculinity to which the latter will eventually accede, a masculinity of which his penis is the proleptic signifier" (366). What makes the "Greek" model interesting is not whether it happens to fit Winckelmann's own character, although he was ostensibly attracted to a certain type of youth who resembled his beloved Greek statues. More significant are the implications for the history of philosophy and aesthetics of the period, namely, how the ontogenetic age gap between boy and adult male can be inscribed onto the phylogenetic spread between the ancients and the moderns. Thus not only does Winckelmann fall in love with the youth encrypted in the Greek statues, feminized particularly in the figures of Bacchus, but he also positions his own era and its aesthetics in terms of this earlier period. Through his revival of the past, Winckelmann offered his contemporaries an image of what they presently were — in other words, of the vibrancy of their own aesthetic discourse on beauty and grace, suffering and sublimity. Winckelmann's aesthetics thereby stages the identity-forming duality Silverman notes of wanting to associate with a past while distancing oneself from it.

As Peter Szondi has observed, Winckelmann oscillates throughout his writing between these two moments. Szondi argues that Winckelmann inaugurated the shift from a normative poetics to an aesthetics in the service of a philosophy of history: he sees Greek art not as a timeless model but in its historical context, whereby art is a manifestation of a culture that must be grasped in its singularity and the specificity of its age. Paradoxically, however, Winckelmann also advocates copying or imitating the Greeks, an aporia that only subsequently, in the writings of Schiller, Hölderlin, and Hegel, is reformulated as a dialectic. In light of Silverman's paradigm, it appears that, although Winckelmann himself does not map the sexual difference female (boy) versus male onto the epochal difference ancients versus moderns, his successors Schiller, Schlegel, and, above all, Hegel do in privileging the secondary term, encoding it as progressive, more resilient, and more mature (not "naive," to use Schiller's term). In a conclusion that bears some resemblance to Mayer's, Kevin Parker has suggestively explored the repressive implications of Winckelmann's consciously historical separation of the present from the past, which led him to aestheticize and idealize the carnal body. This act of estrangement, though, can be profitably contextualized in terms of the psychoanalytic model: in mourning the past,

Winckelmann incorporates it into the self to form the nucleus of a homosexual identity that finds its origin of identification in ancient Greece. Following Silverman's acknowledgment to Abraham and Torok, we can say that the palid marble sculptures are not so much the crypt of beauty as is Winckelmann's own corpus of aesthetics, which its author took as his expression of commitment and belief — in other words, of his own body's passions.

III

Winckelmann indeed reincarnated the past bodily: his contemporaries, identifying their hero with the ancients, called him "der heilige Winckelmann" after "der heilige Sokrates." In reference to Socrates, however, the adjective *heilig* — its use before a name designating a saint, as in "Holy Mary" — had already developed into an ironic, mildly sacrilegious code word for "pederastic" in the writings of Mendelssohn, Lichtenberg, Hamann, and Herder (Derks 57–78). The epitaph crops up again in *Lucinde*, where Friedrich Schlegel, pleading for the free and daring discourse of love found in the ancients, speaks of the Great Plato and Holy Sappho (*KA* 5:25). The very figure of Winckelmann thus advances a semantics surrounding Greek love that, as Schlegel's passage suggests, feeds into the related eighteenth-century discourses on friendship and love and ultimately modifies them.

With the background Winckelmann provides in mind, it is difficult to read mention of same-sex Greek friendships without noticing the homoeroticism that infuses them. Goethe, for instance, writes of the affectionate women friends Chloris and Thyia lying in each other's laps (*WA* 48:111). In Hölderlin's poem "Sokrates und Alcibiades," sensuality, as in Winckelmann, prompts the recognition or realization of beauty:

> "Holy Socrates, why always with deference
> Do you treat this young man? Don't you know greater things?
> Why so lovingly, raptly,
> As on gods, do you gaze on him?"

> Who the deepest has thought loves what is most alive,
> Wide experience may well turn to what's best in youth,
> And the wise in the end will
> Often bow to the beautiful. (*Poems and Fragments* 67)

"Warum huldigest du, heiliger Sokrates,
Diesem Jünglinge stets? kennest du Größers nicht?
Warum siehet mit Liebe,
Wie auf Götter, dein Aug' auf ihn?"

Wer das Tiefste gedacht, liebt das Lebendigste,
Hohe Jugend versteht, wer in die Welt geblikt,
Und es neigen die Weisen
Oft am Ende zu Schönem sich. (*Sämtliche Werke* 1:260)

Here, too, as with Winckelmann (see Richter and McGrath 50), one is invited to consider the possibility of homoeroticism grounding the concept of the beautiful, for Hölderlin a dynamic ideal that incarnates love itself and in contemplation of which the antinomies of life and spirit, intellect and intuition, are aesthetically united and resolved. Despite Diotima's embodiment of this ideal in *Hyperion*, as the example of Alcibiades shows, beauty and grace are not invariably associated with the feminine, as scholarship is wont to claim.[6] To push the argument further, one is tempted to trace a lineage from Winckelmann to Hölderlin of the homoerotically beautiful, a tradition running counter to the (post)-Kantian disinterested study of beauty, a model whose dominance perhaps explains why homoeroticism has been edited out of scholarship on German Classicism despite the period's strong identification with Greek antiquity.

The theme of erotic, ennobling Greek brotherhood also surfaces in other writings of the period. Herder, for instance, observes about ancient Greece: "Manly hearts were tied together in love and friendship, even unto death: the lover pursued the beloved with a kind of jealousy that was on the lookout for even the slightest imperfection, so that the beloved feared the eye of his lover as the purifying flame to the most secret inclinations of his soul" (14:116). Although Herder claims he is far from trying to dissimulate the Greek decay of morals, he also acknowledges that such friendship acts as an effective mechanism (*Triebfeder*) for the state (14:117). For Wilhelm von Humboldt, too, Greek love gives rise to experiencing the gamut of human emotions and inevitably leads to noble heights (*zum Edleren und Höheren* 2:50). Moving away from the specifically Greek context, Schiller planned to write a drama about the heroic amity between two Maltese knights, whose love, although of the purest beauty, could not be denied its sensual nature (*sinnlichen Charakter*) and symptoms of passionate love (*Geschlechtsliebe*).

Schiller, moreover, writes that in this play the love between/for/of men (*Männerliebe*) functions as a complete surrogate for the love of women (*Frauenliebe*) and indeed surpasses the latter in its effect (3:172–73).[7]

As these examples indicate, the eighteenth-century cult of friendship begs to be reassessed in the light of homosexuality, an area of research that is largely unexplored (Mauser and Becker-Cantarino, Rasch) but into which several of the essays in this volume make significant forays (especially those of Richter, Pfeiffer, and Kord). By ignoring the issue of homosexuality in eighteenth-century discussions on friendship, scholarship closets only itself in the dark, blind to such crucial tensions as how brotherhood, where virtue is all-important, becomes a vice or, as in Schiller's case, how fraternity invites jealousy. The cult of friendship is ripe with such paradoxes precisely because it claims to contain sexuality, yet by perpetuating the impossibility of intimate bonding it arouses desire even more. In addition, the entry of sexual attraction into the social discourse on friendship, as into the aesthetic discourse on beauty, is dangerous precisely because it can occur surreptitiously: the result is that its potential for the subversion of social norms is easily overlooked.

By now it is clear that in order for such tensions to be studied, homosexuality must be unhinged from a solely sexual definition: it cannot be conceptualized apart from homoeroticism, homoplatonism, homoaesthetics, and passionate friendship. Furthermore, Schiller's example illustrates that the discourse on same-sex desire is not restricted to evocation of ancient Greek culture. In mentioning the love of Greek youths in his plans, Schiller alluded to the specifically sexual nature of the knights' passion, using the term to describe a transhistorical form of love. If this widening, universalizing view of eighteenth-century Socratic or Platonic love leads to a confusion of categorization, the disorientation is at the very least productive for recognizing a plurality of sexual expression. Moreover and more important, the permeability of boundaries—as between friendship and sexual desire—caution against essentializing and dehistoricizing differences between homo- and heterosexuality.

IV

If Winckelmann by and large encountered acceptance of his homosexuality and Schiller conceptualized a play about same-sex love, at what point did overt male erotic friendships begin to face more pronounced stigmatization, and why? What forms do the increased (internal) editing, concealment, and silencing of homoerotic expression assume? A distinct sign that a radical shift had occurred can be observed in the case of the eminent Swiss historian Johannes Müller, whose known penchant for men was generally accepted until 1806, when it was almost universally condemned once he was perceived to have betrayed his country in his admiration for Napoleon (see Richter's opening article in this volume). What makes Müller's case so fascinating was that he was denounced not for "sodomy" — that is, for having committed a sexual crime — but for his entire moral posture. Here we have an example, perhaps the first of its kind in the modern period, of personality being assessed in terms of homosexuality, which is to say that homosexuality becomes imbricated in such other issues — as it is today — as moral virtue, social interaction, national defense, and patriotism. Prior to this scandal in 1806, however, Müller's passionate friendships with men were not seen to rob him of his manly virtue; on the contrary, Caroline Schlegel, reviewing his letters to his friend Karl Victor von Bonstetten for the *Athenäum*, observed that these epistles are like true love letters: "Although the grown man may smile over the warmth [an allusion to "warm brothers"?] of his younger days," she writes, "he only becomes a man by following this path" (*Athenäum* 2:316).

Although it is difficult to enumerate exhaustively all the reasons for the epistemic shift to which Müller fell prey, one salient cause can be isolated in the changing views of gender and sexuality the turn of the century witnessed. In his book *Making Sex*, Thomas Laqueur has fascinatingly described the movement in the eighteenth century away from a one-sexed to a two-sexed model of the human reproductive system. New biological discoveries revealed that women's reproductive physiology differed substantially from men's, meaning that the former was seen not merely as the latter's invisible inversion (such that "the vagina is imagined as an interior penis, the labia as foreskin, the uterus as scrotum, and the ovaries as testicles"; 4). Whereas previously, all experience to the contrary, it was thought that women could conceive only upon having orgasm (following the male standard), a tremendous amount of literature now speculated on women's imputedly passive and passionless nature. Woman was indeed so passive that she resembled immobile vegetation: Friedrich Schlegel commented that one measures a woman's charm not by her beauty but by her "vegetability" (*Literary Notebooks* 152 #1487). Novalis similarly compares women to plants (2:812, 2:487 #81) and has the hero of his novel *Heinrich von Ofterdingen* fall in love with a flower. As these examples suggest, the "new model of radical dimorphism, of biological divergence" (Laqueur 6) did not only pertain to matters sexual, but stipulated thorough gender segregation in the arenas of social, cultural, and even economic construction as well: women were so passive they were unfit for work outside the home. In all respects, then, men were considered to be male and incommensurably different from women: "Not only are the sexes different, but they are different in every conceivable aspect of body and soul, in every physical and moral aspect" (Laqueur 5).

Given this scenario of increasingly reified gender differentials, it is not surprising that the crossing over or merging of gender opposites would be unsettling and ever rarer. Conceivably, homosexuality is maligned, as in the case of Müller, precisely because of its threat to stable, socially constructed gendered identities. Once stigmatized, moreover, homosexuality, like femininity, can be co-opted into defining what masculinity is not; thus homophobia and misogyny converge (see in this volume Graf, Wilson, and Gustafson).

The essentializing of biological difference that Laqueur descries did meet with skepticism, though, in the form of oddly gendered characters in Romantic tales. Just as the Romantics' stories of *Doppelgänger* and madmen illustrate how insecure the identity of the self-positing ego was and how epistemologically unreliable one's own senses were, so too did they experiment with queer gender — and in works that by now have become canonical (meaning their gender dissonance is usually overlooked). Frequently, these characters materialize in a dreamlike world, as if to suggest the psyche's resistance to mechanical gender binaries. Christian in Ludwig Tieck's "The Runenberg" ("Der Runenberg") cannot determine the sex of a figure who approaches him, whereas in his tale "The Blond Eckbert" ("Der blonde Eckbert") the characters Walther, Hugo, and the old hag collapse into one and the same character. One's *Doppelgänger* can belong to the opposite sex and even be composed of one's own body parts, as in E. T. A. Hoffmann's "The Sandman" ("Der Sandmann"). Achim von Arnim's and Joseph Eichendorff's characters frequently cross-dress and are mistaken for the opposite sex. And in Schlegel's *Lucinde*, Julius and his partner reverse gender positions during sex, so that the reader wonders: If a woman makes love to a man as if she were a man, are they then not both men — or women? Such examples promise to provide exciting ground for future research.

The Romantics' play with gender confusion appears that much more daring when one considers the new social function of the marriage vow, a contract that rewrote the cult of friendship in terms of the gender dyad Laqueur describes. At the end of the eighteenth century, marriage was entered by choice and in the name of love. As Jutta Greis has documented, late-eighteenth-century bourgeois drama developed a new social discourse on love that soon gained widespread cultural application (176): through the person of one's lover/spouse, one expected to discover the profundity of one's being, what is proper to it and gives it its truth. In other words, it was through the intimate sphere of the bourgeois marriage that one's individuality was to be found: love was an unduplicatable experience that insured one's uniqueness and enabled the unfolding of emotional depths. As Greis observes (177), the reterritorialization of divine love as human love endowed this new discourse of love with the promise of meaning and happiness.[8] Given the strength of this new paradigm of marriage — compulsory no longer because arranged but because regarded as existentially vital — is it even conceivable that one could fall in love with someone of the same sex? Clearly, if one were to become enamored of one's own sex, the results could be explosive — all the more reason, then, to contain, hide, or eradicate the attraction. Goethe thus attributes same-sex fascination to transitory, youthful infatuation and, as Robert Tobin argues in this volume, regards it solely as a supplement, albeit an indispensable one, to heterosexual love. Such passion, by contrast, erupts in Kleist but, as Joachim Pfeiffer here argues, must be read alongside Kleist's other attempts to undo stable identity positions. Unlike in friendship, where homosexuality operates from within the discourse, in love it stands on the outside, where its marginalized position is visible and threatening.

This opposition between love and friendship, however, easily deconstructs. Insofar as friendship was held up as an ideal to the marriage contract, so too could male homosexual bonding serve as an inspiration to heterosexual couples. Bettina Brentano quotes Müller's letters to Bonstetten when writing to her future husband,

Achim von Arnim: "You are myself more than I myself am, and what are you not, since you are my only friend?" (quoted in Derks 338). Writing in 1808, after the Müller scandal broke, Bettina received a defensive, harsh response from Achim, who must have felt threatened by the comparison of his relationship to Müller's *Freundschaftsgeschichten* (which can be translated as tales — but more derogatorily, affairs — of friendship; cited in Derks 339). Inversely, the closeness of male bonding invited analogy with marriage: Friedrich Schleiermacher wrote to his sister Charlotte that his friends enjoyed calling his joint household with Friedrich Schlegel a marriage and joked about his being the wife (December 31, 1797). Indeed, Schleiermacher voiced in other letters his desire to be a woman (March 23, 1799, and August 4, 1804), again illustrating the degree to which the Romantics were fascinated by the discourse of essentialist gender difference even as they toyed with imagining transsexuality.

V

Was it only possible, though, for men to give voice to a longing to be women, or could women assume male-gendered roles? Did society permit them to love other women, and if so, what expression could this love take? As far as I have been able to discern in my readings and conversations with other scholars, mid-eighteenth- to early-nineteenth-century Germany did not have the likes of England's renowned cross-dresser Charlotte Charke (Trumbach, "London's Sapphists"; Straub) or the erotic diarist Anne Lister (Castle). Nor, apart from the earlier example of Catharina Linck, who was executed for sodomy in 1721 (Eriksson), are there examples of women who, passing as men, were brought to trial for their deception (Friedli). When women did cross-dress, it was to gain more freedom, especially to travel; their cross-dressing did not signal sexual interest in other women. Presumably traces of lesbianism are hidden in documents coming from the recesses of women's lives that the social historian has yet to unearth. In his otherwise exhaustive book on homosexuality between 1750 and 1850 in Germany, Derks devotes a short chapter to the history of the word "lesbian" but also notes in his introduction that female homosexuality was rarely a topic of discussion because no one knew actual women who could be called lesbian, sapphist, or tribade (10). In editing this volume, I had great difficulty locating scholars prepared to write on lesbianism in the Age of Goethe, and deeply regret that the collection has only one article, albeit a long and excellent one, on the subject. My only hope is that the inventive ways in which the contributors to this volume read for homosexuality might inspire others to read likewise innovatively for lesbianism in earlier periods.

Nevertheless, the documentation of passing and cross-dressing women in England and Holland suggests that these practices must have been present in Germany as well. If they are not there, we must ask why not. But before the archives have been thoroughly exhausted, it is necessary to proceed cautiously in speculating about the reasons for the absence of alternative sexualities available to women. One tentative explanation, though, can at least elucidate why lesbianism is not a more prevalent topic of debate in the period. Since women were believed to be passive creatures—domesticated angels of the hearth—they were inconceivably sexual initiators, especially where other women were concerned. If we take it as unlikely that there were no eroticized relations between women, it is reasonable to assume that they were simply overlooked and disregarded because women were considered asexual in the first place.

A long tradition exists in this invisibility of lesbians, a problem that recent scholarship has attempted to face by broadening what one can understand by the term "lesbian." As Terry Castle observes in her aptly titled book *The Apparitional Lesbian*, "What the advocates of the 'no lesbians before 1900' theory forget is that there are myriad ways of discovering one's desire" (9). Likewise Woodward, in her article on lesbians in eighteenth-century British fiction, writes: "I would define as lesbian any desire for intimate connection between women" (845). And Vicinus notes: "The polymorphous, even amorphous sexuality of women is an invitation to multiple interpretative strategies" (436). Adrienne Rich is arguably the originator behind these strategies by virtue of her now (in)famous notion of a lesbian continuum: many female-female relations, although not genital, partake of an eroticism and closeness that one can anaclitically call lesbian. In *Between Men*, Sedgwick has borrowed Rich's idea of a continuum to establish desire as a thread linking the homosocial—male bonding—with the homosexual. A number of essays in this volume are indebted to Sedgwick's argument in favor of opening up possibilities for eighteenth-century male homoeroticism (especially those of Schindler, Graf, and Gustafson). Indeed, as the preceding discussion on friendship has shown, the notion of a continuum widens what one can count as sexuality and thus helps uncover what language, in either its metaphoric or, conversely, straitjacketing circumscription, would otherwise cloak.

These two contradictory moments require explanation. On the one hand, in the countless constellations of human relationships that it articulates, literature allows desires to be couched tropologically, obliquely, or, if you like, queerly. It forces one to read for what is not overtly said and encourages listening for innuendo. On the other hand, in its historical contingency, language is also a prison-house that constrains sexuality by limiting ways in which desires can be uttered and hence conceptualized. Unconventional sexualities must maneuver between these two poles of license and restraint. Given this problem of naming, a study of past homosexualities necessarily involves discourse analysis, which is why literary scholarship is so vital to the field. Not only do letters, diaries, and autobiographies materially document personal longings that would otherwise remain hidden, but they also, like novels and plays, function as experiments in gender nonconformity. In their rhetorical representation of homosexual desire, they call attention to its ambiguities, nuances, and silences.

These considerations thus point to a reading for lesbianism as the paradigmatic model for reading not just male homosexuality but female desire in general, whose verbalization has likewise been traditionally muted. This exemplary decoding is performed deviantly and cunningly, both acknowledging the phantasy world of sexuality as possessing its own reality and attentive to sudden silences on the topic as suspicious evidence of forbidden passion. Thus, although there is to date little documentation of eighteenth-century lesbianism, this very default is paradoxically productive. It is the concept of eighteenth-century lesbianism that gives privileged testimony to the evasiveness of all sexual discourse, including the circuitous discourse of a love oxymoronically deemed straight.

VI

I shall discuss the final essay in this volume first precisely because its ingenious method of discovering signs of female-directed passion among women can serve as a model for reading the slippages and displacements of erotic difference. Susanne Kord takes one step further Lillian Faderman's argument in her now classic *Surpassing the Love of Men* — that friendship was the traditional domain for the expression of lesbian relationships — by showing how the vocabulary of conjugal love infiltrates the discourse of friendship. Kord compares two sets of correspondences: the arduous exchange of letters between Luise Gottsched (1713–62) and Dorothea von Runckel (1724–62) with the emotionally cool epistles Luise forwarded to her husband, Johann Christoph (1700–1766), a major literary theoretician of his age. Kord then contrasts the two women's erotic openness with the strained mutedness among a later group of literary women: in letters home, Caroline Pichler (1769–1843) and her friends cautiously described their intense collaboration during summers spent together, as if they needed to reassure family and society of the propriety of their relationship. Their silence makes their passion both for each other and for their work truly suspicious. Attuned to discursive obliqueness, Kord refuses to overlook the elliptic expression homosexuality may take and the degree to which the specter of illicit friendship lurks behind male-female gender tensions.

Like the last, the opening essay in this collection documents the diachronic shift in the degree of tolerance eroticized homosociality encountered. Simon Richter provocatively dubs the Age of Enlightenment the "Age of Homosocial Friendship and Cultural Production," citing in support of his historical recasting examples from Frederick the Great and J. W. L. Gleim to Winckelmann and his followers, including the ill-fated Johannes Müller, whose story marks the close of the epoch. Like Kord, Richter analyzes same-sex epistolary exchanges — as well as the cult surrounding the reading of Winckelmann's letters — as a kind of homosocial networking analogous to the formation of a gay community. Richter's second contribution again deals with male reader reception, this time exploring the seductive effects of Wieland's erotics of the breast on the body of his male readers. Richter here articulates scintillating points of convergence between the eighteenth-century physiological discourse on the breast and such diverse topics of contemporaneous debate as masturbation, erection, the powers of imagination, and the aesthetics of purposiveness without a purpose.

Karl Philipp Moritz is an author not represented in this volume but whose eighth issue of the *Magazine for the Experiential Science of the Human Soul* (*Magazin zur Erfahrungsseelenkunde*) reinforces Richter's assessment that homoerotic relations between men were not perceived as unusual or marginal. This text merits a brief excursion here. Moritz's widely read journal discussed various cases of psychological atrophy that could be positivistically observed, rationalized, and eventually cured, the underlying conviction being that the behavior examined was not aberrant but explainable with reference to social circumstance. The aim of the magazine was to encourage in its readers empirical self-observation and critical self-monitoring (as differentiated from pietistic self-absorption). The case in question is narrated in the first person (conceivably by Moritz himself) and concerns the crazed passion that the speaker once developed for a fellow university student. The episode is told as an example of how common (read: normal) the "aberrations of nature" (*Verirrungen der Natur*) were (160). The narrator recounts desiring the most exact union with a man he worships from afar, wanting to merge totally with him (*mich ganz in ihn hineinziehen*, 164), a description that is as graphically sexual as it is mystic, suggesting that what is troublesome about the captivation is less its sexual deviancy than its excessive adoration, pietism being the topic Moritz broached earlier in the same issue of the *Magazine*.

After detailing the progression in his passionate longings, which include wanting to emulate the beloved, the speaker abruptly closes by saying that now that he has actually befriended N. his lethal restlessness has abated. Rather than read this about-face as a repression of homosexuality, I would argue that, since physical attraction to the same sex is not considered pathological or even unusual, it is not conceived to be problematically constitutive of one's general makeup, and thus its sudden cessation does not give rise to surprise. This difference does not mean, however, that amorous feelings for someone of the same sex are acceptable. Indeed, their social etiology is retraced for the benefit of parents and educators. The narrator recalls that as a child of five or six he was always fondled by male adults (women being absent from his upbringing), and as a boy between ten and twelve by his classmates. He even remembers in his youth having tenderly loved certain men, while being indifferent to women. The matter-of-fact attitude that prevails throughout this story prevents it from acquiring a confessional, revelatory, or shocking tone. The guilt-free account is not contextualized, moreover, as one today might expect, among a set of cases devoted to sexual self-questioning (the topic of sexuality hardly being addressed in the *Magazine*). Yet the piece does fold homosexuality into the discourse on *Bildung* and the role that emulation plays in it — which brings us, somewhat circuitously, to Stephan Schindler's contribution.

Schindler investigates the classic autobiographical novel of pietist upbringing, Jung-Stilling's *Life Story* (*Lebensgeschichte*), for the homoerotic impulses that arise within a patriarchal familial configuration where women are marginalized. Moritz could have been extrapolating on the effects of homosocial pedagogy in the Stilling household, even to the point where the socialization of the male subject is predicated on the exclusion of women. In contrast to Moritz, however, Schindler extracts the macabre implications of misogynist homosocialization: homophile desire becomes necrophilic once it is mediated through the body of the dead mother. In his complex remapping of oedipal relations, Schindler continues Richter's investigation of the eighteenth-century peregrinations of the breast into the domains of vampirism and other forms of oral gratification, including induction into the language of the Father. What is so striking about his investigation is that the family does not try to exorcise male-male love; rather, it is itself queer: familial order creates all-male bonds as part of its system of self-regulation.

In Foucauldian terms, the closet functions today to name homosexuality by stigmatizing it. This concept, as I have argued, is foreign to the late eighteenth century, which explored various expressions of same-sex desire without accompanying them with a pathologizing discourse. In his essay on Jakob Michael Reinhold Lenz, however, Roman Graf examines precisely this issue of not naming homosexuality. He rereads some of the most notorious passages penned by this Storm-and-Stress writer as symptomatic of anxieties about heterosexuality that point to the workings of the closet. One such example is the colonel's suggestion, in *The Soldiers* (*Die Soldaten*), that female prostitutes be provided for the army. Here the excessive demonstration of virile heterosexuality, commingled with the trafficking in women, deflects attention from the strong homosocial bonding in the play even as it surreptitiously enables it. With this and other dissimulative swerves Lenz constructs his own closet. Along with Susanne Kord and, as we shall see, Robert Tobin, Roman Graf brings the deconstructive model of writing as silence to bear on sexuality.

Lenz composed a piece, now lost, entitled "Our Marriage" about his relationship with Goethe. I have said relatively little in the introduction about the canonic master from whom this volume derives its title, leaving it to the next four essays to speak instead. They form the centerpiece to this collection. The first piece, by Robert Tobin, shows how far-reaching Goethe's interest in homosexuality was. Tobin finds a consistent supplementary logic of homosexuality operative in several of Goethe's works, including the famous early poem "Ganymede," *Faust*, *Wilhelm Meister's Apprenticeship* (*Wilhelm Meisters Lehrjahre*), *Wilhelm Meister's Journeymanship* (*Wilhelm Meisters Wanderjahre*), the *Roman Elegies*, and the *West-Eastern Divan* (*West-östlicher Divan*). Here homosexuality — which Goethe in a conversation with Johannes Müller had called both in and against nature (or, as Tobin states, following Derrida's notion of the *pharmakon*, both a poison and cure) — repeatedly comes to represent nature itself, whereby the binarisms of the homo- and heterosexual chiastically collapse into each other. In addition, Tobin takes up the issue of how homosexuality relates to aesthetics by examining its interconnectedness to the trope of writing in Goethe.

Like Stephan Schindler, Susan Gustafson looks at how male desire circulates and is sanctioned through the tie to the paternal ego ideal. With recourse to the Lacanian model of identity formation, she demonstrates how in Goethe's play *Götz von Berlichingen* desires are socially instilled, organized, and manipulated. But whereas Schindler shows how the grandfather transsexually emulates the woman's position so as to maintain stable familial order once she is gone, Gustafson demonstrates how masculinity itself is anxiously imitated and acted out. Both are cautious not to reaffirm homosociality lest it perpetuate a patriarchal order. For in *Götz*, too, the male economy of libidinal energy excludes women, except for when the threat of a too intense male friendship requires a female intermediary as a control release. Ironically, were the erotic dimension to have been recognized, Goethe seems to suggest, it would have bestowed an affective wholeness to the subject.

Susan Gustafson's essay raises the issue (as do other contributions, such as Schindler's, Wilson's, and Helfer's) of how feminist and queer readings are to intersect. Does the notion of homosociality bridge or confuse the differences between the two? How does homosociality function as a breeding ground for the development of sexual subcultures, the closet, and gender definitions? To what extent and in which instances does the term "queer" appropriately characterize homosociality? These are pressing questions that, in the wake of Sedgwick's inaugural *Between Men*, gender theory has yet to confront definitively and with which these articles also grapple. The particular readings just mentioned, which stem from a strong feminist conviction, reveal the degree to which issues of male bonding and parenting influence the stature of women in a society where male and female roles, as I argued earlier, are becoming increasingly divergent in response to biological discoveries. They also illustrate how feminist inquiries into the period can profit from gay studies, indeed, cannot afford to overlook homosocial constellations. To use a term from gay parlance in application to heterosexuality, these essays "out" masculinity in the sense that they uncover the social and historical mechanisms behind its construction, including its dependency on a female Other. But these essays "out" masculinity in another way as well: by showing how it veers into queerness. Homosexuality cannot be erased from homosociality, which is not to argue for a homophobic feminist perspective, a view that all these essays consciously skirt. As the cases of Lenz and Götz so lucidly exemplify, it is precisely when homosexuality is repressed that homosociality hideously transforms into the misogynistic (ab)use of women as substitute sexual objects. Here queer theory cannot make do without feminist insights; reciprocally, recognition of queer masculinity enhances a feminist reading, as the cause of misogyny is revealed to reside in homophobia.

By noting the sexuality underlying homosocial bonding, these articles furthermore reinforce the argument that an erotic intimacy and intensity pervade male friendships, familial ties, rivalry, and role-modeling during this period. Love between men is not denied, silently passed over, or condemned. Although gay studies have made us more attentive to this affective component of male interactions, it is important to stress that we cannot assume that the 1990s first popularized same-sex relations. The passion of such relations is undeniably "out" in German letters of the late 1700s. To be sure, male-male desire plays on various registers. This spectrum means that we cannot be quick to apply the dichotomy of hetero- and homosexual to this era, for it has not yet crystallized, as the absence of the closet prior to the Müller case so illuminatingly suggests, or as the prevalent figure of the androgyne, discussed in MacLeod's piece, also reveals. Furthermore, if this dichotomy is not yet firmly established, then it is difficult to read (except perhaps in Friedrich Schlegel's ever active self-reflexivity or in Kleist's metaphoric hyperbole) for the kind of postmodern queerness we are familiar with today, that is, a self-consciousness about sexual divisions that produces camp and parody and has allowed for the growth of queer theory with its interest in gender performativity and drag. To reemphasize: this is not to say that eccentric gender encodings (including, as we shall see, cross-dressing) do not abound in late-eighteenth-century German literature; indeed, they do so precisely because the homo/hetero opposition is not yet firmly in place.

These fuzzy gender boundaries form the subject of the next investigation. Whereas most essays in this volume address same-sex erotic relations (an issue of sexuality), W. Daniel Wilson's attention to cross-dressing (a function of gender) in Goethe's drama *Egmont* reminds us that the two issues are not indiscriminately interchangeable. He thereby uncovers a complex bisexuality at work in physical attraction, whose oddity elicits denial: Egmont tries to overlook the appeal of both feminized men and masculinized women. By disentangling the various gender reversals in the play, moreover, Wilson shows the political potential that resides in the upsetting of gender stereotypes. Political maneuvers are revealed to be engendered, just as the political agitators embody ideals of gender emancipation. It is worthwhile noting that Wilson joins two previous contributors, Graf and Gustafson, in a study of drama, as if the trying and acting out of masculinity — as Gustafson notes, even in the play of the little boy Georg — required a stage. As Wilson points out, though, the spectacle of *female* cross-dressing, especially in the political arena, poses a threat to masculinity.

The section on Goethe closes with an essay that takes us into the twentieth century. Through the lens of "the first bestseller of modern mass culture," Laurence Rickels gives us another look at homosociality or, as he puts it, the one-sexed organization of the group. Rickels brilliantly dovetails an examination of copycat teen suicides, fantasies of cloning, (Nazi) mass psychology, and homophobia via

The Sorrows of Young Werther (Die Leiden des jungen Werthers).
Complementing Tobin's work on pederasty as pharmakon and its
link to writing as a form of nonreproductive yet disseminatory creation, Rickels's piece explores the inoculative, pharmakonic doses of
tolerated homosexuality in Nazi war psychology as well as what he
calls the "Werther effect": the nonprocreative cloning dynamic of
the group. From here Rickels takes off into the "out space of psy fi";
on the way, Goethe's ghostly brother Werther group-bonds with
other siblings: Goethe's sister Cornelia, the *Schwestern* in Theweleit,
as well as, we could add, Lotte's warm brothers who hotly kiss the
dying hero, especially the oldest boy who hangs on Werther's lips
until he departs.

If Winckelmann's homoaesthetics announces the dawn of Enlightenment and the rise of German neoclassicism, then Friedrich
Schlegel's self-reflexive homopoetics sets the tone for Romanticism.
In an intricate reading of *Lucinde*, the flagship novel of Romantic
irony, Martha Helfer points out hitherto ignored allusions to homosexuality, giving us a better appreciation of why its contemporaries
regarded this "mad little book" addressed to "happy young men"
(*KA* 5:32) as exceptionally lewd and offensive. Like other contributors to this volume, Helfer demonstrates how male sexual identity
plays off of and into homosexuality, thus contributing to a broader
assessment of gender relations than strictly feminist analyses, however enlightening, have been able to provide. Moreover, homosexuality, funneling into the theorizing of male autoengenderment, becomes fundamental for understanding Romantic self-reflexivity: the
subject-text's conceptualization of its own artistic creation and coming into being.

Catriona MacLeod reinforces both Richter's and Helfer's yoking
of homoeroticism to the aesthetics of the period. But whereas Helfer
sees self-reflexivity as homoerotically driven in *Lucinde*, MacLeod
pictures androgynous combination as the model for Schlegel's formal principle of chaotic, capricious play. She also raises the pressing
question of whether homosexuality becomes detoxified as a result of
its aestheticization, as the history of the androgyne illustrates: as
one moves into the 1800s, the androgyne comes to underwrite heterosexual union and conjugal complementarity, while the distinctly
homoerotic valence of Winckelmann's androgynous ideal becomes

forgotten. This amphibian figure thus functions as a key signifier by which to chart the shifting, crosscutting histories of homo- and heterosexuality.

Ambivalent views on androgyny similarly characterize Kleist's life and work: according to MacLeod, androgyny can be monstrous yet also generative of aesthetic and sexual experimentation. Also acknowledging this ambivalence, Joachim Pfeiffer warns against trying to pin Kleist down to a single sexual identity or orientation, despite the voicings of intense male-directed desire in his letters. For if this writer in all other ways de-authorizes identity positions and presents a subjectivity at risk, then it is wrongheaded to ascribe a fixed sexual affiliation to him, even if it is labeled as queer. Instead Pfeiffer perceives Kleist's extravagent, violent outbursts of passion as metaphoric explorations and imaginary stagings of sexuality, ones that are simultaneously literarily stylized (a kind of counter-phobic drag). Ultimately, though, Kleist is too powerfully cognizant of constricting socially determined gender roles to believe in their shattering, a fact that explains the almost exultant despair that permeates his work. Pfeiffer makes a clever move at this juncture: lest we see him as refusing, à la Foucault, to hypostatize homosexuality in a pre-twentieth-century author, he aligns Kleist with such contemporary gay writers as Hubert Fichte and Josef Winkler, who similarly blasphemously and ecstatically undermine the symbolic order and its adherence to fixed, static gender and identity positioning. Pfeiffer thereby reinscribes Kleist into a contemporary queer sensibility.

Taken together, these essays show to what an amazing degree sexual and gender orientation was blurred during the Age of Goethe yet at the same time was constantly being restructured, very often via an inoculative (or pharmakonic) model whereby queerness is co-opted into an emergent heterosexuality. These essays thus join queer theory in investigating what constitutes sexuality and in challenging what a normal or natural heterosexuality would be. As noted earlier, late-eighteenth-century German literature was preoccupied with solidifying heterosexual roles via the inventions of Romantic love, classical femininity, the marriage partnership, and an aestheticized motherhood. But the very effort to pin down heterocentrist categories means that gender affiliations must have been in flux, thus opening the door to queerisms on all levels. To give a salient example: as

Schindler points out, once motherhood becomes worshiped (and the pietistic Stilling household was decidedly not Catholic), male desire is to emulate and then usurp the maternal function. Or, in Richter's terms, the breast and the penis become conflated. Yet if the last part of the eighteenth century witnesses gender experimentation without disparaging it, once one enters the nineteenth century there are signs of distress whenever such entanglement arises. Already in *Egmont* (1788), the title character, although fascinated by virile women, tries to control them by feminizing them; moreover, he remains unmoved by Ferdinand's advances. As Wilson further observes, Goethe became more conservative with age in both political and gender matters. As we have also seen, for Kleist, androgyny harbors a monstrous potential, and his desire to sleep with Ernst von Pfuel is voiced with a self-conscious flamboyancy and willfulness utterly missing from Winckelmann's neoclassical homoaesthetics or Moritz's matter-of-fact account of same-sex attraction. Thus, as a whole, the contributions that span the arch from Richter's to Kord's confirm the paradigm shift that these framing pieces (as well as MacLeod's) outline: by the second decade of the nineteenth century the closet door is shutting, as gender roles and the sexual choices they offer become restricted and the "nonnormative" becomes stigmatized.

The *Goethezeit* or Age of Goethe is an academic institution that under the name of its figurehead signals a canonical body of literature influencing not only German belles lettres but also numerous subsequent artistic movements ranging from French Romanticism and American Transcendentalism to Spanish Surrealism. In its time, though, the equivalent universalizing designations were strikingly different: Goethe called the era "The Century of Winckelmann," while Kant termed it "The Century of Frederick the Great." This nominal dissimilarity hints at a certain denial among later generations of the potential importance of homosexuality, a situation that calls for rereading the institution "Goethezeit" by resurrecting its own self-grounding in a gay-positiveness. The title of this book, though, purposefully evokes the author Goethe and not the statesman Frederick or the art historian Winckelmann. In its day, literature was granted hegemony over the visual arts (by Lessing), history (by Schiller), philosophy (by Schelling and Hölderlin), and science (by Novalis). It is also the privileged discourse in which the subjectivity of the bourgeois individual was forged via its amorous affects, a process that included the carving out of a space for the exploration of same-sex desire. For it is precisely literature (including the epistle self-consciously styled as literature) in which a self-awareness is articulated around homoerotic feelings and where, notwithstanding the distancing such sublimation entails, these emotions often become the object of idealization and nostalgia. This critical period in European literature and thought thus can no longer be underestimated in the reconstruction of a gay archaeology, just as homosexuality can no longer be bypassed in the annals of cultural history.

Simon Richter

Winckelmann's Progeny: Homosocial Networking in the Eighteenth Century

Against their better knowledge, scholars of German culture have for the last 200 years regularly falsified literary history by assuming, consciously or not, that the complex period known as the Age of Goethe was fundamentally structured along heterosexual lines. Such an assumption, though understandable on the face of it, is fraught with difficulties and contradictions. For one thing, it is every bit as anachronistic to assume eighteenth-century *hetero*sexuality as it is to speak of eighteenth-century *homo*sexuality. After all, both terms were first coined in the late nineteenth century. More egregious, however, is the patent bad faith of the main traditions of scholarship. Scholars of German literature — up until recently a group consisting primarily of classically educated men — knew better, for they were, like all who have been so educated, privy to an overarching knowledge that concerned the cultural centrality of male-male friendship and male homosocial culture.

A more accurate characterization of the Age of Goethe would take into account the remarkable fact that men of diverging sexual proclivities nonetheless participated jointly in a consuming enthusiasm for classical Greece and within the structure of male heroic friendship. Almost without exception, the male producers of culture in the Age of Goethe were the inhabitants of a virtual, semi-intimate, public/private space of homosocial and homoerotic encounter, imagined or otherwise. Individuals reputed to have liaisons with other men and boys freely mingled with men for whom sodomitical relations were out of the question. Such a milieu might be termed tolerant, and the designation would not be out of keeping with Enlightenment principles. Nonetheless, an unnecessary distinction is implied between those who tolerate and are tolerated. It may be more accurate to speak of a network in which the participants were virtually and potentially linked in friendship according to a Greek model of varying and blurred dimensions. Several individuals served as hubs or points of reference for this extensive homosocial network, among them Frederick the Great. Without doubt, however, the primary figure and imitative icon of the network was Johann Joachim Winckelmann. It is in his shadow, among his virtual progeny, that the contours of an explicitly homosocial and homoerotic *Goethezeit* become apparent.

I

In Kant's famous essay on the Enlightenment (1783) he declares that this historical period could be called the "Age of Enlightening or the Age of Frederick the Great" (15). To readers schooled in the "dialectic of Enlightenment" (Adorno/Horkheimer), this statement may seem to be a veiled reference to the tensions existing between the project of enlightenment and the absolutist state. The intellectual freedom permitted by Frederick is bought at a price: the large and well-disciplined army that protects and guarantees his authority. Yet if we alter our assumptions to accord full weight to the homosocial, a different reading presents itself.

Rumors of Frederick's homosexuality that circulated in his lifetime have persisted to the present day. Instead of defending Frederick from such accusations, James Steakley has suggested that "if Frederick's manifest homosexuality be granted as a working hypothesis, new interpretive possibilities open up in such diverse areas as the absence of a political network or entourage in his court, his growing misanthropy with advancing age, and his role as a patron and producer of the arts" (167). Among other things, Steakley notes that Frederick had a predilection for representations of Ganymede:

A bronze statue of Ganymede . . . was carefully positioned before his library window at Sanssouci so as to afford an unhindered view. He acquired this statue from Prince Eugene of Savoy, the homosexual commander of the victorious Hapsburg armies with whom he briefly studied the art of warfare as crown prince, thus creating an aesthetic link with a role model of the previous generation. A second Ganymede was the central figure in the ceiling fresco of the New Palace Frederick built in Potsdam after his victory in the Seven Years' War. Near this palace he erected a Friendship Temple decorated with portraits of Euryalus and Nisus, Orestes and Pylades, Heracles and Philoctetis, and Peirithoüs and Theseus. (168)

The Age of Frederick, the consummate soldier, sensitive *artiste*, and notoriously homosocial, if not homosexual, man of letters and state, would amount to nothing less than the Age of Homosocial Friendship and Cultural Production.

Despite the rumors, Frederick was widely admired and idolized, even emulated. Undoubtedly this allowed for discrete homoerotic investments, such that the image of Frederick became a significant token in homosocial discourse. One of his more ardent admirers was Johann Wilhelm Ludwig ("Father") Gleim (1719–1803), whose *Prussian Soldier Songs* celebrated Frederick's military feats. Gleim is best known as an early anacreontic poet and as the premiere figure in the so-called cult of friendship. An embarrassed tradition of scholarship has been inclined to deprecate Gleim's poetic accomplishments, to accuse him of pathological excess in the cultivation of friendship, and to regard him as largely irrelevant after 1770 (Rasch 181–221). A barrier is thus erected between Gleim's homoerotic *Empfindsamkeit* (or sensibility) and the classicism of the Age of Goethe. In point of fact, however, Gleim's career stretches into the beginning of the nineteenth century and may be seen as exemplary of the sort of homosocial networking that undergirded the *Goethezeit*. Summoned to an audience with Frederick in 1785, where he expressed the desire to possess the king's hat as a keepsake, Gleim was later the recipient of not only the hat but also the sash the king had worn during the Seven Years' War, a present to him from Frederick's personal valet. Gleim commissioned rings that depicted on their face both of these fetishes to either side of an urn bearing the inscription "To the one and only." The rings were distributed to Gleim's friends in order "to establish a community for his hero" (Körte 236).

Gleim's bachelor home in Halberstadt was known to him and his friends as his "personal Sanssouci" (Körte 163). For a period of over five decades, Gleim devoted himself to friendship as a lifestyle and an art form. In the beginning, during his anacreontic days, his friends were generally of a similar age and included Ewald von Kleist and Klopstock. As he grew older, he surrounded himself with younger men, often protégés, who remained with him as houseguests and relied on his sponsorship and patronage. Soon after moving to Halberstadt in 1747, Gleim established a Temple of Friendship, two rooms in which he mounted portraits of his friends, among them a pastel of Frederick II (Frühsorge). By the time of his death in 1803 he had collected more than 120 paintings, all of them hanging in the temple, visibly displaying the multiple filiations of an extensive homosocial network.

One of the earliest of Gleim's younger friends was Johann Georg Jacobi, his junior by 21 years. In 1768, Gleim published their brief and intimate correspondence leading up to Jacobi's move to Halberstadt. This work, known as the *Letters of Misters Gleim and Jacobi* (*Briefe von den Herren Gleim und Jacobi*) — with its 13,242 kisses and 260,022 embraces (Hanselmann 13) — almost uniformly vilified by scholarship, is perhaps one of the most emphatic examples of the hyperaffectionate discourse of *Empfindsamkeit*. The provocativeness of its homoeroticism may be measured by the response of Anna Luise Karsch, who reproached Gleim for his rejection of her love: "There are too many kisses in this work to avoid slander, suspicion, and mockery. I understand that such love is possible, I know that one can love that way; yet the more I know this, the more it disturbs me that you disapproved of my equally platonic, pure, and perhaps more upstanding love" (Körte 157–58). Heinrich Mohr calls the letters "erotic poems about the theme of the most tender male friendship" (32).

In *Epistemology of the Closet*, Eve Sedgwick parodies the hundreds of professors and teachers who have sought to defuse the erotic charge of such literary phenomena: "Passionate language of same-sex attraction [they say] was extremely common during whatever period is under discussion — and therefore must have been completely meaningless" (*Epistemology* 52). On the contrary, it was far from meaningless. At the very time that intimate male friendship was being stylized into erotic love, some were attempting to exalt the male-female relation by shaping it after the model of male friendship.[1] In other words, the homosocial relationship, typically understood as a perverse or compensating copy of the heterosexual, was in fact the "original" for the new interpretation of bourgeois marriage. Bettina von Arnim implicitly acknowledged this when she proposed the published love letters of Johannes von Müller to Karl Victor von Bonstetten as a model for her marriage with Achim. She quotes one of them: "You are more myself than I, and what are you not, since you are my only friend!" She adds: "That is what I say and continue to say: what will I yet become, if you remain my friend." Achim is less than gracious in his reply: "How can you even mention Müller's friendship in a love letter to me. Having prided myself on your intimate and stable friendship, suddenly that appalling swine's skin Müller comes between my legs, who lies before friendship's door so that everyone can wipe his boots on him" (quoted in Derks 338–39). With Achim's reply, consistent with the male Romantics' response to Müller specifically and homosexuality generally, we have clearly crossed over into the land of the excluded Other, of homophobic reaction. Only the women of Romanticism, who continued to cultivate the genre of the letter, upheld the tradition and possibilities of straightforward homosocial intimacy, though of a lesbian cast.

II

While Kant may not have wanted to call attention to the homosocial ambiguity contained in the "Age of Frederick," Goethe was almost certainly aware of the provocative accuracy of the title he chose, *Winckelmann and His Century* (*Winckelmann und sein Jahrhundert*, 1805), for a commemorative volume that included Goethe's well-known biographical essay, essays by an art historian (Meyer) and a classical philologist (Heyne), and unpublished letters by Winckelmann. Goethe's essay almost immediately became a touchstone of gay sensibility. In a letter to Wilhelm Körte (Gleim's young associate before his death), the same Johannes von Müller writes: "Read Goethe's chapter on friendship again for me, there is much in this chapter for me and for him who knows" (Derks 298). What justifies Goethe in dubbing the eighteenth century with Winckelmann's name is, as Paul Derks writes, "nothing less than the insight that the classicism inaugurated by Goethe owes its ideal of beauty to a homosexual who was only able to so develop and represent it *because* he was homosexual" (208). The more than incidental significance of Winckelmann's homosexuality seems to be confirmed by the combination of personal letters and art historical discussion in the same volume.[2]

The aesthetic gaze that reconfigured and idealized ancient Greece in the image of his own homoerotic desire is clearly inscribed in

Winckelmann's *Reflections Concerning the Imitation of the Greeks* (*Gedancken über die Nachahmung der Griechischen Werke*, 1755) and *History of Ancient Art* (*Geschichte der Kunst des Alterthums*, 1763), though the nineteenth and twentieth centuries have been reluctant to acknowledge it. This powerful vision of Greece, of aesthetic, moral, and sexual freedom, of a time that privileged male friendship and incorporated it into its social and political institutions, that celebrated the beauty of the male body — this vision generated the entire movement of German neoclassicism (Richter, *Laocoon's Body* 38–61). The generative power of his gaze extends to all theories of the symbol (Goethe, etc.); all aesthetics of "purposiveness without purpose" (Kant, Moritz); all raptures concerning healthy male nudity (Goethe, Schlegel, Hölderlin, etc.); all androgynous women (Dorothea, Johanna, Penthesilea); all intimate male friendships, especially in war situations (Schiller's *Malteserfragment*); all journeys to Italy, especially those where Winckelmann himself served as *cicerone*, but also those of Herder, Moritz, Goethe, and other less known figures; all enthusiastic descriptions of the four most significant statues of the eighteenth century: Laocoon, the Belvedere Apollo, the Antinous, and the Torso — the cornerstones of Winckelmann's aesthetics, all conspicuously male.

The homoerotic contours of the Age of Goethe become especially evident at the point where this relatively tolerant, pre-closet period comes to a sudden end. The relevant date appears to be around 1806, a time when Napoleon invades Prussia and an enlightened, cosmopolitan, homosocial culture accepts him, while in Romantic circles a conservative, homophobic nationalism takes hold. Heinrich Mohr illustrates the transition with the example of Friedrich Jacobi, the brother of the person whose early correspondence with Gleim had served as a model for male friendship. Wilhelm Körte had inherited the bulk of Gleim's correspondence with the charge to publish it for posterity. He was taken aback by the hostile response of several involved parties, particularly Jacobi, for whom the matter was so serious as to warrant a public discussion regarding the impropriety of the project. As Mohr writes: "Jacobi undertakes to sharply separate the private and the literary spheres — a separation whose nonexistence was precisely the condition for the epistolary culture of the later eighteenth century" (49–50). Körte was stunned and published a rebuttal, insisting that for Gleim the arrival of an intimate letter was always a public occasion, "always a feast, which was often celebrated with a certain ritual. Family and frequent guests were assembled, then the letter was opened and read aloud, an office usually performed by Körte; the intimacy of the group, not that of an exclusive pair, predominated." Moreover, "completed correspondences were bound and placed in an unlocked bookcase with glass doors next to Gleim's favorite books, in a room between the so-called temple of friendship and the guest rooms. Visiting friends were encouraged to peruse the collected letters at their pleasure" (Mohr 54).

There is a striking analogy between the communal practices of these eighteenth-century friends and those of the contemporary gay community. The shift delineated by Mohr can be mapped onto the incipient opposition between hetero- and homosexual relations, especially in terms of the exclusive and increasingly heterosexual pair (the ideology of bourgeois marriage) on the one hand, and multiple same-sex epistolary partners on the other. The love letter — shared, transmitted from hand to hand, representing the erotic love of two male lovers (one need only think of the effusive expressions of physical contact), and observed by multiple third parties, either jointly or privately — is obviously the vital condition for the entire homosocial community. Indeed, the love letter substitutes for biological reproduction. It is the seed that assures the transmission of homosocial culture from generation to generation. Winckelmann, the father of this culture, obviously knew this, given his charge in a published letter to his young lover, Reinhold von Berg, that he should "awaken sons and grandsons in his own image" (*Abhandlung* 233). This letter, overtly concerned with aesthetic education, more subtly detailed a program for homosocial reproduction, for the generation of Winckelmann's progeny (Richter and McGrath). Since the father of this plan is Winckelmann, it should not surprise us that the reproductive power of the love letter consists in its ability to stimulate and control imitation (almost like epistolary DNA). What I am suggesting is that the image of Winckelmann conveyed in his letters — his language, his life, his friendships — circulated within the homosocial network in such a way that younger and older men both were able to imitate him. Such imitation, incidentally, would suggest the necessity of a complete reassessment of mimesis from the perspective of queer theory.

When Johannes von Müller, one of Winckelmann's most ardent imitators and another of Gleim's young friends and correspondents, was also approached by Körte for the same edition of letters to which Jacobi objected, he responded as expected:

What shall I say about the publication of the letters, and granting the permission you desire in such a friendly way? You believe they may be helpful to young men. That is enough for me to accede. The idea that friendship and courage may gain in several young souls on account of reading these letters causes me to forget what is in them that might be interpreted to my disadvantage. To say more would be vain, since the book is intended for neither the elite nor immortal fame; it is for boys, in whose hearts the joy, the lament of the loving youth echoes of its own accord, who will be able to share the jubilation of noble projects undertaken in the feeling of awakening power, but also dejection, sadness, and the knowledge that even though a man can seldom do what he desires, he will more or less succeed according to the extent to which he remains true to himself.

In accord with the principle of imitation, Körte had planned for Müller's letters to Gleim to follow those of Winckelmann to Count Schlabbrendorf. Müller was delighted: "Excellent that you are connecting Winckelmann's letters to mine; we had many an analogy in perspectives and feelings of more than one kind" (17:353). Since Müller himself was one of those most strongly affected by Winckelmann's example, his own heart echoing, indeed imitating, the sentiments expressed in Winckelmann's letters, this account of eighteenth-century homosocial networking will conclude with his story as the best exemplification of both the efficacy of the letter and the process of *imitatio winckelmanni.*

III

Johannes von Müller (1752–1809) is not nearly as well known as he should be. By his contemporaries he was regarded as the most significant historian of his age, easily Schiller's better. He wrote both a vast history of his native country Switzerland (Schiller's source for *Wilhelm Tell*) and a universal history. For present purposes, however, it is most important to know that Johannes von Müller was out as one inclined to Socratic or Greek love to an extent unparalleled in eighteenth-century Germany. In 1810, shortly after Müller's death, a friend wrote to Goethe that in reading both the histories he was "especially struck by the red thread that proceeds through the entire work: it is the love between men; even in his Swiss history it was hard to miss" (quoted in Derks 343). Derks provides ample proof that Müller's homosexuality was "not merely an open secret, but rather open as day." Confirming the transitional date of 1806, he states:

Apart from occasional stubborn morosities, before 1806 no one had taken Müller to task for his homosexuality. The sheer number of those whom Müller could call friend, on whom he could rely, is large and significant: it includes Christian Gottlob Heyne, Johann Gottfried Herder, Georg Forster, Friedrich Heinrich Jacobi, perhaps Wilhelm Heinse, Christoph Martin Wieland, Christian Wilhelm von Dohm, Alexander von Humboldt, Goethe, Count Reinhard, and Jacob Grimm. (313–14)

Anecdotal and documentary evidence of real homosexual encounters exists in abundance, as most of his biographers have been aware, but that is not necessary for the argument. What concerns us now is the process of Müller's imitation of Winckelmann.[3]

Müller's first contact with Winckelmann came in 1769, through his professor of classics, Christoph Heyne in Göttingen, who had known Winckelmann personally and later contributed to Goethe's *Winckelmann*. Returning that same year to his birthplace, Schaffhausen, Müller became acquainted with Heinrich Füßli, the young artist for whom Winckelmann had served as *cicerone* in Rome and who now lived in Zürich. Müller begged to be allowed to read Winckelmann's letters to him: "I kiss you in gratitude for good Winckelmann's letters; they are very unusual" (quoted in Rihm 77). There were, in fact, some six friends in Zürich with whom Winckelmann had corresponded, and in 1773 Müller made a similar request of Leonard Usteri, one of Winckelmann's confidants:

The last time I embraced you in your house among the community of the wise, you mentioned a correspondence with your departed friend that is still in your possession. You even fostered a hope in me that I might be allowed to glance at it. It's not such a good idea to promise me a means of becoming more acquainted with a spirit such as Winckelmann, for I will hold you to your word. . . . There is nothing I consume more greedily than letters in which interesting men reveal themselves with the forthrightness of *our* Montaigne. (Rehm 4:326–27)

Usteri obliged, and Müller and his new friend Karl Victor von Bonstetten were able to consecrate their budding relationship by establishing this material and imitative link with Winckelmann.

Müller's fascination with Winckelmann continued. In 1775, he begged Bonstetten to send him everything by Winckelmann he could get his hands on. In 1776, he and Charles Bonnet, his landlord, read and discussed the *History of Ancient Art* together in the evenings. Soon Bonstetten was required to marry for social reasons, though this did not prevent their continued fervent correspondence, or their frequent joint vacations. Müller fantasizes a bizarre triangle of homosocial desire where Bonstetten's wife reads aloud to them the "divine chapters about the Belvedere Apollo and Greek beauty" (13:188). In another place, Müller writes: "It is not Winckelmann who depicts Apollo, but Apollo who speaks through the mouth of Winckelmann" (quoted in Rihm 79). Throughout their correspondence, Müller called his friend Apollo — "You are my Apollo, my muse, my light, my self more than I am" (13:177) — just as he calls himself Bonstetten's "Mülly."

Müller's collected letters to Bonstetten were edited and published by their mutual friend Friederike Brun, first in a series of journals from 1798, and in 1802 as a book. Reviewing them anonymously for the *Athenäum* in 1799, Caroline Schlegel called them "real love letters": "We see here the decisive effect of his familiarity with the ancients, and how they pressed a seal of knowledge on his kindred nature. The friendship that breathes in these letters is evidence: it is a friendship in the style of the ancients, as are his works" (quoted in Derks 307). At the very time that the letters appeared, however, Müller was becoming involved in one of the more bizarre incidents of German literary history. Once again he fell in love. The consequences were disastrous, almost fatal, but the letters that were generated afford the purest glimpse of a completely unhindered late-eighteenth-century homoerotic friendship. The only flaw, as regards Müller, was the fact that, unbeknownst to him, his lover was a fiction.[4]

In 1795, Müller was approached by a widowed noblewoman in the hope that he would watch over her unruly fifteen-year-old son, whom Müller described as a "well-built (rather effeminate) beautiful and talented youth" (Henking 2:548). His name was Fritz Hartenberg, and he recognized in Müller not only his own sexual inclina-

tion, but also an easy target for financial exploitation. Over a period
of seven years, Hartenberg was able to string Müller along with
various scams, until in 1802, when Müller was 50, he launched an
unimaginably brash scheme to defraud him of every last penny. He
invented a Hungarian duke by the name of Louis Batthyani, the
illegitimate son of the duchess Marie Theresia von Falkenstein, destined to inherit a vast fortune, and profoundly in love with the
Müller he had come to know through his writings. Müller could not
believe his good fortune and showered Batthyani with letters. These
were intercepted by Hartenberg, who responded with letters from
the duke, the duchess, and the duke's valet. Between them they
create a fantasmatic family: the duchess charges Müller to love her
son ("Now, Jean, he is yours! Be his brother, father, and friend.
I have taken you up into my motherly heart and I have blessed
and sealed the unseparable bond between you and Louis"; Henking
2:554). Louis suggests that they regard Fritz as their common son,
and continually requests financial advances for him, to which Müller willingly accedes, since there is a promise of imminent wealth.
The duchess informs Müller that he will soon come into possession
of a small castle called Röschitz, and Müller, who is wildly dis-
tracted from his historical studies, is encouraged to indulge his fantasies. Trips to Rome, Greece, Jerusalem, and Spain are planned. He
develops elaborate fantasies of an ideal homosocial existence: "Inseparable brotherly love; tending to our mother; caring for Fritz;
patience; quiet charity, in the meantime, and the noblest cultivation
of our mind and heart; here, or wherever we please, often traveling;
everything permeated with love and with the monuments of our
knowledge and our being for coming generations" (Henking 2:562).
Regarding Bonstetten Müller confides to the duke: "In my first youth
I had a friend, full of grace, goodness, and spirit; however, he lacked
that conformity which we have, but my imagination supplied it. I
never wrote to him as I do to you" (Henking 2:558). To his brother
back in Schaffhausen, who like many of Müller's friends is delighted
at his good fortune, he writes: "The letters to Bonstetten are nothing
compared to these; if they were somewhat purified, I would have
nothing against their being published. Certainly no other writing of
mine contains so much soul, or has been written with such love"
(Henking 2:557).

For nine months Hartenberg succeeded in prolonging this charade, actually sending Müller scurrying across Europe for assignations that were always postponed at the last moment, and taking him for every penny. When Müller was confronted with the fact that the entire affair had been a fraud, he was in a state of financial ruin and on the verge of suicide. Many friends supported him, rendering solace and dealing with his creditors. Among them was Goethe, who invited Müller to Weimar and engaged him in a new journalistic endeavor. Goethe was in the initial stages of writing his Winckelmann essay, having read all the available correspondence, and Derks (321) conjectures that he recognized aspects of Winckelmann in the emotionally devastated Müller—a theory that accords well with our notion of the imitative nature of these friendships.

Certainly one feels pity for Müller. At the same time, these bizarre circumstances provided for a representation of a homosocial desire that was hindered only by the limits of its own imagination. In 1805, when Müller was somewhat recovered from the affair, he read an encomium on Winckelmann by Karl Morgenstern. Once more he was drawn into friendship. In a letter praising Morgenstern for his text, he imagines that in a previous life the two of them walked arm in arm through classical Greece. "We now simply give each other the hand of friendship with the inner and familiar consciousness of many precious secrets of that first life. Is it acceptable to you, since Winckelmann cannot personally thank you, that I thank you for him from my heart? Accept it; it is as was his—in many respects, yes, in all respects" (Bonjour 289). The *imitatio winckelmanni* is fulfilled. Müller extends his hand, in a letter, and the gesture becomes a physical and imitative link between Morgenstern, Müller, Winckelmann, and the inimitable Greeks of the latter's inspired vision. "Your spirit wanders in true antiquity, a *kalos kagothos* from those same centuries" (Bonjour 289).

The network of transhistorical homosocial imitation thickened in the last chapter of Müller's life, even as a malicious homophobic backlash began to make itself felt. In 1806, Napoleon's forces humiliated the Prussian army and occupied Berlin. Napoleon took up residence in Sanssouci. Müller, like Gleim, who shortly before his death wrote a poem entitled "To the Sublime Napoleon of St. Cloud" in which he promised to celebrate the French general as he had Frederick II (Körte 359), had followed Napoleon's career with great interest. Müller recognized this moment of world historical significance, even if his interpretation diverged widely from Hegel's. He saw in Napoleon a classical hero and statesman, in the tradition of both Caesar and Frederick (Rihm 96–129). At the same time, he believed that history was calling on him to be Napoleon's intimate biographer. Already involved in the writing of a biography of Frederick, Müller was granted an audience with Napoleon at Sanssouci, just as he had been with Frederick in 1781. In a letter to von Dalberg, Müller writes: "The great man . . . deserves a historian of the classical style; you know that I belong to those ancient times," signing the letter "Jean de Müller, historiographer" (Rihm 107). Although the conversation with Napoleon took a favorable course, the result was hardly what Müller had wished. Instead of being appointed official biographer, Müller was named minister of education in Westphalia, and as such became an easy target for the combined assault of homophobic and nationalist hostility. While Goethe sought to quell or at least inform the debate about Müller by translating into German Müller's French oration on the "Glory of Frederick," in which the deep connection between Frederick and Napoleon is implied, scores of conservative Romantics took license to excoriate him.[5] This event, in the year 1806, marks the inception of the German closet. The Age of Winckelmann and Frederick, the age of homosocial networking, had come to an end.

IV

The effect that has been aimed at throughout this essay is to create the impression of a substantial and coherent network of friends and patrons, lovers and beloveds, models and imitators — the entire system predicated on Winckelmann and the homosocial culture associated with him. Once this impression has been secured, the consequences are both staggering and far-reaching, and they should not be limited to discourses of aesthetics, art history, and *Empfindsamkeit*. This has *not* been the description and analysis of a marginal subculture. Rather, we have been speaking of the major cultural players, texts, traditions, and structures of the Age of Goethe.

In order to convey a sense of the political and historical stakes of acknowledging the homosocial network, we might consider the consequences for Jürgen Habermas's theory of the public sphere, which has enjoyed an American resurgence since the English publication of

The Structural Transformation of the Public Sphere in 1989. It is during the period under discussion, as Habermas argues, that the bourgeois public sphere originates. But Habermas also participates in the falsification of eighteenth-century culture, blithely affirming the heterosexual order, even though there is every indication that he is aware that the public sphere was initially established within the conventions of epistolary culture, coffeehouse socializing, and a form of intimacy not associated with the home (31–51). In other words, his historico-normative narrative depends on the culture that we have amply shown to be homosocial. This version of incipient modern democracy could therefore be accurately defined as public intimacy between men. Certainly it is true that the nineteenth-century ideology of marriage, respectability, and nationalism, to a great extent dependent on the preceding culture of male friendship, in turn forced the submergence of the homoerotic forms of such public intimacy, as George Mosse argues (66–88) and as we have seen in the Romantic response to Johannes von Müller. But it is precisely this response to its own origins, to the homosocial network, that maps out the space that will eventually be occupied by the homosexual. Modern democratic culture and the pathologization of male-male erotic behavior are linked in the denial of their homosocial origin.[6]

Simon Richter

Wieland and the Homoerotics of Reading

Is not Wieland's poetry Wieland's person?
— Caroline Schlegel-Schelling

Christoph Martin Wieland is about the last person one would expect to find implicated in a homoerotics of reading, even if, as Gleim once teasingly pointed out, it is "from his mouth that the German youth first heard of Greek love" (Derks 234). Gleim was referring to one of Wieland's scandalous *Comic Tales* (*Komische Erzählungen*) entitled "Juno and Ganymede," a story that Wieland himself later expunged from his collected works. Wieland is generally known as the celebrator of heterosexual love, not in its spiritualized form, but in its mildly titillating sensuousness. Perhaps nothing figures Wieland's desire as precisely as the contour of the woman's breast. He never tires of inventing situations in which a woman's breast is exposed, and never fails to linger. These passages themselves become breasts in the text, gratuitous folds for the reader's delectation.[1] How could Wieland, of all people, be involved in a homoerotic network?

The reading that follows is itself like the breast. It will trace the line of a prodigious arc that connects Wieland and his (male) readers by means of the proffered breast. This particular homoerotics of reading might best be understood as an extreme instance of the triangle of homosocial desire (Sedgwick, *Between Men* 21–27) mapped onto a model of reader reception. What enhances and complicates the picture is that the mediating breast itself turns out to be phallic. Wieland is locked in a triple bind that is thoroughly gay, and of which he is the reluctant author.

I

It must have surprised the young Wilhelm Heinse when Wieland, his "wise high priest of the graces and Apollo" (Seiffert 5:210), so vociferously rejected the verses he had submitted to Wieland's literary journal, the *Merkur*. Heinse almost certainly believed that he was merely continuing in the tradition of Wieland's *Comic Tales* and *Musarion*. Wieland, however, was so upset that he refused to communicate directly with Heinse. As if to protect himself from contact, he required the mediation of his older friend Gleim to return the provocative poem. The explanation for his extreme reaction is disclosed in an accompanying letter (Seiffert 5:212–13). Heinse's "entire soul," he charges, is "a Priap." He calls Heinse "Mentula" and "mutoniato," characteristically resorting to Latin and Greek when it comes to naming the phallus.[2] He speaks of the "damned Tentigo that incessantly swells [Heinse's] soul." If Heinse's translation of Petronius's *Satyricon* amounted, in Wieland's opinion, to an assault on Ganymede, then these latest verses are nothing less than a rape of the graces. The sheer coherence of the formulations used to interpret Heinse's text and soul urges the hypothesis that Wieland is not merely indulging in a bit of scatological invective, but that he is vitally concerned to differentiate himself from Heinse, and to do so with reference to the male member. It is this difference and the process of differentiation that we will pursue in what follows.

Heinse's unfinished poem, announced to Wieland in an earlier letter as a "heroic poem," consists of 42 strophes: "a mere episode," writes Heinse, a song "that reveals only the slightest portion of the whole" (Seiffert 5:189). The poem begins with a bathing woman, Almina, and a hidden observer, Kleon. Precisely as in a Wieland text, Almina reveals one body part after another to the gaze of the voyeur:

> Now she began to undo her straps
> Mischievously her young bosom sprang forth.
> Now I saw her remove her dress,
> And seat herself on flowers in the moss.
> Already her thighs begin to spread,
> Here the foot and there the shoulder are exposed —
> My spirit burns! In my heart what tumult! —
> And now everything, and opened is heaven.

Jetzt fing sie an die Bänder aufzuschleifen,
Mutwillig sprang der junge Busen los.
Jetzt sah ich sie das Kleid hinauf sich streifen,
Und setzen sich auf Blumen in das Mooß.
Schon fangen an die Schenkel auszuschweifen,
Hier wird der Fuß und dort die Schulter bloß —
Mir brennt mein Geist! im Herzen welch Getümmel! —
Und alles nun, und aufgetan der Himmel.
(Seiffert 5:191)

Kleon is not content with mere observation, and the scene of voyeurism becomes one of rape. Kleon plunges after Almina, but does not capture her until she has injured herself:

. . . the thorns had scratched open
Cheeks and bosom, and divine blood
Flowed over snow to the shrine of love —
This offering flowed to the honor of you graces.

. . . die Dornen hatten Wange
Und Busen aufgeritzt, und göttlich Blut
Floß über Schnee zur Liebe Heiligthume —
Dieß Opfer floß euch Grazien zum Ruhme.
(Seiffert 5:194)

Three strophes were particularly upsetting to Wieland: "Read, dear Gleim, the 15th, 20th, 21st of these stanzas, and tell me whether I judge too harshly" (Seiffert 5:221). In the latter two, the recurring motif of blood implies the violence involved in the act of love.

XX

She struggled still, and my souls wandered,
Stimulated by this fight to fever pitch,
They wandered full of rage, so that all nerves boiled,
Already injured, stained with sweet blood —
And finally, after a thousand strokes of thunder,
Sweet rain broke forth in joyful storm.

XXI

Kisses flare up like lightning around the lips —
After every pause a stroke of thunder follows —
The blood of mad love's penance sprays —
The drunkenness of pleasure steals the day
Causes hands, body, and feet

Each one, to lie full of enraptured souls,
Coursing with the nectar of sensation
That Amor had poured into the flames.

XX

Sie kämpfte noch, und meine Seelen irrten,
Von diesem Kampf zum höchsten Sturm geschreckt,
Voll Wut herum, daß alle Nerven girrten,
Verwundet schon mit süßem Blut befleckt —
Und endlich brach, nach hundert Donnerschlägen,
Im Sturm hervor entzückend süßer Regen.

XXI

Gleich Blitzen flammen um die Lippen Küße —
Auf jede Stille folgt ein Donnerschlag —
Es spritzt das Blut der tollen Liebesbüße —
Die Trunkenheit von Wonne raubt den Tag
Den Augen, macht, daß Hände, Leib und Füße —
Ein jedes voll verzückter Seelen lag,
Vom Nektar der Empfindungen durchfloßen,
Die Amor in die Flammen uns gegoßen.
(Seiffert 5:195)

The fifteenth strophe is distinguished by a single Petronic verse: "For this arrow is there the most beautiful target!" (*Zu diesem Pfeil ist dort das schönste Ziel!* Seiffert 5:193).

What connects the stanzas that disturbed Wieland, and what separates them from the rest, is that they point to distinct signs of the phallus. The phallus in the text does violence not only to Almina, but to the graces and the reader as well. Wieland instructs Gleim to teach Heinse "that the mysteries of nature and love must not be uncovered, and that one need not rape the graces in order to bring them an offering" (Seiffert 5:212). Silence should cover the male part in the writing of the text; as phallus, the male member is the mystery of nature and love. Wieland does not thereby deny the male part in the writing of the text; rather, he insinuates that the text originates from the phallus. As will become apparent in the course of this reading of Wieland, the phallus is, on the one hand, the hidden condition for the writing of the text and, on the other, the equally concealed object of (male) desire. Between these functions of the phallus the line of an arc extends that is nothing other than the breast and the female body, the rhetoric of male fantasy and of male poetry about women, a triangle of homosocial desire inscribed on the model of reception. Heinse's text violated this poetic logistics: Heinse does not offer the breast, he extends the uncovered phallus. Wieland understandably declined. Perhaps this is how Wieland is to be differentiated from Heinse: if Heinse's entire soul is a Priap, then Wieland's entire soul is a breast. It remains to examine the logic of this differentiation and its tenability.

II

The breast, it would seem, is one of the least deceptive signs of sexual differentiation. And yet the cultural meaning of the female breast in the eighteenth century was far from stable. Analysis of the multiple discourses of aesthetics, fashion, morality, and physiology shows that the more the breast was examined and theorized, the more it resembled the penis.

We will begin with aesthetic discourse in which the discussion of the reproductive body parts anticipates the concept of aesthetic autonomy. In his exhaustive catalog of body parts in the *History of the Art of Antiquity (Geschichte der Kunst des Alterthums)*, Winckelmann writes: "The breast or bosom of female figures [in Greek statuary] is never excessively endowed, since beauty was placed in the moderate growth of the breasts" (*Geschichte* 183). In another place, he speaks of the breasts of the goddesses, which "are like those of young girls, and which have not yet received the fruit of love; I mean to say, the nipple is not visible on the breast" (*Geschichte* 156). By insisting on small breasts and missing nipples, Winckelmann denies the functionality and the sex-specific quality of the breast. In other words, he dismisses the maternal from aesthetic consideration. In a private letter, however, Winckelmann as much as admits that for him the female breast can and should be reduced to its functional aspect: "What beautiful thing does the woman have that we do not also have; for a beautiful breast is but of short duration, and Nature fashioned this part not for beauty, but for the rearing of children, and to this end it cannot remain beautiful" (Rehm 3:277). Beauty and functionality are mutually exclusive, as both Karl Philipp Moritz and Kant would insist some thirty years later.

While Winckelmann's aesthetics seems to be constructed within the visual gaze, Johann Gottfried Herder attempts to develop an aesthetics based on touch. In contrast to Winckelmann, Herder discovers beauty precisely in the functionality of the breast: "Nature gave woman not breast, but bosom, draped therefore the girdle of grace around her — since the springs of necessity and love should be presented here for the delicate suckling infant — and created, as is her maternal wont, sensuous pleasure of necessity" (8:52). It is not only a matter of sucking, but even more of touching — this is the *Urszene* of Herder's aesthetics: "When the drink of innocence is prepared and the immature babe clings to the sources of the first joys of mother- and childhood, and his little hand snuggles and taps and is sated . . ." (8:52). The beauty of the breast is in the touching.

Aesthetic and moral discourse intersect. In the aftermath of Rousseau's *Emile*, many voices protest the use of wet nurses. Women of both the noble and the bourgeois classes, according to the familiar polemic, would rather engage a wet nurse than nurse the child themselves. In the anonymous *Physical Treatise Concerning the Maternal Duty of Nursing and Its Influence on the Welfare of the State, According to the Prescription of Dr. Tissot and Other Famous Doctors*, the author asserts: "Just as soon as luxury, sensuous pleasure and prejudice won the upperhand among people, so the band of motherly love was finally torn without shame" (*Physische Abhandlung* 10). City life is to be blamed for this unnatural practice, and particularly the vanity of women: "The tenderness of German women for their men is now too great to allow them to destroy the firmness and roundness of their bosom in the fulfillment of their maternal duty" (*Physische Abhandlung* 13). The fashion of the 1770s required the décolletage to be so low that "the slightest movement of the upper body was sufficient to expose the breast almost entirely" (Pomezny 112; cf. Hollander 203). The immoral use of wet nurses is combated by the detailed description of all sorts of repulsive conditions that putatively arise from the failure to nurse. The self-centered preservation of the beautiful breast is thus equated with masturbation.

For its part, the physiological discourse concentrates primarily on the nipple and its ability to become erect. In *Treatise Concerning the Inner Construction of the Female Breasts*, Alexander Kölpin writes: "In the middle of the brownish ring, there is the nipple (papilla), about whose spongy substance (substantia cavernosa) much fuss has been made, by means of which in the event of pleasurable sensations it attains an erect state, a certain hardness and stiffness, and becomes very sensitive" (15–16). In his *Primae lineae phys-iologiae*, Albrecht von Haller utters what appears to be self-evident: the blood collects in the nipple "& erectionem facere, ut in pene" (512). The erection of the nipple is irresistibly compared with that of the penis. Kölpin, it is true, is skeptical about the appropriateness of the comparison. In dissecting the breast, he had encountered no muscle that would have been capable of sealing the blood in the nipple. The pleasurable sensation should "merely be attributed to the nerves" (21).

Kölpin's sober analysis is powerless against the irresistible force of the analogy. The comparison is not limited to the erection, but rests on the deep-seated conviction that milk is essentially a diluted form of semen, and that the latter is a precious distillate of the blood, possessed in scarce supply by both sexes and expelled with orgasm—hence the constant diatribes against masturbation.[3] In 1719, Christoph Hellwig theorizes sexual intercourse as an inverse variant of nursing: "Just as the child draws the milk from his mother with the greatest desire, so the vagina draws into itself the semen that ejaculates from the male member during amorous skirmishes" (quoted in Meyer-Knees 52). Even the translator of Kölpin's Latin treatise cannot resist appending a long footnote to indicate his diverging opinion:

It will certainly remain an undeniable experience that, in the case of young fertile women, the nipples, which are normally, in indifferent moments, entirely withdrawn and hidden in a navel-like hollow, will, when stimulated through pleasurable sensations and thoughts, soft rubbing with the tip of a finger, nipping of the lips, and the like, emerge in their true, nearly cylindrical form, standing erect and bursting, and, after some time, once the pleasant tickle has had its effect, disappear again. (16)

Even more important than every anatomical similarity is the question, assumed by the translator, as to whether the nipple, like the penis, can be stimulated by the imagination (i.e., "pleasurable thoughts"). Hermann Boerhaave stated early in the eighteenth century that "the muscles concerned in this action [male erection] are not to be reckoned among the class of vital or spontaneous muscles, since of themselves they do not act in the most healthy man; but they are rather in a class sui generis, being under the influence of the imagination. The will has no influence either to suppress, excite, or diminish their action" (quoted in *Tabes dorsalis* 14). Haller and the

British physiologist Robert Whytt engaged in a hotly contested debate concerning the erection (Gilman, *Sexuality* 194–97). The penis, to use Haller's terms, is neither irritable nor sensitive, but somehow both. The penis is governed by the imagination, a dubious (and feminine) power, that mediates between body and soul in mysterious ways. The eighteenth century was inclined to accord this same unique status to the nipple.

Already in Herder a connection between the breast and the sense of touch had emerged. He could have found corroboration in seventeenth-century emblems of touch (Gilman, *Sexuality* 148–60). Typically they show a woman whose one hand is injured by a bird while the other fingers a tortoise's shell, thus displaying the passive and active aspects of touch, as well as the fact that touch is essentially a form of pain. The invariably naked bosom of the woman combines these opposing aspects in the erect nipples. The papilla becomes a physiological emblem of the sense of touch merely by virtue of its Latin name: the term "papillae" (nipples) also designates the vascular protuberances of the dermal layer of the skin which often contain the tactile corpuscles. One sees in the nipple what transpires microscopically in the finger — the papillae become erect. As Haller writes in the *tactus* chapter of his anatomy:

The papillae of the fingertips on the inside of the hand, which are somewhat larger and arranged in regular, ring-shaped folds, can receive an impression of an object in their nerve tissue and transmit it to the nerve fibers and the brain, when they erect themselves somewhat through a psychical effort — in the manner in which a shiver shows itself in female nipples [*papillae muliebres*] — and when they, under the pressure of gentle friction, are pressed against the tactile object. (241)

The papillae rise both when touched and in order to touch. Thus the discourses of the breast proceed — from aesthetics, by way of morality, fashion, and physiology — back to art. The undecidable oppositions are clustered around the related concepts of *Anmut* and *Reiz* (cf. Richter, "Ästhetischer und medizinischer Diskurs"), two German versions of the word "grace," and constitute what Wieland called the philosophy of the graces. The concept of grace in German anacreontic poetry was virtually coined on the female breast. But grace itself is riddled with the same ambiguities. Pomezny notes that

Anmut belongs to those words that have undergone a notable change of meaning. *Anmut* — meaning desire, lust — became the quality of stimulating desire. The word occurs as masculine and feminine. The former has the exclusive meaning of *affectus*. Regarding the latter, Grimm states: "The feminine word also shows in the sixteenth and seventeenth centuries that masculine meaning of desire and lust." (15)

This is an all too familiar figure: the image of the attractive woman is inserted into the scene of rape, displacing all questions regarding the perpetrator and the violence of his act (cf. Heinse's poem). Either the sexual charms of the woman are blamed, or the "charming" image covers the violence of the rape. The older language use, by contrast, conceded that the woman — the feminine — could also be conceived of in terms of desire and lust, which by the eighteenth century was the exclusive resort of the masculine. In all of these discourses, and in the very language itself, the breast emerges as a highly unstable sign of difference, a final characteristic that it shares with the phallus — except for the fact that one speaks of the breast and reveals its forms.

III

The emblem of touch also occurs in Wieland's *History of Agathon* (*Geschichte des Agathon*). Hippias, sophist and materialist philosopher, visits the bathing Danae, a hetaira, in the hope of persuading her to seduce Agathon. Asked what shape he would choose if he were Jupiter, Hippias replies:

What shape could I choose that would be more pleasing to you and more amenable to my intention than this sparrow that so often has provoked justified envy in your lovers; encouraged by the most tender names, it flutters impertinently around your neck, or mischievously nips at the most beautiful bosom, and is rewarded with double the caresses it bestowed on you. (*Agathon* 121)

The bosom-touching bird, emblem of touch, mediates in the imagination between male desire and female body. *Agathon*, along with the *Comic Tales*, is one of Wieland's first works since his break with Breitinger and his turn to empirical psychology. This turn was reinforced by his friendship with Johann Georg Zimmermann, who had published a dissertation on *Reizbarkeit* (irritability) under Haller in Göttingen ten years earlier. Zimmermann is one of the many readers who watched with fascination as Wieland presided over the seduction of his hero as if it were a scientific experiment. The remaining interpretation will concentrate on the meaning of the breast in the seduction and the connection between text and body.

Hippias's sophistics, his theory of rhetoric, is based on what he has learned from the persuasive powers of the female body:

> He was so clever as to have discovered very early how important the favor of these charming creatures is, who in the more polished parts of the world possess the real power; who, with a single glance, or through a small shift of their scarf, are more persuasive than Demosthenes and Lysias with their long speeches; who, with a single tear, disarm the general of an army; and who, through the mere advantage they extract from their shape and a certain need in the stronger sex, raise themselves to become the unhindered rulers of those in whose hands the fates of entire peoples lie. Hippias had found this discovery to be so useful that he spared no effort in bringing its application to the highest degree of perfection. (*Agathon* 44–45)

The cliché-ridden stereotypes are, of course, annoying. What is crucial for the interpretation, however, is that according to Hippias, rhetoric achieves with words what women achieve with their bodies. This body-rhetoric consists in "a single glance," "the shifting of a scarf," or, as in *Musarion*, the exposing of the bosom (Wieland, *Musarion* 41); in other words, in "grace," beauty in motion. The woman who was a master of this rhetoric was Aspasia, the famous hetaira, wife of Pericles, and the frequent object of Wieland's fantasies.[4] She is alleged to have established a school of rhetoric and love in Athens. Wieland strives to recuperate her honor in several texts.[5] The Danae in *Agathon* is reputed to have been schooled by Aspasia. As Wieland says, "This group of women was to its sex what the sophists were to theirs" (*Agathon* 119) — one more indication of the equivalence of female grace and sophistic rhetoric.

Hippias attempts to persuade Agathon of the validity of his philosophy of pleasure by laying out its theoretical principles. The central concept is that of sensuous pleasure — for every pleasure can be reduced to the senses. Three maxims can be deduced from the concept of pleasure: "Satisfy your needs, delight all your senses, and spare yourself as much as possible from all painful sensations" (*Agathon* 77). Hippias speaks theoretically, not rhetorically, of the body and its senses. That is why he fails to convince Agathon. (To that extent, Hippias could be compared to Heinse: both expose the part of the phallus.) If Agathon is to be persuaded, then only through rhetoric — that is, through the female body. Hippias deploys Danae.

She knows that she must conquer Agathon's imagination in order to seduce him (*Agathon* 131). What else does this mean—to speak with Haller—but that she must cause him an erection? The first encounter and the first mimic dance, in which Danae plays the part of Daphne entirely according to Agathon's desire, make a big impression on him. Yet his imagination transmutes the actual, corporeal Danae into "an ideal perfection" (*Agathon* 144), thus neutralizing her body-rhetoric.

The vision of this ideal image "set his spirit in such a pleasant and calm ecstasy that he, as if now all his wishes were satisfied, did not feel the least bit restless, nor suffered, on account of desires, inner ferment, the alteration of cold and fever" (*Agathon* 144). Agathon negates the signifier, the body, in order to loll in the signified, the spirit, as in an undeserved afterglow; thus Wieland skirts the erection. If Danae should ever succeed in seducing Agathon, she will have to draw his imagination back to her body; she will have to understand and use his imagination rhetorically.

Agathon had to be manipulated into deceiving himself without being aware of it; and should he be made sensitive to subaltern stimuli, then it would have to be through the mediation of the imagination and in such a manner that the spiritual and material beauties were mixed in his eyes so that he would believe he saw in the latter nothing but the reflection of the former. Danae knew very well that intelligible beauty arouses no passion and that virtue itself (as Plato said), should it appear in visible form, would awaken ineffable love, but that this effect would be more attributable to the blinding whiteness and the charming contour of a beautiful bosom than to the innocence that it shimmered forth. (*Agathon* 145)

The bosom is not merely the image of what Danae hopes to achieve, the confusion of signifier and signified; it will be *her* bosom against which she will press Agathon's head, through which and for which she will master his imagination. The body, the sign, is more powerful than the spirit, its meaning—not innocence, but breast, blindingly white, with a charming contour. In *Musarion*, Wieland footnotes a passage regarding the "bursting contour" of the bosom: "Contour actually designates the representation of a corporeal form that we have acquired by means of feeling and touching" (41). Vision is blinded; touch takes over. The signified is dissolved in the signifier.

Danae's success confirms our reading. Agathon finds her in feigned sleep in a tiny hut. He observes her "for a long time in immobile ecstasy and with a tenderness, the sweetness of whose inner feeling surpasses all bodily pleasure until finally - - - - compelled by the power of almighty love, he can no longer constrain himself, kneels at her feet, takes one of her casually outstretched hands, and kisses it with an ardor few lovers would be capable of imagining" (*Agathon* 172–73). There is the erection, plainly indicated in the physiognomy of the text. One senses the movement in "finally"; one sees it in the four hyphens "- - - -,"[6] and measures it in "longer" — and yet there is a slippage: he kisses her hand passionately. Because of the previous analysis of the discourses of the breast, however, we realize that the hand substitutes for the breast; the word "papilla" alone guarantees it. Further confirmation comes when Danae wakes from her feigned sleep:

O Callias [her name for Agathon] (she called with a tone of voice that resounded on all his heartstrings, while she wound her beautiful arms around him and pressed the happiest of all lovers into her bosom,) — what new being you give to me? Enjoy, o! enjoy, you most lovable among the mortals, enjoy the entire unlimited tenderness that you have poured into me. (*Agathon* 176)

Here is the pleasure of which Hippias spoke: "Enjoy, o! enjoy" — this is virtually a pictograph of the body she offers him. And Agathon does enjoy: the breast, at the breast. Wieland declines to sketch the scene further; he leaves "the paintbrush to a Correggio" (*Agathon* 176) — which in itself is ambiguous, since Correggio was commonly known as the painter of grace. The act of love for Wieland amounts to pleasure at the breast. What differentiates him from Heinse, it would seem, is that he describes the female seduction of a male, and not a rape. Wieland offers his reader the breast.

IV

There is no greater indication of the interaction between text and body than the reader's erection while reading. The seduction of Agathon by means of the rhetorical body/female rhetoric — that is, by means of the breast — is repeated on the body of the reader. The role of the phallus, in spite of its concealment, protrudes. Wieland is aware of this, though ambivalent. In a letter to his friend Zimmermann, he writes: "I'm glad that the *Comic Tales* appeal to you, but shall I tell you the truth? I was not glad to hear that they even caused such an older married man and such a wise man as yourself to have erections" (Seiffert 3:345). Wieland is in a triple bind. Confronted by Heinse, he conceals the phallus in the text. His text, in turn, cross-dresses the phallus as breast. The relation of the text to the reader is precisely analogous to that of Danae and Agathon. Wieland seduces the imagination; he offers his reader the breast. In the eighteenth-century discourses of the breast, however, it seems to be impossible to decisively differentiate between the female breast and the male member: the apotheosis of the breast in Wieland is at the same time the disclosure of the breast as phallus. The phallic breast enables the seduction of the reader; if the seduction is successful, then there is nothing Wieland can do to prevent the reader, stimulated by this breast/text, from finally - - - - also having an erection. Everywhere he turns, Wieland encounters the erect phallus. While Zimmermann may seem to be admitting to masturbation, Wieland must deal with the realization that through *Agathon* and similar writings he has established a homoerotic network of readers in which he is impli-cated as chief seducer. The breast, where the seduction of Agathon is duplicated by the seduction of the reader, is an arc that connects the desire of every possible (male) reader with Wieland himself.

The key to understanding this eighteenth-century reading net-work is to be found in the numerous and popular antimasturbation treatises of the time. An analysis of the endless anecdotes that fill their pages indicates that masturbation is irrevocably linked with the imagination, the imagination with reading, and, most important, that masturbation is *not* by definition a solitary vice. Indeed, be-havior that we would call homosexual or homoerotic at the very least is classified as onanism and spared any taint of sodomy. One of countless examples will suffice to display the analogy between Wie-land's reading network and that of eighteenth-century group mas-turbation. In a book entitled *Regarding the Secret Sins*, Christian Gotthilf Salzmann writes:

I know from the story of an older colleague that a young man, now a pastor, was seduced by a boy in school and practiced the vice. The entire school, primary and secondary, became infected. I know from experience that dur-ing lectures, while the professor held forth, this disgrace was practiced under the long cloaks worn by the students. Some of my acquaintances have ad-mitted that they did the same thing in school. They had no cloaks, nor did they sit behind benches, but since there were few of them, they simply sat on chairs around a table. I know that two of them performed this service for each other at the deathbed of a fellow student. (Quoted in Villaume 54–55)

Wieland's effort to distinguish Heinse's poetics from his own by reference to the phallus fails in the final analysis. Not only can the distinction between penis and breast not be maintained insofar as both are phallic, but the moral implications of reading Wieland are even more dubious than those of reading Heinse. The repugnance and discomfort he showed in dealing with the rapacious desire of Heinse's verses may, according to eighteenth-century morality, be even more appropriate for the homoerotic community formed in the contact between Wieland and his readers, between text and body. This is one conclusion that cannot be skirted.

Stephan K. Schindler

Homosocial Necrophilia:
The Making of Man in Jung-Stilling's
Idyllic Patriarchy

Eighteenth-century male subjectivity is constructed via the (auto-)biographies and novels of the period, specifically in their account of family affairs. According to Jürgen Habermas, Enlightenment literary discourse constitutes the autonomous bourgeois subject by depicting his "subjectivity discovered in the close relationships of the conjugal family" (49). What a Habermasian historiography of subjectivity fails to recognize, however, is that the space of this private "psychological emancipation" (46) — or what historians have characterized as the "closed domesticated nuclear family" (Stone 147, 411–14) — is itself a discursive construction that intertwines gendered fantasies with educational and sexual politics. One could easily argue that the entire unfolding of philanthropic pedagogy in Germany is an imaginative-fictional enterprise. Following the narrative example of Rousseau's *Emile*, major German speculations on education occur in fictional texts, such as Campe's *Robinson Junior* (*Robinson der Jüngere*) or Pestalozzi's *How Gertrud Teaches Her Children* (*Wie Gertrud ihre Kinder lehrt*), which generate the modern notion of ego formation within planned child- and parenthood.

This enlightened project of "becoming human" (*Menschwerdung*) through education almost exclusively signifies "becoming a man" (*Mannwerdung*), a process wherein women had to "learn" to become mothers in order to further the autonomy of their sons. The educated (M)Other as agent for primary socialization was thought to implement the subordination of the modern subject under its discourse (Mücke 115–60). As Friedrich Kittler has pointed out, a complex system of discursive networks ranging from poetry and philanthropic pedagogy to state administration invented the affectionate mother-child dyad. This interpersonal dynamic, symbolized in the mother's breastfeeding, was regarded as the intimate sphere for the making of the new man. The maternal voice replaced the breast, and her oral teaching of the alphabet became the "natural" process of acculturation (Kittler 25–69) that transformed the authoritarian patrilinear household as a locus of social continuity and reproduction into a motherly center of identity, desire, and fulfillment. In Goethe's *Werther*, for example, the formation of the ideal maternal family appears at first to originate from the coincidental disintegration of traditional households into single-mother families, but this reorganization of the family is also entangled with Werther's fantasies about playing the eternal child in an incestuous matrilinear family (Meyer-Kalkus). Thus, the literary invention of childhood and motherly love as an idealized space for male ego-formation becomes the source for neurotic/psychotic behavior usually associated with the Freudian family: Werther's narcissistic self is doomed to cling to the maternal other whose absence or denial has a cataclysmic impact on the male hero, who subsequently commits suicide.

While the discursive remodeling of bourgeois familial relations seems to culminate in the romantic apotheosis of the mother as educator and primary love object of her son (Poster 166–78), eighteenth-century literature did not attribute the emotional basis of the family exclusively to women. Writers from Lessing to Schiller attempted to rescue the domain of the traditional household for masculinity through the restoration of a compassionate patriarchy in which the absolute despot becomes the loving and beloved father (Sørensen 37–44). This "feminization" of the father must be seen in the context of regulative discourses that initiated but also questioned female participation in the raising of children. Whereas uneducated women in particular were considered unreliable owing to their presumed negligence and negative (i.e., sexual) influence on children (Campe, *Über die früheste Bildung* 135), devoted mothers were criticized for being too affectionate and spoiling their children instead of disciplining them (Wild 210–18). It seems that the discursive production of the overpowering mother as the new center of the family led to a certain envy among male pedagogues, whose writings first constructed and then deconstructed that figure by reempowering the father (Wild 221–57). The literary staging of these ongoing transformations of familial identities reveals male fantasies circulating around the position of the mother. It is therefore not surprising that the engendering of educational roles — "the real nurse is the mother and the real teacher is the father" (J.-J. Rousseau 18) — could be reversed to the extent that the nurturing maternal sentiment, the counterpart to paternal rationality, could be provided by men who take over exactly that position which the philanthropic discourse on childhood ascribes to the mother. This scenario of subject formation within a male family in which women are no longer needed is staged in the first modern German (auto-)biography, Heinrich Jung-Stilling's *Life Story* (*Lebensgeschichte*).

Oscillating between pietistic depiction of providence and secular "self-fashioning," Jung-Stilling's (auto-)biography is appraised still today as "a key transitional text" (Kontje 277) within German literary history. While the entire (auto-)biography — published in six volumes between 1777 and 1817 — represents the pietistic exegesis of the hero's ascending career as teacher, physician, professor, civil servant, and writer, scholars have given special attention to the first part, "Heinrich Stilling's Youth," because of its acclaimed poetic beauty and psychological introspection (Engel 112–14; Niggl 72–75; Pfotenhauer 77–81). Jung-Stilling's contemporaries already classified this text as an unrivaled prototype for autobiographical writing by the underprivileged (Bräker 194) and even compared its autobiographical honesty and veracity to Rousseau's *Confessions* (Moritz, "Aussichten" 89). The success of Jung-Stilling's idealized representation of (his) childhood in a patriarchal rural environment can be attributed largely to Goethe's secret participation as the ghostwriter who not only published but revised and edited his friend's work. Goethe apparently not only reduced Jung-Stilling's lengthy religious contemplations, but also instrumented the idyllic closure of the text, the integration of folk songs and tales, and the depiction of the child as genius, features that have been attributed to his style of the Storm-and-Stress period (Engel 112; Niggl 72–73). Predictably, the scholarly evaluation of the text focuses on authorship, genre questions, and the representation of the pietistic public/private sphere, but it almost entirely ignores the very core of modern autobiographical writing: the depiction of a self that is formed through individual experiences within a distinctive social and familial setting. Whereas all researchers mention that the hero, Heinrich Stilling, grows up under the influence of a harmonized patriarchy, they do not investigate its unique structure. Yet it is exactly this familial framework of ego constitution that reveals an uncanny complexity: Heinrich Stilling's family is epitomized as a homosocial community of men in which the fathers inscribe on the son a homophile desire through the dead body of the mother.

Already in the act of narration, the third-person perspective distorts the formation of the ego. Whenever the child Heinrich Stilling opens his mouth to say "I," paternal representatives speak instead; the story of the hero is subsumed under the history of the grandfather, the father, and indeed all male progenitors. Although the child is positioned as the thematic subject, his grandfather Eberhard Stilling is the subject of the action. He functions as the driving force of the narrative, which opens with anecdotes about him and ends with his death. In order to illustrate the grandfather's central prominence, the narrator identifies him not according to his position in the generational succession but with regard to his status as head of the household — as father Stilling (26–27, 78–82). Further underlining Eberhard's unquestioned power within the three-generation home, the narrator describes in detail how the grandfather enforces the ranking order at communal meals, how he represents the family to the outside world, and how he influences all decisions made by its members. By contrast, the patriarch is also presented as an affectionate honorable old man (10), who follows the enlightened idea of "companionate marriage" (Stone 217–53) by allowing his mature children to choose their own marriage partners. He separates his children according to sex, however, by considering only those as adult who have reached their "male age" (*männliches Alter*, 36).

Although Stilling's household, consisting of three generations, is built on the (re-)productive energy of wives, mothers, and daughters, women do not have a distinct place within the representation of the protagonist's youth. Rather, they function as markers of a threat: death and sexuality seem exclusively to symbolize their sphere. When the narrator introduces Heinrich's mother, Dortchen, into the narrative, he mainly characterizes the way in which her physical and mental weakness immediately becomes a danger for the proper functioning of the household: "But Dortchen had delicate limbs and hands, she tired very fast, and then she sighed and cried" (29). Dortchen's depression displays all the signs of that psychological disorder of the late Enlightenment called melancholia. Whereas men infected with this malady — like Heinrich's father or, more prestigiously, Anton Reiser and Werther — are still able to convert the asocial welt-schmerz and obsessive self-analysis into cultural productivity (e.g., writing, reading, teaching), women are doomed to die from it because of their exclusion from the realm of letters.

A closer look at the disposition of Dortchen's melancholy bares its clearly gendered construction. Under the influence of the pietistic command of mourning (Schings 75–81), she renounces profane pleasures and instead enjoys the "joy of melancholy" (37). Transcending secular and carnal passion, she believes that real fulfillment happens only after death. She visualizes the ultimate union with her husband in heaven and consequently wishes to die, although her marriage is legal and seemingly happy. While her melancholy counterpart Werther hopes to legalize his love to a married woman in paradise, it becomes obvious that in Dortchen's death wish female sexuality in general is at stake. Almost as a prologue to her own end, she sings a song about three virgins who seem to desire their own death by sexual penetration, represented as metaphorical defloration: "The man took a knife sharp and pointed, / and pushed it into the little gentle virgins: / into their sad little hearts" (42). Throughout the novel, all the women's folk songs and tales as well as their personal accounts depict the female experience of sexuality within a realm of violence that ultimately leads to death: women are abducted, raped, and murdered. If they survive deadly penetration they are expelled from society. Thus Dortchen cannot prevail, for she represents the woman who desires. Besides openly displaying her affection for Wilhelm, she accomplishes nothing in Stilling's house, as the narrator points out several times (28–29, 37).

Dortchen does not die, of course, after having had sex with Wilhelm, nor even after having given birth to the child, but only after Heinrich has reached the age of one and a half, when she has completed her services as mother. Her death coincides with the end of the child's weaning because, as a mother, her entire love of life is reduced to nursing her child: "She suckled her Henrich at all times because nursing was all that she had" (36). This suggestion of female fulfillment in the exclusive mother-child relationship seems to be a reference to the contemporary philanthropic and sociomedical discourse on mothering, which constructed the ideal family on the shoulders of the nurturing mother for the sake of the child's needs and emotions (Niestroj 31–48). In family portraits of the late eighteenth century, painters such as Chodowiecki, Edlinger, and Tischbein depicted the new emotional bonds of the family by foregrounding the breastfeeding mother, while relegating the father to the background (Lorenz 55–68). The degree to which paternal supervision is involved in this mother-child relationship, however, becomes clear when one looks at its legal codification. Still in 1794, the "Prussian General Provincial Law" (*Allgemeines Landrecht für die Preussischen Staaten*) calls breastfeeding an indispensable duty of mothers but subordinates its duration to the dictates of the father.[1] Thus, the promise of pleasure through nursing functioned as a discursive strategy to press women into service as wet nurses for their own children while at the same time disciplining mother and child alike (Niestroj 14–17). Aside from the state's interest in controlling the core of the family in the name of the newborn, this emphasis on breastfeeding can also be explained by means of a traditional physio-psychological belief: the mother's milk was supposed to influence the child's physical and moral qualities (Campe, *Über die früheste Bildung* 129). That is why Heinrich inherits "the mother's lineaments and her gentle sensitive heart" (36). Clinging to her breast, the child slowly incorporates the mother: she literally becomes a part of him. As he prospers and grows "pretty, thick, and fat" (36), the mother vanishes, because Heinrich sucks on the motherly breast like a vampire until only the shape of a "faded angel" (43) remains of the giving mother. Although Dortchen never enters the stage of (verbally) educating her son, she nevertheless serves as the disguised center of the emerging male socialization.

When Dortchen expires, her dead body is transformed into the poetic icon Elisabeth Bronfen has described in her analysis of eighteenth-century "deathbed scenes" (76–94): the dead woman as the double embodiment of the "unfamiliar Other" (92) transcends the living family, places threatening female sexuality out of reach, but also becomes the ultimate object of desire by preserving her beauty for reunification with loved ones in heaven. As a living and desiring woman, Dortchen seemed to have endangered the patriarchal order; as a deanimated body, she facilitates its reconstruction by leaving an empty space that forces her survivors to reorganize familial relations and identities. Being confronted with the absolute lack that the dead mother as corpse and woman poses, the men narcissistically reassure themselves by taking over her functions. In this regard, Dortchen's death — the death of the maternal — enables the men of the family to become all they ever wanted to be. Having exploited her biological nurturing of the male heir, men alone become the main agents of the child's education within the idyllic patriarchal household, which is represented as a male triangle. Rousseau's project of producing male subjects through male education seems to have reached even the outskirts of Westphalia. The men have to follow the path Dortchen forged to socialization, however, because her initiation of Heinrich into oral pleasures through breast-feeding functions as the gateway for others into the boy's psyche.

Immediately after Dortchen's death the father sinks into a depression that obliges the women of the traditional household to take care of Heinrich's needs. Again the text shifts the reader's attention to the grandfather Eberhard, who seeks to occupy the position of the lost mother. Already at Heinrich's birth he had hoped to sing his old lullabies and to demonstrate his child-raising abilities (30). His entrance into the boy's life as the provider of food and entertainment is depicted in a scene that incorporates all the features of the literary idyll as exemplified by writers such as Gessner and Voss (Schneider 86–90). As in most representations of harmonious family life, the devoted and "natural" relationship between grandfather and grandson seems to help overcome the objective socioeconomic and personal misery of the boy's childhood (overcrowded home, malnutrition, his mother's death, his father's depression). With the child sitting on his lap, the caring grandfather knows how to make a "dried-up sandwich" (45) palatable to the child by singing children's songs. Yet the grandfather does not only take over the motherly functions of primary socialization (nurturing, orality), thereby altering his generational position; he also combines the satisfaction of the child's needs with the simultaneous creation of an exclusive feeling for its provider: Heinrich "learns" to love his caretaker. When the boy's physical needs are satisfied, he is still hungry, longing for something that goes beyond satisfaction and is spelled desire. Through the exclusive relationship to his grandfather, Heinrich is introduced into the modern structure of familial love that appears as a "gift" (recognition, presence, proof of love) at the site of the (M)Other (Lacan, *Écrits* 286–87).

The text presents this familial drama with the grandfather as a modern Rousseauian educator whose actions are embedded within a philanthropic discourse. After the failure of authoritarian, disciplinary educational practices in the early Enlightenment, the modern idea emerged that love and affection provided by the mother were the best means for the "breaking-in" of children (Glantschnig 11–13). Eberhard Stilling seems to follow these directives. On the basis of personal emotional bonds within the educational relationship, he forms the boy's psyche by using the child's pleasures for didactic purposes: "Father Stilling knew the art of children's education, he always invented new amusements for Henrichen. . . . The child thereby gained a love for his grandfather that exceeded anything else, and that allowed all the ideas the grandfather wanted to teach to easily enter the boy's mind. Whatever the grandfather told him, he believed without further thought" (45–46). Modern family education reproduces precisely this structure, replacing external restraints (religious predestination and physical discipline) with internalized principles whose control mechanisms remain unconscious to the one being coerced. In order to accomplish this "art of controlling without precepts" (J.-J. Rousseau 99), parental love becomes the *via regia* for the child's total subordination to the Other's voice. When Heinrich no longer directs his libidinal energy toward objects, he enters the realm of identification. The shift from pleasure in the "dried-up sandwich" through "amusements" to "love for his grandfather" illustrates this fundamental change in educational practices. Thus, when Heinrich is assured of himself, his needs, and even his desires, he fails to recognize that they are put in place by others. The grandfatherly educator implants within the child a/his "self" by transforming "his desire into the desire of the Other." Here, Lacan's standard formula for determining the structure of desire — "desire is an effect in the subject of the condition that is imposed on him by the existence of the discourse" (*Écrits* 264) — can easily be associated with the making of man in enlightened pedagogy: "Are you not master of his whole environment so far as it affects him? Cannot you make of him what you please? His work and play, his pleasure and pain, are they not, unknown to him, under your control? No doubt he ought only to do what he wants, but he ought to want to do nothing but what you want him to do. He should never take a step you have not foreseen, nor utter a word you could not foretell" (J.-J. Rousseau 100).

Henceforth, all of Heinrich's wants are resolved according to the internalized paradigm or what one might call a narcissistically embraced superego. This unconscious subordination under the fatherly law seems to be the ultimate goal of modern pedagogy. Again, it is the peculiar familial position of the grandfather that makes the educational master-slave relationship so successful. Replacing father and mother alike, the grandfather operates within a same-sex dyad that conflates the child's love object with the introjected superego and the "ego ideal" (*SE* 12:65). Although at first Heinrich only wants to possess his motherly grandfather as his love object and never leaves him voluntarily, in the course of the story it becomes clear that he wants to be like his grandfather. This difference between "to have" and "to be like" corresponds with the ontogenetic phases of "object-choice" and "identification," one compensating for the loss of the other (*SE* 12:63–64). Thus, after the grandfather's death the child occupies his place at the dinner table and symbolically reconstitutes the endangered patriarchal order in the name of the dead. Paternal primary socialization determines this imagined identity of the child: the grandfather assigns to his grandson a place within the all-male lineage. Interestingly, these dead men are not characterized by their social or symbolic status (Lacan's *je*) but by their narcissistically projected recognition (what Lacan called *moi*) in a patriarchal chain of love, the agency of grandfatherly education: "Let it be your greatest honor that your grandfather, great-grandfather, and their fathers were all men who had nothing to say outside of their home but were loved and honored by all" (61).

On the level of plot, however, Heinrich's natural father, Wilhelm, disrupts the grandfatherly educational idyll and extends the grandfather(mother)-child dyad into a triangle. After having overcome his depression about his wife's death, he attempts to instruct the child himself. He rejects Eberhard's loving care and, following his quietistic convictions, tries to make Heinrich submissive and obedient (53). Although Wilhelm pursues the traditional strategy of disciplining the boy's body, he nevertheless utilizes in his private education the principles of modern schooling. Like a professional teacher he replaces Heinrich's "negative" uncontrolled space of experience with "positive" learning worlds: "Wilhelm never allowed the boy to play with other children, keeping him so isolated that at the age of seven the boy did not yet know any children from the neighborhood but rather a lot of beautiful books" (51). The father separates the child from family and society, locks himself in with his son, and even oversees the child's playgrounds. As harsh as his methods may sound, Wilhelm simply practices at home what all pupils will soon face in public education. He destroys traditional, natural, and nonintentional socialization by forcing the isolated child to become accustomed to the compartmentalization of his living space, as well as to scheduling, restrictive codes of communication, and the symbolic representation of the outside world through texts. In other words, Wilhelm employs those disciplinary learning techniques that are executed in all state institutions (prison, school, army) in order to create "docile bodies" (Foucault, *Discipline* 135–69).

A conflict between Wilhelm and his father seems to be inevitable because they compete with apparently different concepts of how to educate the male hero. It is this pedagogical contest between love and breaking-in, between ego ideal and superego, that draws the reader to the grandfather's side. The narrator (and following him, the Germanists) juxtaposes the father's restraining symbolic-formal education (discipline, reading, writing) with the "motherly" socialization of the grandfather (satisfaction of needs, play, orality) and thus splits the two complementary functions of the superego (prohibition and ideal) by assigning them exclusively to each of the two characters. The difference between the fatherly technology of supervision and grandfatherly love is irrelevant, however, because the grandfather has already established his surveillance system in the child's soul. During eighteenth-century educational debates, it became obvious that the patriarchal norm of governing through fear had lost its validity because it proved to be more successful to gain the subject's obedience with compassion and empathy (Sørensen 34–44). After the grandfather has convinced his son that love and devotion are better educational means than force, Heinrich returns under his grandfather's wings and utilizes what he has learned from his father.

Ultimately, this paternal legacy leads to the boy's embracing of the symbolic order that assigns identity in the name of all dead fathers. Following the educational concepts of pietism, Heinrich's desire/identity is guided away from his and the other's body and directed toward the dead and writing. His identification with the figures in "Gottfried Arnold's Life of the Old Patriarchs" and "Reitz's History of the Born Agains" (52) is so strong that he uses these idealized biographies as a model for his own writings. As if to prove the success of the fathers' education and methods, the young Heinrich becomes the scribe to the history, as related by his grandfather, of his own dead male ancestors. Thus Heinrich fulfills both of his fathers' educational intentions: already as a boy he is loved by all members of the household, and he even supersedes his forefathers because he is able to recite and understand Latin chronicles as well as to speak and write in Latin (69).

The absence of women and thus the disavowal of sexual difference, though, generates a problematic set of psychological conditions for the formation of the male ego because it equates the subject of identification (man) with the object of desire (man), subjects the male child to identify with the phallic signifier, and introduces him to the dead-end street of a masculinity that represses sexuality. With the mother's replacement by the grandfather and the subsequent dismissal of all women, the child's identification with the other is limited to a circulation between grandfather and father. The child's narcissistic identification with the beloved and loving grandfather and his initial rejection of the strict father suggest a reading of this triangulation as a displaced Oedipal configuration. But such an interpretation is contradicted by the fact that all men are so entangled in mirroring each other that they expel any potential third player. Although the grandfather takes over the mother's familial position, he remains in the paternal sphere because he identifies with his own dead ancestors and desires in Heinrich his own introjected self. Furthermore, despite their different methods, Heinrich's father and grandfather nevertheless pursue the same goal: the successful writing of their own male imago into the child's soul.

Compared with other contemporary (auto-)biographical novels (Bräker, Moritz, Goethe), the entire field of an imaginary that resists the fathers' inscription is left out. Even the child's fantasies are so preoccupied with the voices of the dead fathers that at the end of his youth Heinrich has only one goal: to become his own (dead) grandfather. One can find neither subversive fantasies nor the playgrounds of polymorphous-perverse child sexuality (Heinrich is not a lover of dainties). He also does not regress into the mother-child dyad that resists phallic signification. The child's desire converges instead with that of his fathers, as when Heinrich's daydreams begin simply to paraphrase the pietistic confessions and biblical legends his father gave him to read and the histories of his male ancestry his grandfather narrated to him. Simultaneously, Heinrich explicitly rejects the oral (sexual) cultures of the women of the household, which fill him with fear (74). Even his lies to avoid physical punishment from his father do not threaten paternal authority, for they are sanctioned by his grandfather and thus forgiven by his father. Any potential conflict between the competing fathers is resolved in the name of the child whose self is their own mirror image, the reason for which the patriarchal idyll remains stable.

This educational regime of the brotherly fathers grants Heinrich fraternity, equality, and righteousness because the all-male family is built on what Flower MacCannell has described as "egomimesis" (43–84): the narcissistic modeling of Heinrich's self, which doubles the imaginary identity of father and grandfather alike. This modernization of the traditional patriarchy, in which the grandfather is supposed to rely on absolute power, is only possible through the exclusion of women. While the living women symbolize a transgression of the paternal order (e.g., the unmarried mother, Dortchen's egocentric revelry), the dead mother serves in the construction of male bonds leading to a confusing "male homosocial desire" (Sedgwick, *Between Men* 1–20). Her empty place is occupied by men in such a way that the child has access to the mother only through the paternal sphere: not only does the grandfather take over her mothering role, but the father also represents her voice for the son. Even any possible recollection of the child's symbiotic relationship to the mother, which was probably established through the long duration of breastfeeding, is converted to an identification with the father's speech. Showing Heinrich "every footstep of his transfigured mother" (56), Wilhelm creates her as the dead object of desire: "Heinrich fell so much in love with his mother that he would transform everything he heard about her into his own; Wilhelm was so delighted about this that he could not hide his joy" (56). Loving the dead mother as a relic, the child himself becomes entangled in the logic of objectifying the living, as when Wilhelm abandons his purely educational relationship to his son to desire him physically once Heinrich represents the dead wife. In his boy's face Wilhelm sees only Dortchen's lineaments; when he sleeps in the same bed with Heinrich he dreams about his dead wife; finally, he "threw all his affection on Heinrich and he found again Dortchen in him" (59). This incestuous reinscribing of (fe)male identity reaches a climax when the homophile organization of the father-son relationship breaks the armor of the pietistic denial of the body in an *Urszene* of physical affection. When Heinrich finds a little knife with Dortchen's initials, the fetishized presence of the dead mother provokes vehement eruptions in both men. The boy faints and "lay like a corpse" (57), thus resembling even physically the dead mother. When the father embraces him, he feels "a pleasure that prevailed over anything else" (57) and imagines to be in heaven with his dead wife. The son awakens and, realizing the unfamiliar paternal embrace, asks his father if he is fond of him (57). Over the signifier of the motherly corpse, "both lovers of the blessed Dortchen" (56) are able to declare their love for each other. While the father experiences a completely new, warm affection for his son, Heinrich finally declares his ultimate obedience to his father, an obedience the grandfather had already erected in him: "I want to do anything you want me to do" (58). Father and son are so preoccupied with each other and their new emotional bond that they lose the newly found precious fetish, making even more obvious what function the mother as dead body has: she reconciles father and son, who find their affection for each other only through the maternal corpse. Twenty years later, the marquis de Sade composed a similar but much more drastic image of two men simultaneously loving one woman: the traffic in women becomes literal when double penetration unveils homosexual desire — a desire expressed in the same image in the classical films of twentieth-century heterosexual pornography (e.g., *The Devil in Miss Jones*, 1974). Jung-Stilling's (auto-)biography, however, complicates any assessment of the object of desire and the subject of identification because the third player (woman) is constantly substituted by the second (man), who nevertheless inherits the characteristic of the former: being dead.

Looking at the replacement of women by men, one is tempted to explain the all-male triangle in Stilling's family along the lines of Silverman's paradigms of "femininity in male homosexuality" (339–88). All men identify with and/or desire the female position. What makes things complicated, however, is the fact that every subject of desire is also the other's object of desire within a different triangle. Wilhelm, Heinrich's father, seems to follow the "Greek" model of homosexuality (Silverman 365–69), identifying with the symbolic position of the "father" and desiring the boy Heinrich as the reincarnation of his young wife. In a patriarchal society that assigns the receptive sexual position to women, the not yet mature son can easily replace the mother as his father's passive love object. While the relationship between Wilhelm and Dortchen was already described as a narcissistic one — they retreated from the family to share their mutual melancholia — the combination of Heinrich's masculine body with the mother's face and heart creates an even more perfect mirror object for the father's narcissistic desire. From the moment he begins to love his son, the change in sex also entails a change in generation. Subsequently, Wilhelm desires not merely his wife in his son but, narcissistically, the child he once was himself. Heinrich, on the other hand, escapes becoming the father's love object by desiring the dead mother, whom he identifies not with the father but with the grandfather. Here, the necrophilic tendencies of the homosocial family come into play. At the very moment when a physical bond seems to be established between father and son, the maternal corpse between the two men directs Heinrich's desire back to the motherly grandfather, who himself has to die in order to physically become the mother.

Following his father's embrace, the son is completely preoccupied with his dead mother. On his first visit to Dortchen's grave, Heinrich wants to excavate the remains of his mother, wishing only to see her remaining bones (59). As if to divert Heinrich's attention from his bizarre request, the grandfather surpasses it: after having a vision of Heinrich's dead mother as a magnificent angel (74–75), Eberhard himself wishes to die — expressing his desire with the same words Dortchen used — in order to reunite with (become) his daughter-in-law in heaven. Although this proximity of mother and grandfather in heaven could be explained by the fact that in pietism the woman as dead mother symbolizes God himself (Langen 309–11), the grandfather's vision has a different function. When Heinrich attempts to find out more about his "dear mother" (75) in heaven, the child depends again on the report of his grandfather, who seems not just to control access to the mother in heaven but to reinforce the homosocial community even beyond earth by replacing the dead mother in the afterlife. As the dead Dortchen becomes a sign (a grave, a memory, an angel), the motherly grandfather as love object is also transformed into an icon that reaffirms the paternal agency of signification. With his own death he stresses again what he mentioned while narrating the family history: the domesticated heaven as the extension of the familial order is a male one in which "our kin/sex" will "flourish and blossom" (61).

Heinrich's search for his dead mother comes to an abrupt end when the grandfather himself dies. His ecstatic deathbed scene and the description of his grave dominate the end of "Heinrich Stilling's Youth." As if to further underline his replacement of the mother both in heaven and on earth, the grandfather's grave is depicted with the same natural design as that of the mother. As in Goethe's *Werther*, the death of a man outshines the previous death of the mother. Although the man's death meticulously restages hers, its representation occupies a much more central position within the text. In this way Heinrich's identification with the motherly grandfather is again reinforced by narrative displacement. Already in the second part of the (auto-)biography, Heinrich has forgotten his mother and only imagines "father Stilling with a bright glow around his head" (83). Subsequently, Heinrich's desire and identification can no longer be addressed to a living body but only to a corpse. This development follows the same path as the course of Heinrich's education, which switches from orality to the realm of the letter. At first, he serves as the medium between heaven and earth, communicating the speech of the dead grandfather to the remaining family members; but already at the age of fourteen he explains the ultimate book of the patriarchy when he becomes a teacher of the catechism (90). The circular structure of inscribing the identity of the dead onto the living becomes evident at the end of the text. The grandfatherly legacy comes to an end when Heinrich's own grandson (and not his children) concludes the last volume of the *Life Story* by placing the now aged Heinrich "on the comfortable chair of the grandfather" (599).

The representation of the other as dead brings together the object of desire and that of identification while crossing all four generations. The grandfather identifies with his dead daughter-in-law, with her familial position as mother, and thus also with his own (dead) mother; he desires his grandson as his alter ego and thereby the boy he once was himself. He educates his grandson in such a way that Heinrich doubles his identity and thus identifies with and desires the grandfather as the dead mother. What Silverman calls the "Leonardo Model" of homosexuality seems to work at the very center of Stilling's homosocial family: "Having 'become' the mother, the subject can only love others as she loved him, which means that he is attracted to those particular others who occupy in relation to him the position he himself earlier occupied in relation to her" (368). This narcissistic structure of desire and identity can also be attributed to Rousseau's educational same-sex relationship and Werther's invention of romantic love within a mother-child dyad. Both texts share with Jung-Stilling's (auto-)biography an undermining of the Oedipal configuration of familial relationships by reducing the triangle to a relationship with only two players. Already at the historic moment when the nuclear family is fantasized into the social norm, the figure of the mother is so desired by men that they seem to wish to erase their own sexual and generational identity in order to become mothers or children themselves. What is so disturbing about Stilling's patriarchal homosocial idyll, however, is the fact that it literally kills women in order to represent familial love between men. For Heinrich, the position of the mother as object of desire is deleted the moment the grandfather occupies her place and authorizes familial love in the Name-of-all-dead-Fathers. But even these emotional bonds between men cannot develop when the loved ones are placed in heaven, becoming ghosts for cultural production instead of being bodies for physical affection. Whether it represents an aberration or the ultimate result of the dominant discourses on mothering, one can only wonder how Jung-Stilling's glorification of a homosocial, antifeminine family, in which homophile desire transforms itself into the desire of (for) the dead man, has influenced other male fantasies about the making of man.

Roman Graf

The Homosexual, the Prostitute, and the Castrato: Closet Performances by J. M. R. Lenz

The works of J. M. R. Lenz are permeated with precarious constellations in gender relationships, causing seemingly erratic forms of behavior in the characters of his plays and prose. In his play of 1776, *The Soldiers (Die Soldaten)*, an army colonel proposes the institutionalization of prostitution as a solution to the continuous sexual exploitation of young women by the soldiers of the time. Sexuality and its prescriptive function in a social setting also determine the action in Lenz's earlier play of 1774, *The Tutor (Der Hofmeister)*. In this work, initially attributed to Goethe, the tutor Läuffer escapes social constraints through his desperate act of castration. In Lenz's short novel *The Hermit (Der Waldbruder)*, first published by Friedrich Schiller in 1797 in *Die Horen*, the protagonist, Herz, physically flees civilization and leads the life of a hermit in a forest. Although he removes himself from society, he nevertheless is bound to it by his desire for a countess, a woman he knows only through the reports of others. The reasons for her unattainability, for the demand for an army of prostitutes in *The Soldiers*, as well as for Läuffer's emasculation in *The Tutor*, have posed almost insurmountable problems for Lenz scholarship.[1] The resulting inaccessibility of these texts has forced Lenz to assume a peripheral role in the canon of German literature.

Since the problematic issues in the works above center on the concept of sexuality, Lenz's understanding and treatment of sexual relations become pertinent to the reading of his literature. This approach to his oeuvre finds further justification in Lenz's anthropological endeavors. He is unique among eighteenth-century German authors in viewing sex as a primary driving force of the human condition. For him, "the sex drive is the mother of all our emotions" (*Philosophische Vorlesungen* 68) and needs to be discussed openly.[2] But *The Soldiers*, *The Tutor*, and *The Hermit* are not motivated only by questions of sexuality; they develop Lenz's anthropology by exploring the bizarre permutations of the sex drive and the yet stranger emotions they produce. These "deviances" are the focus of this article.

According to recent developments in queer theory, especially Eve Kosofsky Sedgwick's *Between Men: English Literature and Male Homosocial Desire* and *Epistemology of the Closet* and Judith Butler's *Gender Trouble*, one cannot assume a heterosexual matrix for gender relationships. Embedded in heterosexual gender constellations are homosocial relationships — bonds between people of the same sex — that harbor a potential eroticism. Homosociality includes elements of desire and intimacy, thereby intersecting with homosexuality, which becomes a topic of medical and psychological discourse around 1900: "I think that a whole cluster of the most crucial sites for the contestation of meaning in twentieth-century Western culture are consequently and quite indelibly marked with the historical specificity of homosocial/homosexual definition, notably but not exclusively male, from around the turn of the century" (Sedgwick, *Epistemology* 72). Although Sedgwick specifically situates these "crucial sites" at the turn of the twentieth century, her distinctions also apply to earlier periods. Investing the human sex drive with a potential for homosexual desire enables one to establish connections in Lenz's texts that otherwise elude heterosexist interpretations.

In *The Soldiers*, Lenz portrays the demise of Marie, the daughter of a jewelry merchant, who falls victim to the desires of soldiers. After one soldier, Desportes, seduces, betrays, and leaves her, she acquires the reputation of a whore and is driven out of her home. Her story, though, is also influenced by her ties to two other men: Mary, best friends with Desportes, gains her trust but not her love, while Stolzius, her fiancé, is left with nothing except his revenge for Marie's destruction. At the end of the play a colonel suggests a seemingly outrageous solution to the problematic situation of women and soldiers: an army of whores subsidized by the emperor. Granted, Lenz himself later revised this suggestion in his treatise

On the Marriages of Soldiers,[3] nevertheless, the colonel's solution demands to be taken seriously in the context of *The Soldiers*, since it proves consistent with the dichotomized gender relationships in the play that arise from the incompatibility of homosociality with homosexuality.

Although Marie has to be viewed as the protagonist of *The Soldiers*, the title distinctly alludes to the soldiers as a focus of attention. Their existence and actions at the end of the eighteenth century form the roster in which individual destinies inscribe themselves. Since the army is an all-male institution, the relationships among the soldiers are perforce homosocial. In this context, Marie finds herself entering what Gayle Rubin describes as the "traffic in women,"[4] the gaining of male power through the trading of women as commodities of sexuality. Marie assumes the role of the gift in an exchange between men: she becomes the item of commerce between Desportes and her father, Wesener, who, as is customary for the times, gives his daughter away to a man, who, in this case, disappears. Desportes takes advantage of Marie and never returns, despite his promise to do so. Instead of relying on her father's efforts, Marie tries to regain her lover herself by attempting to negotiate a deal with him. She plays the bargaining role of her father, trying to escape her function as trade object in order to become an active subject instead. However, Marie cannot be both subject and object at the same time — or, in other words, perform a male part and still remain female. Gayle Rubin states: "To enter into a gift exchange as a partner, one must have something to give. If women are for men to dispose of, they are in no position to give themselves away" (Rubin 175). Since Marie is trafficked as a woman, she is trapped in her role as object of barter. Of consequence to this study is the fact that, via the trade, the two men create a homosocial tie between each other.

Not only is Marie trafficked in an exchange between Desportes and Wesener, but she also constitutes the object of a deal between Desportes and his friend Mary, who becomes Marie's second beau. The similarity of the names of the soldier Mary and the woman Marie already alludes to a possible interchangeability of these two characters in regard to Desportes: again, the "traffic in women" establishes a homosocial tie. Traditionally, same-sex bonds, especially among men, have been regarded as untouched by eroticism, and therefore the opposite of homosexual. Once the denied erotic element is displaced onto heterosexual intercourse, however, women are transformed into mere receptacles for sexual frustration. The suppression of same-sex desire thereby contributes to homophobia as well as misogyny in modern Western society. Counteracting this insidious conjunction, Eve Sedgwick's notion of "homosocial desire," articulated in her book *Between Men*, establishes a continuum between the homosocial and homosexual that results in an incorporation of eroticism and desire into homosocial bonds.

Keeping in mind a slippage of the homosocial toward the homosexual and relating it to the concept of the "traffic in women," we come to a new understanding of the relationship between Mary and Desportes. Mary's desire is exposed as directed toward Desportes and displaced onto Marie. In this respect, Marie assumes a dual function: she could fulfill Mary's sexual desires and at the same time keep him close to Desportes, whose woman he now possesses and whom he shares with her. Lenz himself, during his stay in Strasbourg in 1772, seems to have experienced emotions very similar to Mary's. He writes to his close friend Daniel Salzmann on June 3, 1772, alluding to their close personal friendship: "I love you—my heart forbids me to tell you more, eloquent wit has never been its translator" (*Werke und Briefe* 3:253). On June 10, Lenz relates to Salzmann his encounter with Friederike Brion, whom he adored, and it is not difficult to recognize the homosocial/homosexual tensions in his description:

The day after my last letter to you, I went to her: we spent the evening alone in the gazebo; the modest and angelically good sister hardly ever interrupted us, and if, then always with such amiable wittiness—you were the only subject of our conversation—yes, you, and the friendly girls almost cried out of desire to meet you. (*Werke und Briefe* 3:256)

Lenz's desire to remain close to the man Salzmann finds expression in his conversation with the woman Friederike.[5] In discussing his male friend, Lenz is able to keep him present to mind while at the same time displacing his own sexual desires onto the female. Here we find mirrored Mary's situation in *The Soldiers*: in order to remain close to Desportes and his experiences, Mary tries to gain Marie's love. He displaces his sexual desire onto Marie and achieves the connection with Desportes.

Homosocial desire is not revealed only in the similarity of the protagonists' names and the triadic constellation of Marie-Desportes-Mary; it is emphasized by the very structure of the play. Act 2 ends with a sexual encounter between Marie and Desportes that occurs backstage and is conveyed to the audience via the song of the grandmother. Act 3 then opens with Mary's prank on two other men who have entered this almost entirely male lineup of characters: an old Jewish man, Aaron, and Rammler, one of the soldiers.[6] By arranging a potentially homosexual meeting, Mary tries to embarrass Rammler and call his sexual prowess into question. He convinces Rammler that he is going to bed with a beautiful young woman, while in the meantime informing Aaron of a possible burglary and guaranteeing his assistance. In order for Mary to expose the criminal, however, he tells the Jew that he must remain silent in bed pretending he does not realize that someone has broken into his room. Before Rammler actually gets into bed with the Jew, other soldiers, who had hidden in the dark room, appear and resolve the would-be homosexual encounter. In this scene, Aaron, the Jew, functions as an imaginary woman. He is used by the soldiers to teach one of them a lesson; in other words, he fulfills the function of an object in homosocial relationships and is thereby devaluated. Anti-Semitic, misogynist, and homophobic attitudes thus converge in this scene, which not insignificantly follows a pivotal meeting between Marie and Desportes.[7]

The (hetero-)sex scene between Marie and Desportes is brought into direct connection with the potentially homosexual meeting between Rammler and the Jew via Mary.[8] The homosexual confrontation with Mary as the director and instigator, a scene in which the interchangeability of the gender of potential sex partners is emphasized, follows the heterosexual encounter between Marie and Desportes. Mary's homoerotic awareness is revealed and indirectly, on a structural level of the play, related to Desportes and Marie. The resulting potential homosocial tie between Mary and Desportes then manifests itself openly in act 4, scene 9, when Desportes cannot help but constantly think of Marie and is brought face to face with his past sexual encounter with her when Mary laughingly puts a piece of licorice in his mouth. This gesture ambiguously suggests either fellatio or the penetration of the vagina, but I would propose a reading that includes both sexual acts. On the one hand, Mary's gesture alludes to Desportes's having sex with Marie, and on the other, it retains the image of one man fellating another — Mary Desportes, or vice versa. This allusion to an erotic bond between Mary and Desportes finds its final and climactic realization in Desportes's death scene. Marie's fiancé, Stolzius, after having remained rather passive throughout the play, poisons Desportes, who is seeking help yelling, "Mary!" Stolzius, however, responds with "Marie! Marie! Marie!" The convergence of the names Mary and Marie in this scene not only intensifies Stolzius's revenge for the soldiers' betrayal of Marie, but it also reveals a firm grounding of the play in homosocial norms. Instead of remaining in a homosocial/homosexual relationship with a man, Desportes "betrays" Mary with Marie, and vice versa. He initially leaves his friend Mary to be with Marie, then separates from her to be with Mary again.

Homosocial desire is omnipresent. Yet the categorical repression of such desire, of erotic tension within homosocial relationships, leads to misogynist tendencies. In the last scene of the play, the colonel, in a conversation with the countess Sophie de la Roche, suggests a solution to the problematic relationship between soldiers and young women: "If the king would put up a band of soldier women . . ." (*Werke und Briefe* 1:734).[9] The establishment of an army of prostitutes is supposed to alleviate sexual frustrations among the soldiers. The colonel is trapped in a homophobic, misogynist worldview. He assumes a stance that is rooted in homosociality as opposed to homosexuality, without Sedgwick's potential slippage. Although Lenz alludes several times in this play to a continuum between the homosocial and the homosexual, thus beginning to deconstruct traditional gender norms, he is not able to escape the overall homophobic and misogynist attitudes of his times. Ultimately, he cannot transcend the barriers of compulsory heterosexuality and so sanctions the establishment of an army of whores as a logical conclusion to homosociality.

Whereas prostitution frames the events in *The Soldiers*, castration ushers in the gender and sexual play in Lenz's earlier work, *The Tutor*. As the title suggests, the story focuses on the destiny of one person, thus shifting the action away from the homosocial realm of *The Soldiers*. Nevertheless, the two plays are connected not only through the significance of sexuality, but also through similarities between Stolzius and the main protagonist in *The Tutor*, Läuffer. As stated above, in *The Soldiers* Stolzius remains in the background of the main events until the end of the play. He serves Desportes and

Mary, wears a piece of cloth around his head when seen on stage for the first time, and proves to be the only character who is susceptible to the power of Marie's words. He represents an odd or "queer" male, lacking the stereotypically male qualities of leadership and intellectual rationalization, and expressing an array of emotions, which draw him closer to the realm of the stereotypically feminine. He is the emasculated male, never being able to enter the sphere of homosocial relationships of the other male characters. Läuffer in *The Tutor* actually emasculates *himself*. A "straight" reading of his act of castration refers to his inability to cope with the guilt of having impregnated Gustchen and focuses on the aspect of penance. I suggest a "queer" look at the events.

After an alleged affair with Gustchen, the daughter of an army major in whose house he had been a tutor for a while, Läuffer has to leave town and find shelter at a school in a neighboring village. In a desperate attempt to stifle his sexual desires, he castrates himself. Nevertheless, he is able to win the heart of Lise, a young girl in town, who is willing to marry him despite his "deficiency." Reading the play with a focus on homosexuality allows for a new understanding of Läuffer's situation and explains his plea for a marriage without sex: "And is it even necessary to the happiness of marriage that one satisfies animalistic desires?" (*Werke und Briefe* 1:117). With this rhetorical question, Läuffer hopes to appease the village schoolmaster, Wenzeslaus, who, referring to Läuffer's act of castration, tries to argue the impossibility of a marriage between Lise and Läuffer. Wenzeslaus bases the institution of marriage on the procreation of the human race and prioritizes sexuality in marital relations. Läuffer, however, shifts the emphasis from sexuality to asexual emotions. Lise, who supports Läuffer's argument in front of Wenzeslaus, enables the tutor to argue that she only demands love from him. He then concludes with the rhetorical question just cited. In turn, Wenzeslaus answers with the authority of Latin: "A marriage without a child is like a day without sun" (*Connubium sine prole, est quasi dies sine sole*).

A closer analysis of this conversation reveals the establishment of a distinct matrix of gender relations that manipulate the interpersonal relationships within the play. Läuffer posits the separation of sexual desire from an emotional bond between two people. He emancipates sex, providing it with an autonomy that enables him to reject it as harboring fundamentally negative forces. Since the human sex drive escapes reason, it becomes ultimately uncontrollable and potentially dangerous: it remains in the realm of animalistic desires — "tierische Triebe." With Läuffer's interpretation of these drives, Lenz plays on a gender dichotomy that Fritz von Berg, Gustchen's lover, voices in the last scene when he explains to Gustchen: "Now this child is mine as well; a sad pledge of the weakness of your sex and the foolishness of ours" (*Werke und Briefe* 1:123). Women cannot rely on their intellectual faculties to conquer their sex drive, since their domain is the emotional and nonrational. Men, by contrast, are potentially able to conquer sex through their rational powers. Should they fail, it is as a result of their *Torheit*, a term that, in contrast to *Schwachheit*, remains in the realm of the intellect. Thus, the affirmation of a "cultural association of mind with masculinity and body with femininity" (Butler, *Gender Trouble* 12) functions as a subtext in *The Tutor*.

Lenz confirms these presuppositions by juxtaposing the behavior of two young couples with the life of the tutor Läuffer. The lovers Gustchen and Fritz, as well as a young girl called Jungfer Rehaar and the student Pätus, adhere to traditional heterosexual gender conduct. Gustchen cannot help but remain in love with Fritz even though he leaves her, and the Jungfer Rehaar devotes her life to Pätus. In the framework of the play, both women are limited to a confrontation of their sexual desires via their emotions, which belong to the realm of the animalistic. In other words, they cannot intellectually distance themselves from sex. In fact, this combination of sexuality and emotion constitutes them as women. Men, by contrast, can separate the animalistic from the emotional through the power of reason and thereby signify themselves as men. In this respect, Läuffer's emancipation of sexuality remains within the established gender dichotomy of the play.

For a while, however, Fritz and Pätus return the affection of their lovers on equal terms — that is, emotionally. Such feminine devotion destabilizes gender relations in the play. In fact, the dramatic action depends on this incongruence in gender-determined behavior. In *The Soldiers*, Lenz acknowledges this gender dichotomy, having Desportes simply move from one woman to another, adhering to the stereotypical gender role of the male by separating sex from love. But the woman Marie challenges the prevalent gender hierarchy, thus lending the play its driving force. In *The Tutor*, Lenz allows Fritz and Pätus to succumb to the forces of emotion. Instead of rationalizing and thus distancing themselves from their love affairs, both men remain true to their first love. They surrender their male rationality to female intuition and emotion, and consequently fail to establish functioning relationships. Instead they depend on the voices of reason, their fathers, to solve their dilemma. The privy counselor von Berg and the elder Pätus assume the role of dei ex machinae in regard to Fritz's and young Pätus's destinies. The privy counselor controls the events in the last scene of the play, conjoining his son and his niece Gustchen and encouraging a union between Pätus and Jungfer Rehaar, which the elder Pätus finally supports and administers. The two fathers thus mutually reinforce male hegemony in the play. Only if the rational powers of male thought govern people's actions is it possible to sustain a functioning family.

In the family, as the smallest social unit in the state, gender becomes political. Although the major is extremely happy to have regained his daughter, a sociopolitical concern lingers when he discovers her marriage plans. He asks the privy counselor: "Is it a person of good descent? Is he of nobility? . . . But not someone too far beneath her social rank?" (*Werke und Briefe* 1:121). This invocation mirrors his plea to God in act 1, scene 5, where he prays for a minister or general to court Gustchen. It is crucial to my reading of this play that the major wants to witness this union, since he needs to win his daughter a fortune, thereby gaining prestige himself. Gustchen, by contrast, has no control over her own destiny, but, according to the major, has to be provided for (*versorgt*). She thus constitutes the object in a hypothetical barter between the major and a general or minister. This fantasized situation is realized when Fritz and Gustchen rejoin at the end of act 5, granting the major his previous wish of being associated with the nobility of his time. In contrast to Marie in *The Soldiers*, Gustchen never tries to escape the role of the trade object. She remains at the mercy of men — her father, Fritz, and even Läuffer. Therefore, although the "traffic in women" does not function as the driving force of the action in this play, it still constitutes an important compositional element within gender relations.

Once we shift our attention toward the traders within the triad of commerce, homosocial relationships emerge. The major, Fritz, and Herr von Berg form homosocial ties. Although in *The Tutor*, in contrast to *The Soldiers*, Lenz does not create character constellations that lend themselves to a closer analysis of a "potential unbrokenness of a continuum between homosocial and homosexual" (Sedgwick, *Between Men*, 1), homosociality still operates among the men. Homosocial bonds create a union among the male characters that excludes the teacher Wenzeslaus as well as the tutor Läuffer, situating them outside the strict gender dichotomy in the play. As noted, Gustchen, Jungfer Rehaar, and Lise, in their role as women, function as objects of exchange between the male characters Fritz and Pätus, whose fathers in turn remain the representatives of male power. But by not successfully being part of this "traffic in women," Wenzeslaus and Läuffer, who happen to share similar professions, remain on the periphery of heterosexual relationships.

Keeping established gender constellations in mind, and combining them with a heightened sensitivity toward homosexual desire, we realize that Wenzeslaus's task as a schoolteacher assumes a normative, channeling function in the play. Consider this statement by him: "For nothing is more difficult for young men to learn than to write straight [*gerade*], to write alike — don't write daintily, don't write fast, I always say, but write straight, because that affects everything, morals, sciences, everything, my dear tutor. The person who cannot write straight, I always say, can also not act straight" (*Werke und Briefe* 1:78). Straight writing leads to straight behavior in society. I read the German word *gerade* in the English sense of "straight" as opposed to "queer," as Judith Butler explicates it in her recent article "Critically Queer," subsuming under the category of "queer" anything that does not "line up." In her usage, "queer" seems to assume an all-encompassing meaning that includes "odd" as well as "homosexual," never ridding itself, however, of derogative connotations. " 'Queer' derives its force precisely through the repeated invocation by which it has become linked to accusation, pathologization, insult" (Butler, "Critically Queer" 19). Applying this definition of "queer" to Wenzeslaus's statement reveals him as devoting his life to a mainstreaming of adolescents — in other words, to the development of their heterosexuality. Heterosexuality no longer remains confined to sexual behavior but slides into other areas of life as well. It determines social behavior as such. In this reading, heterosexuality itself becomes an achievement and is not a stable, innate

human condition. Furthermore, the dichotomy between heterosexuality and homosexuality is broken, since sexuality becomes the
libidinal expression of a network of cultural forces that work on
each individual. Sexuality and culture emerge as inextricably inter-
twined, disclosing innumerable sexualities instead of the one op-
positional pair, heterosexuality and homosexuality.

Surrounded by stereotypically heterosexual couples and fathers,
and a teacher who heterosexualizes students, Läuffer assumes the
role of the "outsider." In his monologue in the first scene of the play,
he introduces himself through a frame of reference that situates him
financially, intellectually, and sexually outside the norm: he depends
financially, he says, on the assistance of his father, lacks the necessary qualifications for a position at a public school, and is too young
and beautiful to enter the priesthood. He leaves the stage with a
reference to von Berg: "That guy has something in his face that I
cannot stand" (*Werke und Briefe* 1:42). This remark could allude to
the general physique of the privy counselor, yet Läuffer's discomfort
could conceivably stem from the counselor's beard, a sign of male
potency and a gender mark that Läuffer is missing. This motif of the
beard recurs when von Berg speculates about his son's future: "Fritz,
who soon will have a beard like mine . . ." (*Werke und Briefe* 1:52).
Läuffer cannot display such masculine attributes. In fact, he demonstrates primarily artistic talent as a dancer, musician, and painter,
which already allots him a place outside of "straight," masculine
society. When the major's wife addresses him with the diminutive
"Männichen," the emphasis lies on the suffix -*chen* rather than the
Mann. Furthermore, this "little man's" attraction to women remains
primarily in the realm of the aesthetic. Over and over again he refers
to pictures of women and to the desire to draw them. In this context
it is not surprising that the first onstage encounter between Läuffer
and Gustchen is dominated by the former's references to drawing.
We meet them a second time in Gustchen's bedroom, a potentially
sexual location. There, however, Läuffer contemplates his financial
future, while Gustchen reminisces about Fritz von Berg, her lover.
Given Lenz's adherence to a fixed gender dichotomy throughout the
rest of the play and its combination with a heightened awareness of
homosexuality through the character of Wenzeslaus, Läuffer indeed
appears "queer" — financially, intellectually, and sexually different.

Linguistic strategies hide this "queerness" and at the same time elucidate it. Again, it is Sedgwick who enables us to discern these strategies. In *Epistemology of the Closet*, she discusses the phenomenon of the closet:

> But, in the vicinity of the closet, even what counts as a speech act is problematized on a perfectly routine basis. As Foucault says: "there is no binary division to be made between what one says and what one does not say; . . . There is not one but many silences, and they are an integral part of the strategies that underlie and permeate discourse." "Closetedness" itself is a performance initiated as such by the speech act of a silence — not a particular silence, but a silence that accrues particularity by fits and starts, in relation to the discourse that surrounds and differentially constitutes it. (Sedgwick, *Epistemology* 3)

Sedgwick analyzes a phenomenon pertinent to the lives of modern gays and lesbians, describing the relationship between homosexuals and their degree of "outness" — open acknowledgment of their sexualities — to their surrounding communities. To be "out" always includes some degree of secrecy, of silence. In fact, it is never a state but always an action. At the same time as one "comes out," one still remains "in the closet," for every new encounter demands a new stepping out of confinement. To remain "closeted" then, means to remain silent; in other words, "closetedness" becomes a performance of silences.

These silences vary in actual life as well as in literature, but they can be undone through a reading of the voices that compose and arrange them. In the case of Lenz's *The Tutor*, the surrounding discourse — the strict adherence to a conventional matrix of gender definitions and relations in regard to the other characters in the play — covers and at once uncovers Läuffer's closet. On the one hand, these constellations allow Läuffer to manipulate them so as to create the closet; on the other hand, they also enable the disclosure of his potential homosexuality. A reading based on conventional assumptions about gender sees Läuffer as a tutor who seduces his student and, being confronted with the negative effects of his hetero sex drive — Gustchen's child — chooses to escape the realm of the sexual altogether and castrates himself. A "queer" inquiry into the individual factors that enable such a reading, however, reveals ambiguities that at once hide and discover Läuffer as potentially homosexual.

Could he have fathered Gustchen's child? It would be easy enough for Lenz to state clearly that Läuffer is the child's father. Yet not only does more than a year elapse between the presumed conception and the birth of the child, but the recognition scene in act 5 retains an essential ambiguity. When Marthe, an old woman who had taken in Gustchen, relates Gustchen's story, Läuffer takes hold of the baby and exclaims: "'Oh my heart!—That I can press it against my heart—I understand you, horrible riddle!' (Takes the child in his arms and steps in front of the mirror.) 'How? These would not be my features?' (Faints; the child begins to cry)" (*Werke und Briefe* 1:100). His question "These would not be my features?" allows for a double reading. Either he recognizes that the child *does* bear his features, or he questions the resemblance, seeking refuge in an act of self-silencing: he faints. Since the above scenes point toward a "queer" existence of Läuffer, I read his castration not as an act of heterosexual erasure, but as the ultimate flight into the closet of homosexuality. It is my contention that in order to create a closet, one does not have to be conscious of that creation, but one is aware of the fact that one's sexuality or sexual preferences differ from a societal norm. In Läuffer's case—that is, in the case of a character in an eighteenth-century play—these considerations become relevant. The tutor knows that his attitude toward sex challenges the surrounding opinions, and he states this in his conversation with Wenzeslaus. It is not necessary to spell out that Läuffer is potentially homosexual; in fact, the concept of homosexuality does not even have to exist at the time, but his specific abnormal behavior within the narrow confines of the established heterosexual gender relationships in this play signal to a twentieth-century reader that Läuffer is homosexual.

The final silence that partakes in the establishment of his closet paradoxically surrounds the complete erasure of his heterosexuality. The subtext underlying Läuffer's act of castration reveals the assumptions on which his seemingly erratic behavior is based. In a conventionally heterosexual context, his castration makes sense only if one assumes that Läuffer harbors an enormous hetero sex drive and that in order to protect society from it he has to relinquish this drive by literally eradicating his phallus. As I have discussed above, though, Läuffer cannot be interpreted as a character possessing phallic power. He gains the status that is connected to it only through his castration. On the one hand, he signals to the people around him that he indeed once had the phallus, and on the other, he finds refuge in a nonsexual relationship with Lise. He has created the ultimate closet, a marriage without "animalistic desires." Läuffer does not have to satisfy these desires, but, by taking advantage of the multiple meanings of the verb *stillen*,[10] he silences them. His question "And is it even necessary to the happiness of marriage that one satisfies animalistic desires?" is answered.

Through the erotic relationships of the characters in his two most famous plays, *The Tutor* and *The Soldiers*, Lenz problematizes sexuality to such a degree that heterosexuality, while remaining the societal norm, becomes only one manifestation of human sexual energy among many. In his prose work *The Hermit*, Lenz transcends the boundaries of the formation of individual sexualities,[11] theorizing the concept of sexuality in general and lending it an element of performativity. Through the epistolary structure of his text and the interaction of the characters in it, Lenz suggests that sexualities are artificially created and reinvented—in other words, performed. Within this system, gender "is performative insofar as it is the effect of a regulatory regime of gender differences in which genders are divided and hierarchized *under constraint*" (Butler, "Critically Queer" 21). Therefore, an individual's gender is governed by a system of always already-present rules that categorize and circumscribe its performance.

In *The Hermit*, subtitled "Supplement [*Pendant*] to Werther's Sorrows," Lenz assembles various pieces of information about the protagonist, Herz, and his love, the countess Stella, through Herz's own letters and those of several of his acquaintances and friends. The protagonist escapes the norms and pressures of society by isolating himself in a forest hut. After falling in love with Stella, being betrayed by his friend Rothe, and leading a disillusioning existence as a hermit, Herz decides to venture to America. In contrast to Goethe's much more focused work, the choice of a multiple authorship within the narrative—featuring seven voices all together—creates a mosaic effect. Reported events seem ceaselessly to escape fixed meaning, since each letter sheds a different light on them.

Reality is a fleeting notion not only for the reader of *The Hermit* but also for its protagonist. At a masked ball, Herz meets a woman whom he takes to be the countess Stella and falls in love with her. She turns out, however, to be not even a countess but Frau von Weylach. More amorous complications ensue: instead of directing his emotions toward this woman, Herz displaces his feelings onto Frau Olinde Hohl, who relates incidents from the "countess's" life. Herz then writes: "All her actions appear to me as shadows of the actions of my countess, all her words as echoes of hers. . . . In short, I love her, this Olinde" (*Werke und Briefe* 2:393). The object of the protagonist's devotion is mediated not only through letters, a mask, and another woman, but finally also through a pictorial representation: a picture of Stella functions as the embodiment of Herz's desire for her. In fact, this continuous mediation culminates in the disappearance of the initial object of desire — the countess at the ball is in fact not the countess — a substitution that challenges the authenticity of Herz's feelings. In other words, the question arises whether he is performing his passion because compelled by surrounding forces to act according to social norms. This ambiguity, enhanced by the mosaic structure of the text, encourages a discussion of the novel's performative aspects. Through the polyperspectivity of its epistolary form, the work allows for innumerable silences that enable its performative function as the closet — a silencing and a voicing at once. With each unclarified, unstated motivation on the part of Herz, Lenz provokes a reading of him as a closeted homosexual.

Herz remains in the closet, yet not without alluding to these confinements. Reflecting on Rousseau, he "comes out" to his friend Rothe as a man unfit for procreation: "If I wish to remain weak, only semi-usable, rather than to dull my senses for that at whose creation all powers of nature had been at work, for whose perfection heaven itself united all circumstances . . ." (*Werke und Briefe* 2:382). Herz wants to remain useless (*unbrauchbar*) and refuses to perceive women sexually, even Frau Hohl, about whom he relates that he loves her, "but not the way she wants to be loved" (*Werke und Briefe* 2:394). Comparable to Läuffer's state of mind in *The Tutor*, Herz's attraction to women remains in the realm of the aesthetic and the constructed. He does not succumb to lust over a woman but reacts to the artistic conception of an ideal. The composition of this work as an epistolary novel guarantees the permutability and thus flexibility in regard to the blanks between various letters, granting multiple combinations and allowing insight into Herz and the reactions of the surrounding characters to him. Honesta, for example, writes about Herz's attitudes toward the countess's letters that he became more taken with her after each account of her daily routine. The object of his desire is thus not Stella but the literary representation of her.

Herz is not the only man in *The Hermit* who ultimately cannot relate to women as sexually as he would like to: his best friend, Rothe, experiences similar problems. He entices women through his open, almost foolhardy nature, yet he can no longer sustain his "love stories" (*Liebesgeschichten*) once he tries to communicate with them on the level of "noble sensibilities" (*hohen Empfindungen, Werke und Briefe* 2:384). As soon as he tries to endow these relationships with deeper emotions, he fails, terminating the "love stories." Again, erotic desire for women is contextualized within the fictional frame of stories. Cross-gender relationships remain in the realm of the hypothesized and the fictional.

In addition, in *The Hermit* women are trafficked once again. The picture of the countess, which Herz assumes to be for himself, is actually commissioned by Rothe for his collection of paintings: thus two male friends strive for the same aestheticized woman. As in *The Soldiers*, woman functions as a figure of displacement for men's reciprocal desire. Once the potentially homosexual attraction is transferred onto a woman and heterosexualized, the slippage of homosocial toward homosexual is prohibited. In *The Hermit*, however, the woman is an aesthetic construct whose erotic power presumably lies in her representation, exposing the men as never having experienced heterosexual intercourse. Indeed, the novel suggests a strong homosocial tie between Herz and Rothe: Herz's own letters, which could be directed to any one of the characters in the novel, always address Rothe, emphasizing a close affinity with him. Given that heterosexuality remains the focus of attention despite the powerful current of homosociality, we are led to speculate that Herz is a closeted homosexual who performs his gender role within a set frame of parameters in society, and that he tries to escape these parameters by retreating first to the forest and ultimately to America.

Since a narrator to this story is missing, individual reports of events centering on Herz combine to form a mosaic picture of his character. As a result, the composition of *The Hermit* as an epistolary novel is foregrounded, drawing attention to the process of its construction. We are aware of connecting various pieces of information to form a cohesive whole. Keeping the "queered" relationships in regard to the protagonist in mind, their "fits and starts, in relation to the discourse that surrounds and differentially constitutes" them (Sedgwick, *Epistemology* 3), the polyperspectival text emerges as the "closet." Whereas Lenz alludes in his plays to homosociality, homosexuality, and the closet, in his prose work he emphasizes the fabrication and performance of the closet. In *The Hermit*, the gaps and silences between individual letters assemble the "closet." The thorough aesthetization and distantiation of personal relationships, evident not only in the epistolary form but also in the ultimately proscribed relationships of the protagonist with women through representations — mask and picture — renders gender constructivist. By investing representations with attributes of originals whom he has never truly known — the countess and Frau Hohl — Herz articulates a gender role for himself that is based on cultural assumptions and retains an arbitrariness that allows for speculations about gender. If "gender performativity is a matter of constituting who one is on the basis of what one performs" (Butler, "Critically Queer" 24), not only does Herz create a potentially heterosexual relationship, but since the formation of his character is the novel's focus — its title implies it — the process of creation itself becomes the very modus operandi of the entire work. Herz performs sexuality at the same time that Lenz emphasizes the construction of sexuality. He focuses the reader's attention on the incongruences of Herz's behavior, illuminating the performative character of his attempts. If we take into account that the story is based on events surrounding Lenz and his devotion to Henriette Waldner von Freundstein,[12] Lenz creates a closet not only for Herz, but also for himself. He performs heterosexuality, but leaves enough gaps and silences for the initiated to unlock the door to the closet of homosexuality.

Robert D. Tobin

In and Against Nature: Goethe on Homosexuality and Heterotextuality

Goethe once reportedly commented, in a discussion about the Swiss historian Johannes Müller,[1] that "Greek love" was as old as humanity, adding that it therefore seemed to be at once rooted in nature and against nature (April 7, 1830; Friedrich Müller 187–88). In describing pederasty as something both natural and unnatural, Goethe grants sexuality the power to disrupt the binarisms that construct our society, in a way that Eve Kosofsky Sedgwick, using English, American, and French authors, outlines in *Epistemology of the Closet* (11). Goethe's reference to pederasty's position in nature suggests that same-sex desire is paradigmatic for literature itself. Pederasty, with its power to unsettle the duality of natural versus unnatural, fulfills a function similar to that of writing in Jacques Derrida's essay on "Plato's Pharmacy"—the function of a *pharmakon* that can both poison and heal. Pederasty and writing, which both refer constantly to diametrically opposed concepts, are "heterotextual" in that they mean both themselves and the other. Pharmakons that are at one and the same time natural and unnatural, poisonous and curative, pederasty and writing, show the link in Goethe's works between sexuality and textuality.

Like Goethe, Derrida goes back to the Greeks, specifically Plato, to talk about the pharmakon, which is both a poison causing forgetfulness and ignorance and a remedy to those conditions, strengthening memory and increasing knowledge. His pharmakon is of course writing, not pederasty, yet there is a link between sex and his drug; indeed, the traditional ambiguity of the pharmakon is present to this day in the word "drug," which has both beneficial, healing and

destructive, addictive qualities. Ronell notes the connection between
the pharmakon and erotics: "If Freud was right about the apparent
libidinal autonomy of the drug addict, then drugs are *libidinally
invested*" (25). Rhetorically, Derrida's examples make clear that
Plato's pharmaceutical writing has an erotic component. The pharmakon operates "through seduction" (70).[2] Socrates allegedly uses
his pharmaceutical powers to bewitch Agathon (117–18). The example of Helen shows that the pharmakon has "the power to break
in, to carry off, to seduce internally, to ravish invisibly" (116–17).
The pharmakon, which can cure as well as poison, is not always
used nefariously, to seduce the unwilling; rather, in its "good" and
"beautiful" manifestations, its rhetoric relates to reproductive sexuality: some writing can "engender," "regenerate," "bear fruit"
(152). Language is a "pharmakon which can equally well serve the
seed of life and the seed of death, childbirth and abortion" (153).
Regardless of the outcome, then, writes Derrida, "the entrance of the
pharmakon on the scene" necessarily leads to "games and festivals,
which can never go without some sort of urgency or outpouring of
sperm" (149–50). Clearly, if writing is the pharmakon, then it is, in
Derrida's view of Plato, linked to a sexuality of dissemination.

Although language can give both life and death, Derrida emphasizes nonreproductive sexuality when looking for metaphors for the
pharmakon. He "takes off" from the *Phaedrus*, a text famously
associated with male-male love. Remarks explicitly on homosexuality in "Plato's Pharmacy" link it with writing, Derrida's primary
concern: "One could cite here both the writing *and* the pederasty of
a young man named Plato" (153; see also 164 n. 80). In this passage,
Derrida links up not just sexuality, but specifically homosexuality,
with not just language, but specifically writing: pederasty, like writing, is "a lost trace, a nonviable seed, everything in sperm that over-
flows wastefully," whereas reproductive sex, like "living speech,"
bears fruit (152). Throughout the essay, Derrida describes the pharmakon of writing in ways that could easily also refer to nonreproductive sexuality. Writing as a pharmakon substitutes "the prosthesis for the organ, . . . a limb by a thing, . . . the passive, mechanical . . .
for the active" (108), just as the nonreproductive sexuality of, say, a
marquis de Sade, emphasizes the mechanical nature of what was
allegedly once a wholesome, organic act.

Derrida emphasizes the nonreproductive aspect of writing, instead of the fruitful aspect of living speech, because he doesn't want to push potentially dangerous drugs. For Ronell the addict needs a drug to fill the lack that ultimately derives from the signifier's inaccessibility to the signified. Addiction stems from that condition which renders literature necessarily ambiguous: we can never know if the work is supposed to mean one thing or another. Derrida uses metaphors of nonreproductive sexuality to describe writing because literature is nonreproductive to the extent that it does not transmit the meaning — the genes, so to speak — of its author to future generations. The pederast and other practitioners of nonreproductive sex stand for a sober understanding of the limits of literature's ability to mean. Their sobriety will help them withstand the temptations of addiction, confirming Ronell's psychoanalytic observation that "the pervert does not do drugs" (17). The metaphor for the spoken language that the addict wants is reproductive — not perverse — sexuality that transmits presence and meaning from author to reader. If homosexuality appears in literature as a pharmakon or drug, it is because it characterizes, with its nonreproductive sexuality, literature itself, which is the drug that can either cure (if this condition of "nonreproductive" textuality is accepted) or kill (if it is not) the addict. Thus the pervert, the homosexual, understands the nonreproductive nature of literature and avoids addiction, while the addict yearns for a reproductive writing.

In a footnote Derrida declares the role of the pharmakon "analogous . . . to that of *supplément* in the reading of Rousseau" (96 n. 43),[3] a reading that, on the one hand, emphasizes the diametrically opposed tendencies (both adding to and replacing nature and speech) of writing as a supplément and, on the other hand, stresses Rousseau's use in the *Confessions* of the phrase "dangerous supplément" to mean masturbation (*Of Grammatology* 144–45, 149–50). Once again the deep ambiguity of writing is linked, this time via the concept of supplément, to nonreproductive sexuality. Derrida's comparison of Plato's ancient Greek pharmakon to Rousseau's eighteenth-century European supplément pivots the discussion back to Goethe and his age. When Foucault moves from the erotics of the ancient world to the love of the modern world, he sees Goethe's *Faust* as emblematic for the shift from the love of boys to that of women (*History* 2:229–30). Goethe's comments about pederasty — about its ancient, original ambiguity, its naturalness and unnatural-ness — suggest, however, that for him, male-male love had not yet completely lost its value as a pharmakon or supplément.

Although Goethe drank many a bottle of red wine on the way to the twelve-step programs of his late writings, he takes the recommended dosage of this drug, pederasty, under the doctor's supervision. As Ronell suggests, Goethe is almost the opposite of the "addict": "a non-renouncer par excellence (one thinks of the way *Goethe* mastered renunciation)" (9). Goethe uses the twin pharmakons of writing and homosexuality to renounce the kind of textuality that claims presence, that corresponds to procreative sexuality, in favor of a textuality more comparable to nonaddictive pederasty.

The Italian trip seems to have brought out the value of homosexuality as a pharmakon for Goethe. On the biographical level, the trip to Italy seems to have been generally important for the development of Goethe's sexuality, as Eissler, for instance, documents. Goethe's art work from Italy, especially his images of male nudes with prominent genitalia, suggests that male as well as female sexuality preoccupied him in this period of time.[4] The letter written from Rome to Weimar's Duke Karl August on December 29, 1787, demonstrates Goethe's discovery of Italian male-male love. After complaining that the female prostitutes had venereal diseases and the unmarried maidens insisted upon marriage, Goethe explains that the men in Italy love each other: "After this contribution to statistical knowledge of the country, you will judge how tight our circumstances must be and will understand a remarkable phenomenon that I have seen nowhere as strong as here, that is the love of men among themselves." Goethe's assumption that this love "is rarely driven to the highest degree of sensuality but rather dwells in the more moderate regions of sensuality" implies that it sometimes does go beyond the bounds of propriety. Nonetheless, he praises it as a beautiful example of something that "we only have from Greek traditions." Goethe's references to the traditions of ancient Greece reveal his era's emphasis on the classical heritage of male-male love, but his next comment, that he, as a "researcher of nature," was able to observe "with his own eyes" "the physical and moral" aspects of this phenomenon, illustrates his understanding of it as natural. The fundamental difficulties in talking about sexuality, about whether it is present only in "traditions" (in this case, Greek ones) or also in "nature," difficulties that have to do with its status as a paradigmatic pharmakon, show up in the final line of the paragraph, in which Goethe uses a pre-Wildean version of the trope of the love that dare not speak its name when he writes: "It is a material about which can scarcely be spoken, let alone written." Interestingly, especially with regard to Derrida's work concerning the masturbatory supplément in Rousseau, the next paragraph of Goethe's letter to the duke about sex begins: "Now commences the time of diversions" (*WA* 4.8:314–16). Diversion or *Zerstreuung* (literally, "scattering" or "dispersing"), with its waste, its unproductive strewing, has much to do with masturbation. The letter thus moves from the impossibility, owing to disease, of potentially reproductive heterosexuality to varieties of nonreproductive sexuality such as homosexuality and masturbation.[5]

In fact, homosexuality appears frequently in Goethe's literary works as well as in his biography. Two works in particular raised eyebrows when they first appeared because of their alleged endorsement of pederasty. Although he generally liked the *Roman Elegies* (*Römische Elegien*), August Wilhelm Schlegel objected to a passage in Goethe's tenth elegy that, in a list of great warriors, included Frederick the Great along with Alexander, Caesar, and Henry IV, who would gladly exchange their victories for a night in bed with the speaker's lover. He apparently found the passage problematic, according to Derks, because of the rumors surrounding the sexuality of Frederick the Great (268). More clearly provocative in the *Roman Elegies*, however, is the reference in the nineteenth elegy to Amor, who attempts to steal heroes away from Fama by offering them first women, then men:

> Girls he offers; whoever foolishly scorns them
> Must bear truly grim arrows from his bow;
> He excites man for man, drives desire to the animal.

> Mädchen bietet er an; wer sie ihm töricht verschmäht,
> Muß erst grimmige Pfeile von seinem Bogen erdulden;
> Mann erhitzt er auf Mann, treibt die Begierden aufs Tier.
> (*HA* 1:172)

This passage incensed Schlegel and other contemporaries because of its casual treatment of "unnatural" passions (Derks 268).[6] The four elegies that were not published might have outraged audiences even more. One calls upon the phallic god Priapus to sodomize all those hypocrites who read the *Elegies* voyeuristically:

> Now watch the hypocrites . . .
> If one should near . . .
> . . . then punish him from behind
> With the pole that springs red from your hips!
>
> Nun bemerke die Heuchler . . .
> Naht sich einer . . .
> . . . so straf ihn von hinten
> Mit dem Pfahle, der dir roth von den Hüften entspringt!"
> (*WA* 1.53:6)[7]

On the one hand, this passage emphasizes the violent, nonerotic use of sodomy; on the other hand, the use of sodomy to punish voyeuristic readers points to Goethe's constant interest in linking homosexual behavior metaphorically to writing.

Much later in life, Goethe continues to use homoerotic motifs in his poetry, specifically in *Das Schenkenbuch*, the book in the *West-Eastern Divan* (*West-östlicher Divan*) that most emphasizes the pederastic slant of the Persian literature that inspired Goethe to write the *Divan*. The title of *Das Schenkenbuch* bears some discussion. It stands out in the table of contents of the *Divan* because, whereas all the other titles of the *Divan* are structured as genitives, along the lines of "The Book of the Singer" (*Das Buch des Sängers*), "The Book of Hafis" (*Das Buch Hafis*), or "The Book of Love" (*Das Buch der Liebe*), only *Das Schenkenbuch* is constructed as a compound noun. The unique structure within the *Divan* of this book title allows Goethe to leave pointedly unclear whether this is the Book of the Cupbearer [*der Schenk[e]*] or the Book of the Inn [*die Schenke*]. In fact, in the inn, the poet dallies amorously with the cupbearer, so it is a book about both. Goethe's linguistic subterfuge does not work in English, so translators must choose between inn and cupbearer; those who, like a recent translator,[8] opt for "The Book of the Inn" eliminate what Goethe's contemporaries felt to be the subject of the book. In their dictionary, the brothers Grimm credit much of the modern nuancing of the word *Schenk* (cupbearer) to precisely this book, adducing "Goethe's procedure in *The West-Eastern Divan* (Book of the Cupbearer)" (8:2539). The "Announcement" for *The West-Eastern Divan* that appeared in the *Morgenblatt* of February 24, 1816, also refers to "The Book of the Cupbearer" (*Das Buch des Schenken*; WA 1.6:430).

But when recent translators ignore what Goethe's contemporaries considered to be the book's centerpiece, they merely pass on the opinion of critics like Trunz, who, anxious to allay fears about homosexual tendencies, have hastened to reassure readers by giving Goethe's word that the book depicts "a truly pedagogical relationship" (*HA* 2:202, 649). Goethe must have had a different view of pedagogy than most modern readers, though, for this student-teacher relationship is replete with love of a decidedly physical kind — the cupbearer, a wily student indeed, exclaims:

> But I love you more
> When you kiss to remember;
> For the words pass,
> And the kiss — it stays inside.

> Doch ich liebe dich noch lieber
> Wenn du küssest zum Erinnern;
> Denn die Worte gehn vorüber,
> Und der Kuß, der bleibt im Innern. (*HA* 2:95)

To find this relationship innocent of all erotics is to disagree both with Goethe, who emphasized the erotics of the passage, and his contemporaries, who found the passage morally objectionable. In his commentary to the *Divan*, Goethe writes: "Neither the immoderate taste for half-forbidden wine, nor the tender feeling for the beauty of a growing boy, could be absent from the "Divan"; the latter was to be treated however — in accordance with our traditions — in all purity" (*HA* 2:202). Goethe apparently treats this subject "in all purity" only because that is "in accordance with our traditions." As for Goethe's contemporaries, Chamisso, for instance, after reading the *Divan* accused "father Goethe" of setting a precedent for "coquetting" "with the love of boys" (Derks 271).

The *Roman Elegies* and the *West-Eastern Divan* both show Goethe's willingness to use the motif of homosexuality in his writing; they also show the unwillingness of critics from both Goethe's and our era to accept this homosexuality. More important, however, they also point to Goethe's linking of the motif of homosexuality with the theme of language and writing. The connection between sexuality and poetry is one of the famous points of the *Elegies*, particularly in the fifth elegy, in which the poet uses his hands in the daytime to leaf through the works of the ancients and in the night-time to feel his lover's body. The dream of a union of lived sexuality and poetry reaches its apogee when the poet taps out hexameters on his lover's back (*HA* 1:160). In his commentary on the *Divan*, Goethe follows his reference to the "tender feeling for the beauty of a growing boy" by recounting in some detail one of the stories by the Persian poet Saadi about teacher-student relationships, a story that resembles Plato's *Phaedrus* in its blending of erotics and grammar, of high-minded education and carnal manipulation. The poet Saadi likes the boy, partly because of his looks, but also because the boy, grammar in hand, is learning pure language thoroughly (*HA* 1:203). In fact, the "pedagogy" in "The Book of the Cupbearer" has to do with teaching language. The book begins with a poem that asks:

> Where was the parchment, the pen where,
> That captured everything?
>
> Wo war das Pergament, der Griffel wo,
> Die alles faßten? (*HA* 2:89)

It continues to circulate around the theme of inspired, intoxicating, beautiful writing, speculating that one poet wrote beautiful letters despite drunkenness and discussing the inspired nature of the Moslem scriptures. With the cupbearer himself, the poet discusses the nature of poetry and song, teaching the cupbearer otherwise when the youth says he prefers kisses to words.

Homosexuality and language are both present in the *Roman Elegies* and the *Divan* because they are both pharmakons. In another poem, written while in Italy, Goethe makes clear the relationship between eros and those characteristics that identify the pharmakon. In 1788, Goethe wrote a poem to Cupid, who fills a role analogous to the Amor of the *Roman Elegies*:

> Cupid, loose, stubborn boy!
> You asked me for quarter for a few hours.
> How many days and nights you have stayed!
> And now have become imperious and master of the house.
>
> Cupido, loser eigensinniger Knabe!
> Du batst mich um Quartier auf einige Stunden.
> Wie viele Tag' und Nächte bist du geblieben!
> Und bist nun herrisch und Meister im Hause geworden.
> (*HA* 1:237)

While the more usual, heterosexual, interpretation of this poem might assume that Cupid is the spirit who caused the singer to fall in love with a woman, Sander Gilman intriguingly suggests that this "paean" could in fact address "the young and beautiful boy" (*Sexuality* 228), a suggestion made more plausible by the poet's conclusion that Cupid has "warped and misplaced" his "tool" (*HA* 1:237).[9]

Goethe, who reused parts of this poem in *Claudine of Villa Bella* (*WA* 1.11:230), comments on the self-contradictory nature of eros in its broadest implications when he reprints the poem yet again in the *Italian Journey*: "If one does not take the following poem in a literal sense, doesn't imagine that spirit that one usually calls Amor, but rather imagines a collection of active spirits that speak to the innermost part of humanity, challenge it, pull it back and forth, confuse it with divided interest, then one will participate in a symbolic way in the circumstance in which I found myself" (*HA* 11:478). Regardless of whether this Cupid is homosexual or not, he is definitely a pharmakon, a pleasure and a pain. Here Goethe explicitly asks the reader to dismiss the idea of sexuality, Cupid or Amor, as a single demon, and see it as a complex of self-contradictory impulses that affect humanity in the deepest way. He points here to the pharmaceutical nature of sexuality, its inborn ambiguity, which relates it so closely to textuality.

In an important recent article, Helmut Müller-Sievers correctly argues that "every interpretation that still tries to reconstruct some liberating sexual experience of which the poems [in this case, the *Roman Elegies*] would be the embellished report refuses to acknowledge their poetological cogency as well as their literally vital place in Goethe's oeuvre" (442). Goethe's own understanding of the figure known as "Amor" supports Müller-Sievers's case that Goethe's sexually liberating experiences — in Italy or anywhere else — are not interesting only in and of themselves. Rather, they are interesting because Goethe sees them as apt symbols for poetry. In a number of Goethe's poetic works, the literary ambiguity of sexuality, its pharmaceutical nature, becomes clear.

Many of the passages cited from Goethe indicate that the duality that he saw as most immediately affected by sexuality was that between the natural and the unnatural. The disruptive effect of sexuality upon that duality becomes quite clear in the pair of poems

"Ganymede" and "Prometheus," written in the early 1770s and always published together after 1789.[10] The litany of critics all too anxious to assure us that the name Ganymede has no relevance to the poem to the contrary,[11] the name Ganymede was in fact a code word for homosexuality for centuries (Bredbeck). "The Book of the Cupbearer" bears further witness to his knowledge of the erotic possibilities of Ganymede's position. Thus it is fascinating, even radical, that precisely Ganymede, a mythological figure who had come to represent unnatural sexuality, should be associated with images of nature. The poem speaks ecstatically of "flowers," "grass," "morning wind," "the nightingale," and "clouds," all symbols of a nature with which Ganymede eventually becomes one. Conversely, Prometheus, with his hearth and hut, is alienated from nature, yet his sexuality, although admittedly nonheterosexual insofar as he produces his own young, remains reproductive and thus natural enough to leave readers comfortable. At least, no one has ever wanted to dissociate him from his mythological antecedent. In these poems, Goethe outlines the chiasmic effect of sexuality on the dichotomy natural/unnatural: Ganymede's unnatural sexuality is part of nature, while Prometheus's alienation from nature does not stem from an unnatural sexuality.

Pederasty makes an even more brazen appearance in *Faust*, where, in the final scenes, Mephistopheles falls victim to the charms of the angels. Mephisto's desire for the male angels disrupts conventional boundaries between male and female, as he notes when he calls them "the true arch-conjurers" (*die wahren Hexenmeister*, line 11781; *HA* 3:354) because they seduce both men and women. Mephisto's own sex change from avarice to greed in *Faust II*, act I (lines 5664–65; *HA* 3:176), as well as his cross-dressing as Phorkyas in the Classical Walpurgisnacht (line 8026; *HA* 3:243), further demonstrates his disruptive effect on male-female dichotomies. When he, a devil, falls in love with the angels and calls them "the true arch-conjurers," Mephisto underscores his complication of another dichotomy, one that grounds the entire play: that between heaven and hell. Gilman writes that Mephisto, homosexually tinged throughout the play, is defeated by homosexuality at the end of the play (*Sexuality* 224). But Mephisto's defeat does not have to be seen as an unalloyed critique of homosexuality. Mephisto's self-description as "a part of that power that always desires evil and always does good" (*ein Teil von jener Kraft, die stets das Böse will und stets das Gute schafft*, lines 1335–36; *HA* 3:47) — confirmed by the Lord's admission in the prologue in Heaven that the devil does God's work (lines 340ff.) — makes him (and by extension his sexuality) a paradigmatic pharmakon, a poison that cures.

Two of the protagonists in Goethe's novels show the way in which this pharmakon can poison and cure growing young men. In 1796, Goethe published in *Die Horen* two collections of "Letters from Switzerland" ("Briefe aus der Schweiz"),[12] the first of which purportedly consisted of letters from Werther's youth. Werther, a product of the Storm and Stress, with its emotional cult of friendship, is no stranger to effusive declarations of love to other men, yet in *The Sorrows of Young Werther* (*Die Leiden des jungen Werthers*), it is clear that he is obsessively in love with a woman, Lotte. It turns out, however, that in his youth his desire developed less straightforwardly. Although Werther and his friend Ferdinand mention female beloveds and flirt with the women they encounter, Werther nonetheless develops an appreciation of the male body before encountering the female body:

I arranged for Ferdinand to bathe in the lake; how splendidly my young friend is built! how proportionate are all his parts! what a fullness of form, what a splendor of youth, what a profit for me to have enriched my imagination with this perfect example of human nature. . . . I see him as Adonis felling the boar, as Narcissus mirroring himself in the spring. (*WA* 1.19:213)[13]

Adonis and Narcissus are doomed to an early death, both in mythology and in Werther's desire, so Werther begins to look for Venus and Echo. The gender restrictions of the time make it more difficult for him to find a naked woman, so he must hire a prostitute, who is less willing to pose nude for his observation than to have intercourse with him.

Once the prostitute poses for him, however, Werther shifts his desire from his fellow man to his fellow woman. Even though his discovery of this beauty occurs in the most unnatural situation possible — a brothel, where sex is sold, being used as an artist's studio, where reality is portrayed — Werther declares that her unclothed body is nature revealed: "What a strange sensation, as one piece of clothing after the other fell off, and nature, stripped of its foreign shell, appeared strange to me and — I'd like to say — made almost a frightening impression on me" (WA 1.19:217–18). As strange as it is, this is nature. Homosexuality becomes a phase, albeit also a natural one, through which Werther grows. Its naturalness in his development becomes clear in its setting — the beautiful lakes of Switzerland.[14] Goethe thus holds fast to the belief he expressed in the conversation with Müller that homosexuality was in, although against, nature.

The passage in the "Letters from Switzerland" also shows the relationship between homosexuality and language that recurs in Goethe's writing, for a diatribe against high society, in which Werther particularly objects to speaking French, a language in which he believes he sounds "silly" (*albern*), immediately follows Werther's discovery of the beauty of the male body. Werther observes that the "dunce" expresses himself, "just . . . as in a foreign tongue," "with already coined, traditional phrases," whereas the "witty person" "quickly, vivaciously, and characteristically grasps and easily expresses that which is delicate and proper in the present" (WA 1.19:215–16). Werther's early encounter with sexuality coincides with his discovery of the power of language or textuality.

The same year that Goethe published the flashback to Werther's youth saw the arrival of the first of the Wilhelm Meister novels, *Wilhelm Meister's Apprenticeship* (*Wilhelm Meisters Lehrjahre*), in which a similar pharmaceutical use of homosexuality also appears. Although the *Apprenticeship* begins with Mariane's blissful love affair with Wilhelm, his love for Mariane has an interesting parallel to Werther's admiration for the female body. Just as Werther had discovered "nature" in the artificially lit brothel, Wilhelm discovers "much natural" [*manches Natürliche*] in Mariane's boudoir filled with makeup, cosmetics, and all the decidedly unnatural accoutrements of an actress (HA 7:19). Mariane herself hints at Wilhelm's sexual ambiguity when she identifies him with the figure of Jonathan from his puppet theater. Jonathan, because of his love for David, was in the eighteenth century, like Ganymede, a signifier for homosexuality (Faderman, *Surpassing the Love of Men* 107, 121).

While it might seem eccentric to emphasize the homosexual in Wilhelm, who notoriously goes through a chain of women and even fathers a child along the way, there is something remarkable about his relationships with women. Philine, the most entirely and aggressively feminine among the female characters of the novel, discomforts him (for instance, when she kisses him on the street; *HA* 7:133). While he is fascinated with the fight over her between Friedrich and the supermanly stable-master, he doesn't honor her with a glance (*HA* 7:140–41). In fact, he cannot even remember who is in bed with him when he sleeps with her (*HA* 7:327, 523): so immaterial is the identity of the person with whom he sleeps on that night that he even thinks it might be Mignon, who by all accounts has a considerably different body type than Philine. Indeed, the famous point about Mignon is her youthful androgyny, bringing Wilhelm even closer to the reproach of pederasty! While few critics have accused Wilhelm of pederastic desire, many (MacLeod is one who has done an excellent recent job) have noticed his attraction to androgynous women, the most important of whom is Natalie. He falls in love with her when she is dressed as a man and constantly refers to her thereafter as "the beautiful Amazon" (*HA* 7:226).

Natalie first appears on the scene not only as an Amazon, but also as a bringer of medical care for the wounded Wilhelm. She warms him with her masculine cloak, has her surgeon attend to his immediate needs, and leaves twenty gold pieces behind to pay for his subsequent medical care (*HA* 7:227, 234). Thus her androgyny, which Wilhelm finds so fetching, is intimately connected with her cure of Wilhelm. Friedrich puts his finger on her pharmaceutical nature[15] when he compares her to the princess whose love both poisons and cures the prince, with whom he compares the sick Wilhelm: "What is the name of the beautiful woman who enters and carries in her demure rogue's eyes poison and antidote at the same time?" (*HA* 7:606). Friedrich identifies that "poison and antidote" (*Gift und Gegengift*) that is so typical of the pharmakon[16] as Natalie's erotic appeal, which is initially androgynous and thus homoerotically tinged — a poison — but leads to the cure of the prototypical nuclear family consisting of Wilhelm, Natalie, and Felix.

In 1796, Goethe clarified the homosexuality inherent in Werther's youth and alluded to homosexuality in Wilhelm Meister's personality. Apparently the allusions in *Wilhelm Meister* were not suggestive enough, however, for several decades later Goethe provided his readers with a subsequent flashback to the homosexuality of Wilhelm's youth, just as he had in Werther's case. The importance of the homosexuality for Wilhelm's subsequent "healthy" development into a heterosexual is stressed in *Wilhelm Meister's Journeymanship* (*Wilhelm Meisters Wanderjahre*), in which the reader learns of only one new incident in Wilhelm's life before the *Apprenticeship*: the story of the fisherman's son, with whom Wilhelm falls in love.

As Eissler notes, the story is told haltingly, divided into several sections by dashes or asterisks in the text, suggesting its emotional import (2:1449). Wilhelm was supposed to visit some friends, but in such a way that he would be at home by nightfall, "for it seemed an impossibility to sleep out of his long-accustomed bed" (*HA* 8:270). The parental concern about sleeping arrangements proves justified, because Wilhelm spends the afternoon with a friend, "a youth, who had especially attracted me at his first entrance" (*HA* 8:271), in a sultry, sensual environment, learning to fish — which in this case turns out to be a metaphorical activity. He is surrounded by dragonflies, for which his friend uses the unusual name "sun virgins" (*Sonnenjungfern*, *HA* 8:272), suggesting that virginity is at stake. Eventually, he and the friend are both naked together in the water, overwhelmed by each other's beauty, and, after dressing again, exchanging fiery kisses: "So beautiful was the human figure, of which I had never had a concept. He seemed to observe me with the same attentiveness. Quickly clothed, we stood, still undisguised, in front of each other, our spirits were attracted to each other, and we swore an eternal friendship amidst the most fiery kisses" (*HA* 8:272). The scene has the same erotic implications as the scene in the "Letters from Switzerland" in which Werther watches Ferdinand bathe. Even Trunz has to remark on the "soft erotic tones" of "the first friendship" (*HA* 8:636). Within the narrative, the pastor's wife also suspects that something is wrong when she refuses to let Wilhelm take his new friend home "with a quiet remark on the impropriety" (*HA* 8:272).[17] Wilhelm never sees his friend, who dies trying to rescue some wayward swimmers, alive again.

Just as Werther had associated Ferdinand with doomed figures from Greek mythology, so Wilhelm links his friend with Hyacinth, one of Apollo's male lovers who is killed by Zephyr, who is also in love with the youth. As his friend is — unbeknownst to him — dying, Wilhelm falls in love with a girl, with whom he walks in a garden where the beautiful hyacinths are past their prime. Goethe provides the readers of the *Journeymanship* with one flashback on Wilhelm Meister's youth to emphasize the importance of Wilhelm's male-

male attraction at the beginning of his development. Like the hyacinth, this development is natural, but it blooms in the early spring of the young man's life and passes away before the peak of the human cycle.

Although the flowers in the garden point to the fleeting nature of Wilhelm's homosexual desire, Wilhelm himself is still overwhelmed by the death of his friend when he sees "nude, stretched out, brilliant white bodies, glowing even in the dim lamplight" (*HA* 8:275–76). Seeing his friend's body among the dead, he floods the youth's "broad chest with unending tears" (*HA* 8:276). That these unending tears flooding the beautiful body of his nude friend might be a euphemism for another, less easily mentioned bodily fluid becomes possible when Wilhelm admits: "I had heard something about rubbing that was supposed to help in such a case, I rubbed my tears into him and deceived myself with the warmth that I aroused" (*HA* 8:276). The masturbatory nature of this "rubbing" is further intimated by its pointlessness: this necrophilic pleasure has no living object, does not further a relationship with a living other. Like Rousseau's supplément, this rubbing arouses only deceptive warmth. The final indication of the erotics of this mortuary encounter comes when Wilhelm tries to resuscitate the dead boy artificially, an effort that glides smoothly into memories of their kiss in the lake: "In the confusion I thought I would blow air into him, but the pearly rows of his teeth were clenched tightly, the lips, upon which the farewell kiss seemed yet to rest, denied the lightest sign of response" (*HA* 8:276). The deathbed scene further emphasizes the erotic nature of the friendship between the boys. This homoerotically charged episode is also intimately linked with medicine, as it determines, supposedly, Wilhelm's desire to become a surgeon. Thus homosexuality—both a disease and a drug, and medicine; both the supplier of metaphors for Wilhelm's development and the product of that development—are reinforced as basic structures in Wilhelm's growth.

The list of Goethe's erotic writing is of course long. A number of critics have noted that Goethe links the "act of love" with the "act of writing" (Vaget 5), perhaps even creating—to use Marcel Duchamp's terminology—a "bachelor machine" that manufactures literature out of the raw material of sexual desire (Goethe, *Erotische Gedichte* 236–38). The question arises, though, why Goethe so fre-

quently links explicitly homosexual desire with writing. Biographically, Goethe may well have, as Eissler contends, used homosexuality to strengthen heterosexual bonds (1:636), thus inoculating
himself against this "disease." Historically, it is probably true that
homosexuality was increasingly more likely to be repressed or subli-
mated in this era and therefore more likely to be used as raw material
by the "bachelor machines" who wanted to generate more art. Similarly, Goethe may have felt the need to give a positive portrayal of
homosexual desire in the wake of the increasingly strident antiped-
erastic rhetoric of early-nineteenth-century Germany (Derks). The
inclusion of homosexual allusions in Goethe's erotic poetry allowed
him to make a statement for the urbane, cosmopolitan, and therefore universal in contrast to the increasing tendencies of Romanticism toward nationalism, parochialism, and conservative religion.

Goethe's writings are not, however, undiluted statements in support of homosexuality: his positive understanding of homosexuality
rests in large part on his belief that it points to heterosexuality.
Goethe relies on homosexuality in his literature, just as Derrida
emphasizes nonreproductive sexuality in his writings, because homosexuality is for him "heterotextual" in that it points to both itself
and the Other. Homosexuality in Goethe's works always also points
to heterosexuality. In the Wilhelm Meister story, the male-male desires are not an end in themselves but, by dint of Natalie's cross-
dressing, lead to and thus mean a healthy heterosexual desire. Similarly, in the "Letters from Switzerland," Werther's appreciation of
his male friend's beauty in nature gives way to an appreciation of the
nature in female beauty. By allowing Ganymede's unnatural sexuality to become part of nature, Goethe suggests yet again that sexuality can collapse the dichotomy of natural and unnatural. In Faust,
the pederast Mephisto is opposed to the divine order, which could be
called nature, but remains nonetheless within that order. Goethe's
observation that pederasty is both in and against nature applies
therefore in Faust and throughout his works.

In the final analysis, pederasty is for Goethe always part of the
cure. A pharmakon, with all the medical connotations of that word,
is the drug that endangers many of the characters of Goethe's world,
but also cures them. For the reader, homosexuality functions similarly: as a metaphor for the text. Like pederasty, the text should be a

pharmakon, both natural and unnatural, meaning both itself and the Other—in a word, heterotextual. This equation of pederasty, pharmakon, and writing suggests that sexuality in Goethe's works refers finally to the textuality of these works. Indeed, perhaps it goes beyond the works themselves, to point to the textual nature of sexuality in general.

Susan E. Gustafson

Male Desire in Goethe's *Götz von Berlichingen*

Reviewing Goethe scholarship, one would presume that *Götz von Berlichingen* has little to contribute to our understanding of eighteenth-century German conceptions of sexual preference. Yet Goethe's play actually dramatizes the psychological effects of the familial identifications that steer its male characters toward the choice of specific love objects. Goethe's drama is significant as a historical document of a major eighteenth-century poet's struggle to understand the genesis of male bonding. In it he strives to explicate in dramatic form various possibilities of male-male, in counterpoint to male-female, attraction. I neither want to suggest that Goethe's discernments in *Götz von Berlichingen* concerning the socialization of male desire approach the complexity of Freud's or Lacan's,[1] nor do I underestimate the limitations of his psychological insights; nevertheless, his play does accomplish a rudimentary analysis of the influence a child's identification with his father or mother exerts on the erotic feelings he experiences later as a young man. *Götz von Berlichingen* demonstrates Goethe's endeavor in a pre-psychoanalytic era to elucidate the factors that affect the male child's amatory disposition. Intriguingly, the play portrays the beginnings of a child psychology with striking parallels to the theoretical work of Lacan and Freud.

If we consider *Götz von Berlichingen* in the context of eighteenth-century thought, Goethe's views mark a tremendous divergence from traditional Enlightenment presumptions concerning the "natural character" of male-female union and conjugal families. What radically distinguishes Goethe's play from Enlightenment dra-

mas is its problematization of preferred object-choices. Enlightenment predecessors, such as Lessing, concentrated the erotic tensions
of their works exclusively within the boundaries of male-female
ties. The bourgeois tragedies scrutinized the dynamics of the family
in microscopic detail. Typically, the reputedly improper fancies of
daughters (and their mothers; Gustafson) were regarded as the quintessential threat to the stability of middle-class virtue. Ultimately,
fathers and daughters colluded in such dramas to reaffirm patriarchal family structures. In Lessing's *Miß Sara Sampson*, for instance, the ideal family is finally attained through the sacrifice of the
daughter (who represents desire) and is reconfigured as an adoptive
(nonbiological) family with the virtuous father as its center. The
supposition underlying Enlightenment plays is that sexual yearnings
are inherently illicit. The dramatic tradition Goethe confronts with
Götz von Berlichingen not only restricted its advertence to male-
female relationships; it strove to suppress ardor of any form.

In contrast to Enlightenment family drama, which aimed to illustrate the daughter's questionable sexuality, Goethe turns his attention especially to the formation of the desire of various sons. He is
concerned with how passion comes into being and how men and/or
women become an individual man's chosen object(s) of love. Goethe
exhibits an astute sensitivity to the complexities of erotic predilection by not presupposing natural affinities between men and
women: men bond with men in the play. Nor is male-bonding reduced to "acceptable" forms of knightly camaraderie. *Götz von
Berlichingen* explores as well the reality of male-male orectic attraction. Surprisingly, it is precisely the drama's rather obvious enuncia-
tion of the diverse possibilities of male-male affection that has es-
caped notice throughout Goethe scholarship.

In order to explicate the genesis of male desire in *Götz von
Berlichingen*, Goethe focuses on the childhood memories and experiences of his male characters. In accord with basic hypotheses of
modern psychoanalysis (and particularly those of Freud and Lacan),
Goethe portrays the manner in which these men began to form sexual preferences. During the course of the play several male characters accentuate the salient erotic events of their boyhood. Each of
these accounts concerning the formation of male longing is different — and yet the stirring and sometimes traumatic moments these
men recall share critical similarities. With this in mind, it seems

appropriate to examine closely the narratives of male sexual orientation presented in the play.

The first scenes of *Götz von Berlichingen* already focus in on the issue of male fantasy. The introduction of the play's hero, Götz von Berlichingen, revolves around two interrelated encounters: one between Götz and a young boy who yearns to become a knight, Georg; and one between Götz and an adoring monk, Martin. Martin and Georg converse with Götz separately, but both dialogues function to frame, complicate, and mirror the dynamics of male-male attraction that constitute the central concern of *Götz von Berlichingen*. These stories of male desire acquire additional import later in the play when the audience is presented with Götz's son, Carl, a young man whose childhood experiences draw him away from (what the play implies is) the ideal object of male identification and attachment. These preliminary stagings of variant socializations of male love set the scene finally for Götz's later recollection of his own boyhood dreams, visions, and yearnings.

Götz's discussions with Georg and Martin detail crucial specular influences upon young men. Both characters sketch out largely analogous descriptions of the visual sensations that ignite their passions. They are enamored of ideal knights and they each indicate how eager they are to mimic Götz. Indeed, upon hearing Götz's call, the boy Georg arrives onstage dressed in a man's armor. His masquerade immediately draws Götz's attention, who, it appears, threatens to chide him. But before he can do so, Georg divulges his compulsion to practice his role as a future knight. He admits how he donned a knight's armor and, wielding his father's sword, performed fictional battles across the meadows. Throughout the play, Georg's identification with Götz as a perfect male and as a patriarchal model is suffused with his idealizations of Hans (from whom he has the armor), of his father (from whom he has the sword), and of Saint George (from whom he has his name). The male paragon Georg envisions is associated predominantly with visual and physical signs of knighthood. Moreover, the boy's play-acting serves to make his own fantasies visible.

Similarly, Martin highlights the specular nature of his attraction to Götz. He asserts continuously how imperative it is for him to see his idol: "How constricted my heart felt when I *saw him*. He didn't say a word and my spirit could still perceive his. It is a pleasure, *to see a great man"* (*MA* 1.1:557; emphasis added). Martin continues by thanking God "for having let him see" (*MA* 1.1:556) such a knight. Male-male attraction is inextricably conjoined to visual signs, and Martin foregrounds this fact when he offers Georg a holy card with a picture of his patron saint on it, instructing him to follow the latter's example. The only "example" that Georg has is the ocular image itself. As the boy views the likeness, he lists the alluring objects he sees: "Such a beautiful white steed, if only I had one like it! — and the golden armor! That is a vile dragon! — I only shoot sparrows now — Saint George! make me big and strong, give me such a lance, such armor, and such a horse — then let the dragons come!" (*MA* 1.1:557). Georg's male ideal has a big, strong body, bears armor, and carries a sword. The image of Saint George provides a visual summary of the desired characteristics or trappings of knighthood. The boy perceives in the visual representation his own potentially ideal body. Like the child in Lacan's mirror stage that first conceives of its body as a whole, complete entity in its mirror reflection, Georg anticipates his own corporeal perfection — physical size and prowess — in the image of the saint. And in the manner of Lacan's infant, Georg aspires immediately to become that illusory, perfect body. The simple act of viewing the male paragon (in the form of the saint) excites Georg's fascination for a kind of mirror-stage emulation. Peering at the perfect image, the boy discovers that which lures him and that which he wishes to become.

In an entirely separate passage Martin gazes at Götz (another perfect man/knight) and isolates the same visible signifiers of the male ideal that Georg did. The monk exclaims: "If only God would fill my shoulders with the strength to bear the breastplate, and fill my arms with the strength to knock an enemy from his horse! Poor weak hand, accustomed till now only to guide crosses and flags of peace and to swing censers, how is it that you desire to rule lance and sword?" (*MA* 1.1:555). The breastplate functions for the monk as an exteriority, a surface, a kind of mirror across which and in which he recognizes the ideal male he loves and would like to be. Martin admits that he is "in love with your [Götz's] armor" (*MA* 1.1:554). Whereas Georg concentrates above all on his potential corporeal completeness in the image of Saint George, Martin underscores his corporeal deficiencies in comparison to Götz: his shoulders and arms are so weak that they preclude his ascendance to knightly society. According to Lacan, the child's desire to obtain the illusive corporeal totality she or he perceives in the mirror leads simultaneously to a sense of physical inadequacy or loss as the child compares its own body to the unified image of the reflection. Much in the manner of Lacan's mirror-stage infant, Martin's sighting of Götz triggers his recognition of the fragmentary character of his own body. He notices only a weak arm here and insufficient shoulders there. His body appears to him as disjointed bits and pieces, not as the coveted corporeal whole. In contrast to Georg, Martin does not entertain the fantasy of becoming, like Götz von Berlichingen, a model of complete maleness. While Lacan maintains that the infant perceives simultaneously her or his self-totality and corporeal fragmentation in the mirror reflection, Goethe evinces a similar notion of a split in self-conception through the juxtaposition of Martin and Georg.

Not only does Martin fail to see his potentially complete self in Götz, but in the course of his profuse venerations of the knight he also reveals the male delusion underlying the adulation of a perfect male imago. Both Goethe and Lacan suggest the illusory, phantasmic character of the idealized body reflected in the mirror (or by the armor). The monk undermines the visual paragon as he recounts the story he heard of how Götz forfeited his hand.[2] Martin insists that Götz's mutilation was such a heart-wrenching, distressing story that it can never be forgotten. The monk's reminiscences remind us that even the supposedly perfect male imago is also marked by loss. Indeed, Martin isolates a tension that manifests itself throughout the play: although the characters (and the drama as a whole) locate male perfection in Götz, at the same time, reminders of his physical lack resurface relentlessly. Nonetheless, despite Martin's recollection of the knight's mutilation, he strives to isolate corporeal completeness in Götz. In an effort to mask the disquieting realization of Götz's wounded body (essentially a fear of male castration), the characters of the play, like Martin, invest the iron replacement (a symbolic substitute for the real body) with the significance of a religious relic. According to Martin, the iron hand is one through which "the holiest blood has flowed" (MA 1.1:556). But it is precisely not the iron hand that has surged with blood, but the real hand that has been severed from Götz's body. The iron prosthesis has no blood. It is what Lacan would call the phallic signifier, the great mask, the "stand-in" for that which is absent. The knight's injured body reveals that the phallic signifier is a sham and consequently that no ideal male imago really exists. Thus, paradoxically, the mutilation of the male paragon's supposedly flawless body can only be hidden by an exaggerated consecration of its iron replacement. The "dead tool" (*totes Werkzeug, MA* 1.1:556), as Martin refers to it, is the substitutive signifier, the symbol that diverts attention from the ideal man's torn body and conceals the physical loss. For precisely this reason, the iron hand comes obsessively to the fore throughout *Götz von Berlichingen.*[3] It is the most cherished object, valued as the quintessential sign of Götz's perfection.

Significantly enough, Goethe also intimates not only that loss creates desire, but also that the knight's physical handicap obstructs male-male attraction. Götz cannot offer the monk the knightly sign of alliance: he cannot extend his right hand in a handshake. Martin is offended when the knight offers him his left instead, understanding in the gesture a refusal of honor and male bonding. At this point Götz finally discloses to Martin that his right hand, the iron one, is "insensitive to the feeling of love" (*MA* 1.1:556). Whereas symbolically the iron appendage represents passion and functions as a focal site of male longing (as a culturally determined signifier), in reality it is divorced from all feelings of love, incapable as it is of transmitting sensation or registering affection.[4] Götz's physical injury represents essentially not just the loss of a hand, but the ultimate lack as well: the incapacity to feel and love. Despite tendencies throughout the play to assign all deficiencies in male bonding to Martin and Carl, the discussion of Götz's lost hand discloses his incapacity to reach out to other men and thus his own truncated desire.

Götz von Berlichingen makes male fantasy and its contingent relationship to specularity and linguistic articulation visible. As Martin gives Georg the image of the saint he says, "There you have him. Follow his example" (*MA* 1.1:557), implying that the boy now has what he needs and wants. But both Martin and Georg also see in the armor and the picture precisely what they do not have, that which does not really exist (i.e., Götz's perfection) and that for which they still long. Their descriptions of tantalizing male perfection mark their transition to a narrative of lack — to their verbalized realization of the gap between themselves and the ideal man they

envision. Ultimately the boy's visual experience results in the articulation of his own passions. The child's identification with and emulation of the men around him require his appropriation of certain
crucial visual cathexes, which he endeavors to lend form through
narrative expression and physical enactment. As in Lacan's conception of the mirror stage, the specular image in Goethe's play causes
the viewing subject to recognize an unattainable and desirable (in
this case, male) imago; the simultaneous furor for that which has
been lost encourages in turn the viewer's attempts to substitute language for loss, marking his first step into the symbolic order (language and representation).

What distinguishes Georg's desire from Martin's is both its supposed potential for realization and the child's ability to see, narrate,
and stage his wants. Both men can narrate their fantasies, but while
Georg is capable of acting out his identification with the male paragon, Martin insists on his own inability to translate language (or
longing) into action. He remains then a monk, a man destined to
suppress at least in part "the best desires — those through which we
[men] become, grow, and flourish" (MA 1.1:555). Goethe asserts
that a successful entrance into the symbolic order mandates more
than the simple transition to language: the subject must also act out
his solicitude. Indeed, Götz von Berlichingen itself constitutes a dramatic, multifaceted enactment of male-male attraction.

When it comes to the question of gender preference, Götz's son,
Carl, is perceived by most other characters in the play to be on an
aberrant course. As opposed to Georg's socialization, which takes
place among men, Carl's early life is guided by his aunt and mother-
surrogate, Maria. Carl does not commune with men. He prefers to
keep company with his mother in the kitchen rather than follow his
father to the stables. As one knight comments: "He will never be his
father" (MA 1.1:561). During the first encounter between Carl and
Götz it becomes evident that the father feels his son has somehow
missed the "mirror stage." The boy does not identify with Götz as
either his father or the paragon of male perfection. This failure on
Carl's part comes immediately to the fore when he tries to tell Götz
what he has learned while his father was away from home:

Carl: I know something else.
Götz: What would that be?
Carl: Jaxthausen is a village and castle on the Jaxt and has belonged for two

hundred years to the lords of Berlichingen by hereditary and right of possession.

Götz: Do you know Lord Berlichingen?

Carl stares at him blankly

Götz (to himself): He doesn't know for sheer edification — who his own father is. — To whom does Jaxthausen belong?

Carl: Jaxthausen is a village and castle on the Jaxt.

Götz: That's not what I am asking. — I knew all the paths, ways and fords, before I knew what the river, village, and fortress were called. (*MA* 1.1:563)

The boy has somehow entered language without the prerequisite stage of recognition, without seeing his father as an emulatable and attractive model. Unlike his father, Carl recognizes neither his relationship to his father nor the symbols of paternal existence. Götz, in the manner of Georg and Martin, first saw and identified the signifiers of paternal legacy before he entered into language, before he attempted to give expression to his own relationship to his father, ancestry, and the society of men (knights). As Nägele (75–76) has pointed out, Carl merely repeats words without understanding their connection to specific signifieds. I would add that the crucial signs that he fails to discern are those which represent the father. In accord with Lacanian psychoanalysis, we might say that in Carl's case the mirror stage (because of its apparent absence) has not paved the way to an identification with the "Name of the Father" or with signifiers of paternal power and potency. Because Carl does not recognize his father (or a paternal ideal in the mirror image) and his own lack in relationship to him, he does not enter into signification. The search for gratification, as we know from Lacan, is the veritable foundation of language. Without desire — without the cognition of loss — Carl's language is at best dysfunctional. He speaks, but his words express no want and still no yearning. The boy's utterances are a meaningless exercise in recitation. Goethe's play, like Lacan's psychoanalytic theory, implies that the subject enters language through the illusory fantasy of and identification with a perfect, imitable male/paternal imago — and that is exactly what Carl does not do.

In the first version of the play, *Gottfried von Berlichingen*, Goethe explicates fully Carl's obliviousness to his father and his inclination instead toward priests and women. Rather than following his father's example, Carl is encouraged by Maria to adopt the virtues of monks. As far as Götz is concerned, that is "how women raise their children" (MA 1.1:402). Maria and Carl's mother, Elisabeth, engage in a pedagogical debate over the manner in which boys should be guided. Elisabeth chastises Maria for telling Carl fairy tales about good monks, for they will transform him into a priest: "You will ruin the child with your fairy tales. He is already of a stiller nature than his father approves, and you will make him into a priest" (MA 1.1:397). As a priest, Carl is destined to a life of unmanly weakness; he will be "no better than people incapable of holding their urine" (MA 1.1:397). He will spend his life "in holy idleness" (MA 1.1:398). Carl's future mirrors Martin's present life to the extent that both are unable to be active participants in society. While Martin cannot translate his fantasies into action, Carl has no desire, no masculine strength, and no power. Elisabeth asserts that the only correct way to raise Carl would be through stories about his father's heroic feats. But despite Elisabeth's adhortation, the monastery remains Carl's final destination. Within the theoretical economy of *Götz von Berlichingen* it is evident that what is perceived as healthy, acceptable sexual attraction must be formed in relation to the ideal father. The boy who models himself after priests, follows his mother, and fails to mimic male perfection (Götz) never leaves the state of impuissant childhood.

Yet Carl is faced with still another cheerless fate. Elisabeth accentuates the necessity of interning Carl in a monastery, averring that weak men and women should seek refuge from the world of "real men": "The weak have no place in this world. . . . For this reason prudent women stay home and weaklings creep into a cloister. When my husband rides out, I have no fear. But if Carl were to march off, I would be in eternal anxieties. He is safer in a cowl than behind armor" (MA 1.1:431). Elisabeth insists that Carl has no place in the social order of his father because his weakness marks his affinity to women. Not only does Carl prefer to be with his mother and aunt, but he is also identified by his mother as being like women. As such, the play asserts that Carl is a "failed man." According to his mother, the boy is too effeminate to be of use to a society that demands men: "Now that the possession of our estates is so uncertain, we require men as the pater familias. Carl, if he took a wife, she couldn't be more of a wife than he is" (MA 1.1:431). Carl is more womanly than any wife he might marry. While in Elisabeth's opinion Carl is insufficiently heterosexual and/or not manly enough, the men in the play ostracize him because of his attraction to women. Carl's upbringing among women, the influence of priestly models, and his nonsignificatory language mark his position outside the paternal order and his exclusion from the male desire that, as we shall see, forms the basis of male-male attraction in *Götz von Berlichingen*.

Immediately following the childhood stories of Martin, Georg, and Carl, Weislingen and Götz reminisce about the erotic nature of their youthful relationship. The salient memories are of male communion. Götz enthusiastically recounts their knightly escapades: "Do you still remember how I got entangled with that Pole . . . ? I really beat him stoutly that time, and you later challenged his comrade as well. We stuck together honestly as good brave young boys, and for that reason everyone referred to us as Castor and Pollux! I always felt so good when the margrave toasted us as such" (*MA* 1.1:564). Götz's account of early squabbles imply that he and Weislingen, like Georg, were practicing for their future role as knights. They were parroting the men around them. Weislingen immediately remembers this community of men upon entering Götz's fortress. His initial recollections are of the intense emotional bonds that existed then between himself, Götz, and Götz's father: "Led back, Adelbert, into that hall where we boys romped around. There where you loved him, and hung on him as on your own soul. . . . The joyous times are past when old Berlichingen sat here before the fireplace and when we played chaotically around him and loved each other like angels" (*MA* 1.1:564). Weislingen laments the forgotten love once shared by the two young men. Götz embellishes Weislingen's account of their affection for each other in his own rememoration of their physical closeness: "Indeed we won't ever again find days so pleasurable as those at the margrave's court, where we still slept and roved around together" (*MA* 1.1:564). Götz highlights specifically the attraction of sleeping together with Weislingen at a time when he believed that both their physical and emotional bonds would continue throughout their lifetime:

After work I know of nothing more pleasurable than to remind myself of the past. Particularly when I contemplate again how we bore pleasures and sufferings together, were everything to each other, and how I imagined then that it should be so our whole life long. Wasn't that my entire consolation when my hand was shot off at Landshut. And you nursed me and cared for me more than a brother would, and I hoped that Adelbert would henceforth be my right hand. And now— (MA 1.1:565)

Adelbert is more than a brother to Götz: he ought to be his soul, his love, his right hand. Like the iron hand, Adelbert should function to hide Götz's physical and psychic imperfections. Together the two men are perceived to constitute a whole, unified male totality (Nägele). Throughout the play it becomes evident that the restoration of the perfect male imago is contingent upon the re-union of Weislingen and Götz, that is, through male bonding. Male-male attraction is what Götz and Weislingen had and want to recapture. Carl does not have erotic feelings for men, Martin cannot act upon his idealization of knights; only Georg recognizes and strives to solidify his attachment to the men he idolizes. The entire play is structured around the reality of men loving men. The radical subtext of Goethe's play is that it asserts (at least for men)[5] that same-sex attraction is the most viable answer to the perception of loss produced by the mirror-stage experience of the self as inherently lacking. To this extent, Götz von Berlichingen diverges remarkably from the general suppositions of modern psychoanalysis (and particularly of both Freud and Lacan), in which it is assumed that any sense of subjective wholeness or completion would be possible only by means of a fulfilled desire for someone of the opposite sex.

But if a sense of male totality is only possible through the re-union of Götz and Weislingen, and if the two men genuinely care for each other (as they seem to), one might ask: Why do they never form a lasting alliance in the play? What obstructs their mutually solicited communion? Despite the prominence of male-male attraction in the play, most of the characters seem to assume that each man will inevitably and finally attach himself to a woman. Götz is married to Elisabeth. Weislingen pursues various women. Carl is banished to a monastery because of his inability to assume his proper role as a man and husband. Martin envies Götz's robust lifestyle and the fact that a woman awaits him after a long day on the battlefield.

Not only are men expected to ultimately settle down with the women of their choice, but the only option left to Götz and Weislingen in the play is a substitutive bonding mediated through the exchange of Götz's sister.[6] As he offers Maria to Weislingen in marriage, Götz emphasizes above all his hopes for unity with Adelbert:

Adelbert, you are free: I demand only your hand, nothing further. . . . Give each other your hands as I say Amen! . . . My friend and brother! . . . You don't look very free, Adelbert! What is wrong? I—am completely happy; that which I only hoped for in dreams I now see, and am as if dreaming. Ah! my dream is over! I felt last evening as if I gave you my right iron hand, and you held me so tightly that it came out of the splint as if broken off. I started and woke up. I should have just gone on dreaming . . . then I would have seen how you grafted a new living hand on me. (*MA* 1.1:574–75)

The two knights ought to be brought back together, not as lovers, but through their ties to Maria. She should now be the thread that reunites them. In spite of Götz's aim to celebrate their newly arranged union, his speech reveals relentlessly the tentative and intrinsically unsatisfying character of such an indirect connection. Götz obtains Weislingen's hand (or Weislingen as his lost hand) only through the communal embrace with Maria. The insufficiency of the transaction manifests itself in Weislingen's obvious discomfort. He does not look "free" (available for Götz!), and Götz must ask him what is wrong. Without waiting for Adelbert's answer, Götz launches into an account of a dream that condenses Weislingen into both his lost hand and the man who will once again sever his hand from him. Precisely at the moment of Weislingen's engagement to Maria, Götz relates the subtext of the scene: that the union between Weislingen and Maria signifies a renewed mutilation of Götz's hand. The iron prosthesis and Weislingen merge in a dream-vision of the impossibility of actualizing the passions of their youth. Upon awakening, Götz may assert that male unity was attained through the betrothal of Weislingen and Maria—"I should have just gone on dreaming . . . then I would have seen how you grafted a new living hand on me"—but his hesitations reveal the fanciful nature of those visions. As he himself admits, that which he "only hoped for in dreams"—his fantasy of a re-union with Weislingen—"is over." Maria fails to unite Weislingen and Götz, and indeed, as the play proceeds, the weakness of her fetters comes to the fore as Weislingen abandons both Maria and Götz for a life at court.

Women cannot mediate between desirous men, and an erotic relationship with a woman cannot substitute for the attraction Götz and Weislingen feel for each other. Indeed, Götz insinuates that his close relationship to Weislingen was initially undermined by the women at court to whom Adelbert was drawn. In Götz's view,

Weislingen left him in order to form "shameful ties" (*schändliche Verbindungen, MA* 1.1:565) with women: "The unhappy court life and flirting and company with women held you back." Had Weislingen only stayed with Götz, everything would have been fine. *Götz von Berlichingen* stresses not only Götz's jealousy, but also the melancholy that besets Weislingen once he is erotically attached to Adelheid (a woman of the court) and severed from Götz. Adelheid describes the transformation in Weislingen's character: "Suddenly you were lamenting like a sick poet, melancholy like a healthy girl, and more lazy than an old bachelor" (*MA* 1.1:593). She attributes his despondency to his "accident" (*Unfall, MA* 1.1:593)—to what amounts to Weislingen's amputation from Götz. His severance from Götz marks irrefutably the laceration of the erotic tie that unified them. What is highlighted in Weislingen's relationships with women is less a misogynistic rejection of the female sex than a melancholic mourning of the original, ideal male-male bond that no longer joins him to Götz.

Goethe's predominant interest in the development of male-male desire manifests itself in the multiple stories the play tells of the cardinal events influencing boyhood relationships. The drama highlights the fact that neither Weislingen nor Götz can be satisfied with female companions. Weislingen despairs in his relationship to Adelheid. Götz expends all of his energies trying to re-unite with Weislingen: in other words, his wife is not the central object of his attentions. Two contradictory suppositions concerning male passion thus constitute the core dramatic tensions of *Götz von Berlichingen*: first, several characters express the general expectation that the "normal" course of erotic longing will lead inevitably to male-female attraction; and second, the rather extensive anatomy of male-male desire and its genesis throughout the play point to the radical assumption that any sense of ideal, corporeal wholeness experienced by the male subject after the discovery of self-deficiency during the mirror stage can only be attained through an orectic relationship with another man. Goethe explores in *Götz von Berlichingen* both the reality of male-male erotic attraction and the social forces by which it is thwarted. The melancholy mourning of the male characters in the play results essentially from a societal insistence on male-female attraction as ineluctable.

For men like Götz and Weislingen, Goethe suggests somberly,

existence within an exclusively male-female relationship is simply impossible. As the tragedy approaches its denouement, all impressions of male-male bonding and male community dissolve. The final scenes foreground visions not of the ideal man's flawless body and male union, but of castration and separation. Weislingen and Götz have declared war against each other. In his last hours Weislingen laments his physical weakness and recounts a "poisonous dream" in which his hand (!) fails him in a battle against Götz. Berlichingen himself deplores the transition from knightly unity to a vicious new world of division. He then dies of multiple wounds. The world in *Götz von Berlichingen* has sunk to a ghastly state as the community of men has turned against itself, inflicting wounds upon its own body (bodies) as hundreds are broken on the wheel, impaled on spears, decapitated, and drawn and quartered. The frustration of male-male desire through compulsory bonds with women and the incapacity of Weislingen and Götz to recapture the alluring unity of their youth create a gruesome backlash. The fantasy of male perfection and corporeal wholeness evoked early in the drama by the narratives of young men dissipates entirely. All that remains as *Götz von Berlichingen* draws to a close is a nightmarish countryside strewn with bits and pieces of male flesh.

W. Daniel Wilson

Amazon, Agitator, Allegory: Political and Gender Cross(-Dress)ing in Goethe's *Egmont*

The beginnings of 1970s Germanist feminism were concerned largely with studies of "the image of women" in works by canonical male authors — an understandable project before many texts by women had been (re)discovered. The laudable turn to "gynocriticism," to uncovering and analyzing the considerable corpus of women's literature and the lives of women writers, however, foreshortened the critique of gender in works by male authors. A few of these earlier studies of male authors only began to scratch the surface of gender issues. In the case of Goethe, they (and even some later ones) concentrated almost entirely on two texts: *Iphigenia in Tauris* and *Faust*.[1] More recently, corresponding to the general scholarly shift in interest from the amoral unboundedness of *Faust* to the social project of *Wilhelm Meister's Apprenticeship*, a mass of criticism has uncovered gender complexities previously unsuspected in Goethe's quintessential *Bildungsroman*.[2] But Goethe's other works, too — from *Hanswurst's Wedding* to *Elective Affinities*, from *Roman Elegies* to *Wilhelm Meister's Journeymanship* — contain a dizzying gender complexity that has gone largely unexamined. Although analysis of this gender unsettling in male literature should not, of course, replace "gynocriticism," but only supplement and enrich it, it is of crucial importance — if only to foreground readers' obliviousness to intriguing gender constellations, which raises the most fascinating questions regarding canonization of a bowdlerized Goethe — via unbowdlerized texts.

This feminist critique, however, must also be informed by issues arising from gay studies in order fully to appreciate the breadth of gender issues in these texts. The phenomenon "Goethe and homo-sexuality/homosociality," too, has hardly been exhausted, despite very promising beginnings. Unfortunately, some of those beginnings were studiously ignored. The shoulder was coldest in the case of K. R. Eissler's monumental psychoanalytic study of Goethe; originally published in English in 1963, the work was practically ignored until its translation into German in 1983. Despite the methodological problems of this traditional Freudian study, it contained productive observations on Goethe and homosexuality. More recently, the equally monumental study by Paul Derks of homosexuality in German literature has done a great deal to illuminate this theme.[3] To summarize a complex phenomenon: Goethe at times had a remarkably uninhibited attitude toward homosexuality, conjuring up the old image of the "heathen" Goethe in a new transformation. His attitude could range from apparent casual approval (and even defense of publicly attacked homosexuals like the historian Johannes von Müller) to conventional phobia. But as some of the essays in the present volume show, the topic is hardly exhausted — or easily characterized. Consider, for example, the violent language of erotic desire spoken by Beaumarchais near the end of the tragedy *Clavigo* (1774) as he imagines killing Clavigo: "I am hot on his trail, my teeth lust after his flesh, my palate lusts after his blood. Have I become a raging beast? Every vein in me, every nerve trembles with desire for him, for him!" (*MA* 1.1:738). Gender in Goethe clearly deserves a closer look, and gay studies, particularly with their emphasis on transvestism and performativity, can enrich the analysis.

Homoeroticism in *Egmont* (written 1774–87, published 1788) is a function of the broader fuzziness of gender boundaries, which in turn is expressed mainly in the phenomenon of cross-dressing (themes with which Goethe was confronted especially during the last stages of writing the play, in Italy).[4] At various points in the text there are intriguing homoerotic suggestions. For example, Clärchen first appears in the play singing a soldier's song, her favorite song. But what is supposed to be prototypically masculine performance is actually sung by a female poetic persona, whose "lover" (*Liebster*, grammatically masculine) commands the troops; it culminates in the woman's desire to wear soldier's clothes: "O, would I wore doublet / And breeches and hat!" (94) and ends with the wish to become a man: "[There's no happiness on earth / Like being a man!]" (94–95;

"O hätt ich ein Wämslein / und Hosen und Hut . . . Welch Glück sonder gleichen / ein Mannsbild zu sein," 260).[5] Paradoxically, however, if Clärchen's fantasy were to come true — if she were not only to dress like a man, but to *become* a man — her love for Egmont would be homoerotic. And even if she were only to *dress* as a man, she would be imitating a practice that was widely associated with lesbianism (Dekker and van de Pol 358–59). Such ironies — we will examine a more pronounced suggestion of homoeroticism further on — point to the broader issue of crossing gender boundaries, and cross-dressing is merely a sign for these complex confusions.

Gender images were undergoing a significant retrenchment in late-eighteenth-century Germany. The early century's tentative steps toward including agendas like women's education and promotion of women writers in the program of enlightenment had been overwhelmed by sentimentalism and by economic developments that affected the social structure of the family. As more and more middle-class men began to work outside the home, their wives found themselves cut off from the primary economic activity of the family, in which they had formerly participated in the home. As the family shrank from the larger, premodern "household" family that included servants, relatives, renters, and others, to the modern nuclear family with its stress on intimacy and attention to the child, women were increasingly restricted to the work in that sphere (which was no longer characterized as work, but as "love"). Toward the end of the century, especially under the ideological influence of Rousseau and sentimentalism, strict gender codifications began to provide legitimation for the existing economic and social situation (Hausen: "secondary patriarchy"): women were passive (thus suited to household duties), nonaggressive (thus unsuited to the competitive world outside the home), emotional and religious (thus equipped not for the rationally oriented sphere of the state and business, but for the religious upbringing of the children), and beautiful (thus a decoration suited to entertainment). Such "inborn" and thus "natural" characteristics, which German feminist historiographers call "New Femininity" (*Neue Weiblichkeit*), obviously precluded women's participation in literary discourse.[6] Above all, they gave decisive impetus to modern conceptions of gender roles.

Egmont, like many other works by men in this period, is deeply involved in a dialectic ambivalence toward this new gender discourse.[7] The central passage that reflects an unsettling of gender boundaries is at the end of act 3, which contains one of the most bizarre dialogues in eighteenth-century literature. It begins innocuously enough: Egmont converses with Clärchen about Margarete of Parma, the daughter of Charles V and Spanish regent of the Netherlands. After he describes Margarete's courtly skills of dissimulation, Clärchen responds: "I could never be at home in the great world [i.e., the courtly world, politics]. But then she has a masculine mind; she's a different kind of woman from us seamstresses and cooks. She is noble, brave, resolute" (119; "Ich könnte mich in die Welt nicht finden. Sie hat aber auch einen männlichen Geist, sie ist ein ander Weib als wir Nähtrinnen und Köchinnen. Sie ist groß, herzhaft, entschlossen," 289–90). Striking here is Clärchen's positive valorization of "male" virtues in a woman; she does not allow her opinion of Margarete to be diminished by the regent's supposedly masculine characteristics. At the same time as she voices admiration for these qualities, Clärchen does not let Margarete's "masculine" characteristics prevent her from calling her a woman; if Margarete is "a different kind of woman," it is mainly on the basis of social distinction (". . . from us seamstresses and cooks"). Egmont responds by saying that Margarete is "a bit disoriented" this time, because of the political situation (119). The word I have translated as "disoriented," *auseinander* (literally "separated," "disconnected" — changed in most editions to Herder's emendation, *aus der Fassung*), expresses succinctly Egmont's perception of the dislocation of gender categories presented by a woman in public office. For, responding to Clärchen's puzzlement at why he says this, Egmont "explains" by delivering one of the most striking nonsequiturs in Goethe's oeuvre: "She has a little moustache too, on her upper lip, and occasional attacks of gout. A real Amazon[!]" (119; "Sie hat auch ein Bärtchen auf der Oberlippe und manchmal einen Anfall von Podagra. Eine rechte Amazone!" 290). This physical description of Margarete manages to combine sexism with a closely related ageism directed against the postmenopausal woman. Although the word "too" (*auch*) tends to disqualify Egmont's statement as an elaboration on his previous passage describing Margarete's inadequacy in political matters, the continuity is clear: she is a *Mannweib* or virago, not androgynous but simply an abomination of nature, a being of neither sex who can neither serve men in a subservient role as mate and mother nor meet the intellectual and physical demands of public leadership. Significantly, then,

Egmont disqualifies Margarete *both* as public persona *and* as mate (more on this later). At this point, it is important to see that Clärchen attributes masculinity only to Margarete's mind, while Egmont attributes it to her body.

Clärchen continues doggedly to value Margarete's character positively (119/290), though with a certain awe; to Egmont's "A real Amazon!" she responds provocatively: "A majestic woman!" While this expression may have been an oxymoron for Goethe's age, Clärchen's description is manifestly more positive than Egmont's; furthermore, she (for the second time) stresses that Margarete is *not* a virago — however different she may be from Clärchen herself and other "seamstresses and cooks" — but a woman. She again expresses her feeling of distance from Margarete, now by imagining that she would be intimidated by her, "afraid to enter her presence" (119; "Ich scheute mich vor sie zu treten," 290). In Clärchen's responses to the imagined Margarete we find a balance of distance and identification — even though she knows Margarete only through Egmont's grotesque depiction of her.

The conversation now takes a turn that reveals even more clearly Egmont's motivations. Clärchen imagines that she would be timid in Margarete's presence; this timidity is based on *power*, especially since a few minutes earlier Clärchen had expressed a similar timidity on seeing Egmont's courtly clothing (more on this later). But Egmont attempts to assign her timidity to *gender*, to extremely "feminine" characteristics (thus emphasizing Margarete's "masculinity"): "You're not usually so shy. But then it wouldn't be fear, only [virginal] modesty [*jungfräuliche Scham*]" (119/290). At the mention of virginal coyness, Egmont's facade collapses — not through Clärchen's words, but in her gestures: she averts her gaze shyly, takes his hand, and leans on him. Egmont immediately says that he "understands" the pantomime. Reacting to the imputation of virginal shyness, Clärchen has indicated by her averted gaze that she is no longer a virgin, as Egmont well knows (a fact that the critics usually ignore).[8] He has attempted to distance Clärchen as far as possible from the male-female Margarete, in part by assigning her the role of pristine virgin, the most desired object and fetish of male desire — though he knows differently. Clärchen foils this strategy, and we begin to see that Egmont's typology — Amazon versus virgin — may be less than adequate to *either* woman.

This impression is borne out by the rest of the play. The Margarete *whom we see on the stage* is hardly the caricature that Egmont—and other male characters—make of her. Even in Strada's depiction, she is highly intelligent and capable, and Goethe's portrayal conforms with that estimation. She deals with the rebellion with an even hand that fails only when the situation created by her brother becomes impossible. Her only weakness is imposed on her by men: she is a regent, a surrogate for her brother who rules "through a woman" (101/268). She is thus not fully in power, and this lack of power is the fatal flaw (in the situation, not in her character) that causes her to abdicate and admit defeat; clearly, if she had ruled unhindered, her political savvy would have defused the rebellion. Goethe borrowed Egmont's physical description of Margarete's facial hair and gout from his historical source, Strada, but placed it in Egmont's mouth; we have no independent confirmation of it. The only independently verifiable description that Goethe took from Strada is the indication that she wears hunting attire—that is, pants (89/253).[9] Margarete's manly dress takes on added significance when we juxtapose it to Strada's insistence that Margarete is not so much a woman with the spirit of a man as "a man in woman's clothes," a strategy that enables Strada to reserve masculine qualities of intelligence and strength for men—but paradoxically, for cross-dressed men. Goethe reverses Strada's poles by presenting Margarete as a cross-dressed woman, not a cross-dressed man, and by marking her *Mannweib* characteristics as Egmont's invention.

Historical studies have established that women cross-dress much more than men, mainly in order to partake in the *power* that comes with male identity.[10] This power is normally on a mundane level, such as in giving the ability to travel; if we can extrapolate from the experiences of literary women from Z to A, from Sidonia Hedwig Zäunemann early in the century to Bettine von Arnim at the end of it, women frequently dressed as men in order to travel. In Goethe's play, this tendency is taken to an extreme, since Margarete partakes in very serious power. Of course, she is not fully cross-dressed, since she is identifiable as a woman. She thus parallels many other strong female characters who cross-dress but are still identifiable as women, and potentially retain their attractiveness for men dissatisfied with traditional gender types (Mariane in *Wilhelm Meister's Apprenticeship* is the prominent example in Goethe's oeuvre; he openly expressed the attractiveness of such cross-dressed women in

Italy.)[11] In this way, Goethe has made her much more attractive (in his own eyes) than she is in Strada's depiction of the cross-dressed man. By remaining identifiable as an (only partly cross-dressed) woman who encroaches on the male sphere of power, Margarete does open herself up to the withering attack of men, who will not let this access to power have any permanence. But Margarete herself critiques the male prejudices that undermine her authority: she imagines the male advisers of the king, especially Alba, "mumbling between his teeth of female softheartedness, misplaced indulgence [*Weibergüte, unzeitigem Nachgeben*], and that women may sit a horse already broken, but make poor equerries themselves, and other such pleasantries to which I once had to listen in the company of the political gentlemen" (115/284; cf. 253, 256). Her situation could hardly be clearer: the male rulers place her in an impossible situation and then blame her lack of masculinity ("female softheartedness," etc.) when she fails. No character in the play is more skilled politically than Margarete, and yet the men blame her failure on her feminine nature — in Egmont's depiction, a feminine nature that is made monstrous by male characteristics but is no less doomed to failure as a consequence.

But Egmont's obsession with gender issues betrays his tactics; not only do we never hear independent confirmation of Margarete's supposed male physical features, but Egmont suggests in another passage that his deep-seated fear of and simultaneous fascination with gender ambiguity is at the bottom of his scorn for Margarete: "She is a woman, . . . and women always wish that everyone will meekly creep under their gentle yoke, that every Hercules will doff his lion's skin and join their knitting group [*Kunkelhof*]" (109/278). Again, the reference to cross-dressing conjures up an image of a topsy-turvy gender world: Hercules served the Lydian queen Omphale for three years, indicating submission by wearing women's clothes and carrying out women's work like spinning wool (Egmont's word *Kunkelhof* implies a sort of *court* of knitters or spinners, stressing the *political* power of Queen Omphale/Margarete), while the queen wore his lion's skins and wielded his club (Wagener 18). Today this legend reverberates with historical implications, since Omphale is an incarnation of the Great Goddess served by the sacred king in what many see as historical matriarchal societies; this arrangement provided ritual functions for cross-dressing.[12] Although Goethe lived too early to benefit from this knowledge, he was clearly fascinated by the image of the powerful woman enslaving a man, who then does woman's work and wears her clothes, for the Omphale motif also appears in the *Roman Elegies*.[13] But Egmont uses this myth to disqualify Margarete; he summons up the specter of female power to suggest that Margarete is driven by a desire to dominate men — a suggestion that is nowhere borne out in the play. While Margarete certainly enjoys power (113/283; 115–16/286), she wields it responsibly and refutes the eternal male fears of the woman in power.

Is Margarete, then, Egmont's "real Amazon" (the figure that the *Apprenticeship* later promised but did not deliver),[14] the powerful woman whose attraction for him he feels compelled to repress? This suspicion is bolstered by a curious passage that has seldom been remarked on by the critics. In a long monologue in prison (act 5), Egmont once mentions Margarete's "friendship, which — why not admit it now? — was almost love" (140; "der Regentin Freundschaft, die fast, du darfst es dir gestehen, fast Liebe war," 315). Nowhere in Goethe's sources and, more important, *nowhere else in the play* is there any confirmation that Margarete "almost loves" Egmont — despite the fact that this motif was important enough to Goethe that he stressed it in a conversation more than forty years later.[15] The obvious conclusion would be that Egmont is here employing a common psychological maneuver, attributing to Margarete the erotic attraction that *he* feels for *her*. Another passage gives credence to this reading: the beginning of the bizarre conversation between Egmont and Clärchen about Margarete. It is Clärchen who brings up (abruptly) the topic of Margarete, after discussing how the Netherlanders love Egmont (thus hinting at matters of the heart), and she immediately asks: "Are you on good terms with her?" to which Egmont answers rather officiously: "It looks that way. We are amiable and helpful to each other" ("Bist du gut mit ihr?" "Es sieht einmal so aus. Wir sind einander freundlich und dienstlich," 289). Clärchen then presses the issue: "And in your heart?" ("Und im Herzen[?]"), a question that Egmont evades, speaking of his good wishes for Margarete and of her political suspicion of him. Taken together with Egmont's later monologue, Egmont's avoidance hints at a nascent attraction to Margarete, unlikely though that may seem. If such a liaison seems unlikely, it is primarily because of Egmont's grotesque characterization of Margarete as a mustachioed Amazon a few lines later, a juxtaposition that suggests even more strongly that he may have ulterior motives for his caricature of Margarete. Is he concealing from a suspicious Clärchen his attraction for this powerful woman — behind an implicit disclaimer based on her physical gender ambiguity, her manliness? Is he attracted precisely to what Clärchen describes as Margarete's "masculine mind" that is so skilled in the manly world of power? And does Egmont exaggerate Clärchen's femininity (her "virginal shyness") in order to assure her of *her* attractiveness to him?[16]

Even if we did not argue that Egmont is attracted to Margarete, his attraction to Clärchen herself and his foiled attempt to shape her feminine mystique bolster our suspicions that it is not really feminine mystique that interests him. For Clärchen's bursting of Egmont's virginal fantasy, and her rejection of his caricature of the powerful woman, are paralleled by other passages that show her to be anything but a conventional shrinking violet. In fact, the first appearance of Clärchen is in the scene where she sings a soldier's song, and Brackenburg, her suitor, holds the yarn for her as she coils it[17] — *he* is her distaff, and this scene enacts exactly the sort of "Kunkelhof" that Egmont had attributed to the masculinized Margarete, complete with Brackenburg shedding tears as Clärchen fantasizes about cross-dressing as a male in her song. Clärchen's "Omphale fantasy" draws a clear parallel between her and Egmont's image of a masculinized Margarete, suggesting his attraction to that image; it expresses a spirit of independence and rebellion in Clärchen that belies Egmont's evocation of her "virginal modesty." She, too, is a "real Amazon."

In a gesture of unconventionality that would have been shocking for most people in Goethe's day, Clärchen rejects the very thought of marriage (with Brackenburg); she is revolted by the notion that happiness amounts to being married off and living quietly ("versorgt . . . ein ruhiges Leben," 261). She doesn't worry about the future, but is happy if Egmont loves her (96/261); like Gretchen, who knows that she cannot marry the "traveler" Faust, Clärchen lives entirely for romantic and erotic fulfillment in the here and now.[18] But unlike Gretchen, Clärchen feels no guilt for her transgression of social norms. She vigorously rejects her mother's suggestion that she is a fallen, ruined woman (96/262), the "whore" she would be in the eyes of her society; she is apparently careless enough about her nocturnal meetings with Egmont that the townspeople gossip about an affair between them (98/264). If she is nevertheless passive, it is because of social restrictions on her as an unmarried woman who cannot move about freely (138/313), so that she repeatedly fantasizes crossing gender boundaries and partaking in the most aggressive of masculine activities: "If only I were a boy [Bube] and could go about with him all the time, to Court and everywhere! If only I could carry his standard for him in battle!" (97/262–63). To which her mother responds that Clärchen has always been a "tomboy" (97; "Springinsfeld," 253) and refers immediately to Clärchen's inappropriate clothing.

In the last act, of course, Clärchen *does* manage to break out of the bounds of house and family, and to realize her fantasies of (figuratively) carrying the flag into battle: on hearing of Egmont's imprisonment, she goes out into the street and seeks to rally the timid Dutchmen to revolt and free him. Like the mistress Orsina in Lessing's tragedy *Emilia Galotti*, the "mistress" Clärchen is the only reliable character who carries the play's political action onto the streets, into the public sphere of rebellion.[19] And the Dutchmen react with misogynist horror at this unseemliness, which suggests that her political action is *gendered*. They attempt to reduce Clärchen to the status of a child, piling on diminutives to deplore the inappropriateness of her action ("Darling" [Liebchen], "child," "girl," 135–36/309–10), and when Brackenburg patronizingly asks what her mother would say to this behavior, Clärchen contemptuously rejects this diminutization: "Do you take me for a child, or [mad]?" (137/311). Brackenburg clothes his horror in the conventional insistence that as an unmarried woman Clärchen is out of place in the "streets where you walked only on Sundays, through which you passed [with hands modestly folded,][20] on your way to church. . . . Here you stand and talk and act in full view of the public. Only try to think, my dearest!" (138/313). Of course, Clärchen's sexual liaison with Egmont betrays the emptiness of Brackenburg's image of her going to church with hands piously folded — just as her sophisticated political rhetoric refutes his insistence that the public sphere is inappropriate for women, who are not even to appear in public except on Sundays. Clärchen perceptively points out that it is the men who fail in their political mission, despite their superior physical strength and training in using weapons. She envisions herself as an inspiration to revolt, a rallying spirit:

And I have no strength, no muscles [*Mark*] like yours; but I have what all of you lack—courage and contempt for danger! If only my breath could [inflame you]! If only I could lend you human warmth and vigour by pressing you to my breast! Come with me! I shall walk in your midst! Just as a floating banner, in itself defenceless, leads a band of noble warriors on, so, flaring over all your heads, my spirit [will hover], and love and courage will weld this wavering, scattered people into a terrible army. (137/312)

We have now come full circle: Clärchen shows herself to be "noble, brave, resolute," precisely those characteristics that she had admired in Margarete while distancing herself from these qualities supposedly of "a different kind of woman" from her (119/290).

The image of Clärchen stirring up the populace to free Egmont will trigger objections to the interpretation of her as an independent and active woman with characteristics that Goethe's age attributed to men. For her "political" action derives entirely from her love for Egmont (as the erotic imagery of the above passage suggests), from her attraction to his charisma and power; she is slavishly devoted to him, and it is only in the context of her wish to be closer to him that she fantasizes crossing gender boundaries. Even the imagery of this action is gendered: Clärchen appears as standard-bearer, as catalyst for the actions of men, and finally as allegory of freedom—in the familiar model of Lady Liberty and other allegorized females who only inspire men and do not act, who as idealized, static monuments discourage (public) activity by real flesh-and-blood women. Finally, Clärchen ultimately carries out the suicide that makes her yet one more example of the sacrificed woman of domestic tragedy (see Stephan, "Tugend"). She seems entirely ancillary to Egmont, even calling herself "the smaller part" of him (141/316). These objections cannot be easily dismissed. They reveal the limits of Goethe's disruption of gender stereotypes. However, there are significant differences between Goethe's portrayal and those of some of his contemporaries (and even Goethe's own in works like *Iphigenia*; see Wagner). In order to understand these differences, we must look more closely at Egmont himself.

"The vexed question of Egmont's political judgement"—thus the title of an article by John Ellis—has exercised critical controversy for decades. But common to most readings is a recognition that

Egmont is either politically naive or irresponsible — something of an unpolitical man in a political world, in Ellis's formulation. When we engender this problem, we see that Egmont is essentially *passive*. His political "principle" is inaction where action is desperately needed. And it is telling that Egmont's reputation, the basis for the love he enjoys, is his past, not his present behavior — a past that is full of masculine military exploits and thus contrasts glaringly with his present passivity. Significantly, Clärchen admires the Egmont she finds on a woodcut of a battle, and though she contrasts this "woodcut Egmont" with the real-life man whom she loves, it is not insignificant that she had formed an image (*Bild*) of Egmont even as a girl, based on popular narrations of his exploits (263). This image of the active, heroic Egmont seems to play a major role in her love for him; the present, passive Egmont lives on mythic capital from his past.

In this light, Clärchen's "sacrifice" and apotheosis take on a different hue. Her suicide, which on the surface is an expression of powerlessness, must be seen in the context of her entire life. We take our cue from a female writer, Marie Luise Kaschnitz, who argues that Clärchen wants to break out of the oppressive life represented by her mother: "In her capacity for love and passion, Clärchen differs from her mother and the other middle-class women of the city. Only she is aware of the chains that bind her gender. 'If only I were a boy' [97]: here we see the still childish pleasure in taking part, not sitting at home, doing what her lover is doing" (104). Although Kaschnitz tends to reduce Clärchen to a lover and child, she pinpoints Clärchen's yearning for freedom from the narrow confines of her conventional life — a rebellion expressed in the desire for gender cross(-dress)ing. But can Clärchen truly break out of these restrictions? As Kaschnitz writes, "Clärchen's mother, with her fussiness, her housewifely worries, her anxiety over her family's reputation: that is Clärchen's own future, which she recognizes with horror" (102). Is not rebellion, the fight for "better times" (137/311), a logical response of a woman who cannot accept the inevitability of this suffocating future? Nor should we assume that Clärchen does not fully imagine how this "better," utopian future might look under the rule of the likes of Egmont; after all, the first three administrative cases that we see him deal with as feudal lord benefit women (at least in Goethe's perspective, if not in a modern one,[21] which would critique the expectation of reform from above, through "enlightened" male, feudal power).[22] And when she is finally cut off from this "better" future, is not suicide the only alternative? Significantly, after her mother suggests that her youth and passion will one day be gone and she should marry while she still can, Clärchen's thoughts turn immediately to death (116/287).

Regardless of how Clärchen's death is to be interpreted, Egmont's allegorization of her is clearly incommensurate with her actual life. The ending of the play has drawn criticism ever since it was published, notably from Schiller, who chastised its operatic jump ("Salto mortale in eine Opernwelt," *MA* 3.1:848) into a musically accompanied fantasy of Egmont's dream-vision of Clärchen visible on the stage. But the most bizarre part of the ending is perhaps that Egmont, about to be executed, falls asleep (Egmont's lying down and going to sleep at this crucial moment has to be seen on the stage for its strangeness to be appreciated).[23] Sleep, of course, gives occasion for the symbolic dream-image of Clärchen to appear on the stage. But it also symbolizes perfectly *Egmont's passivity*. As Goethe's friend the painter Angelika Kaufmann remarked, his sleep and dream remind us that he has gone through life as in a dream ("durch sein ganzes Leben gleichsam wachend geträumt," *MA* 3.1.842). Furthermore, the passive sleep produces an image of woman's passivity. However, we must remember that the vision of Clärchen as (passive) allegory of freedom is clearly marked in the play as *Egmont's* dream. The allegory rises up and acts out in pantomime the future liberation of the Netherlands, which will be triggered by Egmont's impending death — not by his life.

The context of this dream is important: we have just seen the fruition of a truly homoerotic relationship between the young son of Alba, Ferdinand, and Egmont — but Ferdinand is the wooer, and Egmont resists his advances. Ferdinand is on a gender mission to Egmont's cell: his "cruel" father, the tyrant Alba, despises both Ferdinand's "feelings" and his "principles," "rebuking" them "as the inheritance of a tender mother," and sends him to the cell to "mould" him in his own "image" by exposing him to Egmont at the brink of execution (146; "Grausamer Vater! . . . Du kanntest mein Herz meine Gesinnung, die du so oft als Erbteil einer zärtlichen Mutter schaltest. Mich dir gleich zu bilden, sandtest du mich hierher," 323). Ferdinand subverts his father's design. After wishing that he were a woman (146; "O daß ich ein Weib wäre!" 323) so that his feelings would be taken more seriously, the sentimental Ferdinand embraces Egmont (147; *Ihm um den Hals fallend*, 323) and declares his love in terms that are so like Clärchen's that he seems destined to become a replacement for her as Egmont's "lover." Egmont's impending death castrates his designs; Ferdinand says: "at last I hoped to see you and did see you, and my heart went out to you [*flog dir entgegen*]. You I had chosen for myself, and confirmed my choice when I saw you. Now, only now, I hoped to be with you, to live with you, to grasp you, to — Well, all that has been cut off [*weggeschnitten*] now" (147/324). With Egmont's death, Ferdinand will lose all "joy and zest [for life]" (148; "Lebenslust und Freude," 325). It is not insignificant that Egmont's last words with Ferdinand involve turning over to his new friend his lover Clärchen; he thus struggles to return both himself and Ferdinand to heterosexual "normality." More important, both Ferdinand and Clärchen, the "lovers" of Egmont, represent an unsettling of traditional gender norms, Clärchen in her desire to be a man, Ferdinand in his desire to be a woman. Thus, if Egmont "tears himself" from Ferdinand's arms, it is so that he can restore forcibly his stable gender world. He falls asleep superficially without cares (149–50/327), but the dream itself reveals his deeper obsession with restoring gender stability.

The characteristic features of the dream-figure with Clärchen's features are her deference to Egmont and her silence. But the *real* Clärchen is not silent. In her first speech on the street, she refers to herself as a *voice* that initiates action (136/310); as we saw, her voice had also expressed discontent with the gender roles forced on her by society. Yet, like the men on the street who try to make her into a child and to silence her voice ("What does the child want? Tell her to be quiet," 136/310), Egmont silences Clärchen in his vision of her and transforms the flesh-and-blood, sensual woman into an allegory — perhaps the reason for Herder's consternation at what he apparently called the missing "nuance between girl and goddess" in the play.[24] The allegory's validity as a representation of the silent Clärchen is, furthermore, even more inappropriate because Egmont *does not know* of her public incitement, her rhetorical action on the streets, or her desire to become a man, or of her reenactment of the "Omphale scene" that he had conjured up with horror: his dream represents a silent Clärchen, not the voiced one to which the spectator has access. Egmont's laconic handing over of Clärchen to Ferdinand in the last scene offended Goethe's female friends in Weimar, apparently because of Egmont's cavalier treatment of Clärchen as a sexual object (literally a thing, a jewel [149], "Kleinod," 327) who can be disposed of with no regard for her own will.[25] But this treatment only reflects his ignorance of her transgression of gender boundaries, his renewed reduction of her to one pole of gender oppositions: the easily dominated, devoted maiden. This misogynist gesture also bolsters his damaged gender identity by fending off homoerotic feelings — feelings that are, however, suggested in another of his laments in his cell: "Oh, Clare, if you were a man, I should surely see you here, the very first to welcome me" (140/315). Thus Egmont directly echoes Clärchen's earlier wish that she be a man and hints at both his and her deeper dissatisfaction with gender strictures. As usual, the homoerotic theme points to wider gender issues: while Egmont accurately captures Clärchen's spirit and courage in these lines, he implies that she would have to be a man in order to do what she has, in fact, done — to go out on the street and incite rebellion. Contrary to what Egmont suggests, it is the men who do not show the courage and activeness of Clärchen, and who doom Egmont. The real Clärchen is active, independent, and finds a strong voice; the men, *especially* Egmont, attempt to reduce her to a virginal girl or a voiceless allegory.

The other possible objection to this reading, however, is that in her "political" activity on the streets, Clärchen is driven by her deferential love for Egmont, by private motives that again associate her with the world of "feminine" feelings and not with the masculine world of public activity. However, Goethe consistently undermines the supposedly idealistic, political motivations of *all* the characters in the play, not just Clärchen — and in this respect, Clärchen comes off rather well. Most strikingly, Goethe portrays Alba's conflict with Egmont as the result of a childhood slighting (145/322) — a twist that for some critics ruins the play's political dynamic and makes it into a "tragedy of arbitrariness" (*MA* 3.1:882). These mixed motives extend to the political players from the lower classes, too; Jetter seems to hate the Spanish troops mainly because they invaded his conjugal bed (89/253), and, most significantly, Goethe undermines the ideas of the agitator Vansen — ideas with which Goethe demonstrably identified — by depicting him as propelled by lower drives such as hunger, alcoholism, and lust for power (see Wilson, "Hunger/Artist"). Egmont himself seems driven mainly by his carefree nature, his desire to enjoy life and avoid the messy world of politics; although he gives lip service to freedom and is basically a generous noble lord, he draws the line at feudal dues, which must be collected at all costs (106/274). Most significantly, we hear that it is the civil "disturbances" that have led to a decrease in his feudal dues (106/274), so it is clear that his failure to support the rebellion against the Spanish has a very personal class interest.[26]

It would seem, in fact, that the female characters, Margarete and Clärchen, are the only ones with relatively pure political motives. In contrast to Vansen, who earlier in the play tries to stir up the peaceful burghers from impure motives, Clärchen tries to do so from a deep love for Egmont. This love is (in Goethe's eyes) itself political; it stands for the love that the people have for Egmont — "You, whom all the people loves," Clärchen says to him (118/289) — and it is their "love" for him, their "burning desire [*Brennende Begier*] to save him," that she evokes in order to free him and with him the Netherlands (135–36/309–10). Although Clärchen is tragically mistaken and obviously projects her own (sexual) desire onto the masses, her love is a model of the sort of bond that the Dutch commoners *should* have to the nobles. We must be careful not to project our own postfeudal political culture onto a patriarchal and patrimonial age and onto a conservative thinker for whom politics always rested on the affectionate bond between rulers (particularly the landed nobility) and subjects.[27] Clärchen's attempt to rally the Dutchmen is as close as Goethe ever came (after the unpublished manuscript of *Gottfried von Berlichingen*) to valorizing insurrection; it is precisely *because* her motives seem based on affection for the feudal lord that Goethe approves of her political activity (just as Schiller's *Wilhelm Tell*, echoing the last lines of *Egmont*, justifies insurrection only as defense of family and home). That Clärchen's love and her action are truly political (from Goethe's perspective) can be seen in her own argumentation, which points to Egmont — the local nobility — as the only protection from despotism and argues that only he can guarantee "better times" (136–37/310–11).[28] It is only "love and courage" (137/312) that will insure freedom; only when Clärchen sees that the Dutchmen will not act on their love for Egmont ("But they loved him!" 137/312) does she give up her mission — thus showing that only a true personal bond can lead to true political action. It could be precisely *because of* her "political" love for Egmont that Goethe included Clärchen in the play (she is his major departure from the sources, since the historical Egmont was married and had a large family): as a lover from the unprivileged classes, she effectively symbolizes the affection that Goethe idealizes in those classes.[29]

The dream-image is thus entirely inappropriate in its depiction of a silenced Clärchen, who has a strong political voice in the service of both positive political goals and gender emancipation. We can therefore question whether the deference that the dream-figure shows toward Egmont — glorifying him as the catalyst of revolt — is an appropriate representation of Clärchen; she has, after all, engaged in agitative activity such as Egmont himself had earlier condemned in Vansen. Clothing brings out the absurdity of this representation of Clärchen; the figure is in "heavenly," and thus presumably feminine, dress ("in Himmlischem Gewand," 328), but Clärchen has herself expressed the opposite desire to wear men's clothing — that is, a hat, for her a symbol of gender freedom (94/260), but which Egmont's dream-Clärchen points out to Egmont as a symbol of Dutch freedom (150/328). And is it not highly ironic that it is only through death — through absence — that Egmont can contribute to Dutch freedom (150/328), whereas Clärchen has actively worked to bring about this goal? In fact, we might ask whether Egmont does not have more of the traditional female "victim" about him than Clärchen — that is, the victim who passively, in her death, inspires men to revolt. Critics have failed to notice that the dream-figure holds out the laurel wreath to crown Egmont as victor but never actually places it on his head. Would it not be entirely inappropriate for the courageous agitator to attribute the future freedom of the Netherlands to a privileged rake who did not lift one finger for the cause, but who somehow passes as its symbol?

The passivity of sleep that produces the dream of a passive woman: if this image is inappropriate for Clärchen, it can apply only to Egmont himself. After his encounter with gender ambiguity in the form of Ferdinand — and, earlier, Clärchen and Margarete — Egmont conjures up his passive, female self in the image of the conventional, allegorized woman. It is not accidental that he describes sleep as a disintegration of the self: "Sweet Sleep! . . . You loosen every knot of strenuous thought, [mix] all the images of joy and pain; unobstructed flows the circle of inner harmonies, and swathed in agreeable delirium, we sink and cease to be" (150; "Süßer Schlaf! . . . Du lösest die Knoten der strengen Gedanken, vermischest alle Bilder der Freude und des Schmerzens, ungehindert fließt der Kreis innerer Harmonien, und eingehüllt in gefälligen Wahnsinn, versinken wir und hören auf zu sein," 328). Gender boundaries have become fluid in Egmont, and the dream, inappropriate as it is as a depiction of his beloved as passive female, turns on him and betrays his own passivity, his own femininity. When he awakens, he returns to the world of masculine aggression and purpose; "I too [stride] from this cell to meet an honourable death; I die for freedom, for which I lived and fought and for which I now passively offer up myself" (150), he claims, but we certainly have not seen him fight for freedom, and he hardly "sacrifices himself" purposefully — he was captured because of his own political miscalculation. The only accurate word in this interpretation is *leidend*, nicely ambiguous as either "suffering" or, as Michael Hamburger translates it, "passively." His martial rhetoric of male protector of the family — "swords are flashing . . . friends, more courage! Behind you parents, wives, and children wait!" (151/329)[30] — is stated with a forced emphasis that betrays knowledge of a world in which gender is not quite so simple.

Clärchen's status as the embodiment of a "politicized" love of the commoners for their feudal lord is clearly invested in a political agenda that was close to Goethe's heart: the stabilization of the social status quo in a period of grave threat to feudal society. At this point, numerous axes of power become apparent in the play. The gender axis, the power of men over women, is analogous to two others: the hegemony of the Spanish over the Dutch (under which the hegemony of Catholic over Protestant is subsumed), and of the privileged (primarily the nobility) over the unprivileged. As woman, commoner, and Dutch, Clärchen is on the powerless end of each of these three axes, but Egmont is on the powerless end of only one of them: as a Netherlander, he should be fighting for the Dutch cause. However, the threat to his feudal dues from the rebellion — as well as a snide remark by Alba (133/307) — highlight the dilemma of a nobleman like Egmont, who fears destabilization of the social order and thus of his privileged status in the Dutch/Protestant rebellion. Thus, at the beginning of act 2 Egmont quells a disturbance fomented by the illegitimate agitator Vansen, who nevertheless voices legitimate grievances that eventually lead to a revolt that Goethe — and Egmont — glorify.

Goethe mobilizes the theme of cross-dressing to highlight Egmont's paradoxical political position: just after he leaves the scene of the disturbance, one of the Dutchmen says of him, "A gracious gentleman! A true Netherlander! Nothing Spanish about him"; but just a few lines later, another character remarks on Egmont's clothing: "Did you notice his dress? It was in the latest fashion, the Spanish cut" (104/271). By cross-dressing as a Spaniard, Egmont displays his divided loyalties; he cannot resist Spanish domination because he has too much invested in it, including his feudal dues (106/274), his very livelihood. His error is in thinking that the very privileges granted to him by the former Spanish king (the Order of the Golden Fleece) will protect him from the present king's power. But until his self-delusion becomes clear, he remains firmly on the side of power — a hidden reason for his passivity.

In the central scene in act 3 in which Egmont and Clärchen discuss the "Amazon" Margarete, Egmont surprises Clärchen by fulfilling a promise to "come dressed in Spanish [courtly] fashion one day" (118; "Ich versprach dir einmal spanisch zu kommen," 288). Significantly, Egmont at first conceals the clothing under his cape, so that he cannot embrace Clärchen, which annoys her (117/287). When he finally reveals his clothing and thus frees his arms to embrace her, Clärchen is so impressed with the courtly dress that she can hardly speak — and her immediate response is to avoid his embrace, to shrink from touching Egmont and his "splendid" attire (118/288), thus symbolizing the distance between the privileged and the unprivileged.[31] The impeding of sexual contact suggests that Clärchen's love for Egmont — which is later transformed into political action and provides a model for the people's active devotion to Egmont — runs up against a barrier: his privileged status as a nobleman, which results in a "secret" alliance with the Spanish (hidden by his cloak) and helps prevent him from acting on behalf of the Dutch *or* the unprivileged. Thus, in the celebrated lines at the end of this scene, in which Egmont splits his public, political self off from his private, personal self that loves Clärchen (120/290–91), we see an entirely appropriate bifurcation stemming from his awareness that his public persona — represented in this scene by the Spanish clothing — is incompatible with the affection of the lower classes for him. These lines are also yet another attempt to relegate his Clärchen and his relationship with her to the private sphere — an attempt in which the real Clärchen partakes for now, but which is contradicted both by her childhood admiration for the *public* Egmont and by her later political activity on his behalf.

It is important to see that positive political action is gendered female in this work. Not only are the female characters Clärchen and Margarete the only political actors whose motives are relatively pure, but Ferdinand's liberal political "principles" (*Gesinnungen*) — though a Spaniard, he empathizes with Dutch freedom — are also explicitly marked as an inheritance of his mother,[32] part of the feminine traits that his father is determined to eradicate. And we have seen that from Goethe's perspective, Clärchen is fighting for "better times" for women. Paradoxically, Egmont is paralyzed and unable to partake in this fight. He becomes a fetish, an empty signifier for political struggle, passive and inert. Clärchen, in contrast, is an active political rebel whom Egmont attempts to transform into just such a fetish; she is *for him* a signifier of femininity, but the reader perceives her incompatibility with traditional femininity. Cross-dressing (or the desire to cross-dress) reflects this difference in signification; it ultimately plays different roles for the women and for Egmont. Representing historical practices, all the cross-dressers in the play hope to partake in the power represented by the opposite pole: the women in male power, the Dutchman in Spanish power. All of them fail, but for quite different reasons, all of them historical. The women fail because men resort to misogynist stereotypes in order to block the usurpation of power (Margarete as a man-dominating Amazon, ultimately too weak to tame a "horse," the Dutch people; Clärchen as a harmless girl-child, banished from public rebellion). Egmont's cross-dressing fails because of his ambiguous position along the various axes of the play. Though a Dutchman, he partakes in feudal power and thus has a concealed affinity to the Spanish; he miscalculates by assuming that his power privilege can be unproblematically transferred to the axis between Dutch and Spanish, and that he is guaranteed the power of the Spanish. His confusion of the two axes suggests that his cross-dressing as a Spaniard might be read as a metaphor for cross-dressing on the gender axis, but the analogy would require reading Egmont as a male cross-dressing as a male, striving to attain the pole representing (male) power. Though a man, he does not conform to prevailing gender codes, because he is attracted by the ambiguity of powerful women — and he denies the gender ambiguity by warding off the homoerotic affections of a man who associates himself with the feminine. Egmont's cross-dressing is thus a *masquerade*, representing an unsettling slippage between two poles rather than the imagined attainment of the pole of power. Catriona MacLeod has recently argued that Goethe, in his remarkable essay "Women's Parts Played by Men in the Roman Theater" (1789), anticipates Judith Butler's argument that transvestism "reveals the imitative, performative nature of gender itself" (394). Egmont cross-dresses for success, but his performance is unconvincing; he merely reveals the performativity of his masculinity. Like Goethe's cross-dressed male actors, whose performance evokes a "third, alien nature" ("eine dritte und eigentlich fremde Natur") because of the "self-conscious illusion" ("eine Art von *selbstbewußter Illusion*") created by the attention to the performance itself (*MA* 3.2:173–74),[33] Egmont's performance of his own gender is ultimately unconvincing.

The French Revolution, with its threefold images of radical feminism, of violent and bloodthirsty lower-class women on the streets of Paris, and of women in uniform,[34] radicalized and politicized gender issues, contributing to the backlash toward gender codification and hierarchy. The previous gender ambiguity in fashion, including masculinized "Amazon" dress for women, was suppressed after about 1789.[35] Remarkably, gender ambiguity became no less pronounced in Goethe's works after the storming of the Bastille; however, he evidently attempted to channel it into more acceptable forms. The specter of the violent woman found its expression in two more of Goethe's works in which gender issues have received far too little attention; in both of them, the woman is armed, reflecting the Revolutionary age's discomfort at this threat from both gender and political unrest. In the antirevolutionary play The Rebels (*Die Aufgeregten*, probably from 1792),[36] a woman hunter (reminiscent of Margarete) resolves the play's dramatic conflict with a rifle in hand, but her femininity is stressed by the authorial voice, which calls her "an ingenuous, purely natural, and fundamentally righteous and feminine being" ("ein unbefangenes, rein natürliches und im tiefsten Grunde rechtliches weibliches Wesen," *MA* 4.1:163). Goethe's favorite work among the nineteenth-century bourgeoisie, the epic tale *Hermann and Dorothea* (1797), contains a notorious glorification of feminine subservience ("Let woman learn to serve according to her destiny"; "Dienen lerne bei Zeiten das Weib nach ihrer Bestimmung," *MA* 4.1:608). However, the speaker, a woman who is expected to be "a domestic girl" ("ein häusliches Mädchen"), had only a few lines earlier been depicted as "courageous and powerful" ("tapfer und mächtig"), slicing up French soldiers with a sword to prevent them from raping young girls (*MA* 4.1:596–97), and her physique is anything but the weak and traditionally "feminine" one that could be expected in this age. Nevertheless, in these two works, Goethe *attempts* to "contain" gender ambiguity by channeling female strength into acceptable models of domesticity[37] — unconvincingly, I think. This forced gender stability in the age of the French Revolution, in two works devoted to counterrevolutionary goals, suggests the strong parallel in Goethe's imagination between gender and political unrest that we have seen in his earlier play. In the prerevolutionary *Egmont*, however, gender and political issues were not yet explosively threatening enough to provoke Goethe to attempt to contain them (though he reports wanting to eliminate the "all too unbuttoned" nature of the play ("ich will nur das Allzuaufgeknöpfte, Studentenhafte der Manier zu tilgen suchen")![38] Later he became more conservative in both political and gender matters. It is telling that when embellishing her letters to Goethe for publication after his death, Bettine Brentano provocatively quotes Clärchen's fantasy of military gender-crossing ("O, would I wore doublet / And breeches and hat!" 94/260) in a "revolutionary" setting, imagining herself joining the rebellious Tyroleans;[39] she thus mobilizes Goethe's brash gender images against his later conservatism. Still, with respect to gender as well as politics, Goethe *never* seemed quite to manage a clear-cut message; his works can never be comfortably squeezed into the aged Goethe's own cliché of "the eternal feminine."

Laurence A. Rickels

Psy Fi Explorations of Out Space: On Werther's Special Effects

> Husband, wife, and friend, one is injured in the other.
>
> — Goethe, *Roman Elegies*

> Homosexual love is far more compatible with group ties, even when it takes the shape of uninhibited sexual impulsions — a remarkable fact, the explanation of which might carry us far.
>
> — Freud, *Group Psychology and the Analysis of the Ego*

> The cult of Werther was exploited by the trade: *eau de Werther* was sold, and Charlotte and Werther, figures long as familiar and ubiquitous as Mickey Mouse or Donald Duck today, appeared on fans and gloves, on bread-boxes and jewelry.
>
> — Atkins, *The Testament of Werther in Poetry and Drama*

> It is a thing so unnatural for a man to tear himself loose from himself . . . that he in most instances uses mechanical means to carry out his intention.
>
> — Goethe, *Poetry and Truth*

The Sorrows of Young Werther was the first bestseller of modern mass culture; from its anonymous authorship on out it folded open along an installment plan of self-help or how-to. It was the book that installed an identificatory understanding or following in a readership of actors-out who dressed up as Werther look-alikes and, in the season finale, copycut their take on or intake of their leading man's suicide. Billed in the novel as outlet for a "creative freedom" (Tellenbach 16) otherwise blocked by a mounting sense of absence and backed up against the off limits separating him from all outside connections, Werther's closing shot of suicide was the hit copped by every fan male. This direct hit has since gone all the way to creating a fit between *Werther*'s outer-literature experiences and the medical and social-scientific examination of "suicide by suggestion." And it's fitting that the foreign body of one example standing for many others available within a factoid discourse working out on stats should be strewn across this threshold, intact and undisclosed:

In September 1774 Goethe published his first novel, *The Sorrows of Young Werther*, whose hero shot himself, unable to bear his desperate love. The book was a sensation and became a European bestseller. Many romantic young men identified themselves with the hero and subsequently the number of suicides rose dramatically. The authorities in Italy, Germany, and Denmark banned the book in hopes of putting a stop to the suicide epidemic.

Emile Durkheim, who wrote the first scientific study of suicide in 1897, was also the first to define the word "imitation" in the context of suicide. He came to the conclusion that, even though imitation can cause clustering of some individual suicides, it can never be the original reason for them. He assumed that the suicides triggered by imitation would have eventually happened, even without the effect of suggestion. Durkheim took a skeptical attitude toward the censorship of news about crimes and suicides demanded by his contemporaries.

In 1974 Phillips introduced and defined the term "Werther effect" to denote an increase in the number of suicides caused by suggestion. Phillips was the first to study systematically and empirically the effect of suggestion on suicide. In his classic paper, Phillips used American and British statistics to show that the number of suicides increased after the story of a suicide was published in the press. Phillips's results contradicted Durkheim's claim that the effects of suggestion are only local. (Taiminen, Salmenpera, and Lehtinen 350–51)

The local activity of imitation, suggestion, and suicide can be thought globally only by summoning an effect that is at once literary and extraliterary, in other words, psychoanalytic. But the summons must be served: Freud's second system, a public address system broadcasting his theory of group psychology, is always one context away from the meeting above of the identificatory "Werther effect" with its match and maker, the same context of journalism and social studies. For example, the unsexed look of mass suicide we find in the generic studies of "the Werther effect" has in the other context of psychoanalysis a unisex appeal. Freud's genealogy of group-level identification, from the Christian mass to the modern masses, follows out the replacement of all that's fair, including love and war, with friendship and suicide.[1] But that's also the genealogy of cuteness or replication: the suicidal teen androgyne — whose adolescent boy body, at once hard and feminine, is not into retro repro relations between the sexes — is spectacularly at the group's disposal. Group psychology is, then, by any other name, the psychology of adolescence.

Teens, who get their sexual license not from their parents (they're too out of it or off limits anyway) but from the unisex group, are into groupwide self-replication: they only want to be different like the friends they like to be like. Reproduction is the traditional frame (and stress) put on the adolescent group, which reserves mega-ambivalence for the couple, both the parental one (that's off in the master bedroom grossing out the masturbating group-of-one) and the futural one every group member is supposed to become or come like for the survival of the group or species (the group doesn't have a reproducing plan of its own). The mourning after separation is the motor that couple formation and reproduction keep running: the group, which never mourns, tries to find different ways of getting around getting stuck on loss. That's why suicide bears the reversible seal of group approval. Checkout time at the same time for the whole group (or group-of-one) folds back onto the wish that is a group-level command: replicate, don't reproduce.

Adolescents already had that cute look of the alien or outsider when they were first invented in the eighteenth century as originals. That's why teen passion was taken over by the newly founded institutions of higher learning as their charge. This is how modern mass culture — the Teen Age — began, intramurally, inside the institution of academe, which has always been fast on the intake. Modern educational institutions were erected on top of a mounting impulse to absorb the overload of this surge. But already in *Faust* we read in the fine print that the university alone could never contain this striving without a cause. Transferential precincts, in other words, could not provide the setting for a set of responses that would, in time, act out in front of the TV set. From the eighteenth century onward the mobile unit or union of conversion shock-absorbed the overload of adolescence that was being institutionalized back in school: the early history of the first American universities and colleges overlaps with the outbreak of mass conversions, which by the turn of the century had gone on the record of psychological study. On his first trip to America Freud made contact with this modern science of conversion, which his host Stanley Hall had established with a two-volume work entitled, simply but subtly, *Adolescence*.

"Hysterical conversion" was one of the missing links between this encounter with adolescence and later developments in Freud's thought. It made a disappearance inside its reformulation for the new and improved concept and context of projection. What relocates early hysterics (like Dora) and the upward mobility of their symptom formations to the media-delusional sensurrounds of Freud's Schreber or Tausk's Natalija A. is the post–World War One zoom onto group psychology's psychotic and perverse structures. That's where the sexual content of hysteria went and came. Interpersonal sexual difference, which has its focus fixed on reproduction, drops out of the group plan.

How Many Siblings?

Eissler set up Goethe's bond with his sister Cornelia as the standard edition of his object choice and frame of preference. For example, he carefully calculated that the onset of Werther's decompensation is set on or by the date of Cornelia's birthday (1:99). *Werther* was first conceived and executed on parallel tracks with the course of his sister's initiation into reproduction, the race set going by her marriage in November 1773 to a certain Schlosser (whose name resonates with variations on "locking up"). By February 1774, when Goethe carried *Werther* to term by term of fulfillment of the suicide contract, the family had every reason to assume Cornelia's expectancy (she delivered in October). In fact, Goethe's own explosive reactions while staying in Wetzlar in 1772, the stopover that provided models for *Werther* (and perhaps, in varying degrees, for every one of Goethe's novels), first went off, according to Eissler's resetting of the timer, with the news break that a courtship was on and going strong between friend Schlosser and Cornelia (1:95). But the direct connection Eissler puts through between Goethe and Cornelia, and which he sees as establishing the incestuous resource center of Goethe's complete portfolio of self-identifications, was also jamming with an excess of murderous static crossing over from other lines.

First there's the mother, for whom Werther's effects pose no problem: according to Goethe's mother, *Werther* accomplished proper burial for actual events in Goethe's life, which are thus commemorated and put to rest (Graham, *Goethe and Lessing* 136). But Goethe was haunted by *Werther*. The book was indeed pursuing its author, Goethe had to admit, like the unlaid ghost of a murdered brother (*HA* 1:558). Werther's improper burial at the novel's close, which was doubled by Goethe's originally having published *Werther* anonymously, thus kept on putting in ghost appearances with the copycat suicides.

Eissler reconstructs Goethe's self-identification with the pregnant mother (beginning with the drag show on ice Goethe pulled off when he skated past his mother with her red coat on) as the one way out of suicide left over after Cornelia was gone (1:104, 105, 112). But when Goethe returned to *Werther* to fine-tune its reception in the final version (this time after Cornelia was gone *and* dead, a double departure that attended her second childbirth), he described this work of revision as Werther's return "into his mother's body" (Eissler 1:81). Eissler's upbeat account of Goethe's bonding with a mother's reproductive capacity (1:113) leaves out the body opened up to this return and thus to the suicidal ready position networked with a Jonestown-style readership and with ghosts. The mother's body, as secret bearer of the undead, is the other medium of identification, the one turning in the ghostly returns; but the maternal body is also the body of the group, a formation or transformation that issues its first bonds as identification going down between siblings, who start out as each other's total rivals for the direct line to the mother. If you can't lick the newly arrived rival, because the conflict, like the sex, is too total or suicidal, then you're joined at the rip-and-tear line of one identification. The fraternity or sorority thus established (with a love right above the death wish) pledges internally or eternally to siblings dead or alive. That's why ghosts can always be seen making the in-crowd of the group bond.

In his essay on a singular childhood recollection recorded by Goethe in *Poetry and Truth*, Freud unpacked the little one's antics at the window as acting out his bond with mother to the point of magically expelling all rival siblings back through the window womb. It is this relationship—Freud refers to it in shorthand as Goethe's close rapport with his mother—that was the source of Goethe's great success. And yet Freud is also moved to list those missing in action: the four dead little ones who found no place in Goethe's autobiography. The first fulfillment of Goethe's death wishes was thus the departure of his younger six-year-old brother, Hermann Jakob, whose death was also the original occasion for Goethe's legendary refusal to mourn.

Dead siblings are the encrypted ones along for the death drive in cases of melancholia. It's a mother of an identification that makes the first deposit; mother's unmourning transfers an undead child to the joint account she opens up inside her surviving child, who is filled out with the missing persons reports of an unknown sibling. For Goethe (and Kafka, whose plan to write an essay on Goethe's "monstrous being" fits right in here), the funereal zone occupied by ghostly, reanimated, or "warm" brothers was also the secret society in which the homosexual component or contingency checked in.[2]

But the haunting fallout of group identifications in Goethe's readership was rehearsed or repeated in Werther's attraction to a couple of live ones, which already packed the double whammy of projective displacement; his suffering or passion, which is out of place, is bound not only to Lotte, the off-limits woman, but also or especially, at the outer limit, to a homosexual object choice. At this end Werther borrows the warm gun of his suicide from Lotte's betrothed, Albert (nothing could be hotter or better). But Eissler's main evidence for his reading of *Werther* as the stations or station-identifications of Goethe's being crossed by Cornelia's couplification with Schlosser is that, in the novel, Albert bears way more resemblance to Schlosser (and to the way Goethe mixed his feelings toward Schlosser) than to Kestner, the apparent model for Werther's Albert (1:98). The going assumption about the fiction's working relationship with what had been a happening event back in Wetzlar went far enough to leave Kestner real hurt. It's the misrecognition some call love. It doesn't require much of an outing to get to the panoramic view that Goethe's correspondence with Kestner about his impossible love for Kestner's wife was homosexual, not in follow-up action, but in frame. It inspires Eissler to imagine that Goethe might have thought, latently that is, that Schlosser married Cornelia only because he was in fact in love with Goethe.

We are desperately familiar by now with the monitoring or administering of degrees of homosexuality attained on the way to an all the more potentiated heterosexuality. But we saw it first with Goethe, who made the ambiguous phasing and phrasing of heterosexual couplification his signature piece. One need only read between the lines of Eissler's analysis, lines too far-flung by half—by the missing half of the homosexual connection—to watch the making and shifting of the perfect fit between the ultimate catch, the whole of heterosexual adjustment, and the bypass operations of Eissler's analysis, which leave out the part or past exceeding that whole. For example, Eissler pursues the Cornelia connection throughout the story of Goethe's attachment to Lili Schönemann, the only girl he ever loved (1:117–22). Eissler's stress is on Goethe's need to recreate an ancillary relationship with a sister to diversify the portfolio of his interest in Schönemann: Goethe turned to Countess Stolberg, whom he had never met and would know only through their correspondence and her two brothers, with whom he connected in real time, Big Time. In the letters she is addressed as "sister," and her brothers are his too; indeed, he tends to establish contact with her inside his relationship with her brothers: "In them I had you, best Gustgen, for you are all one in love and essence." This sister figure thus goes by a unisex nickname that nicks a notch on a conveyor belt of ambiguities: "No female being, after all, loves me as much as Gustgen" (120–22). What fits below the belt (and sets the ambivalence machine running) is also the name Schönemann, which breaks down literally as "beautiful man." "In my relationship to Lili," Goethe would reflect, "it [the demonic] was particularly effective" (118). What is elided but also included by the ellipsis is not only the demonic but also its synonym, the surname that bears the attractiveness of men.

Same Differences

As a work of caution to culture critics against overuse of latent homosexuality as a cure-all explanation for group or psychotic bonding over a long-distant woman's body, Theweleit's *Male Fantasies* at the same time cannot pick up the frequency of ghosts in cases that do, however, come directly out of the loss or losses of World War One. Theweleit's focus on identification is fixed on the sexual combo of merger and murderousness, but with a difference, with one substitution please: he relocates the sister figure at the cathexis center of the para-Nazi fantasies shared by the soldier brothers. Theweleit makes his move to get around the psychoanalytic automatism that rushes to read the itinerary of homosexuality inside the psychic makeup of all-male representation and repression. The sister figure (often, in wartime for example, a nurse who, in German, is thus doubly "sister") is a safe choice because she's linked and limited to the family value of super savings in libido. In fact, however, as the sister of a best friend, her own exogamous availability opens up a libido outlet that stands in for and in the way of the homosexual connection between the soldier bros. But for Theweleit such an analysis moves too quickly, like a guilty assumption or a countertransference.

Theweleit calls for special handling of the shock of recognition that goes down between brother and sister, and thus for more time with the material or text, the biology or biography (before shortcutting, that is, to the castration complex of psychoanalysis). While that opens up psychoanalytic theory to in-session temporality and materiality, the shorthand of theory is still on primal time. In other words, the sister's hard body, which stands in for all women on the outside and defends against the prospect of their dreaded amorphous corporeality, is at the same time, or rather the first time, the mother's body. Every relationship to the body, even one's own body, is to the mother's body. It's the only body around, and it's off limits. It sets a limit to pleasure (and a half-life to material reading) that in turn sets the place of tension between the sexual couple and the group. The group's "body" is the maternal one, the one that can never be consumed in the one-on-one. This maternal body asserting itself in shared fantasy — in other words, in groups — will always be same-sex (even or especially for the soldier boys).

Theweleit is not alone in sizing up Freud's investment in the group's psychology as the oedipalization (or homosexualization) of psychotic structures. The rejection of oedipally directed readings that restrict admissions to homosexuality and then award homosexuality degree status within the range of components making up psychotic delusions belongs right up there with all the popular breakaway movements that split Freud's turn to group psychology. It was against this homosexual tendency of the psychoanalytic group conspiracy (which asserted itself as a nonreproductive exclusion of women) that Adler championed women's rights: the supplemental movement that accompanied the establishment of equal rights within a heterosexual bond of therapy was Adler's persistent demand for therapeutic eradication of homosexuality. He dismissed the it-takes-one-to-know-one view that one's homophobia only reflects the press of one's own repressed homosexuality; that was one of those inside views based on nothing but psychoanalytic theory, which had something to hide and protect (149–70). Reich's resistance to Freud's psychology of groups and, in particular, to their insurance policy, the death drive, is legend. But at the high point of his close encounter with psychosis (which featured sci-fi delusions about invasion from outer space, which he, son of spacemen, was alone fit to withstand, and alternated with that sense of betrayal that invites identification with Christ) Reich specifically denied homosexuals entry into his cure-all organon boxes. It was the first backfire of his remobilization of the notion of libido around which he had retrenched during his save sex campaign against Freud's alleged tampering with the original formulation of libido through introduction of the death drive. Reich's sci-fi delusions first took on the death drive, then all of psychoanalysis; first homosexuality, then sex itself. The equation of homosexuality and Freudian analysis asserts itself Big Time in all the registers of resistance. Deleuze and Guattari's *Anti-Oedipus* thus only reset the trend for reversing the one way psychoanalysis oedipalizes even the psychotic material it interprets. The anti-Oedipus complex is still taking sides against Freud with Reich's special controlling interest in energy flow. This time around it is "perverse reterritorialization" that is internal to the automatic interpretation by psychoanalysis of homosexual dispositions and positions inside psychosis. In the schizophrenia-compatible model Deleuze and Guattari propose as antidote to oedipalization tendencies that work (both overtime and in session) to pervert or reterritorialize the psycho trying to go with the flow, there is, accordingly, one thing missing from an embarrassment of readmissions. When the anti-oedipals muster the interpersonal columns for the social connections excluded from intrapsychic insight, the only thing left to be missing is sexuality. Freud's conception of sexuality has always been one of those unwanted problems, which resistance puts up for adaptation as the related one of homosexuality's continued existence. Once the resistance goes this far the agenda expands or narrows to include the problem of masturbation, which now really has to go. That's why, on this resistance scanner, masturbation, the origin and eternal return of sexuality itself, is already viewed as homosexual, as the other place to get stuck on. If Deleuze and Guattari are merely macho-territorial when it comes to the couplification of these two problems, Adler went so far as to base the community spirit he was setting up as therapeutic norm — as did Reich his superman booths of energy renewal — on the proviso of exclusion of the intimately related diversions of homosexuality and masturbation.

From Adler and Reich to Deleuze and Guattari homophobic interventions are among the scores that are settled with Freud's science. It is a metapsychological fact that in the projectively foreshortened format of these (paranoid) attacks Freudian analysis and homosexuality appear to occupy interchangeable places. According to the lines of these attacks, without psychoanalysis (which introduces an unconscious that has datable origins at the start of the dialectic of Enlightenment in the eighteenth century) homosexuality as we are still coming to know it would not be around. It starts getting around inside the new family pack in which ambiguous identifications get mixed up with denial. Homosexuality was along for the emergence of a new state of tension, that between the group (or group-of-one) and the couple. This group-formatting of desire scores a direct hit or fit with the new ambiguous object, the couple itself. From *Werther* to Kafka's "In the Penal Colony" there is a direct connection riding out this tension, one that makes ambivalent and inevitable room for the homosexual store of identifications. Heading Werther off at his impasse, then, is a closeted point of contact with the other fact of life, which remains beside the point of seeing or visibility but in this way takes the impact of powerful identifications.

Even Adorno, who billed himself as a follower of Freud's double heading of death drive and group psychology, was pulled up short by the prospect of an inversion: Freud's group psychology, it turned out, was not always only a mass or measure of psychopathology but rather addressed the fact of life that we *are* in groups. Adorno fell out of the favor he thought Freud was doing him by filling the prescription of Adorno's humanistic refrains about bad technology, bad groups, bad movies, and so on. He was compelled to put out an interpersonal add for sexual difference, and charge psychoanalysis with replacing the symmetrical differences exchanged in heterosexual couples with the same difference that comes in groups: "Psychoanalysis appears in its flattening out of all it calls unconscious and thus of everything human to succumb to a mechanism of the homosexual type: not seeing what is different. Homosexuals evince a kind of color blindness in experience, the inability to recognize what is individualized: for them all women are in the double sense 'the same'" ("Zum Verhältnis" 84). This homosexual inability to love shares its coldness with Freudian analysis, which puts on rigor to cover its aggressive control tendencies. Along the dotted line of a predisposition going down inside psychoanalysis and out in group psychology, a reversal or inversion can be folded back across psychoanalysis itself, rendering "psychoanalysis in reverse" (Arato and Gebhardt 8) the resource center of those modern mass delusions in which psychotic and perverse positions get acted out. Because the group gives shelter to homosexuality Adorno is able to report in the headline format of one of his minimalist and moralistic aphorisms that homosexuality always goes with totalitarianism (*Minima Moralia* 52). In "Freudian Theory and the Pattern of Fascist Propaganda," Adorno comments on the Freud quote (see epigraph) in which "homosexual love" is declared "far more compatible with group ties" from within a complex Freud shares with Nazi Germany: "This was certainly borne out under German Fascism where the borderline between overt and repressed homosexuality, just as that between overt and repressed sadism, was much more fluent than in liberal middle-class society" (413 n. 7).

Heil Homosexuality

In the suggestion box of literary studies a novel like Karl Aloys Schenzinger's *Hitlerjunge Quex* (1932) has been identified as belonging to the genre of "conversion," which turns out to be another way of claiming for the Nazi novel a *Werther* lineage (Stahl 133). *Hitlerjunge Quex* clearly falls in with a subgenre of novels of "German destiny" (the subtitle or caption regularly appended to them) including Joseph Goebbels's *Michael* (1929) and Hanns Heinz Ewers's *Horst Wessel* (1932). Between *Werther* and these destinal works a few marginalizations have gathered motivation and found completion within the system of displacements *Werther* had already inaugurated.

In these late arrivals of the "Werther effect" the political trajectory of a narcissistic wound mixes up aestheticism and homoeroticism into the doses of inoculation taken in against a crisis in reproductive supply and demand. In Goebbels's novel, Michael's girl friend accuses him, verbatim, of aestheticizing politics (an acting out she considers dangerous to life, and that means to procreation) (40). Michael in turn decides that she can't join the movement of the new: her type, which is good enough, has a half-life that doesn't belong to the future; she represents a reproductive means of "blossoming forth" out of last remaining reserves mobilized one last time (64–65). Politics are defined by Michael as the decision (really: the tenuous will) to procreate: " 'Every father who puts children into the world is pursuing politics. Every mother who makes men out of her boys is a political being' " (21). In other words, war won't go away: " 'The desire to get rid of it is the same as wishing to get rid of the fact that mothers bear children. That too is terrible. All life is terrible' " (22). By the end Michael has his life where he wants it and wants to leave it: reduced to the acting out of the means of production between men, which he now identifies as the lost cause of the German effort in World War One. His work aesthetic, his search for "redemption" (124), bonds him over this lost war with a worker. " 'He calls me thou. I want to embrace him' " (127); " 'I would like to kiss it. How dear this hand is to me, this work hand' " (128). The death that follows for him and others like him in this Nazi genre of final destination is a free gift that comes with group membership: to be innocent bystander at the accident of one's own death, an accident that is always forecast or otherwise foreseeable but that the victim volunteers to attend out of excessive political engagement, the kind that makes him, as dead teen, the best sacrifice or martyr available.

As part of the all-out Allied effort (which began in 1941) to catch up with Nazi military psychology and propaganda (right down to Freud's intrapsychic model, which the Nazis were the first to stick with only because it worked, in particular in treating for or immunizing against war neurosis, and in the preemptive exercise of psychological warfare), Gregory Bateson was invited to locate the intrapsychic battery of the 1933 film version of Schenzinger's novel for Allied use only. In his 1943 lecture at the New York Academy of Sciences Bateson summarized the Nazi psychological advance:

In America we tend to think of propaganda as consisting of a large number of separate utterances, pious sentiments or jokes, inserted into the more or less propagandically neutral matrix of communication. Publicity methods were developed on the basis of rather simple psychological theories of association and Watsonian conditioning and have been comparatively little influenced by Gestalt Psychology or psychoanalysis. The significant propaganda in the German films is, however, not of this sort. ("Section" 72–73)

Bateson also opened up the first reel of the visual evidence with explanatory intertitles. Bateson's version of *Hitlerjunge Quex*, in which the allied effort to understand or follow incorporates the Nazi movie, fixes its focus on the Nazi psychology of adolescence: "If we want to know what makes a fanatical Nazi tick, we must look at how the Nazi propagandists represented the German family — how they made it appear that Youth was infinitely desirable, and what sort of love they took as their model when they set out to build a population of boys in love with Death" (film intertitles transcribed by author).

In his analysis of "the conversion to Nazism of Heini, a twelve-year-old boy," Bateson answers the question "How are the loves and hates in the stereotyped German family invoked and rearranged by the propagandist to make them support Nazism?" The question he doesn't even pose concerns the sex appeal for Heini of the Nazi youths, whom he can refer to only as "the others" (*die anderen*), or, on the other side, the sexual problem Heini has with the Communists, who are coded as flagrant heterosexuals. Instead Bateson shows us — enough to read, between the lines, the tension that's also there between orientations — how Heini's suicidal bond with his mother (who tries to rescue Heini by turning the gas on both of them) is shifted to his bonding happiness with "the others," and how the initial attractiveness of the Communist youth leader, pumped up not only by his muscles but also through association with Heini's mother, gets father-identified with heterosexuality and thus replaced by what "the others" have to offer.

In his lecture, Bateson summarizes in orientation-free terms the Nazi reworking of the family ties to promote these same-sex relations for all but the married women, who must keep the libido pool of applicants for positions in the war machine restocked: "In order to create a violent emotional adherence to Nazism the family itself is unscrupulously sacrificed. The woman's place may be in the home but she need not expect that home to contain a husband or children over six. These others, the men and the boys and the unmarried girls, will be absorbed into 'Youth' organizations which free them from accepting the responsibilities of adult human status" (78).

The core of the displacements going down and out in these Nazi

Werther remakes is what, in Ewers's novel, melts down for Horst Wessel: on a tour of Berlin night life he finds himself barred from reproduction at a gay bar. On the morning after Horst gets advice from his dear comrade:

"That pack of swine will be around everywhere as long as the earth shines through the universe."
"And they are after all people, like you and me!" Horst said. "They sit down on the school bench next to us — back then one didn't notice at all that they were different!"
"No," Richard Fiedler answered. "That comes out later. But it's already inside them right from the beginning." (87)

It's a metapsychological fact: aestheticization of politics (as directly addressed by Benjamin and Goebbels) is the promotion of homo-eroticism as inoculation against the coming out of homosexuality, which is thus, however, admitted as a fact of life.[3] In these Nazi novels the focus on class struggle is coded as heterosexual, and the boys in the bond — that is, the ones unconjugated with means of reproduction — are cute replicants; in *Horst Wessel* there's a wide sampling of boy tans, knees, beautifully shaped heads, figures that are slender, strong, and upright (8, 11, 16).

In a 1937 issue of the pop-psychological Nazi journal *Soldier-hood (Soldatentum)*, which was available up and down the ranks of a military effort being set up at this time as the therapeutic norm for all relations, the reader of Dr. Grunwaldt's "The Erotic Moment in the Life of the Recruit" could learn all about homoeroticism, which was not only admitted as being out there among them but was even advertised as a kind of inoculation against the other H-word with which it stood, antibody style, in a near-miss rapport. At least by facing the fact of what Grunwaldt calls a "unique vibration between man and man in which one somehow discerns a feminine note" (35) homosexuality's takeover can be prevented. For within the unac-knowledged and thus unprotected zone of homoeroticism, homo-sexuality is always a surprise attack facilitated by unequal power relations. Never seduction or connection, but always another case of sexual harassment, homosexuality makes its power moves along institutional lines and under cover of the nonadmission of the homo-eroticism that is there. This harassment that turns a safety zone into the danger zone is the "creeping poison" that must be "annihilated" (36). The total "combat" to which the reader of this article was

summoned required on the erotic, home, or internal front the destruction of whatever was "unclean," and thus the preservation of
"manly discipline" and "womanly honor." These preserved standards would no longer be "phantoms," Grunwaldt assures us, but
would serve as the "guarantors" of the staying power and reserve
supply of the people (36). The Nazis were out to win the war that
wins the race. That's why what Grunwaldt brings into focus as the
"perpetually fluctuating boundary between homoeroticism and homosexuality" (36) requires the kind of all-out surveillance that only
nonphobic tolerance of homoeroticism can bring about.

This calculation of homosexuality as a risk was a Nazi advance.
It was introduced into the American military complex beginning in
1941 via the intensive efforts made to catch up with Nazi-German
psychological research. In a 1941 "Survey and Bibliography" put
out by the U.S. Committee of National Morale under the title *German Psychological Warfare*, the Nazi psychologist Fritzsching is introduced as the authority on individual surrender, betrayal, and desertion, all of which he sees as following out a " 'reversal of the
military conscience' " all the way to " 'perversion.' " "Fritzsching's
advice is to explain this psychological process to soldiers during
peacetime training and thus to expose to the soldier himself all the
subconscious elements leading up to surrender. His knowledge of
these factors usually immunizes him thereafter to voluntary surrender in combat" (Farago 43).

The kind of treatment schedule that goes with the inoculative
approach at the same time requires greater tolerance of the fact of
homosexuality. The Nazi establishment came to face the facts with a
phobia-proofed and psychoanalysis-compatible attitude. But that's
because psychotherapists (including psychoanalysts) in Nazi Germany were eager to apply the success story of Freud's encounter
with war neurotics to a total victory through analysis: the all-out
eradication-through-healing of the homosexual position or disposition (which ever since World War One has marked the spot of the
coming out of war neurosis under fire and the acting out of the
primal submission through betrayal, desertion, even espionage).
Homosexual excess or access could be contained as a danger to
group members trained in the intrapsychic art of battling internal
enemies. Through the homoerotic control releases made available in
the Nazi culture of comradeship, for example, suicide became an

efficient alternative to the breakdowns of war neurosis. This rings up a statistic: Nazi measures taken in against the coming out of war neurosis had permitted only one form of interference to be on the rise—suicide was the only disorder to grow down the ranks of the German group effort totally inoculated with and against war neurosis or homosexuality.

The Buff Object of Identification

In 1938 Herbert Schöffler declared *Werther* to be "the first non-dualistic tragedy of our psychic development" (180). In other words, it is the first modern work of ambivalence, and thus the first to situate itself within the tension between the group (or group-of-one) and the couple. "The absolute value in this artwork is love between the sexes, and if this value cannot be attained, life becomes worthless. A worthless life can, however, be discarded. . . . In the place of the formerly absolute value, the idea of God, another has stepped in, love between the sexes" (175). But this passion gets displaced in the work of its divinization; it gets displaced, son-of-God style, onto the Passion of suicide or, as Schöffler labels it, "passio Wertheri *adolescentis*": "Through his voluntary death, Werther enters the All-mother Nature" (173). But Werther's regressive, suicidal course is not a negative theology of "love between the sexes." Lotte is indeed a maternal figure whom Werther loves, no I mean hates, no loves, no hates. His inability to admit the ambivalence, which takes him through idealization to suicide, follows out the other tension Goethe describes (not only here but also, for example, in "The Wandering Jew") through a juxtaposition of the double trauma of being born to die and of the mother bearing her child—to the grave—with fantasies of self-creation (P. Fischer 548). Certainly Lotte, his one and only true love whom he hates, does not interest him very much.[4] Goethe's revision of *Werther* clarifies the nature of this love interest. A later addition is not always only an afterthought that covers up; sometimes it's a free association that admits what was left out in the first place. Among the add-ons Goethe inserted the second time around, two reflect the pull of Werther's desire: one presses forward the displacement implied in and excluded from the double occupancy of his attraction to the couple; the second tells us right-on just which libido pool furnishes the applicants for Werther's "other" position.

The episodes describing Werther's acquaintance with a peasant boy, who confides in Werther the mounting crush of his interest in his employer, a widowed older woman, frame a route of identification-access that, even at the far remove of displacement, can admit conditions for realistic or realized homosexual involvement. The boy's availability for an attraction across the generation gap (a pull strengthened by the transference that is along for the difference between classes) marks the young man as a prospect at the disposal of all kinds of seduction. It is in this sense that his love is "pure" (that is, not generic). Werther's young man is, in other words, cute, and that means: at the other's disposal. When the widow fires him to make way for another fired-up transferee, the farm-fresh boy must suffer attacks of sexual panic and kill his rival in self-defense. Werther presents the case of the accused to the magistrate (with Albert in attendance) as, it goes without saying, one of sexual harassment or transference transgression, which, under the covers of role reversal, admits all the combinations and identifications.[5]

The second insert folded inside Goethe's work of revision is a narcissistic prop: Lotte's love for him, which he now feels is real, causes Werther to get down on his knees before himself and be his own deity. Being loved means his self-love is real. While not yet reduced to the machinic contours of Olympia (in Hoffmann's "The Sandman"), with all the record and playback functions intact and in push-button readiness, Lotte is nevertheless the placeholder or reflector shield of Werther's own narcissism. Indeed, a course of regression in "The Sandman" overlaps with Lotte's position in *Werther*, the one that introduces Olympia as the new and improved alternative to Klara, Nathanael's humanoid bride-to-be. Their relationship represents Nathanael's first try at replicating himself in or as the other (in other words, as the future). Klara must be replaced when she is seen to embody a contradiction between the mirroring "clarity" she holds up to Nathanael and an other who "speaks against" (*contra-dictio*) Nathanael's self-preoccupation. In the Faustian science fictions *Eve Future* and *Metropolis*, this plan of metabolization of the wound of separation or contradiction into the miracle of merger with the machine also covers the context or contest of reproduction versus replication. This describes the fundamental metapsychological plot of the science fiction impulse. The woman's or mother's body marks the spot of separation or contradiction that works the inside. It is technologized because reproduction, which keeps the separation going as the good news of future generations coming soon, is not what the ego getting into machines of replication or suicide is into.

Nathanael, Lord Ewald, and Rotwang keep in touch with their robots (in fact first fall in love with them) by some long-distancing device, like a telescope, that reenacts a primal scene in which the one getting the picture is always left out of it. The merger will not go through. The reduction of every connection out there to sheer visibility which media-technologization promotes (even the audio portion on the gramophone or phone alone has been brought to us by the desire to make speech "visible") puts the relation between self and other, child and mother, right where ego wants it—and leaves it there, between narcissistic consumer and robot dolly. Sci fi lovers and self-lovers of machines are ego probes that never leave their orbit of techno-vision. Their corporeality, all that's left over, encases a tank or turbo of energy supply. But the miraculous noncontradiction of the machine-being cannot but render the corporeal lover a leftover appendage tagged for evolutionary extinction. Humankind cannot yet beam up into merger with the machine. There's still always a body of separation around that, dead or alive, keeps us close to the traumatic opening of the takeoff of flights of science fantasy. What follows (like clockwork) in these stories of man's infatuation with robot woman is destruction of the machine and the gadget lover's suicide. The merger didn't go through. The destroyed apparatus was his better half, and suicide follows as the down side or slide of fantasies of replication and auto-technologization.

On the Male Nude

In their origin art and technology are just an alternation away from each other: the alternation between sublimation and the other defensive measures metabolizes in techno-fantasy a homosexual predisposition that is back with every crisis in reproduction. The machine connection is born out of same-sex spirits. In Freud's studies of Leonardo da Vinci and Schreber, the return engagements of repressed homosexuality give rise to the emergency projection of delusional technologies. Freud's rereading of the Prometheus myth ascribes technology's origin, primally conceived as control of and access to energy, to the ambiguation (repression, sublimation, or

projection) of homosexuality. The eternal flame of the lost or unknown bond flickers inside the control booth of technology, while a
fast-food temporality of energy waste, early death, and replication
of libidinal connection (group psychology, in sum) drives homosexual object-choosing onward.

In a supplementary episode from Werther's life pre his sufferings,
which Goethe published in 1796, the younger Werther goes to a
swimming hole with his best friend, who agrees to strip down for
Werther's art appreciations:

I arranged for Ferdinand to bathe in the lake; how splendidly my young
friend is built! how proportionate are all his parts! what a fullness of form,
what a splendor of youth, what a profit for me to have enriched my imagination with this perfect example of human nature! Now I people forests,
lawns, and heights with such beautiful figures; I see him as Adonis felling the
boar, as Narcissus mirroring himself in the spring. (WA 19:213)

The early death that these heroes of adolescence share phases out
everything the scene holds in store. Werther must look instead for
Venuses to behold. But when he gains access to his first female
model, what he sees gaining on him is something "strange" that
leaves him behind with a "frightening impression" (WA 19:217–
18). The replicant rapport with the body the first time around has
grown uncanny on the person of the woman. The crisis in reproduction gets its first relief through the upbeat disclaimers of fetishism:
"What do we see in women? . . . A small shoe looks good, and we cry
out: what a beautiful little foot! a narrow belt has something elegant
about it, and we praise the beautiful waist" (WA 19:218).

At a time of all-out gendering even of every category of science
and thought, the adolescent boy body (that of the androgyne), at
once hard and feminine, represents the outside chance of a connection somewhere over the press to reproduce. That's why art appreciation of the male nude, with the androgyne at the front of the line,
requires his early death. The male nude poses as problem, the kind
that only his death seems able to resolve. The life-saving turn to the
female nude (for the survival of the species), which desublimates the
arts (the history of ballet is most instructive re this growing regard
reserved for women only), invites what was in crisis — reproduction — to come on in.

Desublimation or resexualization of an order of identification
(with the father) was, in Freud's reading, the issue of Schreber's

psychosis. Schreber's techno-delusional system keeps the homosexual bonds with dead and dad just a heartbeat away from radical displacement. Emergency measures had to be taken to overcome a crisis in reproduction (he and his wife had failed to have living children). That's how an all-out turn-on gets attributed to the female body (which Schreber is becoming, via replicating changes induced by God's rays, at the same time as he's becoming an android). His is the only body around, and it's at once female and technological. Only this body can receive or conceive the ray beams of a divine force given to recognize only corpses. Only in this way can the crisis in reproduction be overcome for the survival of the species.

The uncanniness of body relations, which transfigured Werther's encounter with the reproductive body in the flesh, always releases, Hanns Sachs argues, the psycho-delusional operations of auto-technologization. In the novel of his teen passion, Werther indeed technologizes on the spot — the spot his narcissistic crisis puts him in. The silhouette becomes the all-encompassing image not only for his attempts at portrayal but even for his every thought. Werther himself comments from another side of the page, in the mode of denial, on the high incidence in his own discourse of dashes or, in German, "thought strokes": "And you see, what oppresses me is that Albert does not seem to be as fortunate as he — hoped — as I — believed to be — if — I do not like to use dashes, but here I cannot express myself any other way — and it seems to me plain enough" (*HA* 6:82). This pushes the dash that's in Werther's typeface up to the front of the line of analogy with the silhouette. The rip-and-tear or dashing off of the inadmissible evidence of his death wishes cannot but shadow his every libidinal relation and tune or turn him into a machine of ambivalence. Werther sees himself now as a magic lantern always projecting funereal silhouettes and dashes, now as a puppet being played by some agency of remote control.

Scratch in the Record

The new ambiguous object of identification that *Werther* introduced is soon found downed by a relay of science fictions as their secret return deposit. Goethe's *Triumph of Sentimentality* (*Der Triumph der Empfindsamkeit*) features a robot queen whose innards enfold a series of books; following this first upsurge of imaginary

titles designed for their mass consumability by women (the direc-
tions recommend improvisation of additional titles with the same
topical fit), the internal sack is once again peristaltically reversed and
the "underlying soup" (*Grundsuppe*) bottoms out. What remains is
a couple of books: *The New Heloise* and *The Sorrows of Young
Werther* (WA 17:56). These, then, are the batteries of a blow-up
dolly that the Prince prefers to its live look-alike, a preference that
belongs in two places at once: in the societywide context of a craze
for monodramas endangering couplification (even though, or especially because, a new line is coming soon that will offer "monodramas for two, duodramas for three, and so on"; WA 17:24) and in
the immediate context of his penchant for "machines" or "boxes"
(*Kästen*) containing "secrets" (*Geheimnisse*), namely artificial means
of producing birdsong and moonlight (WA 17:20). The spread of the
Prince's madness (as in the monodrama fad) is reversed and contained when he is made to choose between the robot and its near-miss
substitute. His object-choice lies with the robot, which forces everyone else's withdrawal from the quarantine of his short circuit.
The outside world of substitution and reproduction thus gets a jump
start back into couplification through this close encounter with the
replicant.

In Mary Shelley's *Frankenstein; or, The Modern Prometheus*, the
monster has filled up his interiority with a triangle of books: in one
corner we find *The Sorrows of Young Werther*. The monster's attachment to families and couples that are forever off limits follows
out the beam of Werther's "monodrama." But beyond this citational
mode of the creature's experience or language, *Werther* also, and in
the first place, programs his suicide (the downside of the fantasy of
artificial creation). One of the models Shelley had recourse to in
portraying the modern promethean scientist was Andrew Crosse,
whose experiments with electricity led to the artificial creation and
replication of what he took to be a new insect species.

The monster's one last wish, to make a match for himself, gets
mixed with Victor Frankenstein's inability to skip the downbeat and
living end of his melancholic science fiction. Dreaming or at her
wake, Victor can embrace his dead mother's substitute, Elizabeth,
only if and when she too fits the part of corpse. And he stops making
the monster's mate dead in her tracks. He cannot risk releasing the
remote controls over the death-wish compact with his original im-

itation monster, the one he built in the missing place of any work of mourning following his mother's unacknowledged departure. Cou-plified and acquitted from the contract out on Victor's family and friends, the monster would begin to slide into focus as the body of the mother, the one that could then only be let go. Instead Victor loves both brides-in-progress to pieces, right down to the corpse parts that, according to his psy-fi fantasy, have a living on and brand-new start that's all their own in the mode of self-replication. "I paused to collect myself," Victor reflects as he leaves behind the remains of what might have been the murdered and mourned mom-ster if he had only first finished building her up.

In *Beyond the Pleasure Principle*, in which the death-drive thesis is first announced, Freud sets up a frame for the drive's introduction into his thought. First he gives consideration to the special psychic access afforded by the evidence of traumatic or war neurosis, and second, on the other side, Freud contemplates the scientific evidence that already advertises a time coming soon when human beings will no longer come in generations but will live on forever within one egoic span of attention through cell-like doubling and division. It is within a certain ring of the Goethe name that the contestants face off in the ring of life versus death. First there's Weismann, to whom not only Freud gives a reception. But then: "Some writers returned to the views of Goette . . . , who regarded death as a direct result of repro-duction" (*SE* 18:47). In Goette's name Freud joins in the writing of a kind of *Bildungsroman* of evolving relations with doubling or repro-duction, in which death develops or becomes but is not a natural.

The natural death of animals cannot be a phenomenon necessarily con-nected as such with organization and life, which would therefore have ex-isted from the beginning. For one thing, a reason for such a connection is simply not apparent, and what is more, natural death does not exist for all animals but rather, according to the current findings and theories about the life of one-celled primordial animals (protozoa), is completely lacking in the latter.

The only phenomenon that might give rise to the assumption of a natu-ral death of these simple creatures, namely their procreation, transpires in such a way that the individual unit, while keeping the continued existence of its organization and life intact, simply splits and then immediately keeps on living in its individual parts. . . . A natural, that is, an internally determined necessary death of the protozoa is also not at all understandable, since, after all, for the preservation of the species one of the individual parts must always in turn procreate through division and at least in one of the thus constituted series live on limitlessly; but then, given the foreseeably complete equality of all parts, the remaining ones would have to possess the same capacity for eternal duration.

As is well known ... the multicellular animals, the metazoa, grew out of the unicellular protozoa, consequently they possessed in the beginning the same immortality. Only now had death become a possibility, insofar as every individual unit, after it reproduced itself through seeds deposited outside itself, could die without harming the preservation of the species. ... The immortality of the metazoa became thus an unnecessary luxury, which was not compatible with the interests of the species, and in this way the natural death of the metazoa emerged as a phenomenon of assimilation according to the principle of utility. (Goette 3–5)

Goette's denaturalization of death, which Freud was writing up as and off to denial, includes on one side an insect analogy—the kind Freud tended to translate in the corner of dream interpretations as melancholic relations or group bonds with the siblings one had also, at one time (and once is enough) wished dead—and, on the other side, the aftershocks of trauma. To this day there are insects that drop dead when they lay the egg or complete the act of siring off. These insects that come and go are wiped out by accompanying overpowering affect; the random catastrophe of sudden death lives on in humans through the same overwhelming affect, though it originates this time in trauma or shock (26). The negative side effect that reproduction first introduced thus became assimilated to the bigger advantage of the "total development of the individual" (37), the individual conceived, that is, in or as groups. Magnified in this way, cells in highly organized animals enjoy a capacity for life that is tied to "their dependency; and their end is not prescribed through their own organization, but they get used up, annihilated in the service of the whole individual" (19). What no longer depends on reproduction is an introductory offer that comes with joining the conditions or concepts of organization and development. But with their innovations in place, it appears that unlimited duration of life is incompatible with life organized for or around reproduction (45). The origin of and explanation for "natural death" lies in development (51), which took over where reproduction left off offing discrete immortalities. Once developmental change starts beginning right from the start, already pre-birth, and reproduction through the mother therefore no longer coincides with her perfect repetition in her progeny

(75), the convergence of death and reproduction characteristic of more primal life forms (69) becomes differentiated, superseded, sublated. The traumatic loss of immortality introduced by reproduction is shock-absorbed by organization into and specialization within larger units that grow reattached in turn to notions of immortality unassimilated to reproduction and its displacement parts.

The two steps or asides of Freud's introduction of the death drive, which, following Goette, first came together for Freud during the first total war, remain the neurosis of trauma or war and the replication fantasies compatible with psychosis, perversion, or group psychology. The modern legacy of doubling or replication was thus created from scratch, the scratch in the war record that keeps the war neurotic's traumatic scene repeating, a scene internally and eternally split between what Freud called in his 1919 "Introduction to *Psychoanalysis and the War Neuroses*" peace ego and war ego or, as Freud would rename the partners one year later, ego and superego. Freud's close encounter with the mass epidemic of traumatic or war neurosis during World War One opened up a no-man's-land or borderline zone between neurosis and psychosis for theorization and treatment. Along this opened-up borderline, group psychology and perversion were made equally accessible to "psy-fi" colonization for the survival of the species. What is always under the threat of extinction in science fiction (or, say, in psychotic delusions) is the couplified means of reproduction and its double native habitat (at once the body and the earth). Freud's World War One essays on war and death and transience gave special mention to the work of mourning as the way through the grief-stuck metabolism of melancholia, a metabolism stuck on irreplaceable relations. Melancholia thus represents a psychotic shutdown that endangers the future of civilization, which Freud charts according to the course of new inventions. In "Thoughts for the Times on War and Death" Freud thus includes attempts at mechanical flight among the types of futurity endangered by melancholia. As the main therapeutic model for the work of psychoanalysis, mourning can keep couplified rapport with the future going along restored access to the libido pool of substitutes. But Freud's emphasis is on promotion of ways or means beyond melancholia. That's how the interest and investment in the diversified structures of psychosis, group psychology, and perversion took over even in psychoanalysis, where pre–World War One they had been left out as limit concepts. In the meantime Freud had discovered ways around the impasse of melancholia that did not first have to do the work of mourning.

Psychosis was already the other place where the crisis in reproduction and its attendant psy-fi fantasies awaited exploration: not until the ready-made cases of war neurosis provided Freud owner-manual access to ego libido, doubling, or merger with the internalized apparatus could Schreber's outer-space fantasies of miraculation, technologization, and homosexual or transsexual replication be visited — visited in the first place on the other, with the enemy or internal enemy at the front of the line. Because already before the war psychotic delusions were seen as following a course of self-help: their endopsychic makeup gives the psychotic the inside view of his psychic apparatus and thus the outside chance of autoanalytic breakthrough. In psychosis, trauma-induced mega-repression reactivates shock waves from the outer reaches of cathected external reality all the way to earliest childhood, and thereby opens up an evacuation chute through which all libido leaves the world and enters the ego. The only way out for Schreber (other than suicide, the route taken by his older brother) is projection of a new delusional world in the place of the one he has lost. The psychotic crisis or break is thus a threat of short circuit or overload that only the emergency projection of a new world out of narcissistic or ego libido can circumvent. As Samuel Weber has described it in his reading of the Schreber case (xlviii), the "wound" of separation is remetabolized through psychotic delusion as "wonder" or "miracle" (as the science fiction of an inner/outer space that awaits colonization for the survival of the species). Schreber made it; his brother, who committed suicide, went out on the downside of replication. In his introduction to *Perceval's Narrative: A Patient's Account of His Psychosis*, Bateson seconds this notion of the voyage-or-initiation character of psychosis bonded to delusions on its way to autoanalytic breakthrough (which is not homecoming but arrival in some other place or cyberspace) (xiv).

Freud's exploration of fetishism also belongs to the thought experiment that began under the new lab conditions of the first total war. In the 1927 essay Freud is clearly less focused on the sexology of perverse acts in the home alone: the two examples of sons who both know and don't know that their fathers are dead take Freud by surprise in the midst of his scan of fetishistic disavowal and splitting. The split that allows this simulcast of wish and reality does not open and shut these cases as psychotic, but rather puts their double vision right on the oscillating borderline between neurosis and psychosis.

Ever since the era of the machine and techno-invention opened at the end of the eighteenth century a crisis in reproduction has been along for the progress. The technological object has always excited egoic fantasies of Immortality Now. That's why Freud's theorization of fetishism, which belongs to his second system, must be kept in context with his turn toward psychosis, perversion, and group psychology. The narcissistic portfolio of investments breaks down into shares of the ultimate science fiction fantasy, that of replacement of reproduction (which is death in life) with a new and improved immortality plan, that of amoeba-like and technology-compatible replication. Rather than fall in with the superegoic standards of tradition and transmission across future generations, the short egoic attention span, which does not want to go (and doesn't want to *be* history), goes for doubling on contact. Fetishism represents a makeshift overcoming of this crisis in reproduction, a compromise formation that shifts gears between the fantastic prospects of doubling or replication and the fact of life that it is still only reproduction that can restock the libido pool for the living on and evolution of the species.

But it was precisely with the introduction of the theory of evolution that fantasy was free to grant invention or other sudden changes the power to switch channels on evolutionary progress and fast-forward plant life or machines to the top of development. As soon as Darwin's theory was out, his fans were hit by fantasies of parallel fast lanes of development that relocated the missing link to interspecial relations between humans and machines (see Samuel Butler's *Erewhon*). Evolution provided the context for imagining that thought can or must go on without the body, and that means beyond the repro-bonds between the sexes. Humans are still the genitals of the machine that is evolving *for* us.

The science fiction or psychotic delusion of merger with the machine thus moves away from any interpersonal relationship of sexual difference. Fetishism is about getting into machines and, at the same time, fulfilling, for the time being, one's commitment to reproduction, which is still the only way to keep the species (and the machines) going. This is where Freud's surprise observation that fetishism saves the man in crisis from becoming homosexual in fact fits in. Nazi Germany, which was one big science fiction, resided within the tension that Freud's theory of fetishism describes: the group psychology that's always along for the psy-fi drive reintroduces the problem of homosexuality, which Nazi therapeutic culture determined to face right on within defense contexts of inoculation. In short, the promotion of homoeroticism right on the face of Nazi culture was part of the all-out effort to inoculate the race (a race that had to be won against all odd-men-out) and grant it immunity from the other fact of life, in particular of life undergoing technologization, namely the real appeal of homosexuality (which comes out on top when the group effort turns on fantasies of cloning). The other side, the downside, of science fictions of survival of the species or group through merger with the machine from *Werther* onward remains the emergency brake and breakdown-prevention of suicide (which was *Werther*'s other special effect). As long as the group remains dependent on the reproductive couple, the "Werther effect" will be the force that is with us when we contemplate replication. What gets you around one crisis goes around as the other crisis or fact of life. Goethe remained convinced that by writing the suicide note entitled *Werther* he was able to do a couple of lines of inoculation against his own urge (or surge) to off himself (or get into machines the fast way). Between the lines, the novel repress-released an ambiguous object of identification, which was the invitational Werther's biggest fans entered to act out what Goethe had put off but kept at long distance and in reserve.

Martha B. Helfer

"Confessions of an Improper Man": Friedrich Schlegel's *Lucinde*

When Friedrich Schlegel's *Lucinde* first appeared in 1799, the novel was considered to be not only shockingly personal and obscene, if not downright pornographic, but an aesthetic abomination to boot. In a representative review printed anonymously in a leading literary journal in 1800, L. F. Huber calls *Lucinde* a work that inspires boredom and repulsion, astonishment and contempt, shame and sadness, a book that represents one of the most insufferable crimes a writer has ever committed against the public (*KA* 5:l). Similarly, August Bode accuses Schlegel of mixing a deluge of pomposity with unmitigated lewdness, while another anonymous critic vows to combat Schlegel's attack on morality and art, as well as his celebration of licentious debauchery (*KA* 5:l). Despite spirited defenses by Schlegel's friends Schleiermacher and Fichte, the outrage created by the "tractatum eroticum Lucinde"[1] continued well into the nineteenth century. Kierkegaard, for example, argues that the novel aims at naked sensuality and attempts to eliminate all morality—an assessment tempered perhaps by Heine's wry comment that the Mother of God may be able to forgive Schlegel for writing *Lucinde*, but the Muses certainly never will (Firchow 5).

Contemporary scholars, by contrast, tend to downplay the text's overt sexuality. In his introduction to the critical edition, Eichner, attacking those eighteenth-century readers who condemned *Lucinde* for being gratuitously explicit in its sexual descriptions (*KA* 5:l), argues that these passages are actually part of an innovative definition of love that combines sensuality and spirituality (*KA* 5:xxix–xxxv). Similarly, Behler interprets the off-color sexual references as autobiographical whimsy, asserting that Schlegel advances a new moral philosophy of love and marriage in his novel (*Schlegel* 66). Firchow's introduction to the English translation makes the more radical claim that the book contains "hardly any graphic description of any sort (let alone sexual)" and that those seeking a racy read will be sorely disappointed (7).

Its sexual dimension thus diminished or dismissed, the novel is now most commonly read either as an instantiation of Romantic literary theory or as a prescient examination of "woman" and women's issues. Two diametrically opposed trends are apparent in the latter category. Traditionally, *Lucinde* has been interpreted either as a revolutionary novel of women's emancipation or as a progressive theory of the androgynous subject. More recently, critics have correctly argued that Lucinde actually plays a very conventional female role in Julius's male fantasy (Becker-Cantarino, "Priesterin" and "Schlegels *Lucinde*"; Eder; Littlejohns) and that the text's treatment of androgyny, which relies on the male projecting himself onto the female, is clearly androcentric (Domoradzki; Friedrichsmeyer, *Androgyne*; Stephan, " 'Daß ich Eins und doppelt bin' "; Weigel, "Wider die romantische Mode"). According to these readings, "woman" as such is absent from the text — a conclusion that should give us pause.

Analyses of *Lucinde* as an instantiation of Romantic literary theory follow Eichner in touting the novel as the most read of the Romantic era (*KA* 5:lv) yet skirt the fact that the text is, in a very real sense, unreadable. Focusing instead on its symmetrical structure (the central "Apprenticeship Years of Masculinity" ["Lehrjahre der Männlichkeit"] is flanked on either side by six sections), these interpretations insightfully trace themes like "love," "marriage," and "religion" throughout the various sections and correctly point to Romantic topoi like "allegory" and "reflexivity" that contribute to the novel's structure, yet never really come to grips with the text itself as a realization of Romantic theory (Behler, "*Lucinde*"; Firchow; Eichner in *KA*; Hudgkins; Sanna; Spuler). If *Lucinde*'s rich metaphoricity and self-referentiality are impenetrable, many of these critics imply, it is only because Schlegel, that well-known advocate of incomprehensibility, was a master of Romantic confusion.

But perhaps there is another reason for *Lucinde*'s layers of metaphorical language, its intratextual cross-referencing, and its programmatic confusion — a reason overlooked by our twentieth-century attenuation of the text's sexuality. Given the fact that *Lucinde* was written at a time when high-society divorce, scandal, and sexual antics were almost de rigueur (*KA* 5:xlviii), it strikes me as odd to argue that Schlegel's contemporaries were a good deal more prudish than we are today when they perceived the book to be sexually explicit or lewd. Moreover, if the novel was indeed pornographic, why didn't it sell well, as erotica generally does (Firchow 7)? And if it wasn't pornographic, why did the older Schlegel, turned conservative and Catholic, exclude it from the 1823 edition of his complete works (Firchow 5)? Could it be that both Schlegel and his eighteenth-century readers were reacting to a sexual subtext encoded in the novel which the critics possibly did not understand fully but nonetheless found highly objectionable?

Perhaps a clue to the scandal the novel created is contained in the astute assessment of one of Schlegel's contemporaries. In an anonymous satire that appeared shortly after the publication of *Lucinde* Schlegel is charged with combining "sparks of swinishness with the steaminess of the Greeks" in his novel ("[Schlegel habe] der Sauheit Funken mit der Griechheit Dämpfen [verbunden]," *KA* 5:l).[2] At first glance this mention of the Greeks might seem anomalous or strange, since, in contrast to his earlier essays where Schlegel had engaged the Classical tradition extensively in order to develop his own aesthetic theory, references to the Greeks are minimal in this text. Clearly the strange turn of phrase does not allude to Schlegel's earlier Classicism, but to "Greek love" or homosexuality. With a heterosexual couple as the focus of the novel, *Lucinde* certainly does not promulgate an overt theory of homosexual love, nor does any text of this period, but this critic's trenchant remark leads us to turn our attention away from the text's female figures, which recent scholars have already established as projections of the male fantasy, and to examine its male characters.

The novel's subtitle suggests that we do as much. Generally translated as "Confessions of a Blunderer," the phrase *Bekenntnisse eines Ungeschickten* has not, I believe, been fully understood. While *ungeschickt* does mean "blundering" or "clumsy," it can also indicate something incongruous, unconforming, false, perverted, or even sinful (Grimm and Grimm 11:842–43) and is applied primarily to men in the text (Littlejohns 609). Hence, *Lucinde* is less about a woman than about a "blunderer," an "improper" or "unconforming" man who has something to "confess." Indeed, I will argue that this "mad little book" addressed to "happy young men" (*KA* 5:32)[3] propounds a graphically explicit, aesthetic theory of a male sexuality infused with homoeroticism. Moreover, this same-sex desire, an expression of Romantic reflexivity, is related, ironically, critically, and self-consciously, to artistic production. The first part of my analysis highlights the homoerotic subtext that subtends *Lucinde*, focusing primarily on the sections surrounding the central "Apprenticeship Years of Masculinity," while the second part interprets the homoerotic aesthetic of the "Apprenticeship Years" as an instantiation of Romantic literary theory.

I

The groundwork for an aesthetic theory of male sexuality is laid in the opening sections of *Lucinde*, where Julius explicitly invites a psychological interpretation of his text (8). Having abolished all "rules of reason and decorum" (8) in his first letter to Lucinde, Julius attempts to explain to her how their life and love animate his spirit and his writing. The first vehicle he chooses for this explication is a "Dithyrambic Fantasy About the Most Beautiful Situation" ("Dithyrambische Fantasie über die schönste Situation"), that is, sexual intercourse. In the dithyramb Julius goes in search of Lucinde filled with amorous intentions. Frustrated at finding a note she has left him in her stead, he sublimates his sexual energy in writing (9). Crudely put, he makes love to the piece of paper. In the act of writing the catachrestic fusion of "mental lust" and "sensual spirituality" (7) results in an ideational erection:

The words are dull and dreary. . . . A grand future beckons me to rush deeper into infinity, each idea opens its womb and produces countless new births. The furthest extremes of unbridled lust and silent intimation live simultaneously in me. I remember everything . . . and all my past and future thoughts are aroused and spring up against my will. Wild blood rages in my swollen arteries, my mouth thirsts for union, and my imagination picks and wavers among the many forms of pleasure and finds none in which my desire could fulfill itself and be at last at peace. (10)

As Julius himself suggests, the sexual scene enacted here is one of autoerotic narcissism: "I don't hesitate to admire and love myself in this mirror [i.e., Lucinde]. Only here do I see myself complete and harmonious, or rather, I see full, complete humanity in me and in you" (10). Julius then proposes that he and Lucinde switch sexual roles, an action he describes as "a wonderfully sensual allegory of the completion of male and female in full, complete humanity" (13). At first glance this might appear to be an androcentric theory of androgyny, but Julius has not broken out of the autoerotic frame-work of his fantasy, and he concludes his musings with a comment laden with sexual innuendo: "Much lies in this, and what lies in this certainly doesn't spring up as quickly as I do when I am overcome by you [when I lie under you;[4] *wenn ich dir unterliege*]" (13). Hence, read against the grain, the "Dithyramb" amounts to little more than Julius inscribing his own sexual prowess in an autoerotic act of aes-thetic intercourse. The product of this masturbatory writing is the text *Lucinde*, which Julius loves (9) and Schlegel calls "my son" (3).[5]

If the novel *Lucinde* is Schlegel's son, the character Lucinde is shaped, procreated, and projected in Julius's own image, an argu-ment I will return to shortly. In fact, Julius freely admits his procliv-ity for superimposing himself on a feminine ideal in the "Character Sketch of Little Wilhelmine" ("Charakteristik der kleinen Wilhel-mine," 15), a short piece he designs to excuse, if not rectify, his seemingly untoward behavior in the "Dithyramb" and in the novel at large. Not only is Wilhelmine the embodiment of the cheerful self-satisfaction that Julius feels in reading his own writing (9, 14), she also represents the novel itself in miniature (15). Julius approvingly describes her complete disregard for decorum when she lies on her back with her legs in the air and her dress up, clearly a sexual de-scription designed as a palliative but made all the more shocking by the fact that he is talking about a two-year-old. He then comments, "And if this small novel of my life should appear to be too wild: then remember it [*er*] is only a child" (15). Julius's statement would seem to establish an analogy, if not an equivalence, between the innocent little girl and the wild little novel, until one notices that the pronoun in his comparison, the German *er*, which means both "he" and "it," refers not only to the novel but also to the girl, suggesting that both *Wilhelm*-ine and the novel are somehow masculine.

The typology of the novel set forth in the ensuing "Allegory of Impudence" ("Allegorie von der Frechheit") clearly indicates that Julius is advancing a male-based aesthetic, and that it would be erroneous to interpret the cross-gendering introduced in the "Dithyramb" and the "Character Sketch" as evidence of true androgyny. Designed to complement the "Character Sketch" and to produce similar results, Julius's "last waking dream" (15) confirms that the novel's aesthetics are closely linked to the psychology of the male ego. Just as his first letter to Lucinde begins with a fantasy of his lover in a lush grove (7), the "Allegory" opens with Julius standing in a magnificent garden inhaling the spicy scent of the flowers and becoming intoxicated with their colors (flowers, of course, being a stock symbol of the feminine [Menninghaus, *Theorie der Weiblichkeit* 208]). This time his fantasy is rudely interrupted when an ugly, swollen monster with colorful, transparent skin suddenly springs from the midst of the flowers. Big enough to arouse fear, the monster appears to be poisonous, its entrails, visible through the transparent skin, are coiled snakelike, and it is surrounded by menacing crab claws. Julius overcomes his terror of this vaginal, Medusa-like apparition by throwing her on her back "with a powerful thrust" (16). Sexually subdued, the monster appears, to his utter amazement, to be nothing but a common frog. As if to underline this description of the feminine as a potentially dangerous froglike monster, Julius later argues that it would be rude to talk of a woman as if she were a sexless amphibian (34).

Schlegel's puzzling equation of the feminine with a frog conceivably extends beyond a representation of male fear of the female genitalia. The frog also reads as a punning intertextual reference to Aristophanes, whom Plato selects in the *Symposium* to introduce what is probably the first documented theory of androgyny in the Western philosophical tradition (Friedrichsmeyer, *Androgyne* 15). According to Aristophanes' account, there were originally three sexes: male, female, and a third that partook of both male and female, the hermaphrodite. These three sets of circular beings were rent asunder by Zeus in order to control their audacious behavior, and each half was left searching for its complement. Hence, while some men seek women, and some women seek men, some men and women seek their same-sex complements. The crucial point is that Aristophanes' discourse is not a theory only of androgyny and heterosexuality, but also of homosexuality, as is the *Symposium* itself, taken as a whole (see Nehemas and Woodruff in Plato xiv). According to his own account, Schlegel had studied the "erotic conversations" of the *Symposium* avidly in preparation for *Lucinde* (*KA*

24:244), and obviously takes Aristophanes' argument to heart in the following discussion in the "Allegory of Impudence."

The demise of the frog paves the way for the next stage of Julius's sexual development, a phase inaugurated when the character Wit appears and identifies the subdued female monster as Public Opinion. Described as a male figure of medium size with Classical Roman features, a friendly fire in his eyes, and two long locks of hair "throwing and thrusting themselves strangely over his bold forehead" (16), Wit presents Julius with a second aspect of male sexuality. In light of the ideal fusion of masculine and feminine that Julius sets forth in his "Dithyrambic Fantasy" one might expect that Wit, generally associated with the *ars combinatoria* in the eighteenth century, might also propound a theory of androgyny, or at least a bringing together of male and female, but he proposes a different kind of combination. With the pronouncement that Julius's "false friends, the flowers [which is to say, the feminine], have all withered already" (16), Wit revives an old drama for Julius, "A Few Young Men at the Crossroads."

In this drama four young men representing a typology of the novel enact an eroticized, androcentric aesthetics.[6] The fantastic novel, flitting across the stage in various stages of undress, seems to incorporate both sexes, since the narrator comments that at times one might take him to be a girl dressed in boy's clothing. The knight in shining armor, the embodiment of propriety, and the serious young man in Greek garb, who represent the sentimental and the philosophical novels, are both lost in yearning for unspecified objects. The fourth young man, the completely modern psychological novel, is surrounded by a group of beautiful girls and women who represent such feminine virtues as decency, decorum, modesty, morality, and the beautiful soul. The women begin to fight among themselves, calling their various virtues into question. This mise-en-scène not only criticizes bourgeois prudery, but obliquely attacks heterosexuality as well: although the frivolous fantastic youth chooses the woman Impudence as his partner, the modern psychological novel announces that he is completely bored by the women's company and leaves. The play's title, "A Few Young Men at the Crossroads," now becomes understandable: the drama is not about young men choosing between virtuous and loose women (Naumann 209; Eichner in

KA 5:xxxix–xl), but about young men choosing what kind of sexuality to pursue.

Julius, too, is caught up in this drama. When the modern novel leaves, Julius notices that, with the exception of Impudence, the women are not nearly as attractive as he had thought. He feels a certain kinship with the bisexual fantastic youth (59), and the male-oriented aesthetic of the novel begins to border on the homoerotic at the drama's conclusion, a path that Julius then pursues in his fantasy. Dismissing the play's characters as mere external appearances, Julius's dream-companion identifies himself as a real person and true Wit. He then grows and elongates. Wit, phallicized, then enters into Julius and becomes a part of him. Feeling a new sense within himself, Julius turns his thoughts inward and sees the figures from the drama engaged in an inner Saturnalia, a spiritual Bacchanalia. Deciding that he, too, wants to enter into this sexual war of passions fighting against prejudices in the name of love and truth, Julius reaches for his weapons, only to find that he has none. He resolves to use art to compensate for this physical lack, but when the feminized Julius opens his mouth to celebrate love in song, he finds that his lips have not yet learned how to imitate the song of the spirit. His masculine mentor Wit then reappears and guides him in learning this new aesthetic, which consists of creating a constant flux of new separations and marriages (19–20).

The text itself questions whether this new homoerotic aesthetic will be viable: the woman Impudence, for whom the "Allegory" is named, has already launched a scathing attack on Wit's previous artistic endeavors. Impudence, clearly a figure of criticism and unmasking (18), berates Wit, the father of the four masculine novels, for having created offspring with little poetic merit (19). Moreover, she accuses those who want to produce children with Wit of engaging in an activity "most unnatural and improper" (19). She herself, however, then disappears arm in arm with one of Wit's sons, the fantastic novel, thereby in some sense approving of Wit's artistic production and drawing her own critique into question.

Wit represents both a sexual and an aesthetic ideal for Julius, and at the conclusion of the "Allegory" he wistfully asks why he, a writer, shouldn't consider himself to be Wit's son (23). With this statement Julius establishes an analogy between himself and Wit's other sons, the four masculine novels. Whereas Fantasy is the mother of the four novels (16), Julius himself, as Wit's feminized homosexual partner, becomes his own "mother." Precisely the same scenario will be repeated in Julius's "Apprenticeship Years of Masculinity," suggesting that it is the key both to Julius's homoerotic fantasy and to *Lucinde* in its entirety. Wit is a figure of autoengenderment. Through him the male subject becomes both "mother" and son: the male subject writes himself as text.

The "Allegory" concludes with a discussion of the rhetoric of love. On the surface a celebration of women, this final section is infused with strong homoerotic overtones that resonate when read in light of the preceding dream fantasy. If the rhetoric of love is to apologize for its directness, Julius wonders, to whom should this apology be addressed? First to women, he reasons, since it is in their hearts that true sensuality lies. But then to youths and men who have remained youths, he continues, since these men have the capacity to learn to love like women. Men must go through three stages of love in order to achieve this goal. The first stage is defined by sensual love, the second by mystical spirituality, and the third and highest level by a lasting feeling of harmonious warmth: "Any young man who possesses this feeling no longer loves only like a man, but also like a woman. In him humanity is complete" (21–22). The attentive reader will recognize this statement as a redaction of the scene from the "Dithyramb" where Julius proposes that he and Lucinde switch sexual roles in "a wonderfully sensual allegory of the completion of male and female in full, complete humanity" (13). Just as the autoerotic narcissism of the "Dithyramb" speaks against reading this scene as one of androgynous love, the "Allegory" contains a clue that Julius is propounding something other than an androcentric androgyny,[7] namely the identification of this highest stage of masculine love as one of "harmonious warmth."

"Warm" was a code word for homosexuality in late-eighteenth-century Berlin (Derks 90–97), where something of a gay subculture flourished under the influence of Frederick the Great (Steakley). Schlegel, who had been living in Berlin since 1797, conceivably was aware of this gay community, although it is unclear whether he knew of the connotations of the term "warm" or employed the expression in this sense in *Lucinde*.[8] The two statements Julius makes explicating the word remain, perhaps intentionally, ambiguous: "It is certain that men are by nature only hot or cold: they must be educated to warmth" (22). While it is possible that this "warmth" refers only to a mental state, one could argue that Wit has just educated Julius to a sexual "warmth" in his homoerotic fantasy, since Julius continues: "But women are by nature sensually and spiritually warm, and have a feeling for warmth of every sort" (22). If "warmth of every sort" is to include homosexuality, then perhaps Julius's celebration of women is not limited to the female sex per se, but also refers to what men must strive to become, namely womanlike men. When he argues that any young man who possesses this feeling of harmonious warmth no longer loves only like a man, but also like a woman, he seems to herald what in the 1860s Karl Ulrichs in his theories of a constitutional or essentialist homosexuality called a woman's soul enclosed in a man's body.[9] Julius's statement about men learning to love like women takes on a further homoerotic cast in light of the feminine sexual role he played in the preceding fantasy, as does his warning that "uninitiated youths" will misunderstand and misuse his text the most (24). The youths are indeed uninitiated in the religion of love, as traditional interpretations would have it (Firchow 23), but the religion of love that is being preached here is not heterosexuality, but one whose "language should be free and bold, according to old Classical custom" (25). As if to explicate this statement as a call to "Greek love," the "Allegory" ends with an encomium to Plato and Sappho.

Up until this point in the text Julius, masquerading under the guise of his heterosexual love for Lucinde, has displayed marked proclivities for both self-love and homoeroticism, and the next two sections, the "Idyll on Idleness" ("Idylle über den Müßiggang") and "Faithfulness and Joke" ("Treue und Scherz"), explore these tendencies in more detail. The "Idyll" begins with a feminized Julius celebrating himself as the best conversation partner he knows for a discussion of idleness: "And so I sat at the side of a brook like a contemplative girl in a thoughtless romance story and looked at the fleeing waves. But the waves fled and flowed so placidly, so calmly and sentimentally, that it seemed as if a Narcissus ought to see himself in the clear surface and become intoxicated with beautiful egoism" (25). Julius declares himself free of such self-centered tendencies, but the very mention of Narcissus makes his claim suspect.

It is no accident, then, that this Ovidean motif is reintroduced in

"Metamorphoses" ("Metamorphosen"), the section immediately following Julius's "Apprenticeship Years of Masculinity." Julius is at the brink of making the transition from egoism to interpersonal love, but despite his professed devotion to Lucinde, this is a transformation that, in Romantic style, is still to come. Although "Metamorphoses" does document Julius's development from the self-love of Narcissus to the object-love of Pygmalion, as Firchow has claimed (34), the object that the artist Julius creates and then falls in love with is himself. As Lucinde puts it at the text's conclusion, "It's not I, my Julius, whom you paint so holily: . . . It's you, it's the wonderful flower of your fantasy that you . . . see in me" (78–79), and she recognizes that Julius, who still loves his namesake Juliane (80), displays numerous narcissistic qualities. Schlegel confirms Lucinde's suspicions in the closing image of the novel's self-critical prologue: the brilliant white swan who is concerned only with nestling in Leda's lap without damaging the beautiful sheen of his own feathers (3) imprints an indelible mark of narcissism on both the text and Julius, who later compares himself to the swan (8).

Although this narcissism clearly has its roots in Classical mythology, the final sentence of "Metamorphoses" suggests that there may be a psychoanalytic dimension to Schlegel's interpretation of the role object-choice plays in artistic production and in sexual self-definition: "Pygmalion's statue stirs, and the surprised artist is seized by a joyful shudder with the knowledge of his own immortality, and like the eagle with Ganymede, a divine hope carries him on powerful wings to Olympus" (61). Whereas the Classical Pygmalion sculpts a female figure who is brought to life by Aphrodite, Schlegel's Pygmalion looks at his statue and sees his own immortality. Schlegel's artist thus creates himself as god: in fact, Julius has already cast himself as a living statue in the section preceding "Metamorphoses," the "Apprenticeship Years of Masculinity" (55). An important sexual component contributes to this aesthetic self-definition. Schlegel replaces the female object-choice in the Classical Pygmalion myth with male self-love, a transport he compares in a homosexually encoded allusion to Ganymede being carried off by the eagle to Olympus.[10] By aligning the two myths, Schlegel explicitly links narcissism with homosexuality.

A second component of the Narcissus motif in "Metamorphoses," once again alluding to Ovid's story, supports this reading, namely the comparison of *Geist* to a flower: "The mind loses itself in its clear depths, and like Narcissus rediscovers itself as a flower" (60). Throughout *Lucinde* flowers are repeatedly associated with the feminine, and occasionally with the union of male and female in "one plant," in true, ideal humanity (12, 74). Menninghaus has suggested that Schlegel is one step ahead of his contemporaries in his use of these botanical metaphors: whereas other writers maintain the traditional flower-female equivalence, Menninghaus argues, Schlegel exploits the fact that many plants are hermaphrodites to advance his theory of androgyny (*Theorie der Weiblichkeit* 208–10).

Menninghaus's interpretation is valid to a large extent, but it does not explain why Schlegel devotes so much attention to the Narcissus myth in this context or why he transforms the flower motif in "Faithfulness and Joke." In this seemingly innocuous spat between our two ideal lovers, Lucinde is upset with Julius, ostensibly because he has flirted with Amalia, but the text contains an oblique suggestion that much more is at stake in this exchange than first meets the eye. When Lucinde rejects his sexual advances, Julius brings her through the garden to the pavilion where the flowers are. Back in her feminine milieu Lucinde, however, remains unresponsive; she then asks Julius to move the hyacinths farther away because their scent is overpowering her (30). If Menninghaus is right to draw attention to the floral semantics of the text, then Lucinde's displeasure with the hyacinths, named after one of Apollo's male lovers, veils ever so delicately her desire not to be overpowered by Julius's homoerotic leanings.

The floral motif reintroduced at the conclusion of "A Reflection" ("Eine Reflexion") also obliquely alludes to homoeroticism. The "Reflection" rewrites Fichtean ego philosophy in sexual terms that "conflict nonsensically at the heart of sensuality" (74) and that overtly criticize definitions and labels: "But what is the definer or the defined itself? In masculinity it is the nameless. And what is the nameless in femininity? — the indefinite" (72). Nothing in the text, however, indicates that the words "masculinity" and "femininity" actually correspond to "man" and "woman." In light of Julius's previous discussion of men learning to love like women, the "Reflection" could just as easily be describing a homoerotic fantasy as a heterosexual encounter: in fact, the sexual play culminates when "a colorful ideal of witty sensuality blooms through allegory" (73), a phrase alluding to Wit's homoerotic aesthetic in the "Allegory of Impudence." Julius then extends a floral appeal to Lucinde: "My dear beloved! Should a complete bouquet of flowers be made up only of virtuous roses, silent forget-me-nots, and modest violets, and anything else that flowers maidenlike and childlike, and not contain whatever else that glows strangely in bright glory?" (74). In the next sentence Julius identifies the glowing object as a wonderful plant that is clearly male in nature: "Male clumsiness is a multifaceted essence and is rich in blossoms and fruits of every kind. Grant even the wonderful plant, which I don't want to name, its place" (74). In this context, male "clumsiness" is obviously a synonym for male sexuality, which Julius describes as "a multifaceted essence rich in blossoms of every kind." Given the other "male" flowers mentioned in the text (hyacinths and narcissus), the marvelous male plant that he prefers not to name, the thing that "glows strangely in bright glory," is clearly a cipher for homosexuality, and Lucinde later accuses Julius of seeing this "wonderful flower" of his fantasy in her (78–79), thereby openly acknowledging his homoerotic desire. Julius then concludes the series of floral/sexual metaphors with what appears to be a call to androgyny: "Or should there perhaps be, instead of this bright abundance, just one complete flower that combines the beauties of all the others and makes their existence superfluous?" (74). This appeal, however, takes the form of a question that Julius implicitly negates in the next sentence: he's counting on Lucinde's objectiveness to understand that "artistic productions of clumsiness often not unwillingly take the materials for their creations from masculine inspiration" (74). This statement serves as an introduction to the male friendship described in Julius's "Letter to Antonio" ("Julius an Antonio"), which even Firchow (36) admits can be read as having homoerotic overtones.

II

The relationship between male sexuality and aesthetic self-definition is explored at length in the "Apprenticeship Years of Masculinity." Rhetorically straightforward in comparison to the rest of *Lucinde*, this central confessional section functions as a self-reflexive novel-within-the-novel, and its narrative simplicity belies a complex examination of the constitutive roles that gender experi-

mentation and artistic production play in the Romantic construction of the subject: the various aspects of Julius's sexuality are revealed to be expressions of Romantic reflexivity, of the self-positing
male subject defining himself as art.[11]

The artist Julius begins his "Apprenticeship Years" with marked
proclivities for self-love and same-sex desire. At first finding women
"wonderfully strange and often incomprehensible, hardly like members of his species," he seeks male companionship, and "young men
who even remotely resembled himself he embraced with hot love
and with a true rage of friendship" (36). These homosexual affairs,
tinged with narcissistic appeal, excite him for a while. "But," as the
narrator indicates in a comment foreshadowing the outcome of his
apprenticeship, "that alone was not yet the right thing for him" (36).
Leaving his male friends, he wallows in his fantasies until "a divine
image of innocence struck his soul like a bolt of lightning" and he
remembers the other sex, "a dangerous dream that was decisive for
his whole life" (37). He then sets out to deflower the young girl
Luise, who willingly succumbs to his advances. Much to her dismay,
however, he refuses to follow through with the act, a decision he
later terms "excellent and interesting" (39). Julius retreats to his
solitary ways until he one day looks in a mirror and sees himself
distraught with yearning (39–40). Overcome by this Narcissus-like
image of himself, he once again turns to women, thereby suggesting
that his heterosexual relationships, like his homosexual affairs, are
grounded in self-love. After a woman toys with his affections and
makes him look ridiculous, he concludes that females in general are
cold and insensitive (41).

Julius then meets the prostitute Lisette, whose extreme corrupt-
ness he finds particularly alluring. She is the first woman with whom
he has a sexual relationship, and his artistic skills begin to develop
in her company: he discusses painting with her, and considers the
sketches produced under her tutelage to be his best (42). When he
somewhat justifiably refuses to acknowledge paternity of Lisette's
unborn child, she kills herself, and the death of this soon-to-be
mother proves devastating to Julius. Plunged into despair, he seeks
solace among his male friends. Predictably, his self-love and homoeroticism surface once again: "He grew aroused in his own thoughts
and conversations, and was intoxicated with pride and masculinity"
(45). Vowing to dedicate his life to the divineness of masculine

friendship, he pursues every man he finds interesting and does not desist from the chase until he has been successful in his quest. Although many scholars have pointedly read this as a description of a spiritual male friendship rather than a physical one (Firchow 36; Menninghaus, *Theorie der Weiblichkeit* 187–88), Julius himself reports: "One can imagine that he, who actually allowed himself everything and who could put himself above ridicule, had a different propriety in mind and in front of his eyes than the commonly accepted one" (45).

He soon finds this homosexual lifestyle psychologically unsatisfying, however, and his painting suffers, suggesting a certain inefficacy of male inspiration for artistic production. Consumed by a "fury of frustration" (46), he becomes suicidal. Two unconsummated heterosexual relationships then help him recover both his mental health and his artistic skills. In the first the woman arouses a sublime passion in him, and, in a phrase invoking the organic metaphor of the novel's prologue where a plant rising from the fertile, motherly earth symbolizes artistic production (3), Julius reports that "standing in truth on the fresh green of a powerful, motherly earth" he recognizes in himself "the high call to divine art" (49). Kuzniar ("Labor Pains") has argued that this maternal image is deployed to make male artistic activity appear natural and spontaneous, a topos that is expanded in Julius's next relationship with a woman whom he loves and honors like a sister (50): when this woman becomes a mother, a new confidence is awakened in his own art (51).

These relationships indicate that woman as "mother" inspires Julius's art. His refusal to accept the prostitute Lisette as "mother" precipitates an artistic crisis, the two unconsummated relationships with motherly women initiate his artistic recovery, and when he eventually meets the young artist Lucinde, who is also a mother (53), his artistic powers reach maturation: the objects he paints most frequently now are bathing girls (heterosexual desire), a youth looking with secret desire at his own reflection in the water (narcissistic homoeroticism), a smiling mother with a child in her arms (motherhood), and embraces of every sort (56). The components of Julius's sexual identity are thus clearly inscribed in a self-reflexive Romantic aesthetic that is inextricably linked to the "mother."

The theoretical significance of this maternal imagery and its relationship to male homoerotic desire become manifest in Julius's purportedly heterosexual relationship with Lucinde. According to his own account, Lucinde is not just a mother, she is also *his* "mother": "Julius rediscovered his youth in Lucinde's arms. . . . The ravishing power and warmth of her embrace were more than girlish; she had an air of inspiration and depth which only a mother could have" (55). Whereas his two previous relationships with maternal figures remain unconsummated, Julius makes love to his own "mother," a detail that would seem to indicate that there is something inherently improper about this intimacy. In fact, the text suggests that Julius's attraction to Lucinde is primarily narcissistic, with strong homoerotic overtones.[12] Julius first falls in love with Lucinde because he discovers a "wonderful likeness" of himself in her: she has a decided bent for the Romantic, she creates her own world, she shuns decorum, and she lives freely and independently (53). Although Julius learns to admire her for her differences rather than her similarities to him, he eventually concludes that these differences are actually grounded in a profound identity (56): he loves himself in her.

Almost paradoxically, Julius's self-love becomes synonymous with homoeroticism when he engages in heterosexual intercourse with Lucinde. The passage immediately following the identification of Lucinde as Julius's "mother" describes his attraction to the soft, gentle contours of her body and then concludes: " — Julius, too, was beautiful in a manly way." The dash that initiates this comment does not indicate differentiation, however, but equivalence, since the ensuing description is of a feminine body: " — Julius, too, was beautiful in a manly way, but the manliness of his figure was not revealed in a pronounced muscular strength. On the contrary, the contours were soft, the limbs full and round, though nowhere fat. Under a bright light the surface of his body formed broad masses all over, and the smooth body seemed as solid and firm as marble, and in their love battles the whole richness of his powerful figure would be revealed" (55). With this description of a "marble" body, Julius casts himself as a statue characterized in the unmistakable manner of Winckelmann, whose discussions of rounded, feminine young men were homoerotically charged (Baeumer). A decisive difference separates this homoerotic encounter from Julius's previous ones: whereas the earlier liaisons were with men, here Julius makes love to a woman. Hence, the feminized Julius enjoys an almost lesbian relationship with Lucinde.[13]

This reversal suggests that we read Julius's desire to switch sexual roles with Lucinde in a new light. This desire is not, as Julius would have us believe, "a wonderfully sensual allegory of the completion of male and female in full, complete humanity" (13). Julius himself later states that this completion takes place in the youth who loves like a woman (21–22), alluding to his own homoerotic relationship with Lucinde. Julius's desire to switch sexual roles and his identification with Lucinde as "mother" are manifestations of a desire to define himself as a woman, specifically, as his own mother, a desire to put himself in a position of autoengenderment, in the privileged feminine position of producing self-reflexive Romantic poesy.[14] For both Schlegel and Novalis the woman as childbearer is the sole source of true poetic production, a thesis that results in a profound identity crisis for the male subject: since the Romantic subject posits itself in and through poesy, and only women can create poesy, a man cannot define himself fully unless he somehow becomes a woman.

The various aspects of Julius's sexuality are all part of a complex equation of Romantic reflexivity designed to bring about this transformation: his narcissism is an expression of the self-positing subject, "I am I"; he overcomes the male subject's limitations both by defining himself homoerotically as a woman and by extending his self-love to Lucinde, hence rewriting the male subject's self-positing as "I am woman." This homoerotic substitution, explicitly effected via gender play in Schlegel's redaction of Fichtean ego philosophy in "A Reflection," allows Julius to conclude "I am mother," therefore "I am poet" and "I can define myself as poesy." Hence, when he learns that Lucinde is pregnant Julius exclaims: "I want to plant myself on the earth . . . I want to refresh myself in the arms of the mother who will always be my bride" (62), thereby using the organic metaphor of "planting" to project himself into a position of autogenesis and to define himself vis-à-vis the "mother." His vicarious appropriation of Lucinde's maternal status then allows him to complete his apprenticeship with the statement that just as his painting has reached perfection, his life has become "a created story" (53), "a work of art" (57): in the self-reflexive act of writing his autobiography, Julius actually transforms himself into poesy. The male artist takes this aesthetic self-definition one step further in the novel's prologue: having invoked the metaphor of the plant rising from the fertile, maternal earth as a symbol of poetic production, the "mother" Schlegel identifies the text *Lucinde* as "my son" (3), thereby equating procreation with artistic creation.

The "Allegory of Impudence" posits precisely the same model of male autoengenderment. At the conclusion of this homoerotic fantasy the writer Julius asks why he shouldn't consider himself to be Wit's son, that is, a novel. As Wit's feminized homosexual partner, he thereby defines himself as both "mother" and son, procreator and text. It is no coincidence, then, that Schlegel returns to the "Allegory" at the end of the "Apprenticeship Years of Masculinity" by drawing attention to the fantastic novel that embodied both sexes, a cipher, Schlegel reports, of his own *Lucinde* (*KA* 24:252): "It was not without reason that the fantastic youth, whom I liked best of the four immortal novels that I saw in my dream, was playing with a mask. Allegory also has crept into what seems to be pure representation and fact, and has mixed meaningful lies with beautiful truth. But only as a spiritual breath does it hover over the whole mass, animating it, like Wit, who plays invisibly with his creation, smiling softly" (59). In other words, what seems to be "pure representation and fact" (Julius's heterosexual love for Lucinde) is infused with an allegorical masking that hides the true subtext (homoeroticism), while Wit, Julius's male mentor, plays gently with the text, animating it with a homoerotic aesthetic that, as Julius puts it, can only be hinted at, but not told (58). As if to confirm this reading, Julius concludes that poems of the "old religion" (read "Greek love") provide the pattern for his own text: "Poesy has shaped and transformed these writings so finely and richly that their beautiful meaningfulness has remained ambiguous, and so permitted ever new interpretations and configurations" (59).

"Triflings of Fantasy" ("Tändeleien der Fantasie") indicates that Schlegel's attitude toward this new homoerotic aesthetic remains ambivalent at best. In this final section of the novel Julius, in a gesture of Romantic self-criticism, strews flowers on the grave of his too-soon-departed son, presumably the novel itself (81).[15] Hence, *Lucinde* is not a miscarriage, as Gundolf would have it (Weigel, "Wider die romantische Mode" 68), but a novel fated to die young: the homoerotic aesthetic of *Lucinde* will not develop into a mature Romantic art form. Julius's male fantasy must fail, a fact alluded to at the end of the "Idyll on Idleness," where he sees a theatrical production comparing Prometheus and Hercules as creators of men. In this "allegorical comedy" (29) the chained Prometheus hastily fashions men out of clay, producing people who all look alike, while the heroic Hercules begets his various offspring together with women. No Hercules, this feminized lover, Julius writes as the artisan Prometheus produces men, alone and in his own image, and Schlegel criticizes Prometheus and Julius for their solipsistic artistic methods (28). *Lucinde* posits a theoretical model whereby the male subject defines himself as a woman who produces self-reflexive Romantic poesy, but this gender play has obvious practical limitations: men are not women and cannot bear children.

Hence the novel dies, but Julius is given a chance to reform himself. After he scatters flowers on his son's grave, "Triflings of Fantasy" continues with a High Priestess reaching out her hand to him to effect "an earnest union, to vow eternal purity and eternal inspiration" (82). Julius enters into this new religion (clearly a heterosexual aesthetic), then hastens from the altar to seize a sword so he can plunge into battle, a gesture reminiscent of the homoerotic aesthetic of the "Allegory," where the feminized Julius tries to rush to war but finds that he has no weapon (20). Although the High Priestess restores his "weapon," Julius soon forgets the battle and stands alone in deepest solitude, gazing only at himself and the sky above (82). Not surprisingly, the narrator concludes that "the soul that slumbers in such dreams, dreams them forever, even when it's awake" (82). In other words, while Julius will never break out of his narcissism, Schlegel clearly understands its theoretical limitations, and undercuts his own homoerotic aesthetic in a self-reflexive act of Romantic criticism.

Given the Romantics' programmatic confusion of the real and ideal, any reading of *Lucinde* as autobiography would be speculative at best. While there is no point in denying the biographical correspondences, there is also no clear way to interpret them. Perhaps Schlegel was gay or bisexual; perhaps the homoerotic desire expressed in *Lucinde* is merely aesthetic in nature. Schlegel was clearly uncomfortable with women as a young man (*KA* 5:xxvi), and when he and Schleiermacher (the Antonio of *Lucinde*) lived together, their friends termed the relationship a "marriage," with Schleiermacher acting as the woman (Naumann 181).[16] If Schlegel was gay or bisexual, was his wife Dorothea aware of it, as Lucinde seems to be? The title of her *Florentin* may be a reference to another code word for homosexuality,[17] and the novel conceivably constitutes an important female response to the homoerotic aesthetic of *Lucinde*.

There has been an unfortunate elision of the feminine in my own discussion here, and if this is justifiable, it is only because Schlegel himself does so in *Lucinde*. Although he was obviously interested in developing a "theory of femininity" (Menninghaus, *Theorie der Weiblichkeit* 185–213), he fell short of this goal in his novel, a state of affairs of which he was keenly aware. Schlegel had in fact planned to complement the one-sided treatment of masculinity evident in "Part One" of *Lucinde* with a corresponding analysis of the feminine in an ensuing installment of the novel (*KA* 24:252–53), an installment that never appeared. As it stands, the text has much less in common with his earlier progressive essays "On the Feminine Characters in Greek Poetry" and "On Diotima" than it does with the later *Conversation on Poetry*, in which men write poetry and criticism, while women play a regulative, interlocutory role. Although *Lucinde* is regrettably regressive in its "theory of femininity," it is astonishingly progressive in its analysis of men: Schlegel experiments with the potential advantages and repercussions of male same-sex desire for Romantic aesthetic theory, rather than adhering to a heterosexual societal norm.

Catriona MacLeod

The "Third Sex" in an Age of Difference: Androgyny and Homosexuality in Winckelmann, Friedrich Schlegel, and Kleist

The "third sex," or in German "das dritte Geschlecht," Magnus Hirschfeld's well-known designation for the homosexual, is not, as this essay will show, an invention of the twentieth century. Fictions of an androgynous "third sex" play a strategic role in German aesthetics and literature of the Age of Goethe, during a period when sexual difference is being inscribed as scientific fact. As Thomas Laqueur has argued in his work on scientific constructions of sex, there occurred in the late eighteenth century a shift away from the old Galenic model, which presupposed a metaphysics of hierarchy in the relationship between male and female, in favor of an anatomy of radical dimorphism and incommensurability: "opposite" sexes.[1]

Typical of utopian appeals to androgyny on the part of German theoreticians of difference is Wilhelm von Humboldt's important essay of 1795 "On Masculine and Feminine Form" ("Über die männliche und weibliche Form"). While the main purpose of his essay is to confirm sexual difference as a biological and social necessity, and a highly desirable one at that, von Humboldt views the androgynous union of polar opposites as the supreme state to be attained by humanity. He formulates this abstract ideal of an androgynous third sex at the opening of the essay: "The highest and perfect form of beauty demands not merely union, but *the most exact balance [das genaueste Gleichgewicht]* of form and matter, of art and freedom, of spiritual and sensual unity, and this is only achieved when the characteristics of both sexes are melted together in thought and humanity is fashioned from the most intimate union of pure masculinity and pure femininity" (1:296–97). Similarly, the theologian Friedrich Schleiermacher, in a women's "catechism" ("Idee zu einem Katechismus der Vernunft für edle Frauen") published in 1798 in the Schlegels' journal *Athenäum*, conceived of a utopian androgynous state in which the "barriers of sex" (*Schranken des Geschlechts*, 285–87) would be overcome. Androgyny promises to be an aesthetic construction that blurs, or indeed denies, binary categories. What may at first glance seem surprising, then, is its insistent appearance in literary and aesthetic discourses such as von Humboldt's essay that are premised on binarism, that uphold heterosexuality as the normative sexuality, and that are repressive of sexual fluidity.

When Carolyn Heilbrun inaugurated the current feminist debates on androgyny in 1964 with the publication of her widely admired book *Toward a Recognition of Androgyny*, it was to recuperate the androgynous ideal as a feminist myth promising both psychological and sociopolitical equality between the sexes. Yet Heilbrun's book, while it alludes to the intriguing fact that such an androgynous ideal flourished in an age of polarization, does not address the possible historical collusion between literary androgyny and the construction of (heterosexual) difference. What is more, Heilbrun's programmatic distancing of the term "androgyny" from homosexuality or bisexuality may even, as I will indicate, be regarded as an uncanny repetition of eighteenth- and nineteenth-century discourses on androgyny.[2] Is the figure of the androgyne, as Jonathan Dollimore has recently suggested, the culturally acceptable, aestheticized face of a threatening third term — homosexuality? The problem with androgyny, writes Dollimore, is that it "typically envisages a unity ostensibly beyond sexual difference, but in fact inseparable from it; androgyny especially has too often been a genderless transcendent which leaves sexual difference in place" (262). In this essay I want to push Dollimore's point several steps further, to propose that androgyny does not simply leave gender binarisms intact; more instrumental than such a definition would allow, androgyny may even serve as a mythical, theoretical vehicle for the inscription of difference, acquiring iconic status as the prime cultural symbol of heterosexual union.[3] I identify a shift that occurs in the late eighteenth century from the (homo)erotic and genuinely polymorphous ideal of androgyny proposed by Winckelmann to a model grounded in heterosexual complementarity, drained of sexuality, and central to the aesthetic program of Wilhelm von Humboldt, Schiller, Goethe, and others. The texts that I consider here, generically varied as they are — Winckelmann's aesthetics, Schlegel's *Bildungsroman*, Kleist's correspondence — nevertheless all share a concern with the dual question of androgyny and *Bildung*, or the education of desire. (On the link between *Bildung* and the sentimental cult of male friendship and letter writing, see Joachim Pfeiffer's essay "Friendship and Gender," in this volume.)

Late-eighteenth- and nineteenth-century fascination with and uneasiness about the androgyne may itself be understood as a coded expression of cultural anxiety about homosexuality, for at the moment when the distinct contours of heterosexuality, with its polar and naturalized attributes of "masculinity" and "femininity," have been crystallized, homosexuality comes into existence as its "unnatural" other. This is a point recognized by Foucault when he links the formation of the modern bourgeois family with the medicalization — and thus date of birth — of the (male) homosexual. Significantly for my arguments in this essay, homosexuality, as categorized in the pivotal work of Carl Westphal, is in Foucault's view characterized "less by a type of sexual relations than by a certain quality of sexual sensibility, a certain way of inverting the masculine and the feminine in oneself. Homosexuality appeared as one of the forms of sexuality when it was transposed from the practice of sodomy onto a kind of interior androgyny, a hermaphrodism of the soul" (*History* 1:43).[4] The historian Randolph Trumbach, who locates the origins of modern homosexuality in the early eighteenth century, uses "androgynous" terms strikingly similar to Foucault's. He has argued that the Enlightenment in Europe marked a new phase in male homosexual behavior: prior to 1700, men married women and had sexual relations with adolescent boys, but after 1700 the prevalent form of relationship was between two adult men, at least one of whom was characterized as decidedly effeminate. Accompanying this shift, Trumbach suggests, is the notion of a "third" gender role, neither exclusively male nor exclusively female, that of the sodomite ("Sodomy Transformed" 106). What Foucault's path-breaking work on the historical construction of male homosexuality does not take into account — and it is a significant omission — is that with all its divergent history the sexual category of lesbianism similarly attracted the culturally unsettling label "androgyny": in German, the lesbian was characterized in medical discourse as a "Mannweib," a direct translation of the Greek term "androgyne."[5] Indeed, Westphal's now famous article of 1869 on "contrary sexual sensations" (*die conträre Sexualempfindung*) would be the point of departure for subsequent medical research on both male *and* female homosexuality, influencing among others the sexologist Krafft-Ebing.[6] (Krafft-Ebing's system of classification in his major work *Psychopathia sexualis* included androgynes — among psychosexual hermaphrodites, effeminates, homosexuals, and sundry other categories; see Jones 59.)

The focus of my inquiry is literary and aesthetic reformulations of the developmental narrative of human sexuality presented by Aristophanes in Plato's *Symposium* (189E–193D). According to Aristophanes' playful account of the primal androgyne, human beings were originally of three sexes — male, female, and male-female — but because of their greed for divine power the gods resolved to split them in half, leaving us today in a perpetual quest for our lost halves. The primordial human being was a spherical creature, bountifully equipped with two sets of hands, legs, faces, sexual organs, and so on. This creature we might describe as belonging to a fundamentally presexual, undifferentiated phase of human development. In the second phase of human evolution, following the divine punishment of differentiation, each creature was doomed to seek its lost half, in a quest to achieve completion. Significantly, Aristophanes notes that this urge for plenitude could be fulfilled through either homosexual or heterosexual union. But the tragedy of this anatomical phase lay in the fact that the human genitalia were now positioned in such a way as to impede internal fertilization. In addition to this reproductive problem, these human beings faced an even more fatal dilemma: now that they had been refashioned as sexual beings, and because of their obsessive pursuit of erotic fulfillment, they were barred from leading socially productive lives, to the extent that the unrelenting urge for sexual union eventually led to death. Aristophanes then tells of the gods' mercy toward these pitiful creatures. In order to make internal reproduction possible, Zeus relocated the genitalia to the front of the human body, thus also permitting social productivity. However, now that the principal goal of sexual intercourse was procreation, human beings found themselves plunged into a new tragedy: that of sexual difference. Aristophanes' androgyne has often been taken as a totalizing, static model of balance, yet his account of human sexual development is in fact anything but symmetrical, depending as it does on a dizzying play of combination and recombination and permissive as it is of all the permutations on erotic union, heterosexual or homosexual.[7] At the same time, his narrative does proceed along developmental lines, moving from an image of primordial, polymorphous unity to the fall into sexual difference. It is apt, then, that the narrative of androgyny achieves central importance in the German literary imagination of the late eighteenth century, a period preoccupied with questions of difference, the construction of the subject, and bourgeois socialization. Importantly for modern theories of sexuality, Freud's reading of the Platonic myth, reflected for example in the *Three Essays on the Theory of Sexuality*, similarly "rehabilitates" heterosexuality vis-à-vis the destabilizing homosexuality present in Aristophanes' speech, positing sexual polymorphousness as the domain of infantile sexuality, and adulthood as the phase entered into through correct socialization and determined by difference (*SE* 7:123–245).

Winckelmann: Contours of Indeterminacy

It is hardly coincidental that Winckelmann, the "prime ideologue of pedagogic eros" (Dellamora 110), chose to have himself depicted, in a portrait by Anton Maron executed during his time in Rome, with an engraving of the youth Antinous emblematically placed across the leaves of his notebook. Antinous, the favorite of the emperor Hadrian, was also the ideal neoclassical embodiment of the androgyne. The Antinous relief, rediscovered in 1735, was the art sensation of its time. Its wild success with contemporary art critics derived from its sexual indeterminacy: the softly contoured torso of the half-naked form made an exquisite contrast with the rather severe profile of the boy's face.[8] Androgyny, as opposed to the perceived monstrosity of biological hermaphrodism, becomes the highest aesthetic manifestation of neoclassicism's desire for seamless equilibrium, "the middle way."[9] Despite his fascination with antique hermaphrodite sculptures, it is important to point out that Winckelmann doubted the existence of genuine physical hermaphrodites, in whom the genitalia of both sexes are present, and stressed that the supreme harmony of an androgynous artwork like the Belvedere

Apollo had nothing in common with these freakish, unnatural creatures. Androgyny, then, is from the outset linked with aesthetics and artifice. For Winckelmann, as he describes it in his *History of Ancient Art* (*Geschichte der Kunst des Alterthums*), the Greek ideal of beauty stems from the fact that it combined in an ideal work the manliness of a beautiful boy with the forms of enduring feminine youth (*SW* 4:73–76). The resulting work of art is neither masculine nor feminine, but rather what Winckelmann terms a "middle form" (*mittlere Gestalt*, 73). The line that describes these contours of indeterminacy, writes Winckelmann, is neither straight nor curved: inexpressible in strictly geometric terms, it evades human rationality. This aesthetic principle corresponds to the imagery that pervades his writings: water and waves; floating, hovering, suspension. The indefinability of art is not merely an abstract aesthetic concept, but is concretized by Winckelmann in the formal demands he places on the artist. Thus, the artist will avoid harsh, jarring moments, and will allow the different components of the work to ebb and flow, wavelike. The Belvedere Hercules, for Winckelmann a pinnacle of artistic perfection, displays taut, well-defined muscles (*sägeformig*); but hard and virile as they appear, they are also soft and sensual, "like the surging of the peaceful ocean, sublime and flowing, in a gentle hovering motion" (*SW* 4:140).

Just as, when the sea is rising, a previously still surface transforms itself, in misty turbulence, into playful waves, as each wave is swallowed up by another and then surges forth again: in just this fashion, softly swollen and hovering, one muscle here ripples into another, and a third, rising up between them and apparently strengthening their motion, is lost in the first two, and our gaze is engulfed with it [*unser Blick wird gleichsam mit verschlungen*]. (*SW* 1:229)

As with so many of Winckelmann's descriptions, this view of the Belvedere Hercules depends on the endless play of seemingly unresolvable tensions: movement and stasis, softness and hardness, fluidity and rigidity, upward and downward motion, water and body, viewer and statue. Indeed, after gazing at the Hercules torso, this fragment that both suggests and demands completion, we can no longer discern where we, as viewers, end and where the statue begins. "Let the artist admire in the contours of this body the continuous flow of one form into another, and the hovering lines that rise and fall like waves and are engulfed in one another: he will find that no one can be certain of reproducing this accurately in a drawing, since the curve he believes himself to be following imperceptibly changes direction, and bewilders both eye and hand [*das Auge und die Hand irre macht*] with its new trajectory" (*SW* 6:98).

What I have called Winckelmann's androgynous aesthetic is premised on erotic desire: it is an aesthetic that depends on the nomadic subjectivity of the viewer, who engages in free play with the sculpture, allowing himself to be seduced by its fleeting contours.[10] The marble statue, focal point of discussions on aesthetics, also becomes central to cultural constructions of gender and difference. If the statue kindles erotic desire in the viewer, it is also true that the viewer animates the statue as a sexual being, Pygmalion-like. The sex of a Telephus statue, for example, is dependent on the perspective of the observer: bewildered as to the correct sex, the viewer perceives the figure as feminine when seen from below, as masculine when seen from above (*SW* 4:141). This eroticized aesthetic experience might be compared with Lacan's analysis of anamorphosis, in which he discusses the "pulsatile" erotic effects generated by the interaction between artwork and gaze.[11] Unlike the gaze of the mystic, whose sensual vocabulary Winckelmann borrows freely, Winckelmann's gaze is outer-directed [*außer sich*], voluptuous. The gaze caresses the curve of the androgynous statue and becomes one with the tactile movement of the hand: Winckelmann's description of the sinuous body of the Belvedere Hercules stresses, as I noted above, that the sculpture seduces and bewilders both eye and hand (*SW* 6:98).

It is important to emphasize Winckelmann's self-conscious twist on the Pygmalion myth: what is posited by Ovid's narrative of creation as the fusion of art and life, female and male, here takes on distinctly homoerotic shades of desire. The eroticism present in the relationship between viewer and statue is, paralleling the focus of Winckelmann's aesthetics, an eroticism of indeterminacy. Winckelmann's most adored androgynes are modeled after adolescent boys — puberty being the supreme moment of sexual indeterminacy and liminality. Indeed, as one critic has recently noted, Winckelmann scrutinizes the youthful male body for the discomforting signs of body hair, the harbinger of adulthood, devoting at least fifty pages of the *History of Ancient Art* to this subject. The most lovely hair, for Winckelmann, is the down on the adolescent's chin, an indication that the coarse beard of manhood has not yet arrived (Parker 540–41). Furthermore, the adolescent god still revels — though fleetingly — in unalienated existence in nature, pursuing his desires undisturbed by consciousness. Winckelmann describes this sensual, supremely "natural" androgyne as a creature eternally poised between sleep and consciousness, between dream and reality, between childhood and adulthood, between femaleness and maleness: "The image . . . of an already full-grown youth, who approaches the threshold of the springtime of life, when sensuality begins to stir like the delicate bud of a plant. So in this statue he seems, between sleeping and waking, wistfully to be recollecting the remaining images of a dream he has just dreamed, as if wishing he could make them real. His features are filled with voluptuous sweetness, but his joyful spirit does not manifest itself fully" (SW 7:112).

It is the moment of liminality captured in the androgynous sculpture that leaves open for the viewer the possibility of Bildung. This play between binaries, with its promise of growth, is, of course, one of the fundamental concepts of classical Bildung, as it is elaborated, for example, in Schiller's Aesthetic Letters or in Goethe's theory of Polarität. However, the eternal liminality of the Greek androgynous youth constitutes a phase that in real life must be overcome through Bildung: a real person could not remain at this stage of arrested adolescence without mummification. Winckelmann's vision of male maturation is defined by the Greek "problem of the boy," as Foucault terms it in The Use of Pleasure.[12] The close attention paid to the type of sexual relationship between an older man and a boy is due less to the fact that this was a dominant mode of sexual behavior in Greek society than to the boy's liminal status: unlike a slave or a woman, the boy would become a man, and would thus enjoy all the rights and privileges linked with this status. And since it was considered inappropriate for an adolescent to pursue his sexual relationship with an older man into adulthood, part of what the boy could expect from his mentor was the correct education to make him into a respectable citizen. As Winckelmann delineates his hierarchy of life stages, the androgynous boy, closely aligned with the imaginary and with unconscious nature, represents the first stage of male development. This is followed by mature adulthood, represented by Mercury and Mars, heroism and energy incarnated. Jupiter, the most important god, symbolizes old age and wisdom (SW 7:102–

14; see also Spickernagel 102–3). Significantly, however, there is no parallel movement of *Bildung* to be found among the goddesses described by Winckelmann. As they age, according to his developmental model, only women's physical appearance changes, never their sex or gender orientation or their alignment with nature. Winckelmann places Venus at the head of his hierarchy of female divinities, largely because she, like the male gods, is depicted in various developmental stages. But her development is presented in quite unambiguous terms: reproductive readiness is what the viewer glimpses in the blossoming adolescent Venus, not androgynous liminality. Woman is defined biologically by her fecundity; in the nonreproductive work of art, for Winckelmann, resides an idealized burgeoning of differences. The association I have discussed in Winckelmann's writings between the androgynous boy and the realms of the imaginary and unconscious nature yield first clues about the tendency, in later German writers, to colonize femininity and childhood as androgynous spaces (a move also evident in Freud's concept of the "polymorphous perverse"). This nomadic bisexual model expressed in the fluidity of Winckelmann's aesthetic writings finds itself in a contested relationship with an ideal of androgyny that posits heterosexual complementarity and procreation as the norm and thus serves as the mythical cornerstone of an ideology of difference.

In this context, it is important to consider briefly the reception of Winckelmann—and, by extension, of "Greek" notions of sexuality—in the latter half of the century. As early as 1769, Herder in his *Critical Forests* (*Kritische Wälder*) coined the epithet "worthy Greek" (*würdiger Grieche*) of Winckelmann (3:186), which, as Paul Derks convincingly argues, may have functioned as a way of avoiding the more culturally charged term "Greek love" (*griechische Liebe*).[13] In 1787 Herder returned to the subject of Greek friendship between men, and, while he did not disguise his distaste for the "moral vices" (*Sittenverderbnisse*) of this practice, he was nonetheless able to explain it as a historical phenomenon reflecting the character of the Greeks and as a social structure contributing to the good of the state (14:116–17; cf. Derks 198). Wilhelm von Humboldt more overtly wards off the specter of homoeroticism, and thus by implication the scandalous body of the aesthetic pedagogue, through his strategic historicizing of the Greeks. In his 1806 essay "Latium and Hellas or Reflections on Classical Antiquity" ("Latium

und Hellas oder Betrachtungen über das classische Alterthum,"
2:25–64), von Humboldt presents a seemingly irreversible historical
narrative that sees the homoeroticism of the ancients as but a necessary preliminary to the securing of heterosexual love by the moderns.[14] Goethe, in his Winckelmann essay of 1805, takes up the
familiar vocabulary of Winckelmann the pagan and antique, once
again viewing the theoretician of Classicism through the lens of classical Greece, situating him in the cradle of civilization (HA 12:96–
129). In Goethe's case, however, this self-conscious anachronism is
coupled with a recognition that his own classical age is predicated
on Winckelmann's pan-erotic gaze. As Sander Gilman reminds us,
the first mention of Winckelmann in Goethe's Italian Journey recounts Winckelmann's delight at a neoclassical forgery of a portrait
of Ganymede, who presents Jupiter with a cup of wine and receives a
kiss in exchange ("Goethe's Touch" 39). Winckelmann's androgynous aesthetic is mediated and historicized through this cultural
sign.

Schlegel: Androgynous Chaos, Androgynous Stasis

If the neoclassical eighteenth century pays homage to the "antique" Winckelmann, the theoretical and poetic writings of Friedrich
Schlegel are also shot through with a vision of androgyny as an
aesthetic and erotic ideal, a vision that doubtless owes much to
Winckelmann, at least in its initial phases. Schlegel is concerned
above all with the radical aesthetic and sexual possibilities opened
up by the figure of the androgyne. In his emphasis on indeterminacy
and chaos he would seem to break with the integrational model of
plenitude and harmony that comes to dominate late-eighteenth- and
early-nineteenth-century writing on androgyny.[15] Schlegel's novel
Lucinde, published in 1799, is the quintessential novel of androgyny—not simply for thematic reasons, though of course its hero
and heroine, Julius and Lucinde, revel in dizzying sexual role-play
and their love relationship is represented as a perfect androgynous
union, but because the novel's whole structure is set in motion by
notions of aesthetic indeterminacy and erotic chaos.

The spiraling "system" of the novel is laid out in its opening
pages, in a letter from Julius to Lucinde. Although Julius ostensibly
begins his letter in conventional narratorial mode, by announcing

his desire to lay bare his past history and the reasons for his current state of bliss, he willfully breaks the narrative thread and declares: "No purpose, however, is more purposeful for myself and this work . . . than to destroy at the very outset all that part we call 'order,' remove it, and claim explicitly and affirm actually the right to a charming confusion" (*KA* 5:9; Firchow 45). Offering the justification that the raw material for the novel, the love affair with Lucinde, is so systematic and progressive that any novel mirroring it formally would be unbearably dull and uniform, Julius asserts his "incontestable right to confusion" (*unbezweifeltes Verwirrungsrecht, KA* 5:9; Firchow 45). His novel will both recreate and enhance "the most beautiful chaos of sublime harmonies and fascinating pleasures" (*KA* 5:9; Firchow 45). The opening section of the novel ends with a telling vignette: from among the many notes composed to Lucinde and scattered all over his room, we see Julius selecting his favorite pages and inserting them, it seems randomly, into the body of his novel. The resulting work does indeed appear anarchic and hybrid: letters are interspersed with dialogues, an idyll, dreams, allegories, and fantasies, and it is known that Schlegel's plans for continuation also stressed the inclusion of poetry (Friedrichsmeyer, *Androgyne* 149). We would, however, probably do best to employ an oxymoron ourselves and call the novel an ordered chaos: that Schlegel in fact carefully contrived the work's overall symmetry is clear from the novel's structure, its central confessional narrative surrounded on both sides by six "arabesques." Androgynous symmetry and androgynous chaos: the strange aesthetic coincidence of the two will become clearer toward the end of my discussion of Schlegel.

In the "Allegory of Impudence" ("Allegorie von der Frechheit"), a section of the novel that frustrates interpretation perhaps more than any other in this multilayered work, the androgyne appears in person on the novel stage. A figure who introduces himself as "Wit" (*der Witz*) presents Julius with the allegorical picture of four youths at the crossroads, who represent, he claims, four types of novel. One is described as a pious knight; one is a melancholic youth dressed in classical Greek robes; one is a worldly young cosmopolitan. The first youth to be introduced is, however, the most capricious and mutable in form, and his fleeting and unpredictable appearances in the allegory punctuate and destabilize the more orderly, unified descriptions of the other youths. His final incursion into the text finds the boy, a figure of literary artifice, in the extravagant carnivalesque attire of a rococo shepherd, mask in hand. The text signals the androgynous disposition of the polymorphous youth by comparing his costume with a girl's whimsical cross-dressing (*KA* 5:16–17; Firchow 53–54). While the novel is not explicit as to the type of novel represented by the boy, Schlegel reveals in a letter to Caroline Böhmer of 1799 that the androgynous youth stands for his own *Lucinde,* while the three others represent plans for future novels (*Caroline* 514). Julius's vision ends with the androgynous boy shunning a group of maidens who represent conventional morality and leaving arm in arm with Lady Impudence. Finally, Julius's companion on this bewildering allegorical journey, Wit, calls upon him to reveal the chaos of nature in a new kind of novel. Significantly, the vocabulary used is the language of erotic combination: "Create, discover, transform, and retain the world and its eternal forms in the perpetual variation of new marriages and divorces" (*KA* 5:20; Firchow 58). Again, this aesthetic principle of constant flux, of incessant combination and recombination, recalls the volatility of the androgynous boy, as well as the virtuosic games of sexual shape-shifting that are described by Julius as an allegory of true humanity (*KA* 5:12–13; Firchow 49). If we take into account the teasing adolescent who represents allegorically this dizzying novel, we can begin to see androgyny as a central erotic and formal principle, fundamentally connected with Julius's "right to confusion" (*Verwirrungsrecht*).

In his earlier essays on Greek literature and history, as well as in *Lucinde,* his contribution to the *Bildungsroman,* Schlegel would seem to propose a bisexual model of androgyny. In his 1795 essay on Diotima, written in part as a response to von Humboldt's standard catalog of sexual stereotypes "Über die männliche und weibliche Form," Schlegel refuses what he sees as an uncritical appropriation of Greek history in order to back up modern assumptions regarding sexual difference, thus pointing to the historical constructedness of sexual stereotypes. It is in this essay that Schlegel famously declares the aesthetic distastefulness and moral bankruptcy of a rigid adherence to binaristic conceptions of masculinity and femininity: "What is uglier than overloaded femininity, what is more repulsive than exaggerated masculinity?" (*KA* 1:92). And in an essay addressed to his future wife, Dorothea Veit, Schlegel radically asserts the right of each individual "to move freely according to his or her own desire, along the whole spectrum of humanity" (*sich nach Lust und Liebe in dem ganzen Bezirke der Menschheit frei zu bewegen, KA* 8:45). Furthermore, in *Lucinde* Schlegel takes up as a positive analogy plant hermaphrodism, opposing the classical notion of *Bildung* and its emphasis on sexual maturation and differentiation with the concept of pure androgynous vegetation (see Firchow 66; *KA* 5:27).[16] Such notions of free-flowing desire, of genuinely polymorphous sexuality, do indeed seem a revolutionary assault on the models of strict sexual complementarity established by, among others, Wilhelm von Humboldt. Certainly many readers were offended by the apparent radicality of the relationship at the center of *Lucinde*, the endless games of combination and recombination, erotic *ars combinatoria*.

I want to stress, however, that Schlegel covertly reformulates the androgynous myth in terms of exclusively heterosexual love. Where the essay on Diotima tells of the giddying powers of each human being to move freely within the whole spectrum of sexual possibilities, *Lucinde* actually places us within a model that culminates teleologically in strict heterosexual complementarity. Schelling's *Of the World Spirit* (*Von der Weltseele*), of 1798, with its view of the natural world as a living organism pulsating with polarities, may have been an influence on the revised Romantic philosophical notion of androgyny, committed to maintaining sexual difference as a biological principle (Friedrichsmeyer, "Subversive Androgyne" 67). Achim Aurnhammer suggests that Schlegel rather nervously begins to accentuate sexual binaries in order to efface the suggestion of homosexual union present in Aristophanes' narrative. Schlegel, Aurnhammer further proposes, is perhaps also capitulating to the moral expectations of his readers by following the Romantic philosopher Franz von Baader's androgynous model, which superimposes on the Platonic model an orthodox Catholic concept of marriage as heterosexual androgynous union, as a return to prelapsarian undividedness (Aurnhammer 199; see also Baader, "Sätze aus der erotischen Philosophie"; and Sill).

To make this argument is, however, to efface the homoerotic elements that undercut the androgynous vision of Schlegel's novel. These form an integral part of the novel's central narrative of erotic apprenticeship, the "Apprenticeship for Manhood" ("Lehrjahre der

Männlichkeit"), and are also characteristic of the androgynous boy who embodies the novel itself. Indeed, the moral outrage that greeted the publication of Schlegel's novel may be more explicable if we turn our attention to this homosexual subplot and away from the heterosexual union with which the narrative ends, and which is, after all, the conventional conclusion of the *Bildungsroman* as genre.[17] As evidence that the homosexual elements of the novel were in fact recognized as such by contemporary readers, Martha Helfer cites an anonymous satire that appeared soon after its publication, which claimed that Schlegel had mingled "sparks of swinishness with the steaminess of the Greeks" (Helfer, " 'Confessions of an Improper Man,' " in this volume; *KA* 5:L).

Julius himself has the indeterminate marmoreal beauty of Winckelmann's sculptures (*KA* 5:55; Firchow 100). Beyond this, the novel reveals that Julius's early, and troubled, erotic encounters with women are punctuated with passionate friendships with men — significantly, it is the latter form of relationship that is described as "divine" (*KA* 5:45; Firchow 88). With one male friend Julius found "more than feminine consideration and delicacy of feeling combined with a sublime intelligence and a firm, cultivated character" (*KA* 5:45; Firchow 88). With another, however, "friendship had become strained and almost coarse [*gemein*]. It had been completely spiritual at first and should have remained so" (*KA* 5:46; Firchow 90). Yet these tumultuous relationships, which lead Julius to a mental state bordering on madness, are ultimately unsatisfactory because of their transitory, irrational, and unsociable nature: as the novel makes clear, true happiness for Julius is to be found in a relationship of domesticized heterosexual complementarity. One of the final sections of the novel, at first glance an irritating and digressive letter to a male friend, Antonio, in fact ironically signals the irretrievable breakdown of a male-male relationship as the affair with Lucinde reaches its apotheosis and heterosexual union is reaffirmed. The irony is further intensified, I would argue, when Julius chooses this epistolary forum in order to express his ideal of friendship, in overtly androgynous terms: "a wonderful symmetry," "this beautiful mysticism" (*KA* 5:77; Firchow 125). A powerful subtext in Schlegel's *Lucinde*, then, is its depiction of male homosexuality as a seductive but perilous phase in the hero's erotic *Bildung*, a phase that is domesticated in favor of the relationship with a woman, and a woman who is also, and importantly, a mother. In doing so, the novel follows the developmental account of homosexuality and heterosexuality traced out by Aristophanes in the *Symposium*, a text well known to Schlegel and one with which he was particularly preoccupied as he came to write his novel (*KA* 24:244; cited by Helfer).

The final rigidity of an androgynous model that might seem to offer free flow is apparent in the section of the novel entitled "A Reflection" ("Eine Reflexion"). Here, Schlegel broadens the vision of androgynous union symbolically, glorifying nature as an entity fueled by the combination and recombination of sexual dualities. Here, too, Julius finally posits woman as the mysterious and unknowable other. What we have learned of Lucinde as an individual is that she functions as a blank mirror to Julius's gaze (e.g., *KA* 5:10; Firchow 46).[18] In a sense, Lucinde can be viewed as a double of the languorous, statuesque beauty who holds Julius enthralled in the "Apprenticeship for Manhood," and who is famed for her erotic arts. However, rather than turning marble into life, the classical aesthetic move that Julius suggests is possible in "Metamorphosen" (*KA* 5:61; Firchow 106), this androgynous desire actually enacts petrification: both the courtesan, described at the center of the novel in her eternally fixed boudoir pose, and her marmoreal twin, the strangely lifeless Lucinde, ultimately function as passive stages along a male trajectory of *Bildung*.[19] What, then, are the implications for the aesthetics of androgynous chaos proposed by Schlegel's novel? Julius expressed his desire to create a "charming confusion" precisely as an antidote to one potential literary outcome of his heterosexual love story, that it become "insufferably unified and monotonous" (*eine unerträgliche Einheit und Einerleiheit, KA* 5:9; Firchow 45). Androgyny, then, as this passage predicts, may indeed function as the absolute antithesis to a nomadic sexuality and a nomadic aesthetic.

Kleist: Androgynous Equivocation

> "As far as I know, in nature there is but
> Force and resistance, no third thing [*nichts Drittes*]."
> —Odysseus, *Penthesilea*, Kleist 1:326, lines 125–26)

As the letters of Heinrich von Kleist show, the coexistence of two competing versions of the androgynous myth—polymorphous eroticism versus heterosexual marriage — powerfully underscores the stabilizing and destabilizing effects of androgynous desire, as well as the precarious nature of sexual identity itself.[20] Kleist's complex rhetoric of sexuality and gender is deployed in what seems to be a strange double-dealing project of simultaneously constructing and disrupting binaristic gender categories. I will be proposing that his creative fascination with androgynous or "amphibian" sexuality is for Kleist a refraction of his own sexuality, which, as much recent research has shown, fits only uneasily within the heterosexual, polar norm propagated at the close of the eighteenth century and, more specifically, within the codified homosocial environment of the Prussian officer class.

In Kleist's relentlessly pedagogical letters and "mental exercises" (*Denkübungen*) to his fiancée, Wilhelmine von Zenge, as well as to his sister Ulrike, he frequently alludes approvingly to the supplemental model of androgyny that had become a convention of literature and aesthetics of the period: that is, woman is conceived of as complementary to man, with the heterosexual union privileged and naturalized as a moment of totality. The quintessential example of such an androgynous bride is of course Goethe's Natalie, fiancée of Wilhelm Meister, aptly referred to by her brother as "the supplement to someone's existence" (*HA* 7:565). Kleist's letter to Ulrike of May 1799 could serve here as one example among many, with Kleist outlining the supplementary nature of woman's relationship with man: woman, this letter insists, occupies a secondary place in the human order, and her supreme destiny is as helpmeet to a man, and as mother (2:486–93). In the same letter, Kleist sets out his own social role in complementary terms, as husband and father. Throughout these letters, the emphasis is on *Bildung*: we read of their author's desire "to fashion a wife" (2:564–65), of his bride as a still formless "mass" which he will sculpt into a perfect being (2:576). Kleist, intoning the word "purpose" (*Zweck*), reserves his sternest words for those individuals who lack a life plan and who luxuriate in a state of existence "without a determinate goal [*ohne feste Bestimmung*], always oscillating between uncertain desires" (2:490). What I want to emphasize here is the antipathy expressed by Kleist toward fluctuation, a lack of firm contours, unclassifiable desires, the flouting of social expectations.

More interesting, in the context of my present argument, than

the well-worn reformulations of supplemental Romantic androgyny, are Kleist's descriptions of his sister Ulrike, a stubborn refuser
both of "life plan" and of conventional sex roles, and the only one of
Kleist's sisters to remain unmarried. In fact, Ulrike's tenacious resistance to the form of gender pedagogy being purveyed by her
brother is censured by him as a criminal offense (*strafbar, ver-
brecherisch*, 2:492). Ulrike von Kleist, it is well known, displayed a
predilection for transvestism and the freedoms it afforded, attending
lectures at Leipzig University, roaming the streets of Paris, and even
visiting the writer Wieland in male dress (Borchardt 201). Indeed,
Kleist sees in Ulrike's passion for travel the expression of her nomadic subjectivity and the obstacle to her supreme calling (*höchste
Bestimmung*), marriage (2:492). In more than one letter Kleist refers
to the heroic spirit of this unsettlingly mannish woman: "She is a
woman with the soul of a hero, but she has nothing of her own sex
except for her hips" (2:664). On two occasions Kleist uses a striking
zoological analogy to refer to Ulrike's anomalous hybrid sexuality: a
New Year's greeting of 1800 implores an amphibian Ulrike with
classificatory zeal to leave the water, element of mutable androgynous desire, and to acquire a unified, coherent gender identity, "a
definite sex" (*ein sicheres Geschlecht*, 1:44). And in a letter to Adolf-
ine von Werdeck, Kleist describes his sister again as a freak of nature: "What an error [*Mißgriff*] nature committed when it fashioned
a creature that is neither man nor woman, and that hovers between
two species [*Gattungen*] like an amphibian" (2:676).[21] Like the term
"androgyny," the zoological taxonomy "amphibian" connotes dual-
ism, "having a double life." Kleist's rhetorical use of the term also
entails a form of double-dealing. The image of the amphibian, the
creature who leads a double life between water and land and who
mutates morphologically at various developmental stages, could not
be further from the supplemental, strictly heterosexual version of
androgyny that informs Kleist's pedagogical efforts. Rather than an
incarnation of harmony, Ulrike represents unresolvable contradictions (*Widersprüche*, 2:489), leading the duplicitous double life that
gives the amphibian its name. Androgyny serves in these letters,
then, also in a duplicitous manner, both as a regulatory and as a
destabilizing discourse. Not even human (*ein Wesen*), Ulrike-as-
amphibian is for Kleist unsettling, if not monstrous, precisely because she shows no sign of evolving toward the "correct" sexual

form, unambiguous femininity. In a related move, Ulrike is situated by Kleist in a watery, unconscious, undifferentiated state, explicitly a less evolved being: "I find you undecided [*unentschieden*], where you should long since be decided, I find you slumbering, where you should long since be awake" (2:488).

Other traces of this unruly story of nomadic androgyny are present in Kleist's correspondence, but they pertain to his own homoerotic desires and, significantly, are not freighted with the negativity contained in references to Ulrike's fluid sexuality. If critics have tended to stress Kleist's notorious "Kant-crisis" of 1801 as the catalyst for his artistic creativity, it is equally valid to view his troubled Würzburg journey in 1800, the confrontation with his own sexual identity, as the pivotal moment (on the journey, see Politzer). Despite a general cultural reformulation of the Platonic myth in exclusively heterosexual terms, Kleist's tendency to apply the vocabulary of androgyny to male friendships indicates that it still circulates, as it had with Winckelmann, as a code for the love between men. In this volume, Simon Richter alludes to the fact that passages from Winckelmann's Belvedere Apollo descriptions were included in love letters between men after Winckelmann's death, thus reinforcing the idea of androgyny as an eroticized homoerotic code ("Winckelmann's Progeny"). The subject of androgynous citation clearly merits further attention.[22] When Kleist describes his friend Brockes to his fiancée, Wilhelmine von Zenge, in a letter of January 1801, he dwells on the fluidity of his personality, his feminine, childlike characteristics, his antipathy to cold rationality, and he situates him in that undifferentiated, androgynous phase between childhood and adulthood (2:619–21). Indeed, he goes so far as to present Brockes to Wilhelmine as a model to be emulated in her one-sidedly "feminine" *Bildung*: ironically, it is a man who most perfectly incarnates womanly, if not wifely, virtue, in that he sacrifices himself completely to the needs of his beloved. "I want to bring out only the most characteristic aspect of his personality — that was his *selflessness*. My dear Wilhelmine! Have you been attentive to yourself and others? Do you know what it means to be *completely selfless*? And do you know what it means *always* to be selfless, and in your *innermost* heart, and *joyfully*?" (2:621).

Quite contrary to the de-eroticized image of heterosexual union, the language of androgyny, in letters between men, is often highly eroticized, even aphrodisiac. This is readily apparent in Kleist's well-known letter of January 1805 to his friend Ernst von Pfuel, with whom he had traveled and shared lodgings and who, significantly, was an inspiration in the writing of Kleist's drama of gender insurgence, *Penthesilea*. The letter mirrors the concern with *Bildung* expressed so relentlessly in Kleist's letters to his fiancée; but here, Kleist expresses his love of the perfectly mutual *Ausbildung* ("formation") experienced with his friend. Clearly signaling the homoerotic subtext with its multiple references to Greek antiquity, and to its author as a Winckelmannian spectator of a nude male form emerging from the watery androgynous realm, Kleist writes that Pfuel has blurred the boundaries between masculine and feminine, between past and present, recreating the world of the Greeks in Kleist's heart: "When you were stepping into the lake at Thun, I often gazed at your body with truly *girlish* feelings. You really could be an artist's model. If I had been an artist, I might perhaps have conceived through your body [*durch ihn empfangen*] the idea of a god" (2:749).[23] Now, Kleist writes, he understands the lawgiver Lycurgus of Sparta, whose state, with its emphasis on the gymnasium, was premised on the love between men. The love letter to Pfuel, a privileged space of ambiguity, concludes with a repudiation of marriage, the conventional context of androgyny, and with the exhortation to Pfuel to "be my wife, my children and grandchildren" (*sei Du die Frau mir, die Kinder, und die Enkel!* 2:750). Thus, Kleist imaginatively subverts the stable subject positions of the bourgeois family and opens them up to a nomadic, androgynous sexuality, multiplying the other into others and breaking with classification. Characteristic of this gender nomadism is its rhetorical gaming, its foundation in aesthetics and linguistic artifice. What could be further from Kleist's own self-stylization in letters of 1801 and 1802 to Wilhelmine and Ulrike as the stolid Swiss paterfamilias firmly possessed of a house, a wife, and freedom?

Furthermore, as is already indicated in the quotations from the letter to Pfuel, in which he speaks of artistic creativity from the biological point of view of a female "conception" (*empfangen*), Kleist defines his own poetic work from a transsexual, feminized perspective: the normative procreative sexuality he urges upon Ulrike is displaced by the aesthetic fertility of the male artist. It is important to bear in mind in this context that the binary biological terms "fertilisation" (*zeugen*) and "conception" (*empfangen*) had entered the realm of aesthetics in essays such as von Humboldt's to define the polarized operations of the masculine and feminine imagination. In a letter to Wilhelmine of October 1801, Kleist describes his writing as "a love child," protected within a holy womblike "vault," like the child of a vestal virgin (2:694). In this letter, Wilhelmine, the passionless bride whose highest calling must be maternity rather than eros (2:577), is led by Kleist to a secret birth-scene: it is the site of an aesthetic of androgyny, supremely artificial, and, in its nostalgic allusion to Greece, locus of homoerotic desire. The poetic child born here is, however, socially stigmatized, a bastard (to use Kleist's own word) or hybrid (2:694). Here androgyny is a fiction of displaced origins and generative aesthetic play. The paradox, as one critic recently formulated it, is that this is a form of bisexual creativity, on the one hand both sacred and desired and yet on the other hand antisocial, forbidden, and repudiated (vestal virgins, to take up Kleist's analogy, could be condemned to death for such a sexual offense).[24] But only a few sentences after this astonishing feminized image of artistic conception, Kleist abandons the vision of art in favor of his patriarchal Swiss farming utopia, now declaring the *fathering* of a (human) child as the will of nature: "A person can do nothing more pleasing in the eyes of God than to cultivate a field, plant a tree, and beget a child [*ein Kind zeugen*]" (2:694).

Kleist, like Schlegel and Winckelmann, engages in the radical desubstantialization of apparently stable sexual identities. As Joachim Pfeiffer shows in his essay "Friendship and Gender" in this volume, it is possible to view Kleist's poetic and epistolary writing as an imaginary space permitting the disruption of binaristic gender categories. The shifting representational ground that results from this experimentation is, as I have been arguing throughout, characteristic of the fate of double-lived androgyny, which in Kleist's letters functions both in a didactic/coercive and in a transgressive direction. Actualized as an equivocal, sensual compound, the figure of the androgyne evokes monstrosity (in the case of the amphibian Ulrike) and a nomadic aestheticism (in the case of male homoeroticism), in both cases denaturalizing binaristic heterosexual norms and provoking gender trouble.[25] But it is important to recognize that even such apparently subversive, nomadic moments as those contained in Kleist's letters or in Schlegel's *Bildungsroman* are shadowed, if not overshadowed, by androgynous discourse that actually serves in a regulatory manner to inscribe binaristic codes and to naturalize the proper unity between love and marriage. In the ultimate equivocation, the androgyne figures as both the nomadic, unnatural "other" of heterosexuality and, in its incarnation as a static model of integrational thought, the symbolic affirmation of supplemental heterosexuality and marriage.

Joachim Pfeiffer

Friendship and Gender: The Aesthetic Construction of Subjectivity in Kleist

On January 7, 1805, Heinrich von Kleist wrote a letter to one of his closest friends, Ernst von Pfuel. Kleist had undertaken several trips with Pfuel, lived with him in Paris, moved into an apartment in Dresden with him, and conceived *Penthesilea* while thinking of him. The letter is a document of an emphatically passionate friendship. Reflecting on their days together, Kleist emphasizes the highly constructive value of this friendship: "In those days we loved in each other the highest in humanity; for we loved the complete cultivation of our natures" (2:749). This "lovely enthusiasm of friendship" (2:749) is a part of that cult of friendship that emerged in the eighteenth century, reaching its high point in the middle of the century and remaining perceptible far into the nineteenth century (Tenbruck 436). It probably has roots in the early Enlightenment philosophies of virtue and happiness from circa 1700 (Barner 23) and represents an important element in the developing self-understanding of the bourgeoisie. The cult of friendship is also related to the tradition of sentimentality and Storm and Stress, which can be understood as critical correctives to the rationalist side of the Enlightenment. The new emphatic, emotional grounding of subjectivity finds in the cult of friendship both an expression of itself and a budding need for community — indeed, some scholars see in the emphatic friendship of the eighteenth century a "utopia of bourgeois community" (Meyer-Krentler 20).

Kleist demonstrates his solidarity with the teleological thinking of the Enlightenment when he refers to "the complete cultivation"

Translated by Robert D. Tobin.

(*die ganze Ausbildung*) that emerged from the relationship between the two men. He thus makes clear the educational aspects (that is, those related to *Bildung*) of the cult of friendship. The early letters of Kleist are also permeated with enlightened concepts in which the goal of a virtuous life merges with the goal of happiness — at first, virtue and happiness construct the pillars of Kleist's enlightened tele-ology: "happiness as encouragement to virtue, virtue as the way to happiness" (letter to Kleist's teacher Martini, March 1799; 2:475).

At the same time, however, a disquiet, a feeling of latent threat, manifests itself at the beginning of the letter to Pfuel — an almost magical power seems to dwell within the exchange of friendly glances, a terror hangs over the image in which the subject recognizes itself in the eye of the friend: "With your eloquence, you exercise, you good dear youth, a strange power over my heart, and, whether I myself have given you the same insight into my condition, nonetheless you occasionally move my image so close before my soul that I start, as before the latest appearances of the world" (2:748–49). As the letter progresses, an erotic attraction, which redirects the love between the souls in the direction of a passion between bodies, joins the "lovely enthusiasm of friendship":

I could have slept with you, you dear boy; my entire soul embraced you! I have often observed your beautiful body with truly *girlish* feelings, when you, before my eyes, entered the lake in Thun. It could truly serve an artist as a study. . . . The entire legislation of Lycurgus, and his concept of the love of youths, has become clear to me through the feelings that you have awakened in me. Come to me! (2:749)

Here the sentimental style of writing seems to turn into homosexual desire, an impression that is strengthened by the subsequent passage, in which the letter writer offers his friend a new model of life — together as man and wife: "Go with me to Anspach and let us enjoy sweet friendship. . . . I will never marry, you be my wife, my children, my grandchildren!" (2:750). Immediately, the urgent, almost imperative request follows: "Accept my suggestion. If you don't, I'll feel that no one in the world loves me. I would like to say more to you, but it isn't suitable for a letter" (2:750). The letter ends in the trope of secrecy and silence — a typical gesture for Kleist, for whom writing's mediated nature makes it so unfit for communication between people that it should be replaced by the materiality of voiced sounds or even the body itself, as he suggests in a letter to his sister Ulrike: "I wish I could rip my heart out of my body, pack it in this letter, and send it to you" (2:730).

Are such passages in letters proof of the homosexuality of their author? The claim has often been made, particularly in psychological and biographical interpretations. Isidor Sadger writes in 1910 that such sentences are "indubitable" evidence for Kleist's homosexual feelings. In 1954, Fritz Wittels also refers to the letter of January 7, 1805, first cautiously pointing out the differing characteristics of sentimental letter-writing ("we are told that the style of letter-writing in his era was different from ours") but then adding: "At least one letter . . . cannot be considered other than a homosexual love letter" — whereupon he cites the letter to Pfuel (20). Lilian Hoverland also writes in an essay on the "openly homosexual letter to Ernst von Pfuel" (67). In a recent work, Gerhard Weinholz is of the opinion that Kleist's homosexuality results "directly" from his letters (206).

We must be very reluctant to come to such conclusions. They are problematic especially because they understand Kleist's letters as unmediated documents of his life history. They misjudge the highly aesthetic status of many of Kleist's letters, and they understand homosexuality essentially, attributing a specific sexual identity to the author, resubstantializing concepts of identity that Kleist had just desubstantialized. Michel Foucault's works have shown that sexuality has no ontological status, but rather always functions as a societal construct, the order (or disorder) of which is inscribed by linguistic codes. This heteronymy continues even in the modern tolerance toward gays: enlightened knowledge produced the type of the "homosexual." In this scientific mania for classification, the terrain is staked out in which the homosexual exists. The multifarious, incommensurable aspects of an individual experience are leveled out in the societal offers of tolerance, because these offers are often only a positive variation of the pathologization with which the nineteenth century gained classificatory control of the homosexual. In this vein Gert Mattenklott asked, in his dialogue with Paul Derks, whether the enlightened desire of gays for societal legitimation was not "an exact complement of their oppression, a formulation of their unfree condition, at every time threatened by the revocation of the concession" (95).

In more recent gender studies, too, there is a tendency to replace essentialist with constructivist concepts. Queer theory should not expand binary construction of sexuality with a third mode ("the third sex"), but rather it should attack fixed gender stereotypes that have developed traditionally. Klaus Theweleit has demonstrated with many examples how the societal production of "male phantasies" in symbols and language has become fixed, and other authors have pointed to the great importance that "stereotypes of masculinity" have had for the psychological integration of men in society and the continuity of social systems (Gilmore). This explains the strong societal proscription of every behavior deviating from stereotypical masculinity. (In German, the word *Schlappschwanz*, with its suggestion of impotence, is a widespread pejorative term, while *weibisch* conveys a high degree of contempt — compare English "pussy-whipped," which implies an "unnatural" victory of female genitalia over male genitalia, and "effeminate," which, when applied to men, is usually negative.) Stereotypes of masculinity have become recurrent myths of occidental culture; the development of "a school of masculinity" in American literature — from Hemingway and Mailer to Stone — is only one example of this.

The discourse of sentimental friendship is therefore of special interest, because it is here, in this fertile ground, that the fixed images of masculinity are disrupted and a gay sensibility can manifest itself linguistically, without being forced to define itself as such. The androgynous visions of Romantic authors are unthinkable without the discourse of sentimental friendship. Moreover, the initial separation between friendship and sensual love gives way to an increasing convergence of the two; the emphatic, passionate content of the sentimental friendship alone makes it difficult to draw a "reasonable" boundary between the categories. As early as 1759, Klopstock has Aristus in *Conversations on Happiness* (*Gespräche von der Glückseligkeit*) say: "Friendship and love are basically one and the same. Whoever distinguishes them a little is not wrong; whoever distinguishes them too much, however, knows neither of them" (961). This careful and simultaneously vague formulation provides evidence for the permeable boundary between friendship and love; increasingly, even the sensual, corporeal components are not excluded, at least in principle (Mauser). Precisely this conceptual uncertainty had to encourage authors to articulate even unconventional feelings in this zone of imperceptible transitions.

Similarly, it is surprising to modern readers of Jean Paul how passionately Siebenkäs and Leibgeber embrace each other, how openly Siebenkäs describes his friend as "Beloved," and how clearly their stormy reunion contains traces of a bodily unification: "Storming up the stairs — breaking through the triumphal gates — falling onto the beloved heart . . . everything was one. . . . They lay clinging to each other," the narrator of *Siebenkäs* informs the reader, "embracing and embraced" (1:713).[1] In the afternoon they go to the "greening pleasure grounds of the hermitage" (1:717), a "locus amoenus" for lovers, which reminds the reader of the earlier passage in the novel, in which Leibgeber is compared with the "Morlacks," who "marry their [male] friends and are blessed at the altar" (1:496). It is owing, undoubtedly, to the tradition of sentimental friendship that these texts could be published without scandal. The astonishingly broad ambiguity of masculine feelings of this era can be seen in both Kleist's letters and Jean Paul's *Siebenkäs*.[2] Who could give the exact boundary between eros and caritas, between friendship and love, when Kleist sings an encomium of his friend Brockes and thereby describes the delicate corporeal proximity that he and his friend enjoyed at night — all in a letter to his fiancée, whom he meets more aloofly: "When I sometimes at night fell asleep on his breast, he held me without sleeping himself" (January 31, 1801; 2:623)?

Kleist seems to transfer the undefined free space of sentiment, a space which the discourse of friendship opened for him, into the undefined realm of his imaginative world. His texts resist classifications: they replace concepts with overdetermined images, and conceptual definitions are undermined by overextravagant metaphors. The symbolic orders, through which language is determined, are subverted by imaginary stagings. Interpretations that force a sexual order onto the letter to Pfuel ignore Kleist's attempts to play with identities and essences in experimental literary formations. In the imaginary, he dissolves these identities and essences, attempts previously unimagined forms of love, even fantasizes marriages between men. Although he invents bold metaphors, however, he aesthetically discards again and again all of his constructions (Pfeiffer 29–36) — frequently with suggestions of anxiety, in a literary sphere of disquiet, in catastrophic images. Thus, in a letter to his friend Rühle (late November 1805), Kleist uses unusual images to express the degree of mutual attraction as well as his disappointment that a permanent nearness is scarcely possible. "Why can't we always be together?" is his first plea — and then a comparison follows in which the rules of attraction and rejection that can be observed in chemical reactions are applied to the structure of human relationships. Thus Kleist anticipates the experiment of the "chemical metaphor" that Goethe would carry out four years later in his *Elective Affinities* (*Wahlverwandtschaften*), but here it takes place in a negative reversal: "I wish I were an acid or an alkali. Then there would be an end, when I was separated from the salt" (2:759). Behind the resigned wish for chemical rejection hides the opposite image: the power of a "chemical" attraction, the unrealizability of which is the occasion for constant suffering.

Karl-Heinz Bohrer has shown in an interesting study on the romantic letter (*Der romantische Brief*) that Kleist's letters increasingly diverge from the enlightened rationality that attributes an autonomous status to the subject. The "aesthetic subjectivity" that emerges in Kleist's letters cannot be described in the categories of a social, bourgeois identity. It does not obey the traditional autobiographical rules of "authenticity" and subjective self-construction. The *autobiographical* "I" wants to achieve itself or defend itself against attacks on its identity; in the final analysis, it strives for its salvation, even when it reveals itself unsparingly in confessional rituals. The radicality of self-portrayal in Rousseau, for instance, serves a deeper truth of the self, which must be defended against all societal attacks and challenges. The literary subjects in Karl Philipp Moritz or Lenz also aim at self-preservation, orient themselves toward the ideal of social identity, and claim this identity especially when it is experienced as endangered or defeated. The "aesthetic subject" in Kleist's letters, in contrast, puts itself on the line; it is ready to lose its identity by dissolving it in aesthetic projects and unconventionally inventing it anew. Maurice Blanchot has defended such radicality as "literature and the right to death."

Kleist's literary and aesthetic deconstruction of identity is of course in no way free of the effort to anchor these subjects in traditions, even literary ones. The "subject's constitution in language" is to be understood as an ambivalent double-movement in which the process of subject formation is both supported and disrupted, as shown by Cullens and Mücke, who use the examples of *Penthesilea* and *Käthchen* (461–93). Alongside Kleist's increasing skepticism with regard to enlightened concepts of reason and the ever more powerful entrance of experiences of contingency and discontinuity, a simultaneous attempt emerges in Kleist's letters to anchor a world that has gone out of joint in literary and aesthetic traditions.

To the literary shape of Kleist's letter to Pfuel belongs the thickness of intertextual references that bind the daring proposals for a different life ("you be my wife") to literary and historical models. The letter contains a series of literary allusions that use cultural authorities to attempt to validate the exaltation of feelings. Klopstock is cited first: "I shall never forget that festive night when, in the worst hole-in-the-wall in France, you scolded me in a truly sublime way, almost as the archangel did to his fallen brother in the *Messiah*" (2:749). This allusion to Klopstock's *Messiah* refers to the thirteenth song, in which the archangel Gabriel has a dialogue with his "fallen brother," Satan. Kleist thereby evokes a poetic form (considered revolutionary by his contemporaries) in which sentimentality was finally helped to achieve its breakthrough against Gottsched's strict, rule-oriented poetics. An emotional agitation that dissolves metric restrictions into free rhythms often permeates Klopstock's poetry. It is no coincidence that Werther and Lotte cite Klopstock in the affectively charged scene of their "unregulated" love affair.

The next literary allusion is to Shakespeare: "What shall I, beloved Pfuel, do with all these tears? To pass the time as they fall every minute, I would like to dig a tomb, like that naked King Richard, in order to lower into it you and me and our unending pain" (2:749).[3] Deep pain stylized in the characteristic poetic manner of a great Shakespearean tragedy: that Kleist here, unlike Shakespeare, unclothes King Richard may be an unconscious attempt at eroticization — or simply a mistake. Nonetheless, in Shakespeare and Klopstock, Kleist appeals to the unconventional guarantors of great literary traditions with the help of which sentimentality and Storm and Stress revolutionized classicist poetics.

Kleist proceeds similarly in the passage of the letter described as "openly homosexual": it, too, is embedded in references to intertextual tradition. "You recreated the age of the Greeks in my heart" (2:749), he writes and thereby places himself in a certain tradition of understanding classical antiquity, the tradition of, for instance, Winckelmann. But Kleist's letter becomes more precise when he refers to the legislation of Lycurgus and hence provides a historical justification for his desire to live together with Pfuel: "The entire legislation of Lycurgus, and his concept of the love of youths, has become clear to me through the feelings which you have awakened in me" (2:749). One can read in encyclopedias that, according to Spartan legislation, as whose father Lycurgus is seen, the Spartans were supposed to live together in a "perfect community of men" (*Pauly* 27/2, col. 1382). The educational system was strictly structured and built upon two pillars: gymnastics and pederasty. The ideal of gymnastic education corresponds with Pfuel's desire to introduce athletic exercises for the physical education of his regimental comrades — an idea that the officers, Prussian Junkers, rejected (Streller 4:588).

This attempt at the embedding of texts in literary traditions is typical for almost all Kleistean texts — in *Penthesilea* there are countless passages that refer to ancient sources and are thereby simultaneously legitimized. Behind this cover, Kleist then carries out incredible mental and aesthetic experiments; one has the impression that these intertextual references represent a counterbalance to the boldness with which he dissolves conventions and constructs experimental formations. This explains the high degree of literary stylization in his letters: the literary "placement" of the untimely quality of his writing, thinking, and life. The unconventional life model that he emphatically suggests to his friend Pfuel is also to be understood in this sense: it cannot be captured with the concept of social or sexual identity, but rather offers imaginative proposals as alternatives to social constructions of identity.

Behind this tendency to replace social subjectivity with an aesthetically constructed subjectivity stands an experience of social homelessness that is very recognizable quite early in the letters. This experience has found its way into the title of Christa Wolf's novel about Kleist and Günderrode: *No Place on Earth* (*Kein Ort. Nirgends*). All preexistent models of socialization, all models of societal subject foundation, were problematic for Kleist: officer, scholar, civil servant, husband, and father — what remained for him was literature, which allowed him an imaginary liquefaction of such identities. This avoidance of the expected male role is all the more remarkable because Kleist grew up in a family tradition shaped by a military, heroic ideal of masculinity: by the end of the eighteenth century, his family had produced eighteen Prussian generals (Apel 8)! Kleist, however, leaves the army, tries life as a scholar, flees into a civilian profession, he travels, goes to France, wants to die in battle, then he wants to become a farmer in Switzerland, and finally returns to Germany. He calls off his engagement to Wilhelmine von Zenge, to whom he has been writing letters without any passion.

Already in an early letter, from November 12, 1799, Kleist complains to his sister not only about the difficulties of intersubjective understanding but also about the foundational traumatic experience of finding *no place* in society — the experience of a far-reaching alienation and homelessness. Kleist writes that, while "a thousand bonds connect people with each other," he is unable to interrelate with humanity, particularly because his interests do not coincide with theirs. Because his attempts to bridge the gap have not been successful, he has turned inward, locking his secrets up "in the innermost recesses of my heart forever." This experience of isolation has caused sudden attacks of "anxiety" and "apprehensiveness" (2:496). This decisive denial of the enlightened ideal of intersubjectivity of thought and the rejection of societal integration (and therefore also of the assumption of social roles and sexual attributes) have literary consequences that are strengthened by the catastrophic experience of the Kant crisis in 1801: the experience of contingency, the relinquishing of the Enlightenment's truth postulate, the experience of a specific displacement give Kleistean texts an original tone that subsequently produces their incomparability and modernity.

It is conspicuous that a similar foundational experience predominates in contemporary texts of gay literature and has manifested itself in analogous textual structures. The "primal anxiety" of the homosexual is falling out of all identity-creating societal referents — the anxiety of groundlessness outside all norms and practices. Tomas Vollhaber and Dirck Linck have in recent times described such experiences and in particular analyzed the aesthetic constructions of Hubert Fichte and the Austrian Josef Winkler. In contrast to the "literature of authenticity" written by gay authors in the 1970s, such writing is no longer concerned with the representation of the arduous fight of gay figures for a place in society, for societal recognition. In the place of autobiographical, mimetic literature steps another, which, like Sade, undermines the discursive orders of society. The exclusion from the symbolic order of the genders, the stigma, does not lead to an attempt at literary emancipation, but rather to a contra-phobic writing, to the blasphemous outbidding and destruction of reality. Through this aesthetic subversion of the symbolic, a new freedom offers itself to the writer: through rituals of destruction the writing "I" disempowers that reality through which it is destroyed. The threatened identity does not save itself through integration, but celebrates literarily the homelessness to which it has been damned. Such a literature is not autobiographical and emancipatory, but rather imaginative, excessive, blasphemous. The affects that have become homeless, including the denounced sexual ones, invest their energy in emotionally inflamed metaphors, in metaphorical violence, in excesses of the imagination. Precisely this "aesthetic mode" creates a radicalization that would not be possible in mimetic, naturalist literature.

In Kleist, textual structures and poetic procedures are manifested that are analogous to those found in more recent authors. Hans Mayer's observation that the homosexual outsider in nineteenth-century bourgeois society is only imaginable as an "aesthetic existence" (262) dovetails with the description of "aesthetic subjectivity" in Kleist's letter.

In their essay, Cullens and Mücke go in some detail into the Kleistean imagology, into the world of images that at times undermines the symbolic order; the authors try "to set in relief how Kleist's plays question the ideals of 'personhood,' hermeneutics, the 'natural' unity of heterosexual love and marriage, and the possibility of a utopian retreat to preverbal communication" (463). It is certainly accurate that the world of images of the Kleistean plays is not unconditionally able to subvert the symbolic order of a patriarchal world (this is true above all for *Käthchen of Heilbronn*). This failure is one more symptom of the aporetic structure of Kleist's literary worlds. In *Family Schroffenstein* (*Familie Schroffenstein*), for instance, the device of switching genders fails. The transformation takes place in a cave, beyond the world of paternal power. Ottokar hopes to fool the murderous paternal world with sexual travesty, saying to Agnes:

> If I place this helmet upon your locks,
> I make women also my rivals.

> Drück ich dir noch den Helm auf deine Locken,
> Mach' ich auch Weiber mir zu Nebenbuhlern. (lines 2501–2)

But the ruse goes awry. The gender switch does not put the world of patriarchal order into question; instead it retains the ideas of identity that are inscribed into the subject. The role-play switches the gender identities, but does not subvert their order. Similarly, the trick of Achilles, laying down his weapons — the symbolic attributes of his manhood — and submitting to Penthesilea in an "unmanly" way, goes wrong: He wants, "as though vanquished, to lay himself down at her tiny feet" (*als ein Überwundener, Zu ihren kleinen Füßen niederlegen*, lines 2493–94) — but only "for a moon," "for one or two, not more" (*Auf einen Mond nur, . . . Auf einen oder zwei, mehr nicht*, lines 2474, 2476). The attempt to lay down temporarily the masculine gender role changes nothing in the violence that dominates in patriarchal systems; this is true even when women take on this power.

The motif of gender-role switches is a common one in the Age of Goethe — in Achim von Arnim's work it returns almost stereotypically (Wingertszahn 372). Arnim's short story of 1824, "The Disguises of the French Tutor and His German Pupil" ("Die Verkleidungen des französischen Hofmeisters und seines deutschen Zöglings"), contains a paradigmatic clothing-exchange scene. Such play is carried further in Friedrich Schlegel's *Lucinde*: clothing exchange is praised here as "dithyrambic phantasy," as an "allegory of the completion of the masculine and the feminine to full, complete humanity" (*KA* 5:13). But here too the androgynous fantasy stands in service of a desire for wholeness that hopes to find its fulfillment in the reciprocal completion of heterosexual lovers. The sexual travesty in Kleist's verse idyll "The Scare in the Bath" ("Der Schrecken im Bade") reveals itself in the end as a joke: Johanna, disguised as Fritz, observes the naked Margarete in the bath and contributes to her boundless confusion — until the deceived lady notices the error:

> It's Johanna, the maid, in Fritz's clothes!
> And makes, hidden in the lilac bush,
> With Fritz's raw male voice, a fool of me!
>
> Johanna ists, die Magd, in Fritzens Röcken!
> Und äfft, in eines Flieders Busch gesteckt,
> Mit Fritzens rauher Männerstimme mich! (1:19)

Very early, Kleist seems to have recognized that societal identity consists of constructed roles that one can analyze, parody, but not necessarily break through. He writes on February 5, 1801, to Ulrike: "The necessity to play a role, and an internal aversion to that, make all society tiresome for me" (2:628). All roles, including gender roles, are societal attributes—leaving the world of the symbolic order (the sign system) behind is only possible as a desire, in a tireless race of language against itself. He repeatedly expresses desires to rip thoughts or even his very heart out of his breast (2:347, 730). The physicality of these images indicates his belief that "language, rhythm, harmony . . . as beautiful as they may be, insofar as they cloak spirit, . . . are . . . nothing but a real, although natural and necessary evil" (2:347). It is, Kleist continues, art's task to make these linguistic elements disappear. The image of nakedness that Kleist proposes in the cave scene of *Family Schroffenstein* also functions as the breakthrough of societal sign systems: Ottokar undresses Agnes so that the naked bodies, without the "foreign shell" of clothing (line 2485), can speak for themselves, for everything beautiful "needs no other veil than its own" (lines 2489–90). But the "movement without moderation or order" (line 2483), in which sexual desire attempts to assert itself as nature against culture, is itself only imagination: a fiction within fiction, a dream of the world of paternal power. The wedding night is directed and stage-managed. A piece of literature. A dream, what else?

Only in such imaginative pictures, characterized as such, does a breakthrough of sexual stereotypes take place in Kleist's literary world. In the fantastic world of the dream, Count Wetter vom Strahl, in the "elderberry bush scene" of *Käthchen*, discovers his gentle, girlish feelings: "When I see her lying there so, the entire sensibility of women comes over me and makes my tears flow" (1:504). The brutal, sadistic man experiences himself as a split existence: "Now stand by me, you gods, I am doubled!" (1:509). In such images of splitting the difficulty of mediating between the sensual, sentimental tradition and the handed-down characteristics of manhood reveals itself. A similar doubling characterizes the Prince of Homburg, who, before he gets the opportunity to prove his masculinity, sits in the opening scene under an oak tree in somnambulistic immersion, "half waking, half sleeping" (1:631), lost in dream, "like a girl" (1:633).

The destruction of societal construction of sexuality thus takes place in a world of imaginary stagings that extends as far as the aesthetic construction of the letters. Because, for Kleist, all pre-given models of socialization were threatening, literature remained for him the only escape; it allowed him to place an aesthetically constructed subjectivity in the place of socially mediated identity. Herein he resembles more recent authors who, in the imaginary realm, undermine the binary codes of Western thinking, transforming them into a dreamlike, ecstatic literature. In Kleist's double suicide, the fiction of the death that he had proposed in the *Engagement in St. Domingo* (*Verlobung in St. Domingo*) has become reality. Perhaps his texts have this ability too: to prefigure a reality in which people are no longer tied down to fixed orders of subjectivity.

Susanne T. Kord

Eternal Love or Sentimental Discourse? Gender Dissonance and Women's Passionate "Friendships"

What Maggiore has found to be "an almost total obliteration of the lesbian in history" (709) doubly appertains to German scholarship, where the subject seems to be even more taboo than in the English-speaking cultures. While overall very few studies deal with lesbianism directly (Hacker; Faderman, *Surpassing* and "Female Romantic Friendship"; Göttert; Linnhoff; Friedli; and Tubach), and none do so for eighteenth-century Germany, a host of literature treats two deceptively related subjects: friendships (mostly between men) and, a recent extension of the subject, what Irigaray has aptly termed "hommosexuality" (de Lauretis 18).

Chercher la femme: Hom(m)osexuality in History and Scholarship

One reason for the conspicuous silence on the subject of lesbianism is that in most historical and philosophical discourse women were considered incapable of either friendship or homosexuality. During times when male homosexual activity was harshly punished (Rousseau and Porter 5, 105), women, lacking a penis, were deemed unable to engage in sexual activity. Whereas male homosexuality has been considered a crime since the earliest laws on the subject were established, female homosexuality remained unthinkable and for the most part went uncondemned.[1] The Bible, inspiration for much antihomosexual legislation in Western societies, employs very clear wording when dealing with male homosexuality: "If a man lies with a male as with a woman, both of them have committed an abomination; they shall be put to death, their blood is upon them" (Leviticus 20:13). For women, the Bible makes no such provision; female homosexuality is mentioned only once, and then rather vaguely and without recommendations for punishment, in a comment concerning "women [who] exchanged natural relations for unnatural" (Romans 1:26). That lesbianism is the very indirect target here must be assumed based on the rest of the sentence, an exclamation against male homosexual activity (Romans 1:27).

Whether based on biblical attitudes or not, there is strong evidence that Western antihomosexual legislation ignored lesbianism almost entirely. From biblical and Talmudic laws to the Prussian Allgemeines Landrecht of 1794, virtually all legislation governing homosexuality refers explicitly and exclusively to male homosexual activity (Tubach 44–46). Of the 44 witnesses, accessories, or direct participants in homosexual activity between 1700 and 1730 listed in the Haustein study of 1930, only one is female (Steakley 164). That one case, Catharina Linck, executed in 1721, has inspired Crompton's attempt to dispel "the myth of lesbian impunity," based on his claim that in Germany, lesbian acts, like sodomy, were punishable by death (11). Despite the theme of his article, however, the majority of executed homosexuals that he cites either were male or their gender could not be established (16–17). In the few instances where women were executed — one German woman, drowned in 1477 for "lesbian love"; two Spanish nuns, burned in the sixteenth century for using "material instruments"; two sixteenth-century Frenchwomen who disguised themselves as men (17), and Catharina Linck — it remains unclear whether they were executed for their lesbianism or for their "cross-living" and assumption of male prerogatives.[2]

Both Faderman's and Linnhoff's findings clearly suggest that in the rare cases where women were executed for crimes connected with lesbianism, their real crime was not lesbian activity but male impersonation (Faderman, *Surpassing* 52; Linnhoff 115). The few contemporary writings that specifically target lesbianism suggest a similar logic. In many cases, use of a dildo, cross-living, or other assumptions of male privileges *in connection with lesbianism* could mean the difference between life and death for the offender. Witness Antonio Gómez's differentiation (mid–sixteenth century): " 'If a woman has relations with another woman by means of any material instrument,' they must be burned. . . . 'If a woman has relations with any woman without an instrument,' a lighter penalty is permissable [*sic*]" (quoted by Crompton 19).[3] With only one possible exception, the female victims of executions cited in Crompton's study were also accused of male impersonation of some sort; the court records and contemporary reports he cites clearly place the emphasis on the women's use of "material instruments" or the "wickedness which she used to counterfeit the office of a husband" (Antonio Gómez and Henri Estienne, respectively; quoted in Crompton 17). The same holds true for the case of Catharina Linck,[4] who used several different male names, dressed as a man, served in the military, married another woman, and had sex with her using an artificial penis. She was executed in 1721; her wife, Catharina Mühlhahn, was sentenced to three years in jail and subsequent banishment, although she had, by her own admission, voluntarily engaged in sex with Linck after she discovered the true gender of her spouse (Eriksson 38–40). The court's rationale makes it abundantly clear that Linck was executed primarily for her use of a dildo (Eriksson 39), thus justifying the difference in punishment for the two women.

The fact that prejudice and legislation almost exclusively targeted homosexual men, while lesbianism *alone* was condoned or ignored, is paralleled by the philosophical discussion of homosexuality as exclusively male. Instances of "hommosexuality"[5] are evident in the often assumed synonymity of "homosexuality" with "pederasty" or even "love between men" (*mann-männliche Liebe*, Hohmann 18–19) as well as in scholarship on the subject which frequently limits its discussion to male homosexuality (G. S. Rousseau, Rousseau and Porter). In eighteenth-century scholarship, female homosexuality is as nonexistent as it was in Western legislature; relationships between women are mostly discussed under the heading of "friendship." However, the discussion of women as friends suffers from the same "phallacies" as that of women as lovers: until very recently, the discussion of friendship in German scholarly discourse has concerned itself exclusively with friendships between men.

Male Bonding, Binding Women: Friendship, Love, and the Sentimental Discourse

Part of the foundation for the exclusively male friendships discussed in scholarly discourse is the late-eighteenth-century myth that women were as incapable of friendship as they were of homosexuality. Writers such as Carl Friedrich Pockels claimed that women, by constantly vying and competing for the love of men, were prevented from forming lasting friendships with either gender (1:349–51, 2:176–88). Adolph Freiherr von Knigge, whose work *Human Interaction* (1788) became the standard text on good manners in Germany for well over a century, strictly differentiates between friendship and love: friendship is characterized by the equality and emotional distance of the partners, who are usually male; love is characterized by exceeding irrational emotionality and the inequality of the partners, *always* a male-female couple.[6]

Until well into the twentieth century, scholarship on the subject took its cue from Knigge especially with regard to the opposition between friendship and love and its mandatory gender distribution (friendship can exist only between a male,[7] love only between a male-female couple). Much of the scholarship on friendship, desexualized and strictly juxtaposed to its "unreasonable" cousin, love, was thus set free to celebrate male bonding in the eighteenth century without encountering the dangerous territory of homosexuality. What made it possible to rescue the Socratic tradition from any hint of homosexuality, to celebrate Goethe and Schiller as having a "male friendship truly inspired by antiquity" (*wahrhaft antiken Männerfreundschaft*, Salomon 303) while remaining within the bounds of nineteenth- and twentieth-century propriety, and to publish the most ardent love letters of the age under the innocuous title *Letters Between Friends* (Schenck), is what scholarship now commonly terms "sentimental discourse": the assumption that even where men and women openly declare their love, they do not mean it unless they are speaking to a member of the opposite sex. The sentimental discourse rests on no basis but the assumption of universal heterosexuality on the part of the reader: since it is impossible to *prove* sexual activity or desire between these "friends," none is presupposed or suspected. In cases of similar declarations of love between heterosexuals where evidence of genital activity is equally difficult to find, however, it is either assumed or hotly debated that the two were lovers: most scholarship on Charlotte von Stein, for example, centers on the question whether she was Goethe's lover.[8]

In scholarship, the sentimental discourse has been employed for a purpose: to place the Socratic tradition of male relationships under the heading "friendship" and thus to free it from the sexual element. Only rarely, and only as long as it does not cross into the genital, is homoeroticism tolerated (Schenck viii); usually the incompatibility of love and friendship is emphasized and the existence of any sexual or erotic attachment between members of the same sex denied (Sweet). Where relationships between women are examined, the friendship-love dichotomy used to establish the universality of heterosexuality is frequently borrowed from the discourse on nonsexual Socratic friendships between men: all bonding between women is discussed under the heading "friendship"; "friendship" implies a nonsexual affiliation, "love" implies a sexual relationship; any evidence of erotic attachment is dismissed as "sentimental discourse."[9]

Like sentimental discourse, eighteenth- and nineteenth-century discussion of friendship and love served a purpose. In the course of the Enlightenment, with its emphasis on virtue and reason, love, with its connotations of passion, fell from favor, while friendship was raised to the status of an ideal mode of human interaction and advocated in novels and the Moral Weeklies as the best reason for marriage (Martens). For women, the new valorization of friendship as superior to love opened the door to establishing passionate relationships with other women under the heading of "friendship." Relationships that frequently fluctuated between *agape*, *eros*, and *sexus* were probably tolerated as an emotional outlet in an age when marriage had nothing to do with emotion and divorce was impossible. By the turn of the century, however, the love match began to replace the enlightened "reasonable" marriage (Friedli 235–36). With the return of love to the marriage, women's passionate relationships lost their official raison d'être: all female emotion was now expected to center on men, and same-sex relationships between women increasingly came under attack during the nineteenth century until lesbianism officially entered the medical discourse as a "disease" in the late nineteenth century (Tubach 4; Hacker 33–92).

At the close of the eighteenth century, at the same time that Pockels deemed women "naturally" male-centered and therefore incapable of meaningful relationships with other women, a flood of works appeared that were dedicated to the task of establishing the "nature" of woman as wife, mother, and *Hausfrau*, to the exclusion of all other relationships or activities.[10] Female traits that had previously been discussed as desirable but not inherent (beauty, pas-

sivity, tenderness, renunciation, devotedness, etc.) were now re-
defined as woman's *nature*, her "sexual character" (Hausen). In the
postrevolutionary age, in which demands for the equality of Man
naturally posed the question of women's parity, this redefinition
provided both the ideological basis for the exclusion of women from
public life and the philosophical basis for the new idealization of
woman's domestic role,[11] all of which served to obscure their loss
of real economic control. As a direct result of these developments,
women's education and intellectual pursuits came under increasing
attack: during the Enlightenment, educated women were ignored,
tolerated, and even occasionally honored, as the cases of the celebrated Luise Gottsched and poets laureate Christiana Mariane von
Ziegler and Sidonia Hedwig Zäunemann attest. During the early
nineteenth century, however, intellectual activities were seen as a
transgression of women's "nature" and "vocation" (Duden; Walter 156, 217) and as detrimental to their domestic duties (Becker-
Cantarino, *Der lange Weg* 174). Pockels, writing in 1797–98,
already voices the fear behind this ideology when he attributes wom-
en's "sentimental friendships" to their reading of trashy novels and
laments that many women are "spoilt and corrupted" by books.
Most of those overglorified friendships, he goes on to say, exist
between women writers, making them "overripe brainy women"
who are neither happy wives nor good mothers (2:215–18).

Woman's "Nature": Gender Coherence,
Gender Dissonance

The connection drawn by Pockels between women's same-sex
relationships and their intellectual life is one that provides the basis
for this article: all same-sex ties between women discussed here, and
in fact most of those that we know about, were those between
women writers. One reason for this is, of course, that the few
sources available to us were provided by writers. Another reason
is the fact that while all female couples known to me engaged in
some kind of intellectual exchange, some of these relationships were
formed and upheld to enable the partners to pursue their mental life.
In many cases, their relationship was the sole area of their lives
where such pursuits were possible. The third and final reason why
the connection between women's intellectual lives and their same-

sex relationships is of particular interest here is what I am judging to be a greater likelihood of gender dissonance[12] among female thinkers of the time. Because women were passing from an age of greater freedom of thought to one that defined any cerebral activity as inconsistent with their gender, I am making the — admittedly elitist — assumption that writing women of the nineteenth century were more prone to gender dissonance, and therefore to questioning the entire structure of woman's "nature," than nonerudite women of the age. Because the new ideology of woman's "nature" and vocation as housewife and mother excluded women from educated public life, gender dissonance is here understood to include not only sexual or erotic relationships with other women, dressing as a man and the like, but also a woman's insistence on intellectual and public activity, which — like the above examples, though perhaps to a lesser degree — would have been judged as an assumption of male prerogative.

The definition of woman's nature as wife and mother in the early nineteenth century leads us straight into the essentialist/constructionist debate (Fuss, *Essentially Speaking*). While the question whether gendered experience is essential or constructed is an especially burning one for both lesbians and gay men, lesbians, because of their obliteration from history, are less willing to depart from the idea of a lesbian essence (Fuss, *Essentially Speaking* 98). The same holds true for heterosexual women (as opposed to heterosexual men): the greater need for an essential female identity is one of the reasons for the opposition of U.S. essentialist feminists to Barthes's theory of the death of the author (Miller, *Subject to Change* 17–18). Many feminists view this concept as a renewed attempt to suppress the female subject, which has finally begun to emerge. Miller, for example, summed up the discussion on identity: only those who have it can play with not having it (*Subject to Change* 75). Other voices in the identity debate, such as Sedgwick's and Butler's, have begun to doubt the existence of a prediscursive gender that could provide the basis for an essential identity as "female" or "male." Sedgwick has posed gender as a construct that allows for the social (re)production of male/female identities and behaviors (*Epistemology* 27–31). Butler reads gender and, to some extent, anatomical sex as a cultural and compulsory performance, involving behavior, self-definition, and habit(s): as Virginia Woolf pointed out, "it is clothes that wear us and not we them. We may make them take the mould of our arm or breast, but [clothes] mold our hearts, our brains, our tongues to their liking" (*Orlando*, quoted in Gilbert 193).

According to Butler, the cultural performance of femininity or masculinity constitutes the gender identity of the actor: without this performance, there is no such thing as gender. What is usually taken to be the source of the performance, the actor's gender, is actually its result. The performance is not individual, that is, not dependent on individual volition, but cultural, social, and compulsory; deviations are punished. For Butler, two consequences emerge from these presuppositions. First, within the parameters of the performance, a seemingly "natural" relationship is created between anatomical sex, gender, and sexual desire that does not exist outside of this performance. "Normally," these relationships demand that the bearer of an XX-chromosome perform in a "feminine" manner (i.e., according to her gender) and desire bearers of XY-chromosomes: that is, identification and desire are diametrically opposed. Second — and this idea will become important in the context of our discussion — a gender identity that is constructed in repeated performances can be subverted, negated, or defined differently.[13]

With regard to the same-sex relationships of German women in the eighteenth and early nineteenth centuries, the following questions seem relevant: In which way(s) did they refuse to perform their "feminine" gender? In which way did their same-sex relationship with other women permit them to explore other forms of gender dissonance? And how were their alternative performances affected by the increased pressure for gender coherence in the course of the nineteenth century?

The same-sex "affairs" that will be discussed here — Luise Gottsched and Dorothea Henriette von Runckel; Therese Heyne and her friends Luise Mejer and Auguste Schneider; Bettina von Arnim and Karoline von Günderrode; Rahel Varnhagen and her friends Pauline Wiesel and Rebekka Friedländer; and Caroline Pichler and her circle of friends — all revolved around the partners' intellectual lives; they all, more or less overtly, displayed homoerotic tendencies; and they all involved a certain amount of gender dissonance. To claim that they were lesbians in the twentieth-century meaning of the word would be inaccurate, since lesbianism — by its twentieth-century definition — involves sexual activity, which is impossible to prove in some cases and unlikely in others. Conversely, unless one subscribes to the directives of the sentimental discourse, it is obvious from their letters that they were not just "friends" but shared a deeper and more exclusive affection for each other.

"Friendship, Tenderness, and Whatever": Eighteenth- and Early-Nineteenth-Century Love Letters

Until the early nineteenth century, the differentiation between friendship and love was widely discussed in letters between women, particularly women who sought to define their own same-sex rapport. "Friendship," considered the superior mode of interaction, could be used to denote the sincerity of the relationship, while "love," with its emphasis on emotionality, proved its intensity. In their love letters to each other, women declared their passion for each other, bemoaned their separation, counted the miles between them, voiced their fears of being "replaced" by other female acquaintances, and insisted on assurances of monogamy. Many eighteenth-century love letters from women to female "friends" not only used the vocabulary traditionally assigned to love; they also explicitly identified friendship with "love," marriage (husbands in the eighteenth century are sometimes referred to as "friends"), or erotic attraction.

The most striking example is the exchange of letters between Luise Adelgunde Gottsched (1713–62)[14] and Dorothea Henriette von Runckel (1724–1800), for two reasons: one, their relationship outlasted most same-sex relationships I know of, and two, Gottsched's letters to Runckel afford easy comparison with her letters to her husband. Her letters to Johann Christoph Gottsched (1700– 1766), written mainly between 1730 and 1735, followed the formula of enlightened reasonable friendship employing an unemotional, distant tone: Gottsched addresses him as her "inestimable," "wrathful," "reconciled," "virtuous," "chosen," or "philosophical" friend (Heuser, "Das beständige Angedencken" 153). While of the 64 letters she wrote to her husband only a few, all written after their definitive engagement in 1734, could be construed as love letters, others abound where she attempts to either postpone their wedding or curb their correspondence (for example *Briefe* 1:12–13, 1731; 42–43, 45–46, 1732; 50–53, 53–55, 1733; 86–87, 92–93, 97–99, 100, 107, 114–16, 120–23, 130–31, 1734). What is most striking in

Gottsched's epistles, besides the emotional distance, is her repeated refusal to define the terms of their relationship. Even after their inofficial engagement, frequent asides in Gottsched's letters show that, for her, it was by no means decided that she would end up marrying Johann Christoph:[15] In her estimation, their relationship was informed not by love but by "friendship, tenderness, and whatever else you would like to call this attachment" (August 21, 1734; 1:122–23). While the terms of intimacy remained largely undefined, the structural aspect of their relationship developed fairly early in their correspondence: as early as 1730, Gottsched referred to Johann Christoph as her "mentor" and emphasized her willingness to learn under his tutelage (1:4–5); in other letters he appeared as her "master" and "kind teacher" (1:26, 33). Johann Christoph Gottsched viewed the relationship in similar terms, as is evident in his biographical essay of his wife, published one year after her death, in which he relates that he sent her books for instruction and "thus made her my helpmeet."[16] The student-teacher relationship was a lifelong one: as Johann Christoph's wife and "industrious helper," Gottsched strove to support his scholarly and literary career. For this purpose, she authored five original plays and seven translations for her husband's anthology *The German Stage*, translated the larger part of Addison and Steele's *Spectator* and Pierre Bayle's *Historical Critical Dictionary*, participated in Johann Christoph's translation of Leibniz's *Theodizee*, cataloged dramas for Johann Christoph's project *An Essential Supply* (*Nöthiger Vorrath*), and researched and compiled a bibliography of his sources. She supplied the etymological basis for Johann Christoph's monumental work *The German Language*, proofread the entire work, hand-copied the Goldast manuscript (one folio!) for Johann Christoph's use, authored a multitude of satires, translations, reviews, and smaller articles, labeled Johann Christoph's entire library, and upheld his correspondence with other scholars in his name whenever, in the words of her husband, "I was too overwhelmed with other projects."[17] Aside from the fact that most of her contributions appeared either anonymously, under a cryptonym, or under her husband's name, her own literary development was hampered by this enormous workload: although she saw herself as an author of tragedies, Gottsched produced only one tragedy in 28 years of ceaseless writing. In one of her last letters to Runckel, she called her forced literary activity her "writing yoke" and her "work on the galleys" (2:82, 211) and blamed it for her ruined health and early death (March 4, 1762; 3:167–68). She died on June 26, 1762.

Gottsched and Runckel first met in 1752 on one of the many journeys Gottsched undertook to repair her ruined health. Her ensuing correspondence with Runckel differs from her earlier letters to her husband in two respects: they display an openness uncharacteristic of Gottsched and an emotionality unprecedented in her earlier letters.

Why did I have to meet you for such a short time? Why did I have to discover in you everything I have sought so ardently, but never found united in one person? Why did you have to grant me your friendship immediately? . . . You are right, nothing is more enchanting than the friendship of two upright souls. Let ours be inseparable and eternal. Permit me to write to you often and often to share with you my sorrows, of which you are the innocent cause. (June 19, 1752; *Briefe* 2:44–45)

Gottsched's letters to Runckel, like those to her husband, define their relationship as a friendship, yet unlike the letters to her husband, they employ the vocabulary of love. In their ensuing correspondence, Gottsched sends Runckel love poems (2:45, 238; 3:53–54), her picture (an emotionally laden gift that she had earlier refused Johann Christoph; 1:15 vs. 2:236–37), her "tender embrace" (2:58), "one thousand kisses" (2:108, 173), and her "most fiery embrace" (2:230). She speaks, moreover, of "unspeakable tenderness" (2:91), "love eternal" (2:94, 3:133), and "tenderness that cannot be matched" (2:131). At times she employs a playful and teasing tone also unknown from her earlier letters (2:109, 121–22) and exhibits clear signs of jealousy with regard to other women. Conversely, she assures Runckel that their relationship has nothing to fear from Gottsched's contact with other women (2:252; men are not considered adequate competition). She rails at the fate and the husbands that keep them separated (2:63, 117) and fantasizes about a life without them that would free the two of them to live together (2:63). In addition, she counts the miles that separate them (2:123, 135–36, 236–37, 302), she swears she lives only for Runckel (2:157; 3:37, 145) and fantasizes about dying with her (2:276–77, 3:138). Gottsched, who in her earlier letters took great care to uphold her image as virtuous wife, went so far as to call housework a miserable occupation for a thinking being (2:151), to wish podagra on her husband (2:152–53), to refer to him as a perjurer for falsely promising to let her visit Runckel (2:305), and to claim that she would rather travel the thirteen miles that separated her from Runckel than go on a nine-mile trip with her husband (3:18). What makes this sudden emotionality on Gottsched's part even more remarkable is that Johann Christoph, despite the Enlightenment rhetoric of "reason," had clearly expected such passion from his fiancée and been refused: during the years of their courtship, Gottsched frequently had had to defend herself against Johann Christoph's accusations of "coldness" (1:121).

"Friendship," a term Gottsched employs with regard to her relationship with both her husband and Runckel, and "love," a term she more frequently uses in connection with Runckel, become constant themes in her letters to her. Gottsched never directly refers to themselves as lovers, although she invokes love constantly and draws the comparison between an amorous relationship and their own several times (2:217; 3:45, 116). Following the dominant discourse of her time, Gottsched viewed friendship as the highest form of human interaction. Breaking with that discourse, however, which limited friendship to men, she considered women more capable of lasting friendships than men, as she wrote to Johann Christoph in 1734 (1:157). In her letters to Runckel, she goes on to claim that "men rarely know the exquisiteness of friendship" (May 29, 1755; 2:289) and that "it would be bad if two souls who love each other as we do should learn the rules of friendship from that deceitful sex [men]" (October 4, 1755; 2:304–5). The Enlightenment discourse, in which friendship was valued higher than love, enabled Gottsched both to define her relationship with Runckel in terms that did not conflict with her role as Johann Christoph's wife and to give it a special validation that distinguished this relationship qualitatively from the one she shared with her husband.

The difference between these relationships is evident not only in her writing, but also in her publishing. Gottsched, who had repeatedly refused Johann Christoph permission to publish her letters (in 1734; see 1:101, 127), granted this permission to Runckel, rejoicing that "the magic of friendship can thus transform miserable remains into relics" (March 9, 1754; 2:177). Runckel not only edited and published Gottsched's letters in three volumes in 1771–72, but also reprinted, in the same collection, Gottsched's favorite drama, *Pan-*

thea (1744), her only tragedy. After 28 years of producing literary works for her husband's projects, many of which were never credited to her, it was Runckel who was finally responsible for publishing the works that Gottsched *wanted* to write — her tragedy and her letters — under the author's name. And it was this last act of friendship for Gottsched that inspired Runckel's own ensuing literary and editorial activity (Heuser, "Das beständige Angedencken" 161–62). As Heuser has pointed out, Gottsched's letters to Runckel represent an emancipatory act directed at both Johann Christoph, her husband, and Johann Christoph Gottsched, the literary "Pope" of her time: her refusal to let him publish her letters permitted her to develop her passionate epistolary style and thus to participate in the development of the new emotional and linguistic culture of the eighteenth century ("Das beständige Angedencken" 160–61). Simultaneously, she managed to preserve the integrity of her relationship with Runckel by conferring the editorship of her letters on her and thus permitting her letters to become "relics" of their friendship.

It is a sign of the male-centeredness of scholarship on friendship and same-sex relationships that the bond between Gottsched and Runckel, with the exception of Heuser's articles on the subject, has received no scholarly attention, although it formed the emotional center of the last ten years of Gottsched's life and although Gottsched is probably one of the best-researched women writers of the period.[18] Her highly erotic relationship with Runckel probably did not involve sexual activity (the two women met only twice, even though, as every reader of Gottsched's letters is well aware, they lived only 26 miles apart — which to Gottsched, without her husband's consent and accompaniment, represented an insurmountable distance). However, it is evident from Gottsched's letters that her tie to Runckel constituted the most intense love relationship of her life, as well as the emotional counterpart to what became an increasingly unhappy marriage.

Because of Runckel's preservation of the relics of their "friendship," Gottsched's affiliation with her is better documented than most other same-sex bonds between women. Despite the sparse documentation, however, one theme recurs consistently in late-eighteenth-century letters between women: the need to redefine same-sex relationships in the tangle of meanings between "friendship" and "love." As "friendship" lost its predominance in late-eighteenth-century discourse, the term became insufficient to describe the intensity of emotional experience. Toward the end of the century, women involved in intense same-sex relationships increasingly turned to "love" as a mode of description: unlike Gottsched, who employed the vocabulary of love but defined her love for Runckel as "friendship," women at the end of the century applied traditionally male-female–defined feelings like love, passion, and jealousy both to their relationships with men and to those with other women. When Therese Heyne (later Therese Huber, 1764–1829) formed an erotic attachment to the actress Auguste Schneider (no dates), she attempted to divert the jealousy of her older friend Luise Mejer (1746–1786) by a division of competencies: while Schneider would be her lover, she promised Mejer the undiminished place in her heart as her "confidante" (*Vertraute*, Leuschner 200). In her letters to Mejer, she described the relationship with Schneider in terms usually reserved for heterosexual romance: "I must love my Auguste as fearfully and as tenderly as a lover," she wrote (1783). In 1784, she spoke of her "dear alter Ego, of Auguste; since she claims that we love each other as man and wife, or rather as lover and beloved, we are One" (quoted in Leuschner 199). In the absence of a tradition governing women's love relationships, this heterosexual discourse is employed to describe homoerotic feelings. Until women's homoerotic and homosexual relationships were codified as sick or criminal, they existed in a discursive vacuum: despite Sappho, there was no tradition, no historical precedence, no point of reference.[19] In the rare cases where the partners clearly stated or alluded to the homoerotic nature of their relationship, their model is *male*, not female, homosexuality: in one love letter to Karoline von Günderrode, Bettine von Arnim compares their love to that between Plato and Dion, not that between Sappho and Anactoria.[20]

With the growing need of female homoerotic couples to turn to passionate discourse, borrowed from either heterosexual or male homosexual love, and with the simultaneous redefinition of love as an *exclusive* male-female pairing, the need for secrecy increased. In comparison to the openly amorous letters by Gottsched, Heyne, and von Arnim, written between 1752 and 1805, Rahel Varnhagen's (1771–1833) letters to Rebekka Friedländer (written between 1805 and 1810) and Pauline Wiesel (written between 1810 and 1831) are a strange mixture of passion and caution. In a letter to

Friedländer (1783–1850), Varnhagen admits that her attachments to other women are the most intense relationships of her life: "Most of the time, I have been disregarded, often despised—for a long, long time I was not loved, often hated—loved supernaturally rarely, very briefly by lovers and only by a few male friends—very sincerely and lastingly by female friends" (September 18, 1810; 291). Varnhagen's correspondence with Pauline Wiesel (1779–1848) is stylistically and thematically similar to Gottsched's passionate letters to Runckel: they longed to live and die together (226, 228, 235–36, 240), assured each other that seeing the other person was the only thing worth living for (266), railed at the fate that separated them (233), and wished that they had met before marriage limited their mobility (239). Interspersed in these love letters are cryptic remarks such as "But in *this* we are and remain unique, and we *want* to be unique, in that we remember how we were, know what we wish for, and still wish for, want and mean the same thing." Following this cryptic remark, which might well allude to a former homosexual relationship terminated by distance, are the words "Destroy this letter, these words *immediately!*" (June 8, 1826; 257, emphasis in the original). That secrecy in the relationship was advisable is also apparent in Wiesel's request for a rendezvous: "I beg you, dear, dear, sweet Ralle, my only consolation *still*, answer me, if you believe in the possibility of seeing me this summer, and *where?* I'd prefer a clandestine meeting" (December 8, 1826; 260, emphasis in the original).

Back to "Nature": Gender Coherence in the Nineteenth Century

In the late eighteenth century, woman's "nature" as housewife and mother had been the overwhelming theme in the works of poets, philosophers, and pedagogues. In 1826, at the time when Varnhagen and Wiesel exercised such caution, it had become a fact of gendered life. While eighteenth-century pedagogy had claimed as its goal the education of "mankind" to "virtue," nineteenth-century pedagogy specifically targeted boys and girls, in whom it sought to instill *gender-specific* virtues (such as bravery, activeness, and academic curiosity in boys versus passivity and domestic skills in girls).[21] The new ideology of woman's "nature" and the definition of love as exclusively heterosexual forced all women, but especially homosexually inclined women, into constant demonstrations of gender coherence. From the early nineteenth century on, it became imperative that women involved in same-sex relationships appear to be not just "friends" but—pointedly—"just" friends.

For Caroline Pichler and her circle of friends,[22] ostentatious gender coherence appears to have been the primary concern. Pichler (1769–1843) was one of the most prolific authors of an age that took a particularly dim view of women and their writing. She was also one of only two or three women authors of the nineteenth century to publish her own collected works during her lifetime. Unlike most of her female colleagues, whose titles appeared anonymously or pseudonymously, she not only brought out most of her works under her name but usually added her birth-name, as if to "overidentify" herself: Caroline Pichler, née von Greiner. The predominant theme in her fictional oeuvre was friendship (her longer narrative texts are all epistolary novels, which take the form of an exchange of letters between friends), while a large part of her biographical work concerns her relationship to her "sisters in Apollo" Therese von Artner (1772–1829), Maria von Zay (1779–1842), and Marianne von Neumann-Meißenthal (1768–1837).[23] Of these three, her closest friend was Artner, whom Pichler met in 1814 at Zay's house, where Artner lived with Zay. From 1814 until Artner's death in 1829, Pichler visited Artner and Zay virtually every summer, frequently joined by Neumann-Meißenthal. Pichler's autobiography treats these yearly visits as relatively minor incidents—and with good reason, since there are numerous facets to them that would have made them appear extremely unusual, such as that these visits occurred on a yearly basis and in each instance lasted for the entire summer. Although three of the four writers in question were married, none of them were inhibited from leaving their husbands nearly every summer for weeks at a time. Pichler's autobiography, an exceedingly meticulous record of even minor events, only rarely mentions the presence of one of the husbands in question, indicating conclusively that most summers were spent without them. Conversely, she frequently (and without explanation) remarks that either Zay's or her own husband were unable to accompany them, or that they picked up their wives at Zay's estate (*Denkwürdigkeiten* 2:73, 98, 143, 148, 173, 229).

Because we have only Pichler's cautious account of these visits, the nature of the personal relationships involved remains obscure. In terms of literary networking, however, these summers were extremely productive. Many of the works written by each of the four authors were written for, with, or about a female friend, usually a member of their annual circle, or inspired by one. A few examples are Artner's and Neumann's collaboration on their first collection of poetry, *Wild Flowers* (Schindel 1:22); Pichler's first poem, written and published at age twelve and dedicated to a female friend (Becker-Cantarino, "Caroline Pichler" 6); and her first longer work, *Parables*, originally dedicated to her friend Josephe von Ravenet. During these visits, with the help of endless coaxing from her friends, Maria von Zay wrote and published six dramas and ten novellas; Artner finished songs for Zay's novella *Ivan and Ilena* (Schindel 2:481); and Pichler composed *The Mountain Castle*, which she dedicated to Zay (Pichler, *Denkwürdigkeiten* 2:454), and *Ghosts of the Mountain*, which she dedicated to Artner. Zay describes Artner in her novella *Serena* and the circle of friends in *Journey to the Mountain*, while Pichler portrays the same circle in her poem "To My Women Friends" ("An meine Freundinnen"; see *Denkwürdigkeiten* 2:422). Pichler, the subject of Artner's poems "The Rescue" and "To Caroline Pichler," responded in "To My Friend Theone" (Theone is Artner's pseudonym), an enthusiastic celebration of writing and literary inspiration (*Sämtliche Werke* 23:5ff.).

Contrasting with the picture emerging from the published fictional writings of each woman and their descriptions of each other in these works — all of which suggest intense emotional involvement leading to poetic inspiration — is Pichler's description of her summers with her friends, which conveys mixed messages to the point of utter confusion. On the one hand, she frequently emphasizes both the feelings of friendship among the four writers and the function of these meetings as a literary support network: she admits that at Zay's house, "four women writers were united through respect and good will . . . amicably, intimately, and free of envy" ("Therese von Artner" 201–2). On the other hand, she attempts to soften by frequent references to housework the potentially threatening image of a fellowship of women writers that excluded men. Readings of the author's literary works, for example, are described as occasions "when we . . . gathered around the lady of the house with our needlework, and one or the other of us . . . read from her own work"

("Therese von Artner" 205). "Housework" and "needlework" loom large in Pichler's writing, particularly when she discusses women's authorship. "In all of these women lived that respect for true femininity, domesticity, and order which alone, in my estimation, can give the writing of women its true value and license, under which it can emerge into the world without fear of justified criticism," she intones piously in defense of Zay, Neumann, Artner, and Johanna Franul von Weißenthurn (1772–1847), whose immense literary production would have made her suspect (*Denkwürdigkeiten* 2:409).

Similar concerns are evident in her biographical essay of her closest friend, "Therese von Artner," written after Artner's death specifically to counter Schindel's biography of Artner, as Pichler herself admits ("Therese von Artner" 191). Schindel, who was sympathetic toward women writers but less astute than Pichler with regard to the damage that any appearance of gender dissonance could do to their image, describes Artner as a voracious learner, artist, and writer, who pleaded with her mother for leftover candlewax to be able to write at night, frequently made herself sick by sheer overwork, and spent years on background research for a historical epic poem (Schindel 1:13–30). Pichler's "correction" of this account is one long poetic eulogy on Artner's domestic qualities: "Her rich spirit, her multitude of talents, especially her excellent poetic gift, did not in any way estrange her from her feminine occupations. With prudence and insight she attended to her domestic duties, which commanded her active presence at the sewing table, at the embroidery frame. She made her own dresses with adroitness and taste, she put up her own hair with extreme care, far from all exaggeration" ("Therese von Artner" 202). In contrast to Schindel's depiction of Artner as an ambitious writer, Pichler takes great care to portray her friend as a "woman in the true, higher sense, whose life and work was therefore concealed ... by the walls of her home" ("Therese von Artner" 192–93), that is, as a housewife without a husband. Pichler thus professed to be at a loss to explain why Artner chose to remain unmarried and instead preferred to associate with other women — Pichler herself included: given "that sense for domestic occupations, that providing love for others that forgets itself and never demands anything for itself, ... in view of this lovable disposition, it must be doubly marveled at and regretted that Therese later never made up her mind to bless a man with her hand" ("Therese von Artner" 194).

The constant need to demonstrate gender coherence, that is, to conform to the mandatory image as a good housewife and mother, asserted itself in Pichler's self-image as well. A sizable part of her own literary production centered on her female friends, yet she credited her husband with her entire literary development, claimed that she wrote her first drama only to please him, and excused the fact that her first longer work was dedicated to Josephe von Ravenet by hastily adding, "but only in the manuscript" (the dedication was omitted when the work was printed; Schindel 2:112, 106, respectively). She wrote ten dramas, most of which portray periods of Austrian history that involved wars, but elsewhere claimed to find an interest in war unfeminine and stated her belief that dramas were beyond the capabilities of women writers, particularly tragedies, of which she herself had authored three (*Denkwürdigkeiten* 1:427–28, 400). She repeatedly stated in her memoirs that women should be permitted to write in their spare time only, if at all, and warned mothers to educate their daughters, especially those endangered by literary ambition, to become "wives, housewives, and mothers in the most noble sense" ("Kindererziehung" 65–66). Yet she herself published her own collected works, of which 53 volumes appeared in her lifetime, and, in letters not intended for publication, refers to writing as her "sweetest occupation,"[24] "the better time," and "the moment of consecration." She likewise privately admits that "writing is one of the highest delights"[25] and that "my most blissful hours have always been, and still are, those spent at my desk."[26]

What makes the research both of women's homoerotic relationships and of their writing so difficult today is the fact that their masquerade, inspired by the need to demonstrate gender conformity, was often so extraordinarily effective. A glance at Pichler's reception history proves how successful she was in passing herself off as the model housewife: although she was one of the most prolific writers of the age, she was also one of few to gain the approval of her male critics (Blümml; Wolf; Schindel 2:97–119). Despite the fact that she wrote and published much more than Artner did, she was never accused of compromising her "femininity" by her literary activity, as Artner apparently was. And unlike Louise Brachmann, whose suicide was seen as the consequence of her madness resulting from literary activity,[27] Caroline Pichler, who committed suicide in 1843, was never accused of similar literary insanity. Instead, her male critics rushed to her defense, attributing her death to "complete exhaustion, which the doctors called senility" (Wolf 2:390–91) or discreetly rewriting her suicide as a "severe, if not unexpected illness, from which she would never recover," until "her body failed and on July 9, 1843, a Sunday, her soul left its fragile shell" (Blümml 1:xxiv–xxv). A similar bias governs the reception of writings that describe homoerotic relationships between women, which are, depending on the degree of explicitness, neatly divided into "documentary" and "fictional" genres: while great care is taken to emphasize the fictional elements in Arnim's passionate biographical novel *Die Günderode*, Pichler's equally fictitious presentation of Artner, Zay, and Neumann as "mere" — that is, nonerotic and nonsexual — friends as well as exemplary housewives is considered trustworthy biography.

Conclusion

In the eighteenth century homoerotic relationships between women, their (often connected) literary activity, or any other evidence of their gender dissonance is frequently obscured by the employment of selective reading or of the "sentimental discourse." Most nineteenth-century authors, responding to increased pressure to demonstrate gender coherence, forestalled their critics both by being secretive and by constantly exaggerating their own wifely, domestic virtues, while downplaying their relationships with other women. In the nineteenth century, women's attitudes toward homoeroticism are characterized by a studious avoidance of the subject, as witness the few literary works by women that could have had homosexuality as their theme but do not: both Amalie von Helvig's drama *Two Sisters on Lesbos* (1800) and Auguste Cornelius's play *Platen in Venice* (1865), for example, are heterosexual love stories.

Despite the fact that women's homoerotic relationships fell into increasing obscurity as the nineteenth century wore on, there can be little doubt that they existed, and that for many women they constituted the most intense love relationships of their lives, as well as the emotional counterpart to their marriages of convenience. Writing about Arnim and Günderrode, Tubach uses the word "homosexuality" "in the sense that Bettina was lovingly, if possessively, devoted to Karoline, that she desired the greatest possible degree of personal intimacy from her including some physical familiarity, that she adopted the language of love to speak to her" (261). This "homosexual[ity] in the broad sense of the word" applies to each of the couples discussed here. In the eighteenth century, we can take their word that they loved each other, if we manage to dispense with the sentimental discourse. In the nineteenth, women's frequent attempts to obscure their relationships with other women can be taken as indication that these relationships were often conceived of as illicit and as evidence that, like female authorship, they increasingly came under attack.

Equally compelling, from the standpoint of researching gender dissonance, is the tight connection between women's homoeroticism and their literary activity. In the cases of Gottsched and Runckel, von Arnim and Günderrode, and Pichler and her friends, the relationship served as the inspiration and the support network for their writing; in some cases, their closeness was seen as the *only* context in which such activity could evolve. That connection is also indicated by the exact parallel between the increasing obscurity that pervades women's documents about their same-sex relationships and their growing anonymity as writers in the nineteenth century: both women's anonymity and the frequency of male pseudonyms increase dramatically between 1800 and 1850 as well as between 1850 and the turn of the twentieth century. Whereas about 80 percent of all eighteenth-century writers who published pseudonymously insisted on being recognized as female (typical pseudonyms are "Jerta," "Minna," "Psyche," or "Therese"), over 60 percent of their nineteenth-century colleagues obscured both their identity and their gender by hiding behind male, often emphatically male names ("Werner Kraft," "Josef Trieb," "Schwucht von Zinken") or abbreviations of their first names that were, in all likelihood, designed to suggest male authorship ("P. v. Husch," "H. Sakkorausch").[28] Increasingly in the nineteenth century, the conviction took hold that a work would have a greater chance of being taken seriously if it was published by a man.

In view of the link between women's writing and their same-sex relationships, it is perhaps not surprising that our knowledge of women's publications before the twentieth century is still so scant. To this day, there is no scholarly monograph on German women poets before the twentieth century, only one collection of essays on contemporary women novelists (Gallas and Heuser), three comprehensive studies on women dramatists (Scholtz-Novak; von Hoff; Kord, *Ein Blick*), and two German-language anthologies (Brinker-Gabler, Wurst). Perhaps our insufficient knowledge of women's writing can be explained by our lack of interest in the homoerotic relationships that inspired and produced much literature by women: until recently, most scholarship on women has concentrated on their connection with men, and in many cases we do not have any biographical information on an author unless she was the wife, mother, sister, or lover of one of the male literary "giants" (Zantop, "Caroline Auguste Fischer" 351). For scholars of either women's same-sex relationships or their writing, a closer examination of the connection between the two could lead to significant rediscoveries of works by women and, perhaps, the bonds that inspired them — a much-needed reevaluation of the personal and literary history of women.

Reference Matter

Notes

Kuzniar: Introduction

1. For the purposes of this study I am bracketing out biogenetic theories of homosexuality as a predetermined constant. Even if sexuality involves genetic factors, its expression does change over time.

2. For another set of categories see Hekma, "Sodomites, Platonic Lovers."

3. Sweet offers a contrasting reading: "Friendships with other men are no more than part of the ancient aura that Goethe constructs about Winckelmann. Because Winckelmann, by this reckoning, is really an ancient somehow misplaced and born into the modern age, he seeks friendships along the ancient model. The issue at stake here is the construction of a normative, neoclassical aesthetics by Goethe and the Weimar Friends of Art bulwarked by a stylization of the famous archaeologist's life and character from the previous generation. The issue is not an uncovering of Winckelmann's homosexuality" (148).

4. See Richter's discussion of the fresco in *Laocoon's Body*, 38–61.

5. Derks similarly disagrees with Mayer (188). On the homoeroticism in Winckelmann's aesthetics, see also Bauemer; Richter, *Laocoon's Body*, 38–61.

6. See Derks's gay reading of *Hyperion*, 393–409.

7. For more extensive discussion of Schiller's plans, see Derks 370–78.

8. Greis revises backward Luhmann's dating on this shift: he attributes the development of this amorous discourse to Romanticism.

Richter: Winckelmann's Progeny

All translations from the German and French are by the author.

1. Cf. Luhmann, who, however, studiously avoids the issue of homosexuality (221 n. 33).

2. As an essentialist, Derks believes that Winckelmann was indeed a homosexual. As a constructionist, I do not. My use of the terms "gay" and "homosexual" in this paragraph is, in my view, historically imprecise, yet accurate in another way insofar as it does tap into a popular gay perspective that recognizes in Winckelmann an important forebear. As such it is continuous with the sort of transhistorical homosocial imitation being explored in this chapter.

3. The most detailed account of Müller's intellectual and emotional interactions with Winckelmann's biography and work can be found in Rihm 68–88.

4. The most detailed account of this affair is in Henking 2:546–83.

5. Derks (313–68) names and analyzes them in great detail.

6. The peculiarly German linkage between democracy and the homosocial becomes evident once again during the Weimar Republic. Thomas Mann's speech "On the German Republic" ("Von deutscher Republik"), for example, which invokes Walt Whitman, is analyzed for this connection in a chapter in Bernd Widdig's *Männerbünde und Massen*.

Richter: Wieland and the Homoerotics of Reading

All translations from the German and Latin are by the author. The original version of this essay, with some differences of content, appeared first in German under the title " 'Erektionen machen': Wieland und die Erotik der weiblichen Physiognomie," in *Geschichten der Physiognomik. Text–Bild–Wissen*, ed. Rüdiger Campe and Manfred Schneider (Freiburg: Rombach Verlag, in press).

1. The Greek word for bosom, *kolpos*, also means fold or pocket.

2. Cf. Wieland's refusal to translate *katapugon*, discussed by Derks 233.

3. With this conviction the eighteenth century duplicated a belief shared by many ancient and contemporary kinship-structured societies. See Gilbert H. Herdt's essay "Semen Transactions in Sambia Culture": "Sambia practice secret homosexual fellatio. . . . The symbolism of the first homosexual teachings in initiation is elaborate and rich; the meaning of fellatio is related to secret bamboo flutes, and ritual equations are made between flutes, penis, and mother's breast, and between semen and breast milk. Boys must drink semen to grow big and strong" (173).

4. Wieland had the habit of calling his girlfriends "Aspasia" and "Diotima"; see Sengle 75.

5. See, for example, *Ehrenrettung dreyer berühmter Frauen des Alterthums, der Aspasia, Julia und jungern Faustina*.

6. In Kleist's *Marquise von O*—these hyphens cover the space of the rape.

Schindler: Homosocial Necrophilia

All translations from the German are by the author, unless otherwise specified.

1. See *Allgemeines Landrecht* 384: "A healthy mother is obliged to suckle her child herself. How long she should breastfeed her child depends on the father's determination."

Graf: Homosexual, Prostitute, Castrato

1. For more traditional readings, see Haffner 89; Rudolf 176.

2. In his comments to the recently found treatise *Philosophische Vorlesungen für empfindsame Seelen*, Christoph Weiß elaborates on Lenz's concept of concupiscence, discussing Lenz's ambivalent relation to sex.

3. In this essay, *Über die Soldatenehen*, which was not published until 1913, Lenz invokes the family as the saving institution for the fate of the army. Through the bonds with their wives and children, the soldiers are supposed to be able to relate to the destinies of their adversaries' kin. Thinking of their own families, they can no longer brutally murder and rape their enemies.

4. "It is certainly not difficult to find ethnographic and historical examples of trafficking in women. Women are given in marriage, taken in battle, exchanged for favors, sent as tribute, traded, bought, and sold. Far from being confined to the 'primitive' world, these practices seem only to become more pronounced and commercialized in more 'civilized' societies" (Rubin 175).

5. It is not surprising that Lenz would fall in love with Friederike Brion, since she had been Goethe's lover. Lenz's feelings for Goethe can best be described as intense. Sigrid Damm mentions a lost essay called "Our Marriage" ("Unsere Ehe"; Damm 141) in which Lenz describes his relationship with Goethe in detail, and in 1992 Egon Günther, in his movie *Lenz*, justifiably portrayed the relationship between the two authors as very homoerotic.

6. Rammler, as others in the play, is given a telling name that in his case alludes to his insatiable sex drive, *rammeln* meaning "to fuck."

7. Lenz is not immune to the anti-Semitism of his time. This scene reveals the close affinity of discrimination on the basis of gender and sexual orientation to religious discrimination. In each instance, a potential subject is reduced to an object position while at the same time functioning as an element of stabilization for the discriminating powers, that is, heterosexist societies. Gender, race, and sexuality become tools of oppression. Accordingly, the closet as a performance act gains relevance for members of each group, however in very distinct ways. Eve Sedgwick explains: "Racism, for

instance, is based on a stigma that is visible in all but exceptional cases. . . . A (for instance) Jewish or Gypsy identity, and hence a Jewish or Gypsy secrecy or closet, would nonetheless differ again from the distinctive gay version of these things in its clear ancestral linearity and answerability, in the roots (however tortuous and ambivalent) of cultural identification through each individual's originary culture of (at a minimum) the family" (*Epistemology* 75).

8. Sexual affinities dominate and connect the play structurally. This scene not only reveals Lenz's awareness of gender roles in his time, but it also suggests insight into the play of gender. Is gender a play of sexualities? How phantasmatic are sexual relations in general? The fundamental structure of Lenz's oeuvre consistently points toward these questions.

9. Lenz changed this final scene, conceding to Herder's recommendations. In the earlier version, the countess, not the colonel, suggests a "Pflanzschule von Soldatenweibern."

10. *Stillen* encompasses the meanings of "to satisfy," "to silence," "to staunch," and "to nurse."

11. A problematization of the sex/gender distinction transcends the confines of this paper. I do think that Lenz assumes a strict traditional correlation between biological sex and sociological gender, which in my reading in turn reveals both gender and sexuality as performative.

12. See *Werke und Briefe* 2:871.

Tobin: In and Against Nature

1. For more about Johannes Müller, see Derks 275–95, as well as Richter, "Winckelmann's Progeny," in this volume.

2. Unless otherwise indicated, all references to Derrida are to "Plato's Pharmacy," in *Dissemination*.

3. See also the translator's note 46 on page 110 of the "Pharmacy."

4. For images of the nudes, see Femmel 3: pls. 221–38. For more on Goethe's artworks, see Gilman, *Sexuality* 229.

5. In addition to Goethe's remark about the historian Müller and Goethe's letter to the duke about Italian homosexuality, a number of other biographical facts suggest Goethe's awareness of lived homosexual desire. Eissler puts together a — by his own admission somewhat sketchy — case for possible homosexual activity in Goethe's youth (2:1456–57). Goethe's essay on Winckelmann (*HA* 12:96–129) is shot through with positive allusions to the art historian's well-known love of men (Derks 203–11). Given Goethe's general knowledge of homosexual relationships between men, it is not surprising to find the following Venetian epigramm:

> Boys I have also loved,
> but I prefer girls;

If I'm tired of her as a girl,
she can serve me as a boy as well!

Knaben liebte ich wohl auch,
doch lieber sind mir die Mädchen;
Hab' ich als Mädchen sie satt,
dient sie als Knabe mir noch. (*WA* 1.5.2:381)

Whether or not this is an autobiographical confession or — more likely — a play on the ancient tropes of erotic epigramms, it points to Goethe's knowledge of homosexual practices.

6. For further reactions to the *Elegies*, see *Erotika* 11–14.

7. Ammer positions this poem as a "guard" at the beginning of his reconstruction of the "original" *Roman Elegies*. Goethe, incidentally, possessed a drawing of a thief being sodomized by a priapic monument (*Erotika* 175).

8. Whaley is the culprit.

9. The warped and (or perhaps because) misplaced tool reflects the idea that pederasty might actually have an effect on or be an effect of the physical construction of the genitalia. Klaus Müller reports that around 1800 physicians were beginning to suspect that pederasts had thin and not very long members (95).

10. A more thorough analysis of these poems and *Faust* is presented in my essay "Faust's Membership."

11. See the essays cited in the commentary of *HA* (1:487), for example.

12. Eissler, incidentally, sees a general pattern in Goethe's life linking homosexuality and Switzerland (1:370).

13. This incident may have origins in the adventures of the two Counts Stolberg, with whom in 1775 Goethe first visited Switzerland and who enjoyed bathing in the nude so much that they were eventually asked to leave the country (Eissler 1:373).

14. In fact, Eissler argues that most of Goethe's homosexual bonding takes place in nature (1:374).

15. See my essay "Healthy Families," in which I call this "pharmaceutical" nature "homeopathic."

16. In fact, Derrida devotes the second half of an extensive footnote in "Plato's Pharmacy" to the word *Gift* (131–32 n. 56).

17. Eissler believes the situation is inappropriate because of the class differences between the two boys.

Gustafson: Male Desire in *Götz von Berlichingen*

All translations from the German are by the author.

1. Freud comes to mind specifically because of his emphasis on the child's sexuality and erotic feelings. Lacan's conception of the mirror stage

(as developed in the first chapter of *Écrits*) and the visual cathexes that influence the course of a child's desire help to illustrate the complexities of Goethe's play.

2. Goethe scholarship has also told many stories about the significance of Götz's iron hand, but none have explored in detail its psychoanalytic implications for the genesis of male desire. Cf. Graham, "Götz"; Wells; Ryder; Nägele.

3. Here I am thinking of Freud's "Medusa Head" essay in which he suggests that the sheer number of snakes in Medusa's hair represents a multiplication of penis symbols that function to conceal castration. The iron hand in Goethe's play is what Freud would refer to as a penis symbol and what Lacan later refines into the "phallic signifier." In Lacan's view the phallus (a sign usually of male power) is not necessarily the penis, but can substitute for it in a string of significations that ought to mask castration, loss, and/or corporeal deficiency.

4. Gilman (*Inscribing the Other* 34), Bennett (344), and Graham ("Götz" 217) all refer to the insensitivity of Götz's right hand. My interest is in the hand's function as both representative of and an impediment to male-male bonding.

5. Goethe does not address in *Götz von Berlichingen* the possibility of erotic attachments between women.

6. See Sedgwick's *Between Men* for a detailed account of the homosocial bonding of men in nineteenth-century English literature.

Wilson: Amazon, Agitator, Allegory

For helpful comments on an earlier version of this paper I am indebted to Alice Kuzniar, Simon Richter, Ellis Shookman, and Susanne Zantop.

1. To cite only a few significant examples: on *Iphigenia*, Reed and Wagner; on *Faust* (where feminist analysis could still do a great deal), Cocalis.

2. From the vast literature on *Wilhelm Meister's Apprenticeship* (and the *Theatrical Mission*) see the entire essay collection edited by Hoffmeister, and the essay by MacLeod (which lists most of the important scholarship).

3. See esp. Derks 247–94. Joachim Campe's anthology of works dealing with homosexuality gathers excerpts from the essential texts, especially *West-East Divan*, *Faust II*, and *Wilhelm Meister's Journeymanship*; other important passages that Derks had analyzed, such as those in the *Roman Elegies* (Derks 267ff.), are not included in Campe.

4. On homosexuality in Italy, see below, note 18; on transvestism, see particularly *The Roman Carnival* (*Das römische Carneval*, 1789), reflecting Goethe's experiences of the carnival of 1787, a year of intensive work on *Egmont*. Although Goethe displays fascination with cross-dressing, the carnival deeply disturbed him, and he clearly politicized it as proof "that free-

dom and equality can only be enjoyed in dizzying madness" (*MA* 3.2:250, incorporated into the *Italian Journey, MA* 15:572–607). See also *Frauen-rollen auf dem Römischen Theater durch Männer gespielt* (*MA* 3.2:171–75, translated by Isa Ragusa as "Goethe's 'Women's Parts Played by Men in the Roman Theater'" in Ferris 47–51), to which I return below. In the auto-biographical *Poetry and Truth,* Goethe remarks that "from my youth on a desire to disguise myself [*eine Lust mich zu verkleiden*] was stimulated even by my severe father" (*MA* 16:462; cf. 580); a Paralipomenon suggests that he planned to portray himself dressed as a girl (*MA* 16:997), and he reports, for example, dressing as a preacher, with a male friend dressing as his wife (*MA* 16:658). These personal experiences (aside from the Roman theater) are not portrayed with the ambiguity and subtlety that we find in *Egmont,* but perhaps provide an impetus for it and indicate the casual attitude to-ward such themes before the French Revolution.

5. I cite the translation of *Egmont* from *Early Verse Drama and Prose Plays,* and the original from the Münchner Ausgabe (*MA*). When two page numbers are separated by a slash, the first refers to the translation, the second to the original. Because Goethe did not authorize Herder's emenda-tions when he sent the manuscript to him from Italy, the manuscript version must be considered the authentic text; among modern editions, it is re-produced only by the Akademie-Ausgabe and *MA.* Both because the editors of the English translation I cite did not use this manuscript German original version and because my analysis sometimes requires a very literal transla-tion, I have occasionally altered the translation (indicated by brackets).

6. Zantop provides a succinct and insightful English-language sum-mary of these trends and their relevance to female writers; besides the litera-ture listed there (especially Hausen and Duden), see Dotzler and Hoffmann.

7. Gender themes in *Egmont* have been almost totally ignored. Most critics adopt the scheme of Clärchen as devoted, feminine "girl" whose entire being is defined by her love for Egmont; gender aspects of the other charac-ters go entirely unnoticed, except implicitly to valorize Egmont's depiction of the woman in power, Margarete, as a sort of gender monster. The only significant exception is Helmut Fuhrmann's somewhat old-fashioned but comprehensive and perceptive article on the contradiction between Goethe's conscious view of women and the depiction of them in his works; Fuhrmann has some insightful comments on the "Amazon" Margarete von Parma (63) and on Clärchen's masculinity and admiration of Margarete (79–80). The amazing fact of *Egmont* reception among feminist critics is their shunning of it. In fact, even most nonfeminist treatments of Goethe's "classical dramas" ignore *Egmont,* probably for three related reasons: (1) it contains significant features of domestic tragedy (particularly the socially charged theme of an affair between a middle-class woman and a nobleman), since (2) it was written beginning in Goethe's pre-Weimar period and published only in

1787, thus showing a hybridity of "Storm and Stress" and Classical features; and (3) unlike *Iphigenia* and *Torquato Tasso*, it was not written in blank verse. Feminist studies of Goethe's classical dramas (such as Prandi, whose topic is especially well suited to the play, and Wagner) should hardly be constricted by such formalist considerations (Prandi does contrast Egmont to Eugenie in *The Natural Daughter*, but almost completely ignores Clär-chen and particularly Margarete, who could have been included in Prandi's discussions of "Amazons and Public Identity" [64–81] and "Women on Horseback" [91–95]).

8. Hartmut Reinhardt is the only commentator in recent times to catch the meaning of these lines (*MA* 3.1:875); they are the only clear indication that the relationship has been sexually consummated, a fact that is therefore usually not addressed by critics.

9. Strada: "She not only had truly a mind that was vastly superior to that of a woman, but she also had a demeanor and bearing that made her seem not so much a woman with the mind of a man, as a man in women's clothes. To be sure, she was so strong that she often changed horses while deer hunting, of which the strongest men are often incapable. She also had some whiskers on her chin and upper lip, which did not so much give her a masculine appearance as it gave her the appropriate authority. And, what is unusual for women, unless they are strong: she was chronically plagued by podagra. Beyond that, she had quick intelligence and presence of mind, and a wonderful skill at following any necessary direction in any of her under-takings" (Wagener 47, with the Latin original and a German translation). In the later play *The Rebels* (*Die Aufgeregten*, probably from 1792), Goethe also has a female character who is a sort of regent and who therefore cannot fully take on the powers of ruling (the Countess) as well as a woman whose "masculine" characteristics are evident in her hunting garb (Friederike); see *MA* 4.1:133–81. See Wilson, "Dramen."

10. See Bullough and Bullough, chap. 6 (on the eighteenth century), who, however, focus on France and England; I am unaware of analogous studies for Germany (cf. below, note 34).

11. "One must confess that they often succeed in being very attractive [*reizend*] in this hermaphroditic form [*Zwittergestalt*]" (*MA* 3.2:225; cf. 221, and MacLeod 393–94).

12. See the articles "Omphale," "Kingship," and "Transvestism" in Walker.

13. *Roman Elegies* 19.11ff. (*MA* 3.2:71ff. and 479).

14. Egmont calls her "a real Amazon" (119; "eine rechte Amazone," 290); see MacLeod's insightful analysis of the "true Amazon" (*wahre Ama-zone*) Therese (and the other cross-dressers in the *Apprenticeship*).

15. On February 19, 1829, Goethe agreed with Eckermann's criticism of Schiller's stage version (which entirely deleted Margarete!), adding: "Fur-

thermore, Egmont gains significance through the glow that the monarch's affection [*die Neigung der Fürstin*] casts on him, just as Clärchen seems elevated when we see that she even wins out over a female monarch [*Fürstin*] and possesses Egmont's undivided love" (*MA* 3.1:862; Wagener 72). While the aged Goethe seems unaware of the interpretive possibilities I draw out here (and his fundamental confusion of Margarete's stature as "Regentin" by inaccurately calling her "Fürstin" betrays poor memory of the text), his perception of Margarete and Clärchen as competitors for Egmont's affections is consistent with my reading of Egmont's construction of gender roles for these two women—*and* of hidden gender parallels between the two characters whom Egmont is determined to differentiate so clearly.

16. It goes almost without saying that this later confession ("why not admit it now?"), along with the prevarications regarding Margarete, gives the lie to Egmont's celebrated claim at the end of his scene with Clärchen that what she experiences is the *real* Egmont (120/290–91), a sentiment that is unanimously accepted by the critics: "he reveals himself as he really is" (Wilkinson 63), he is "completely and utterly himself" (Waldeck 75).

17. In Goethe's "The Good Women, as Contrast to Bad Women" ("Die guten Frauen, als Gegenbilder der bösen Weiber," 1800), one of the women caricatures a male figure on an etching as a "yarn-holder" (*Zwirnhalter, MA* 6.1:817).

18. In his psychoanalytic study of Goethe's first Weimar decade, Eissler attributes special significance to this first portrayal in Goethe's oeuvre of a satisfying sexual relationship (2:1041); had he noticed the homoerotic and cross-dressing motifs in *Egmont*, Eissler might have made a connection between the biographical complex to which he attributes the completion of the play in Italy and Goethe's remarks on homosexuality at about the same time (letter of December 27, 1787), which Eissler had discussed earlier in the same chapter (2:1023–24). See also Eissler's (traditionally Freudian) analysis of homosexuality in the *Venetian Epigrams* (2:1347–48) and of Goethe's relationship with Carl August (2:1315–30).

In an older reading of the play that basically valorizes Clärchen's role as ancillary to Egmont, Marie-Luise Waldeck does emphasize her unconventionality (70)—while somehow entirely overlooking its sexual substrate, even interpreting Goethe's November 1787 letter to Herder (see below, note 24) as meaning that Clärchen lacks "any sensual feeling" (87). Accordingly, Waldeck passes over entirely the dialogue between Egmont and Clärchen about the "Amazon" Margarete, with Clärchen's gestural refutation of virginal asexuality.

19. Orsina says: "The prince is a murderer!" "Tomorrow I will announce it at the market square" (act 4, scene 5; Lessing 185).

20. Herder changed *sittsam gefaltet* to *sittsam* for the published version (see *MA* 3.1:880).

21. Egmont (1) releases female rebels with a warning while whipping male ones; Goethe intended this preferential treatment positively, while a modern critique would see it as a basis for further discrimination (and even a generation later, Caroline Auguste Fischer would argue that exempting women from punishment cemented their tutelage; *Unmündigkeit*, 26). Egmont then (2) upholds the general ban on soldiers marrying, which resulted in just the sort of rape that he then (3) punishes by whipping; the punishment, however, is only to be carried out if the victim is "an honest girl" (106/273), suggesting the rape victim's responsibility for demonstrating that she did not provoke the attack. However, all of these critiques were inaccessible to Goethe—save, perhaps, the critique of military celibacy, but Goethe knew and rejected this critique when Lenz formulated it (see Wilson, "Zwischen Kritik und Affirmation").

22. On Goethe's central concept of "enlightened feudalism" (by analogy with "enlightened absolutism"), see Wilson, "Dramen"; on the structurally similar concept of "enlightened patriarchy," see Becker-Cantarino, "Patriarchy."

23. It is indicative of this strangeness that in the most famous representation of this scene, Friedrich Wilhelm von Schadow's drawing (now in the Goethe-Museum in Düsseldorf and reproduced in *MA* 3.1:835), the passivity of Egmont's sleep is counteracted in his half-upright posture, as he rests against a table with his head on his hand. Of course, sleep's restorative powers are a recurring motif in Goethe's works, primarily in the first scene of *Faust II*; but none of the other occasions where the hero falls asleep are charged with the tension of the tragic denouement, the climactic moment before his execution.

24. In the *Italian Journey*, Goethe reproduced a letter he had written in November 1787, apparently in response to Herder's (lost) critique of the play: "I see very well that you miss a nuance between girl and goddess" ("Ich sehe wohl, daß dir eine Nüance zwischen der Dirne [in Goethe's day, a neutral word for "girl"] und der Göttin zu fehlen scheint," *MA* 3.1:840; Wagener 58); Goethe's answer to these charges concerns, among other things, his supposed emphasis on Clärchen's pleasure in possessing Egmont rather than on her sensuality (*Sinnlichkeit*), so Herder's objection probably addressed the contrast between Clärchen's sexuality and her apotheosis as goddess.

25. Egmont hands her over to Ferdinand, saying that he will not despise her, since she was Egmont's, but this phrase could also be read as "you will not despise her just because she was mine" ("Ich kenn ein Mädchen, du wirst sie nicht verachten weil sie mein war," 327). In either case, this phrase clearly refers to Clärchen's loss of her virginity. Significantly, Goethe sought to counter these objections of his "female friends" (most prominently Charlotte von Stein, but probably also Charlotte von Lengefeld and Caroline

Herder) by appealing to the famous Swiss portrait artist Angelika Kauffmann, who was residing in Rome; according to Goethe, she analyzed the
work with "feminine delicacy" ("weiblich zart") and argued that dwelling
on Clärchen in this scene would detract from the focus on Egmont and
Ferdinand's parting; Kauffmann also said that in his dream Egmont lifted
Clärchen above himself, not up to himself ("das liebenswürdige Geschöpf
nicht zu ihm herauf, sondern über ihn hinauf hebe"; *Italian Journey*, December 1787, *MA* 3.1:841–42 and 15:544–46; also Wagener 60–62). These
arguments seem rather hollow. Schiller also objected to the breathtaking
passage at the end of act 2 in which Egmont calls Clärchen a "means"
(*Mittel*) to bathe away the wrinkles of care resulting from public life (282;
cf. Schiller at *MA* 3.1:844–45, 846). Egmont's instrumentalization of Clärchen thus struck several contemporaries.

26. In this respect, Egmont shows striking similarities to his fictive
"brother" from the same historical period, Gottfried von Berlichingen (in
the manuscript, not in the published version of *Götz von Berlichingen*,
which toned down these issues!); Gottfried is ultimately unable to partake in
the peasant uprising, since it threatens his privilege. Before he dies, Gottfried
expresses his sense of historical superfluity and his ambiguous position as
feudal lord who senses the injustice of his privileges in the striking image of
himself as a crumbling house whose stones are carried off by the peasants to
build their own homes (*MA* 1.1:496).

27. A trivial yet telling portrayal of such a relationship is contained in
Goethe's counterrevolutionary play *The Middle-Class General* (*Der Bürgergeneral*, 1793), where the local squire grew up in close proximity to his
peasant subjects (*MA* 4.1:94–130, here 98; see Wilson, "Dramen").

28. The notion that the local nobility could protect peasants and other
subjects from the abuses of centralized absolutism is a central idea of Justus
Möser, one of the young Goethe's favorite thinkers.

29. As court poet, too, Goethe fantasized this sort of idealized affection
of peasants (*MA* 2.1:12–13) — and particularly female peasants (109–10) —
for Duke Carl August; in contrast to these "poems for occasions" stands the
remarkable poem "In Court" ("Vor Gericht"), with its female voice that
brazenly defies secular and religious authority (*MA* 2.1:32).

30. An even more cynical reading might argue that the hero's backbone
is really made up of the weak, particularly women, since the passage literally
reads, "At [or: in!] your back you have parents, wives, children!" ("im
Rücken habt ihr Eltern, Weiber, Kinder!" 329).

31. This distance between nobility and commoners is brought out in
many other passages in the play, such as by Vansen, who says he could live
for a whole year from what Egmont loses in gambling in one evening (294).

32. Pages 146/323, quoted above (Hamburger translates *Gesinnungen*
as "disposition" rather than as "principles").

33. This essay should receive more critical attention, especially as an aesthetics of proto-Romantic irony; Ferris (51–57) does not do it justice.

34. For an account of these specters of female violence and radicalism, see the essays in Stephan and Weigel, *Marseillaise*; and Schmidt-Linsenhoff. For reflections of this thematic in works by Kleist and Schiller, see Stephan, " 'Da werden Weiber zu Hyänen.' " For female cross-dressing in the Netherlands and France before and during the Revolution, see Dekker and van de Pol.

35. A prerevolutionary encyclopedia defines women's "Amazon dress" (*Amazonenkleid*) as "women's clothing, which is half masculine, namely on the upper half of the body. A kind of men's vest with sleeves, worn over a customary women's skirt, usually buttoned up, but sometimes open and flowing"; it is green and is worn not with a bonnet, but with a man's hat, gallooned and with feathers (*Deutsche Encyclopaedie oder Allgemeines Real-Wörterbuch aller Künste und Wissenschaften* [Frankfurt: Varrentrapp, 1778] 415–16). I am indebted to Susanne M. Zantop for this information.

36. For more detail on this play, including my dating of it, see Wilson, "Dramen."

37. In *Hermann and Dorothea*, Goethe attempts this integration of female strength into traditional patterns through the physical gestures of the "strong" Dorothea's stumbling on the way to become Hermann's wife and her images of dizziness and trembling as she leans on Hermann just before being engaged to him, as well as the suggestion that the above-mentioned "service" of the housewife is really a sort of dominance, with strength greater than that of men (8.89–98; 9.294–96; 7.114–28; *MA* 4.1:617, 629, 608). These issues can only be fully explored in a long-overdue study of gender issues in Goethe.

38. To Charlotte von Stein, March 20, 1782, quoted in Wagener 54.

39. "I, too, am in a ferment, a revolutionary one. . . . 'O, would I wore doublet / And breeches and hat!' I would defect to the Tyroleans with their straight noses and hearts, and I would wave their green standard in the wind" ("Ich auch bin in Gärung, und zwar in revolutionairer. . . . *Ach hätt' ich ein Wämslein und Hosen und Hut*, ich lief hinüber zu den gradnasigen, gradherzigen Tyrolern und ließ ihre schöne grüne Standarte im Winde klatschen," parallel to the "standard-bearer" Clärchen; in Arnim, *Goethe's Briefwechsel* 248–49; Arnim's editors [1044] were unable to identify her quotation as being from *Egmont*).

Rickels: Psy Fi Explorations of Out Space

1. In *The Case of California* I provide a genealogy of adolescent or group psychology that underwrites these briefer contextualizations of "the Werther effect."

2. For the complete funereal reading of Kafka's sibling bonding, see chap. 7 of my *Aberrations of Mourning*.

3. A more detailed account of the homoerotic bonding cum all-out cure-all of homosexuality going down in the Nazi pop-therapeutic culture of total healing can be found in my article entitled "Camp."

4. Barthes writes: "Charlotte is quite insipid; she is the paltry character of a powerful, tormented, flamboyant drama staged by the subject Werther; by a kindly decision of this subject, a colorless object is placed in the center of the stage and there adored, idolized, *taken to task*, covered with discourse, with prayers (and perhaps, surreptitiously, with invectives); as if she were a huge motionless hen huddled amid her feathers, around which circles a slightly mad cock" (31).

5. The peasant boy digression was inserted right before another detour or deviation, the one through Italy, which would be getting Goethe off at eros. Goethe concluded the new and improved *Werther* right before starting out on his Italian trip, during which his anxiety about picking up a tripper through intercourse, which had been keeping up his impotence as maxi-protection, got allayed. In *Inscribing the Other* Gilman has argued that probability is on the side of a homosexual choice having been what Goethe made in Italy.

Helfer: "Confessions of an Improper Man"

1. This according to J. C. W. Augusti's 1799 assessment of the novel (*KA* 5:li).

2. The German phrase is somewhat ambiguous, since *Dämpfen* can refer to both steam and mutedness.

3. Further page references will be to this volume. Although I have consulted Firchow, the translations are my own.

4. The first translation I have given is the literal one, but the German also obliquely suggests the second.

5. Special thanks to Glenn Kurtz, who first drew my attention to this phrase.

6. See Eichner, "Neues aus Friedrich Schlegels Nachlaß," for a discussion of what the various young men represent.

7. Domoradzki ("Und er erschuf die Frau"), Stephan (" 'Daß ich Eins und doppelt bin' "), and Weigel ("Wider die romantische Mode") all point to the contradiction between these two passages and then conclude that Schlegel's theory of androgyny is androcentric, yet none of these critics considers what Julius might be saying when he argues that humanity is completed in a youth *who loves like a woman*. MacLeod ("The 'Third Sex' " in this volume), who reads *Lucinde* as "the quintessential novel of androgyny," sees the undercutting homoerotic elements in the novel's de-

scriptions of androgyny as constituting one phase in the male subject's sexual development, a phase that is domesticated in favor of the relationship with a woman. Julius's relationship with Lucinde, though, I am arguing, is itself profoundly homoerotic.

8. Derks argues that the word took on homosexual overtones when it was used in the phrase "warm brothers" or in a clearly homosexual context (95). The latter seems to be the case here.

9. See Silverman for a recent discussion of the place of the "feminine" in male homosexuality.

10. Ganymede, one of Zeus's male lovers, has been a cipher for homosexuality for centuries. See Tobin, "In and Against Nature," in this volume.

11. See Kuzniar, "Reassessing Romantic Reflexivity," and Menninghaus, *Unendliche Verdopplung*, for recent discussions of Romantic reflexivity.

12. This configuration conforms to Silverman's Freudian "Leonardo model" of homosexuality, where the male subject oscillates between two modalities: he either identifies narcissistically with what he once was and desires his mother, or he identifies with his mother and desires what he once was (366–73).

13. See Kuzniar, "Labor Pains," for a similar male lesbian relationship in Novalis.

14. See Domoradzki (*Und alle Fremdheit*) and Kuzniar ("Hearing Woman's Voices" and "Labor Pains") for extensive analyses of this topos.

15. It is also possible to read this reference to a son autobiographically. The text is ambiguous about whose son is being discussed here, but in the same passage Julius hands flowers to his brother's wife. Caroline did in fact have an illegitimate son by a French officer. The son died young, and Friedrich came to help her during this difficult time (Naumann 173).

16. In two separate letters (March 23, 1799, and August 4, 1804) Schleiermacher also reveals his desire to be a woman (cited in Kuzniar, "Labor Pains").

17. According to Derks, many of these code words were named after geographical places, and he lists *Florenzen* as an example (87).

MacLeod: The "Third Sex"

1. For a fuller discussion of the polarization taking place in the gender debate in Germany at the end of the eighteenth century, see Karin Hausen's influential essay, as well as Volker Hoffmann, whose focus is on literary representations of gender.

2. Early critiques of Heilbrun's position already demonstrated that the myth of androgyny has often been used to shore up polarized heterosexual norms. See the articles contained in *Women's Studies* 2 (1974), especially

those by Daniel Harris and Catherine R. Stimpson. For a detailed historical survey of modern feminist critiques of androgyny, see Weil, 145–69.

3. That this may also be the case in the wider European context is indicated by Boudier de Villemer's appropriation of the androgynous myth as a proof of difference. Stressing the relative perfection of each sex, he notes "that the two sexes, although divided into two individuals, form but one moral entity, emblematized in the fable of the Androgynes. It follows that the more they strive to be reunified with one another, the more they lose their own rights and graces" (*Le nouvel ami des femmes ou la philosophie des sexes*, 1779; quoted in Kluckhohn 105).

4. See also Westphal. For an account of the influence of the medical "third sex" model of homosexuality on German literature between the late 1880s and 1914, see Jones. On the changing status of homosexuals in eighteenth-century Prussia, see Steakley.

5. For an illuminating discussion of the medical categorization of lesbianism in nineteenth century Germany, see Schwarz. The more common term for female homosexuality at the end of the eighteenth century, undertheorized as it was by comparison to male homosexuality, appears to have been *lesbisch*. See Schwarz 79 n. 3; Derks 43 ff.

6. A professor at the Charité Hospital in Berlin, Westphal based his findings on the patients who entered the psychiatric wards there. His theoretical pronouncements on the patient Fräulein N., which have been singled out as the first case study of a lesbian (Schwarz 64), reveal that a defining criterion of female homosexuality would be, for Westphal, "the phenomenon of a reversal of sexual sensation, the sense that she was playing the role of a male" (91).

7. Halperin's reading (18–21) of Aristophanes' speech rightly cautions, however, against uncritically and unhistorically projecting modern "homosexual" desire onto the myth, stressing the sharp distinctions drawn between the sexual practices of men and boys in classical Athens.

8. For a reproduction of the Winckelmann portrait and a discussion of the Antinous relief, see Spickernagel, esp. 99. G. S. Rousseau has presented a paradigm with important implications for Winckelmann studies, "Eros and neoclassical retrieval." The Villa Albani in Rome, which attracted Winckelmann, Mengs, and the comte Caylus, is described by Rousseau as an "aesthetic nerve centre for antiquarian and homosocial behaviour," fertile ground for the cult of Antinous. See his essay "Love and Antiquities: Gray and Walpole on the Grand Tour," contained in the volume *Perilous Enlightenment*.

9. On the eighteenth-century fascination and disdain for hermaphrodites, see Stafford, esp. 265–66. It remains to be seen to what extent hermaphrodism, as a medical subject of investigation, itself becomes implicated in eighteenth-century conceptions of homosexuality.

10. Significantly, Winckelmann also adopts the vocabulary of androg-
yny in his private correspondence, quoting, for example, Cowley's "Ode on
Platonic Love" in a love letter to Friedrich von Berg: "I thee both as Man and
Woman prize / For a perfect love implies / Love in all capacities" (*Briefe*
2:232); quoted in Mayer, *Outsiders* 169). For biographical details on
Winckelmann, see Derks 174–231.

11. For Lacan, however, the effect of this perspectivism is to annihilate
the viewing subject. See his discussion of Holbein's *The Ambassadors* in *The
Four Fundamental Concepts of Psycho-Analysis* 79–80.

12. See Parker's (537ff.) illuminating analysis of Winckelmann's appropriation of Greek philosophical discourse on love between men. I do, however, wish to argue against Parker's point that beauty, for Winckelmann, is
not erotically charged. Parker suggests that mastering the problem of historical difference becomes a way of mastering homoerotic desire. I want to
emphasize, rather, the powerful dialectic in the viewer-statue relationship
between presence and historical absence, eroticism and repression, anima-
tion and petrification, penetration and resistance. To cite just one example
of this dynamic, Winckelmann, as the art historian Hugh Honour rightly
observes, while describing the Belvedere Apollo, a dead marble statue, slips
into a description of a sensual living body with faintly perfumed hair (Honour 60).

13. Derks 193. Sweet reads the repeated connections made between
Winckelmann and classical Greek culture as "only part of a profound styl-
isation of Winckelmann," concluding that "the issue is not an uncovering of
Winckelmann's sexuality" (147–48). Mayer (167–74) makes a similar argu-
ment regarding what he sees as the cultural will to efface Winckelmann's
homosexuality. It would, however, seem clear that the construction of
Winckelmann "the Greek" has everything to do with the defining fact of
Winckelmann's sexuality.

14. For a fuller discussion of this essay, see Derks 80–82. Derks sums
up the views of both Herder and von Humboldt on the Greeks concisely:
"The pederasts, if they remain confined to the Greek world, are quite toler-
able as an early stage [*Vorstufe*] of higher human development, but are not
commensurate with our current advanced state" (82). Ironically, of course,
Winckelmann himself had been instrumental in forging such developmental
historical narratives.

15. Goethe's *Bildungsroman Wilhelm Meister's Apprenticeship*, published three years before Schlegel's *Lucinde*, marks a decisive step in the literary inscription of androgyny as an ideal of heterosexual complementarity.
See my essay "Pedagogy and Androgyny in *Wilhelm Meisters Lehrjahre*."

16. On the relationship between botany and androgyny, see Aurnhammer 177–200.

17. To my knowledge, Derks is the first critic to have acknowledged this

aspect of the novel, although he rather understates what he sees as its vaguely erotic suggestiveness (221).

18. On the Romantic intersection between the myth of androgyny and that of the "eternal feminine," see Hoeveler 11–14.

19. Feminist critics have rightly questioned the revolutionary potential of *Lucinde*. See, for example, Sigrid Weigel's essay on the aesthetic function of femininity in Schlegel's novel, "Wider die romantische Mode."

20. Stephan suggestively reads Kleist's correspondence in conjunction with his drama *Penthesilea*, though without explicit reference to androgyny ("'Da werden Weiber zu Hyänen'"). For a discussion of Kleist's shifting self-identification with Achilles and Penthesilea, see Zimmermann, esp. 263ff. These critics, who emphasize as I do the polymorphous sexual desire present in Kleist's letters, provide a corrective to such approaches as Edith Borchardt's. Borchardt denies the strong bisexual undercurrents to Kleistian androgyny in favor of a metaphysical, Jungian-inspired reading (188).

21. Kluckhohn (567), in his rich collection of sources on Romanticism and love, cites numerous negative responses to women perceived as androgynous, by, among others, Tieck, Brentano, and A. W. Schlegel. In my view, symptomatic of the dualistic vision of androgyny are the writings of Schleiermacher, who on the one hand, as I indicated above, posits androgyny as an ideal state transcending sexual difference, yet on the other hand is not slow to criticize androgyny as it is representationally actualized, for example in the works of Angelika Kauffmann, with their equivocal depictions of effeminate youths (*Athenäum* 1:264).

22. As Steakley notes, contained in the firsthand reports by male homosexuals published under the rubric "Zur Seelenkrankheitskunde" in the groundbreaking journal of psychology *Magazin zur Erfahrungsseelenkunde* (1783–93) is one couched in the idealizing rhetoric of Platonic androgyny: "I desired only the most precise union with him; indeed, in my rapturous seizures I wanted to draw myself into him completely, so that the two of us would make one person. Reason and religion, however, had too much influence on me for me to allow such forbidden wishes to emerge" (quoted in Steakley 172).

23. A similarly sensual atmosphere is evoked in Kleist's essay "About the Puppet Theatre" ("Über das Marionettentheater"), in which men openly admire one another's nude forms and merger-like relationships are envisioned between an adolescent and an older man as well as between puppet and puppeteer. On the homoeroticism present in this essay, see Schaefer, and Popp 139–40. In its presentation of the puppet or *Gliedermann*, an assemblage of limbs awaiting a future condition of wholeness, "Über das Marionettentheater" suggestively recalls Aristophanes' narrative of androgyny. Furthermore, the puppet's grace depends on the paradoxical coincidence between the algebraic precision of the puppetmaster and his own

elliptical movements, an aesthetic effect that might be compared with that produced by Winckelmann's androgynous statues. Herr C., commenting on this movement, remarks that whenever the puppet is directed in a straight line its limbs are already describing curves (2:339).

24. Dietrick 319. On Kleist as a practitioner of the fluid discursive practice *écriture féminine*, see Cixous and Clément, esp. 112–22, and Hoverland.

25. Here my reading of androgyny differs from that of Kari Weil, who in her book *Androgyny and the Denial of Difference* identifies Plato's treatment of the primal androgyne with Classical integrational aesthetics, and Ovid's account of Hermaphroditus with the anti-Classical critique and deconstruction of binarism.

Pfeiffer: Friendship and Gender

1. The "embracing and embraced" (*umschlingend und umschlungen*) is perhaps a parodistic allusion to the "embracing embraced" (*umfangend umfangen*) in Goethe's "Ganymede" (*HA* 1:47), a poem with its own homoerotic implications.

2. In her account of "romantic" friendship among English women of the eighteenth century, Lillian Faderman similarly rejects any clear distinction between the concepts of "friend" and "lover" (*Surpassing* 84, 142).

3. Kleist alludes to a passage from Shakespeare's *King Richard II*:

Or shall we play the wantons with our woes,
And make some pretty match with shedding tears;
As thus to drop them still upon one place
Till they have fretted us a pair of graves
Within the earth, and therein laid? "There lies
Two kinsmen digg'd their graves with weeping eyes." (3.3.164–69)

Kord: Eternal Love or Sentimental Discourse?

1. See Hohmann 22; Tubach 10, 37, 44–46, 58; Faderman, *Surpassing* 80–81, 148–55; Derks 40–41, 54, 157; Friedli 250; Hacker 249.

2. "Cross-living" is used to distinguish women who attempted to live, work, and/or marry as men from women who temporarily cross-dressed, even if they did so for enjoyment of male privileges, but made no attempt to pass for men (like Sidonia Hedwig Zäunemann or George Sand).

3. Similar reasoning pervades the laws that assumed an enlarged clitoris to be evidence of lesbian activity and justification for torture, the assumption being that "such unusual organs" could serve as replacement for the male member. See Crompton 20.

4. The court records of her case are available in translation by Brigitte Eriksson.

5. Irigaray's term is based on the different meanings of the word *homo*, which means "same" in Greek and "man" in Latin. She uses "hommosexuality," playing on the ambivalent meanings of *l'homme*, which like "man" or "der Mensch" at times pretends to include women, to refer to discussions of homosexuality that exclude lesbianism while claiming to be all-inclusive (de Lauretis 18). In my discussion, I will use the word "hommosexuality" to indicate male homosexuality (regardless of its frequent claims to inclusiveness in philosophical, scholarly, and legal contexts), "homosexuality" to mean same-sex love relationships regardless of gender, and "lesbianism" to mean love relationships between women.

6. "Über den Umgang unter Freunden," 130–61; "Über den Umgang mit und unter Verliebten," 81–94; "Von dem Umgange unter Eheleuten," 32–80.

7. Kluckhohn speaks of "male friendship" with "male" meaning "manly" rather than "between men" (181); Rasch's pioneering study on the cult of friendship in the eighteenth century lists only male couples in the table of contents and defines the purpose of friendship as "providing an outlet for the creative powers of male existence, which, owing to the historical situation at the time, were doomed to inefficiency, and which also could not find fulfillment in love for a woman" (101). Trunz, Rasch, Schenck, Salomon, and Mittner discuss male friendships exclusively; where friendship is contrasted with love (Trunz, Kluckhohn), the list of all-male friendships is supplemented with a corresponding list of male-female lovers.

8. See Maurer, Düntzer, Höfer, Petersen, Martin, Susmann, Hof, Voß, Kahn-Wallerstein, Boy-Ed, and Bode.

9. See Weber; and Becker-Cantarino, "Zur Theorie" 58–60.

10. See Fichte's "Erster Anhang des Naturrechts: Grundriß des Familienrechts"; Kant's "Die Metaphysik der Sitten" and "Anthropologie in pragmatischer Hinsicht"; Schiller's "Über Anmut und Würde"; Humboldt's "Plan einer vergleichenden Anthropologie," "Über den Geschlechtsunterschied," and "Über männliche und weibliche Form"; and Hegel's *Philosophie des Rechts. Die Vorlesung von 1819/20.* For a discussion of some of these texts, see Cocalis.

11. The most famous example is probably Schiller's "chaste housewife" in his monumental poem "Das Lied von der Glocke" (1799; 2:810–21).

12. For the purposes of this article, I would like to define "gender coherence" as adherence to the expectations of men and women formed in a heterocentric society, as outlined by Butler ("Gender Trouble, Feminist Theory" 339): the assumption that anatomical sex (XX- vs. XY-chromosome) determines gender (masculine vs. feminine) as well as sexual orientation. In this system, a bearer of the XX-chromosome is of the feminine gender; she

identifies with her own sex and desires the opposite. Gender dissonance is used to mean failure to adhere to the rules of gender coherence, for example homosexuality, homoeroticism, cross-dressing, cross-living, etc.

13. Butler, *Gender Trouble*, "Gender Trouble," "Imitation," "Performative Acts."

14. While recognizing the necessity to distinguish between Luise Adelgunde and Johann Christoph Gottsched, both subjects of scholarly inquiry, I find both "Luise" and "die Gottschedin" unacceptable for L. A. Gottsched. The widespread habit, especially in German scholarship, to refer to women writers by their first names implies the lower competence of women authors and cements their invisibility in literary history; the eighteenth-century designation of women authors ("die Gottschedin," "die Neuberin," "die Karschin") conveys "archaic" connotations, at least to students. Throughout this article, I will therefore refer to Luise Adelgunde Gottsched as Gottsched and to her husband as Johann Christoph or J. Chr. Gottsched.

15. On September 10, 1732 (1:45), she writes to him of "your future wife (whoever she may be)."

16. J. Chr. Gottsched, "Leben," unpag. J. Chr. Gottsched most frequently refers to his wife as his "industrious helper."

17. J. Chr. Gottsched, "Leben." For biographical information on Gottsched, see Sanders, " 'Ein kleiner Umweg' "; Kord, *Ein Blick* 276–83; Richel; Schlenther; Ploetz; and J. Chr. Gottsched.

18. Cf. Becker-Cantarino, *Der lange Weg* 259–78, "Luise Adelgunde Victorie Gottsched," and "Outsiders"; Bohm; Brüggemann, *Gottscheds Lebens- und Kunstreform*; Critchfield; Crüger; Danzel; Dawson, "Frauen und Theater"; J. Chr. Gottsched; Groß 1:28–43; Heckmann; Heitner; Kord, *Ein Blick* 44–48, 94–96, 276–83, 372–74; Petig; Ploetz; Richel; Robinson 115–34; Sanders, " 'Ein kleiner Umweg' " and "Virtuous Woman" 9–15, 51–94; Schlenther; and Schreiber 41–88.

19. As has been frequently and correctly pointed out, Sappho did not become a cultural symbol for female homoerotic tradition that could be said to parallel Socrates and the male tradition (Becker-Cantarino, "Zur Theorie" 59; Tubach 77–89; Linnhoff 116). Both Linnhoff and Tubach speculate that the reason for the failure of Sappho as a tradition-inspiring symbol lies in the repeated burnings of her works (in A.D. 380 and 1072) as Christianity gained hold in the Holy Roman Empire and homosexuality fell under the religious taboo. Both, however, fail to explain why this taboo did not affect Socrates. The difference in the historical treatment of Sappho the homosexual and Socrates the homosexual raises the question which part of Linnhoff's "double stigma" (loving a woman or being one) is more likely to invite social penalization.

20. Von Arnim, *Die Günderode* 49–50. The relationship between Ar-

nim and Günderrode is discussed at length by Tubach 178–262. Tubach quotes this letter on p. 240.

21. This trend is evident in most pedagogical literature of the early nineteenth century, especially in children's theater. See Kord, *Ein Blick* 217–25, and "Frauennatur und Kinderspiel."

22. The section on Caroline Pichler is an excerpt of my findings in "Caroline Pichler's Fictional Auto/Biographies."

23. Pichler also upheld an affectionate correspondence with women writers whom she had never met or knew only slightly, such as Therese Huber and Louise Brachmann.

24. Letter to Goethe, November 28, 1811, quoted in Sauer 2:255ff.

25. Unpublished letter to Zay, no date, quoted in Jansen 37.

26. Letter to Friedrich von Matthisson, March 26, 1829, quoted in Blümml's annotations to her *Denkwürdigkeiten* 1:594 n. 551.

27. See Pichler's eloquent defense of Brachmann's image in "Louise Brachmann."

28. The figures are the results of research for my book on the anonymity of German women writers in the eighteenth and nineteenth centuries, working title: *Sich einen Namen machen*.

Works Cited

Adler, Alfred. *Cooperation Between the Sexes: Writings on Women, Love and Marriage, Sexuality and Its Disorders.* Ed. and trans. H. L. Ansbacher and R. R. Ansbacher. Garden City, N.Y.: Anchor Books, 1978.

Adorno, Theodor. "Freudian Theory and the Pattern of Fascist Propaganda." In *Gesammelte Schriften*, ed. Rolf Tiedemann. Frankfurt: Suhrkamp, 1972. 8:408–33.

———. *Minima Moralia. Reflexionen aus dem beschädigten Leben.* Frankfurt: Suhrkamp, 1971.

———. "Zum Verhältnis von Soziologie und Psychologie." In *Gesammelte Schriften*, ed. Rolf Tiedemann. Frankfurt: Suhrkamp, 1972. 8:42–92.

Adorno, Theodor, and Max Horkheimer. *Dialectic of Enlightenment.* Trans. John Cuming. New York: Herder & Herder, 1972.

Allgemeines Landrecht für die Preussischen Staaten von 1794. Ed. H. Hattenhauer and G. Bernert. Frankfurt: A. Metzner, 1970.

Apel, Friedmar, ed. *Kleists Kohlhaas. Ein deutscher Traum vom Recht auf Mordbrennerei.* Berlin: Wagenbach, 1987.

Arato, Andrew, and Eike Gebhardt, eds. *The Essential Frankfurt School Reader.* New York: Continuum, 1985.

Arnim, Bettine von. *Goethe's Briefwechsel mit einem Kinde.* Ed. Walter Schmitz and Sibylle von Steinsdorff. Vol. 2 of *Werke und Briefe.* Frankfurt: Deutscher Klassiker, 1992.

———. *Die Günderode.* Leipzig: Insel, 1983.

Athenäum. Eine Zeitschrift. Ed. August Wilhelm Schlegel and Friedrich Schlegel. 3 vols. Berlin, 1798–1800.

Atkins, Stuart. *The Testament of Werther in Poetry and Drama.* Cambridge, MA: Harvard University Press, 1949.

Aurnhammer, Achim. *Androgynie. Studien zu einem Motiv in der europäischen Literatur.* Cologne: Böhlau, 1986.

Baader, Franz von. *Schriften.* Ed. Max Pulver. Leipzig: Insel, 1921.

Baeumer, Max L. "Winckelmanns Formulierung der klassischen Schönheit." *Monatshefte* 65 (1973): 61–75.

Barner, Wilfried. "Gelehrte Freundschaft im 18. Jahrhundert: Zu ihren traditionalen Voraussetzungen." In Mauser and Becker-Cantarino, 23–45.

Barthes, Roland. *A Lover's Discourse: Fragments.* Trans. Richard Howard. New York: Hill & Wang, 1978.

Bateson, Gregory, ed. *Perceval's Narrative: A Patient's Account of His Psychosis, 1830–1832.* Stanford: Stanford University Press, 1961.

———. "Section of Psychology" (January 18, 1943). *Transactions of the New York Academy of Sciences,* ser. 2, 4, no. 1 (Nov. 1943): 72–78.

Becker-Cantarino, Barbara. "Caroline Pichler und die Frauendichtung." *Modern Austrian Literature* 12, nos. 3–4 (1979): 1–23.

———. *Der lange Weg zur Mündigkeit. Frau und Literatur (1500–1800).* Stuttgart: Metzler, 1987.

———. "Luise Adelgunde Victorie Gottsched." In *Women Writers of Germany, Austria, and Switzerland: An Annotated Bio-Bibliographical Guide,* ed. Elke Frederiksen. New York: Greenwood Press, 1989. 86.

———. "Outsiders: Women in German Literary Culture of Absolutism." *Jahrbuch für Internationale Germanistik* 16, no. 2 (1985): 147–57.

———. "Patriarchy and German Enlightenment Discourse: From Goethe's *Wilhelm Meister* to Horkheimer and Adorno's *Dialectic of Enlightenment.*" In *Impure Reason: Dialectic of Enlightenment in Germany,* ed. W. Daniel Wilson and Robert C. Holub. Detroit: Wayne State University Press, 1993. 48–64.

———. "Priesterin und Lichtbringerin: Zur Ideologie des weiblichen Charakters in der Frühromantik." In *Die Frau als Heldin und Autorin. Neue kritische Ansätze zur deutschen Literatur,* ed. Wolfgang Paulsen. Bern and Munich: Francke, 1979. 111–24.

———. "Schlegels *Lucinde*: Zur Frauenbild der Frühromantik." *Colloquia Germanica* 10 (1976–77): 128–39.

———. "Zur Theorie der literarischen Freundschaft im 18. Jahrhundert am Beispiel der Sophie La Roche." In Mauser and Becker–Cantarino, 47–74.

Behler, Ernst. *Friedrich Schlegel.* Hamburg: Rowohlt, 1966.

———. "Friedrich Schlegel: *Lucinde* (1799)." In *Romane und Erzählungen der deutschen Romantik. Neue Interpretationen,* ed. Paul Michael Lützeler. Stuttgart: Reclam, 1981. 98–124.

Bennett, Benjamin. "Prometheus and Saturn: Three Versions of Götz von Berlichingen." *German Quarterly* 58 (1985): 335–47.

The Holy Bible. Revised Standard Version. New York: New American Library, 1974.

Blanchot, Maurice. "La littérature et le droit à la mort." In *La part du feu.* Paris: Gallimard, 1949. 293–331.

Blümml, Emil Karl. "Einleitung" to *Denkwürdigkeiten aus meinem Leben,* by Caroline Pichler. Munich: Müller, 1914. 1:vii–lxxvii.

Bode, Wilhelm. *Charlotte von Stein.* Berlin: Mittler, 1920.

Bohm, Arnd. "Authority and Authorship in Luise Adelgunde Gottsched's *Das Testament.*" *Lessing Yearbook* 18 (1986): 129–40.

Bohrer, Karl-Heinz. *Der romantische Brief. Die Entstehung ästhetischer Subjektivität.* Munich: Hanser, 1987.

Bonjour, Edgar, ed. *Johannes von Müller. Briefe in Auswahl.* Basel: Benno Schwabe, 1953.

Borchardt, Edith. *Mythische Strukturen im Werk Heinrich von Kleists.* New York: Lang, 1987.

Boy-Ed, Ida. *Das Martyrium der Charlotte von Stein. Versuch ihrer Rechtfertigung.* Stuttgart: Cotta, 1920.

Bräker, Ulrich. *Der arme Mann im Tockenburg.* Munich: Winkler, 1965.

Bredbeck, Gregory W. "Milton's Ganymede: Negotiations of the Homoerotic Tradition in *Paradise Regained.*" *PMLA* 106 (1991): 262–76.

Brinker-Gabler, Gisela, ed. *Deutsche Dichterinnen vom 16. Jahrhundert bis zur Gegenwart. Gedichte und Lebensläufe.* Frankfurt: Fischer, 1978.

Bronfen, Elisabeth. *Over Her Dead Body: Death, Femininity, and the Aesthetic.* New York: Routledge, 1992.

Brüggemann, Fritz, ed. *Der Anbruch der Gefühlskultur in den fünfziger Jahren.* Darmstadt: Wissenschaftliche Buchgesellschaft, 1966.

——, ed. *Gottscheds Lebens- und Kunstreform in den zwanziger und dreißiger Jahren. Gottsched, Breitinger, die Gottschedin, die Neuberin.* Leipzig: Reclam, 1935.

Bullough, Vern L., and Bonnie Bullough. *Cross Dressing, Sex, and Gender.* Philadelphia: University of Pennsylvania Press, 1993.

Butler, Judith. "Critically Queer." *Gay and Lesbian Quarterly* 1 (1993): 17–32.

——. *Gender Trouble: Feminism and the Subversion of Identity.* New York: Routledge, 1990.

——. "Gender Trouble, Feminist Theory, and Psychoanalytic Discourse." In *Feminism/Postmodernism,* ed. Linda J. Nicholson. New York: Routledge, 1990. 324–40.

——. "Imitation and Gender Insubordination." In Fuss, *Inside/Out,* 13–31.

——. "Performative Acts and Gender Constitution: An Essay in Phenomenology and Feminist Theory." In *Performing Feminisms: Feminist Critical Theory and Theatre,* ed. Sue-Ellen Case. Baltimore: Johns Hopkins University Press, 1990. 270–82.

Butler, Judith, and Joan W. Scott, eds. *Feminists Theorize the Political.* New York: Routledge, 1992.

Campe, Joachim, ed. *Andere Lieben. Homosexualität in der deutschen Literatur.* Frankfurt: Suhrkamp, 1988.

———. *Über die früheste Bildung junger Kinderseelen.* Ed. B. H. E. Niestroj. Frankfurt: Ullstein, 1985.

Caroline. *Briefe aus der Frühomantik.* Ed. Erich Schmidt. 2 vols. Leipzig: Insel, 1913.

Casanova de Seingalt, Jacques. *Histoire de ma vie.* Vol. 7. Wiesbaden: Brockhaus, 1961.

Castle, Terry. *The Apparitional Lesbian: Female Homosexuality and Modern Culture.* New York: Columbia University Press, 1993.

Cixous, Hélène, and Catherine Clément. *The Newly Born Woman.* Trans. Betsy Wing. Minneapolis: University of Minnesota Press, 1986.

Cocalis, Susan. "Der Vormund will Vormund sein: Zur Problematik der weiblichen Unmündigkeit im 18. Jahrhundert." In *Gestaltet und gestaltend. Frauen in der deutschen Literatur,* ed. Marianne Burkhard. Amsterdam: Rodopi, 1980. 33–55.

Cohen, Ed. "Who Are 'We'? Gay 'Identity' as Political (E)motion (A Theoretical Rumination)." In Fuss, *Inside/Out,* 71–92.

Cornelius, Auguste. *Platen in Venedig: Original-Lustpiel in einem Aufzuge. Dramaturgische Probleme, Entwickelungen und Kritiken zur Förderung und Belehrung dramatischer Dichter und darstellender Künstler* (ed. H[einrich] Th[eodor] Rötscher) 3 (1865): 17–26.

Critchfield, Richard. "Beyond Luise Gottsched's 'Die Pietisterey im Fischbein-Rocke oder die Doctormässige Frau.' " *Jahrbuch für Internationale Germanistik* 17, no. 2 (1985): 112–20.

Crompton, Louis. "The Myth of Lesbian Impunity: Capital Laws from 1270 to 1791." *Journal of Homosexuality* 6, nos. 1–2 (1980–81): 11–25.

Crüger, Johannes, comp. *Joh. Christoph Gottsched und die Schweizer Joh. J. Bodmer und Joh. J. Breitinger.* Darmstadt: Wissenschaftliche Buchgesellschaft, 1965.

Cullens, Chris, and Dorothea von Mücke. "Love in Kleist's *Penthesilea* and *Käthchen von Heilbronn.*" *Deutsche Vierteljahrsschrift* 63 (1989): 461–93.

Damm, Sigrid. *Vögel, die verkünden Land. Das Leben des Jakob Michael Reinhold Lenz.* Frankfurt: Insel Verlag, 1989.

Danzel, Th. W., ed. *Gottsched und seine Zeit. Auszüge aus seinem Briefwechsel zusammengestellt und erläutert.* Hildesheim: Olms, 1970.

Dawson, Ruth. "Frauen und Theater: Vom Stegreifspiel zum bürgerlichen Rührstück." In *Deutsche Literatur von Frauen,* ed. Gisela Brinker-Gabler. Munich: Beck, 1988. 1:421–34, 508–10, 551–52.

———. "Reconstructing Women's Literary Relationships: Sophie Albrecht and Female Friendship." In *In the Shadow of Olympus: German Women Writers Around 1800*, ed. Katherine Goodman and Edith Waldstein. Albany: State University of New York Press, 1992. 173–87.

DeJean, Joan, and Nancy K. Miller, eds. *Displacements: Women, Tradition, Literatures in French*. Baltimore: Johns Hopkins University Press, 1991.

Dekker, Rudolf M., and Lotte C. van de Pol. "Republican Heroines: Cross-Dressing Women in the French Revolutionary Armies." *History of European Ideas* 10 (1989): 353–63.

de Lauretis, Teresa. "Sexual Indifference and Lesbian Representation." In *Performing Feminisms: Feminist Critical Theory and Theatre*, ed. Sue-Ellen Case. Baltimore: Johns Hopkins University Press, 1990. 17–39.

Deleuze, Gilles, and Felix Guattari. *Anti-Oedipus: Capitalism and Schizophrenia*. Trans. Robert Hurley et al. Minneapolis: University of Minnesota Press, 1983.

Dellamora, Richard. *Masculine Desire: The Sexual Politics of Victorian Aestheticism*. Chapel Hill: University of North Carolina Press, 1990.

Derks, Paul. *Die Schande der heiligen Päderastie. Homosexualität und Öffentlichkeit in der deutschen Literatur, 1750–1850*. Berlin: Rosa Winkel, 1990.

Derrida, Jacques. *Dissemination*. Trans. Barbara Johnson. Chicago: University of Chicago Press, 1981.

———. *Of Grammatology*. Trans. Gayatri Chakravorty Spivak. Baltimore: Johns Hopkins University Press, 1976.

Dietrick, Linda. "Immaculate Conceptions: The Marquise von O . . . and the Swan." *Seminar* 27 (1991): 316–29.

Dollimore, Jonathan. *Sexual Dissidence: Augustine to Wilde, Freud to Foucault*. Oxford: Oxford University Press, 1991.

Domoradzki, Eva. *Und alle Fremdheit ist verschwunden. Status und Funktion des Weiblichen im Werk Friedrich Schlegels. Zur Geschlechtigkeit einer Denkform*. Innsbruck: Verlag des Instituts für Sprachwissenschaft der Universität Innsbruck, 1982.

———. "Und er erschuf die Frau nach seiner Sehnsucht: Zum Weiblichkeitsentwurf in Friedrich Schlegels Frühwerk unter besonderer Berücksichtigung des Romans *Lucinde*." In *Der widerspenstigen Zähmung. Studien zur bezwungenen Weiblichkeit in der Literatur vom Mittelalter bis zur Gegenwart*, ed. Sylvia Wallinger and Monika Jonas. Innsbruck: Innsbrucker Beiträge zur Kulturwissenschaft, 1986. 169–84.

Dotzler, Bernhard J. " 'Seht doch wie ihr vor Eifer schäumet . . .': Zum männlichen Diskurs über Weiblichkeit um 1800." *Jahrbuch der Deutschen Schiller-Gesellschaft* 30 (1986): 339–82.

Duden, Barbara. "Das schöne Eigentum: Zur Herausbildung des bürgerlichen Frauenbildes an der Wende vom 18. zum 19. Jahrhundert." *Kursbuch* 47 (1977): 125–40.

Düntzer, Heinrich. *Charlotte von Stein. Goethes Freundin.* 2 vols. Stuttgart: Cotta, 1874.

Eckermann, Johann Peter. *Gespräche mit Goethe in den letzten Jahren seines Lebens.* Munich: Beck, 1984.

Eder, Anna-Maria. "Die Metamorphose der Frau: Zur Funktion der Frauenfiguren in Friedrich Schlegels *Lucinde.*" In ". . . *Das Weib wie es seyn sollte.*" *Aspekte zur Frauenliteraturgeschichte,* ed. Anna-Maria Eder, Edda Klesel, and Beate Rattay. Fußnoten zur neueren deutschen Literatur 9. Bamberg, 1986. 55–65.

Eichenbaum, Luise, and Susie Orbach. *Between Women: Love, Envy, and Competition in Women's Friendships.* New York: Viking Press, 1988.

Eichner, Hans. "Neues aus Friedrich Schlegels Nachlaß." *Jahrbuch der Deutschen Schiller-Gesellschaft* 3 (1959): 21–43.

Eissler, Kurt Robert. *Goethe: A Psychoanalytic Study, 1775–1786.* 2 vols. Detroit: Wayne State University Press, 1963.

Ellis, John M. "The Vexed Question of Egmont's Political Judgement." In *Tradition and Creation,* ed. C. P. Magill et al. Leeds: Maney, 1978. 116–30.

Engel, Manfred. *Der Roman der Goethezeit.* Stuttgart: Metzler, 1993.

Eriksson, Brigitte, trans. "A Lesbian Execution in Germany, 1721: The Trial Records." In *Historical Perspectives on Homosexuality,* ed. Salvatore J. Licata and Robert P. Petersen. New York: Haworth, 1981. 27–40.

Die Erotika und Priapea aus den Sammlungen Goethes. Ed. Gerhard Femmel and Christoph Meckel. Frankfurt: Insel, 1990.

Ewers, Hanns Heinz. *Horst Wessel. Ein deutsches Schicksal.* Stuttgart and Berlin: J. G. Cotta'sche Buchhandlung Nachfolger, 1943.

Faderman, Lillian. "Female Romantic Friendship." In *Encyclopedia of Homosexuality,* ed. Wayne R. Dynes. New York: Garland, 1990. 1:438–42.

———. *Surpassing the Love of Men: Romantic Friendship and Love Between Women from the Renaissance to the Present.* New York: Morrow, 1981.

Farago, Ladislas, ed. *German Psychological Warfare: Survey and Bibliography.* New York: Committee for National Morale, 1941.

Femmel, Gerhard, ed. *Corpus der Goethezeichnungen.* 3 vols. Leipzig: Seeman, 1965.

Ferris, Lesley, ed. *Crossing the Stage: Controversies on Cross-Dressing.* London: Routledge, 1993.

Firchow, Peter, trans. *Lucinde and the Fragments,* by Friedrich Schlegel. Minneapolis: University of Minnesota Press, 1971.

Fischer, Caroline Auguste. *Justine.* In *Werde, die du bist! Zwischen Anpassung und Selbstbestimmung. Texte deutschsprachiger Schriftstellerinnen des 19. Jahrhunderts,* ed. Gisela Henckmann. Munich: Goldmann, 1993. 15–39.

Fischer, Peter. "Familienauftritte: Goethes Phantasiewelt und die Konstruktion des Werther-Romans." *Psyche* 40, no. 6 (June 1986): 527–56.

Flower MacCannell, Juliet. *The Regime of the Brother: After the Patriarchy.* New York: Routledge, 1991.

Foucault, Michel. *Discipline and Punish: The Birth of the Prison.* Trans. Alan Sheridan. New York: Vintage Books, 1979.

———. *The History of Sexuality.* Trans. Robert Hurley. 3 vols. New York: Pantheon Books, 1978–86.

Freud, Sigmund. *The Standard Edition of the Complete Psychological Works.* Ed. and trans. James Strachey. 24 vols. London: Hogarth, 1953. Cited as *SE*.

Friedli, Lynne. " 'Passing Women': A Study of Gender Boundaries in the Eighteenth Century." In G. S. Rousseau and Porter, 234–60.

Friedrichsmeyer, Sara. *The Androgyne in Early German Romanticism: Friedrich Schlegel, Novalis, and the Metaphysics of Love.* New York: Lang, 1983.

———. "The Subversive Androgyne." *Women in German Yearbook* 3 (1986): 63–74.

Frühsorge, Gotthardt. "Freundschaftliche Bilder: Zur historischen Bedeutung der Bildnissammlung im Gleimhaus zu Halberstadt." In *Theatrum Europaeum. Festschrift für Elida Maria Szarota*, ed. R. Brinkmann et al. Munich: Wilhelm Fink, 1982. 429–52.

Fuhrmann, Helmut. "Der schwankende Paris: 'Bild' und 'Gestalt' der Frau in Werk Goethes." *Jahrbuch des Freien Deutschen Hochstifts* (1989): 37–126.

Fuss, Diana. *Essentially Speaking: Feminism, Nature, and Difference.* New York: Routledge, 1989.

———, ed. *Inside/Out: Lesbian Theories, Gay Theories.* New York: Routledge, 1991.

Gallas, Helga, and Magdalene Heuser, eds. *Untersuchungen zum Roman von Frauen um 1800.* Tübingen: Niemeyer, 1990.

Gerard, Kent, and Gert Hekma, ed. *The Pursuit of Sodomy: Male Homosexuality in Renaissance and Enlightenment Europe.* New York: Harrington Park Press, 1989.

Gilbert, Sandra. "Costumes of the Mind: Transvestism as Metaphor in Modern Literature." In *Writing and Sexual Difference*, ed. Elizabeth Abel. Chicago: University of Chicago Press, 1982. 193–219.

Gilman, Sander L. "Goethe's Touch: Touching, Seeing, and Sexuality." In *Inscribing the Other.* Lincoln: University of Nebraska Press, 1991. 29–49.

———. *Sexuality: An Illustrated History.* New York: John Wiley, 1989.

Gilmore, David D. *Manhood in the Making: Cultural Concepts of Masculinity.* London: Yale University Press, 1990.

Glantschnig, Helga. *Liebe als Dressur. Kindererziehung in der Aufklärung.* Frankfurt: Campus, 1987.

Goebbels, Joseph. *Michael. Ein deutsches Schicksal in Tagebuchblättern.* Munich: Zentralverlag der NSDAP, Franz Eher Nachfolger, 1929.

Goethe, Johann Wolfgang von. *Early Verse Drama and Prose Plays.* Ed. Cyrus Hamlin and Frank Ryder. Goethe's Collected Works 7. New York: Suhrkamp, 1988.

———. *Erotische Gedichte. Gedichte, Skizzen und Fragmente.* Ed. Andreas Ammer. Frankfurt: Insel, 1991.

———. *Sämtliche Werke nach Epochen seines Schaffens. Münchner Ausgabe.* Ed. Karl Richter, Herbert G. Göpfert, Norbert Miller, and Gerhard Sauder. 24 vols. to date. Munich: Carl Hanser, 1985. Cited as *MA.*

———. *Werke. Hamburger Ausgabe in 14 Bänden.* Ed. Erich Trunz. Munich: Beck, 1982. Cited as *HA.*

———. *Werke. Herausgegeben im Auftrage der Großherzogin Sophie von Sachsen. Weimarer Ausgabe.* 143 vols. in 4 secs. Weimar: Böhlau, 1887–1919. Cited as *WA.*

———. *West-Eastern Divan—Westöstlicher Divan.* Trans. J. Whaley. London: Wolff, 1974.

Goette, Alexander. *Über den Ursprung des Todes.* Hamburg: Leopold Voss, 1883.

Göttert, Margit. " 'Chloe liebte Olivia . . .': Frauenbeziehungen als Gegenstand historischer Forschung." In *Frauengeschichte. Gesucht—gefunden? Auskünfte zum Stand der historischen Frauenforschung,* ed. Beate Fieseler and Birgit Schulze. Köln: Böhlau, 1991. 92–111.

Gottsched, Johann Christoph. "Leben." In Luise Adelgunde Gottsched, *Der Frau Luise Adelgunde Victoria Gottschedinn, geb. Kulmus, sämmtliche Kleinere Gedichte, nebst dem, von vielen vornehmen Standespersonen, Gönnern und Freunden beyderley Geschlechtes, Ihr gestifteten Ehrenmale, und Ihrem Leben, herausgegeben von Ihrem hinterbliebenen Ehegatten,* ed. Johann Christoph Gottsched. Leipzig: B. C. Breitkopf, 1763.

Gottsched, Luise Adelgunde. *Briefe der Frau Luise Adelgunde Gottsched gebohrne Kulmus.* Ed. Dorothea Henriette von Runckel. 3 vols. Dresden: Harpeterische Schriften, 1771–72.

Graham, Ilse. *Goethe and Lessing: The Wellsprings of Creation.* London: Paul Elek, 1973.

———. "Götz von Berlichingen's Right Hand." *German Life and Letters* 16 (1962–63): 212–28.

Greis, Jutta. *Drama Liebe. Zur Entstehungsgeschichte der modernen Liebe im Drama des 18. Jahrhunderts.* Stuttgart: Metzler, 1991.

Grimm, Jacob, and Wilhelm Grimm. *Deutsches Wörterbuch.* Ed. Karl Euling. 16 vols. Leipzig: Hirzel, 1936.

Groß, Heinrich, ed. *Deutsche Dichterinen und Schriftstellerinen in Wort und Bild.* 3 vols. Berlin: F. Thiel, 1885.

Grunwaldt. "Das erotische Moment im Rekrutenleben." *Soldatentum,* 1937, 31–36.

Günther, Egon. *Lenz* (radio version). Saarländischer Rundfunk and Ostdeutscher Rundfunk Brandenburg, 1992.

Gustafson, Susan E. *Absent Mothers and Orphaned Fathers: Narcissism and Abjection in Lessing's Aesthetic and Dramatic Production.* Detroit: Wayne State University Press, 1994.

Habermas, Jürgen. *The Structural Transformation of the Public Sphere.* Trans. Thomas Burger. Cambridge, Mass.: MIT Press, 1989.

Hacker, Hanna. *Frauen und Freundinnen. Studien zur 'weiblichen Homosexualität' am Beispiel Österreich, 1870–1938.* Weinheim: Beltz, 1987.

Haffner, Herbert. *Lenz. Der Hofmeister, Die Soldaten.* Munich: Oldenburg, 1979.

Hahn, Barbara. *Unter falschem Namen. Von der schwierigen Autorschaft der Frauen.* Frankfurt: Suhrkamp, 1991.

Haller, Albrecht von. *Primae lineae physiologiae in usum praelectionum academicarum nunc quarto conscriptae emedatae et pluribus animadversionibus auctae ab Henrico Augusto Wrisberg.* Göttingen: Vandenhoeck, 1780.

Halperin, David M. *One Hundred Years of Homosexuality and Other Essays on Greek Love.* New York: Routledge, 1990.

Hanselmann, Beat. *Johann Wilhelm Ludwig Gleim und seine Freundschaften, oder der Weg nach Arkadien.* Bern: Peter Lang, 1989.

Harris, Daniel. "Androgyny: The Sexist Myth in Disguise." *Women's Studies* 2 (1974): 171–84.

Hausen, Karin. "Die Polarisierung der 'Geschlechtskaraktere': Eine Spiegelung der Dissoziation von Erwerbs- und Familienleben." In *Sozialgeschichte der Familie in der Neuzeit Europas,* ed. Werner Conze. Stuttgart: Ernst Klett, 1976. 363–93.

Heckmann, Hannelore. "Auf der Suche nach einem Verleger: Aus Gottscheds Briefwechsel." *Daphnis: Zeitschrift für Mittlere Deutsche Literatur* 17, no. 2 (1988): 327–45.

Heilbrun, Carolyn. *Toward a Recognition of Androgyny.* New York: Knopf, 1964.

Heine, Heinrich. *Poetry and Prose.* Ed. Jost Hermand and Robert Holub. German Library 32. New York: Continuum, 1982.

Heitner, Robert. *German Tragedy in the Age of Enlightenment: A Study in the Development of Original Tragedies, 1724–1768.* Berkeley: University of California Press, 1968.

Hekma, Gert. "Homosociality." In *Encyclopedia of Homosexuality,* ed. Wayne R. Dynes. New York: Garland, 1990. 1:560–62.

——. "Sodomites, Platonic Lovers: The Backgrounds of the Modern Homosexual." *Journal of Homosexuality* 16 (1988): 433–55.

Helvig, Amalie von. *Die Schwestern von Lesbos. Die Tageszeiten. Die Schwestern auf Corcyra.* Stockholm: Bruzelius, 1818.

Henking, Karl. *Johannes von Müller.* 2 vols. Stuttgart: J. G. Cotta'sche Buchhandlung Nachfolger, 1928.

Herder, Johann Gottfried. *Sämtliche Werke.* Ed. Bernhard Suphan. 33 vols. Berlin: Weimannsche Buchhandlung, 1877–1913.

Herdt, Gilbert H. "Semen Transactions in Sambia Culture." In *Ritualized Homosexuality in Melanesia,* ed. G. Herdt. Berkeley: University of California Press, 1984. 167–210.

Heuser, Magdalene. " 'Das beständige Angedencken vertritt die Stelle der Gegenwart': Frauen und Freundschaften in Briefen der Frühaufklärung und Empfindsamkeit." In Mauser and Becker-Cantarino, 141–65.

——. "Das Musenchor mit neuer Ehre zieren: Schriftstellerinnen zur Zeit der Frühaufklärung." In *Deutsche Literatur von Frauen,* ed. Gisela Brinker-Gabler. Munich: Beck, 1988. 1:293–313, 496–99, 536–39.

Hoeveler, Diane Long. *Romantic Androgyny: The Women Within.* University Park: Pennsylvania State University Press, 1990.

Hof, Walter. *Goethe und Charlotte von Stein.* Frankfurt: Insel, 1979.

Höfer, Edmund. *Goethe und Charlotte von Stein.* Berlin: B. Behr, 1923.

Hoff, Dagmar von. *Dramen des Weiblichen. Deutsche Dramatikerinnen um 1800.* Opladen: Westdeutscher Verlag, 1989.

Hoffmann, Volker. "Elisa und Robert, oder das Weib und der Mann, wie sie sein sollten: Anmerkungen zur Geschlechtercharakteristik der Goethezeit." In *Klassik und Moderne,* ed. Karl Richter and Jörg Schönert. Stuttgart: Metzler, 1983. 80–97.

Hoffmeister, Gerhart, ed. *Goethes Mignon und ihre Schwestern. Interpretationen und Rezeption.* New York: Peter Lang, 1993.

Hohmann, Joachim S. "Der unterdrückte Sexus: Zu einer Geschichte der Homosexualität in Deutschland." In *Der unterdrückte Sexus. Historische Texte und Kommentare zur Homosexualität,* ed. Joachim S. Hohmann. Fulda: Lollar, 1977. 17–58.

Hölderlin, Friedrich. *Poems and Fragments.* Trans. Michael Hamburger. Cambridge: Cambridge University Press, 1980.

——. *Sämtliche Werke.* Ed. Friedrich Beißner. 8 vols. Stuttgart: Kohlhammer, 1943–85.

Hollander, Anne. *Seeing Through Clothes.* New York: Avon Books, 1980.

Honour, Hugh. *Neo-classicism.* Harmondsworth, Eng.: Penguin, 1977.

Hoverland, Lilian. "Heinrich von Kleist and Luce Irigaray: Visions of the Feminine." In *Gestaltet und gestaltend — Frauen in der deutschen Literatur,* ed. Marianne Burkhard. Special issue of *Amsterdamer Beiträge zur neueren Germanistik* 10 (1980). 57–83.

Huber, Therese. "Briefe Huber an Karoline Pichler." Ed. Karl Glossy. *Jahrbuch der Grillparzer-Gesellschaft* 7 (1907): 190–291.

Hudgkins, Esther. "Das Geheimnis der *Lucinde*-Struktur: Goethes 'Die Metamorphose der Pflanzen.'" *German Quarterly* 49 (1976): 295–311.

Humboldt, Wilhelm von. *Werke*. Ed. Andreas Flitner and Klaus Giel. 5 vols. Stuttgart: Cotta, 1960.

Jansen, Lena. *Karoline Pichlers Schaffen und Weltanschauung im Rahmen ihrer Zeit*. Graz: Wächter, 1936.

Jean Paul. *Werke in drei Bänden*. Ed. Norbert Miller. Munich: Hanser, 1986.

Jones, James W. *"We of the Third Sex": Literary Representations of Homosexuality in Wilhelmine Germany*. New York: Lang, 1990.

Jung-Stilling, Johann Heinrich. *Lebensgeschichte*. Frankfurt: Insel, 1983.

Kahn-Wallerstein, Carmen. "Charlotte von Stein und Goethe." *Goethe-Kalender*, 1932, 108–37.

Kant, Immanuel. "Beantwortung der Frage 'Was ist Aufklärung?'" In *Was ist Aufklärung? Kant, Erhard, Hamann, Herder, Lessing, Mendelssohn, Riem, Schiller, Wieland*, ed. Ehrhard Bahr. Stuttgart: Reclam, 1981. 9–17.

Kaschnitz, Marie Luise. "Egmont und Klärchen" (1954). In *Zwischen Immer und Nie: Gestalten und Themen der Dichtung*. Frankfurt: Insel, 1971. 99–109.

Kieffer, Bruce. *The Storm and Stress of Language: Linguistic Catastrophe in the Early Works of Goethe, Lenz, Klinger, and Schiller*. University Park: Pennsylvania State University Press, 1986.

Kittler, Friedrich A. *Discourse Networks 1800/1900*. Trans. Michael Metteer, with Chris Cullens. Stanford: Stanford University Press, 1990.

Kleist, Heinrich von. *Sämtliche Werke und Briefe*. Ed. Helmut Sembdner. 2d ed. 2 vols. Munich: Hanser, 1961.

Klopstock, Friedrich Gottlieb. *Ausgewählte Werke*. Ed. Karl August Schleiden. Munich: Hanser, 1962.

Kluckhohn, Paul. *Die Auffassung der Liebe in der Literatur des 18. Jahrhunderts und in der deutschen Romantik*. 3d ed. Tübingen: Max Niemeyer, 1966.

Knigge, Adolph Freiherr von. *Über den Umgang mit Menschen*. Nendeln, Liecht.: KTO Press, 1978. Vol. 2. (Reprint of the 5th ed., Hannover: Christian Ritscher, 1796.)

Kölpin, Alexander Bernhard. *Abhandlung von dem innern Bau der weiblichen Brüste*. Berlin, 1767.

Kontje, Todd. "Private Life in the Public Sphere: Heinrich Jung-Stilling's *Lebensgeschichte*." *Colloquia Germanica* 21, no. 4 (1988): 275–87.

Kord, Susanne. *Ein Blick hinter die Kulissen. Deutschsprachige Dramatikerinnen im 18. und 19. Jahrhundert*. Stuttgart: Metzler, 1992.

———. "Frauennatur und Kinderspiel: Zur geschlechtsspezifischen Sozialisation in Kinderdramen weiblicher Autoren, 1820–1865." *Jahrbuch des Freien Deutschen Hochstifts* (1994): 221–53.

——. "'Und drinnen waltet die züchtige Hausfrau'? Caroline Pichler's Fictional Auto/Biographies." *Women in German Yearbook* 8 (1993): 141–58.

Körte, Wilhelm. *Johann Wilhelm Ludewig Gleims Leben. Aus seinen Briefen und Schriften.* Halberstadt: Büreau für Literatur und Kunst, 1811.

Kuzniar, Alice A. "Hearing Women's Voices in *Heinrich von Ofterdingen.*" *PMLA* 107 (1992): 1196–1207.

——. "Labor Pains: Romantic Theories of Creativity and Gender." Forthcoming.

——. "Reassessing Romantic Reflexivity: The Case of Novalis." *Germanic Review* 63 (1988): 77–86.

Lacan, Jacques. *Écrits: A Selection.* Trans. Alan Sheridan. New York: W. W. Norton, 1977.

——. *The Four Fundamental Concepts of Psycho-Analysis.* Ed. Jacques-Alain Miller; trans. Alan Sheridan. New York: W. W. Norton, 1981.

Laqueur, Thomas. *Making Sex: Body and Gender from the Greeks to Freud.* Cambridge, Mass.: Harvard University Press, 1990.

Langen, August. *Der Wortschatz des deutschen Pietismus.* 2d ed. Tübingen: Niemeyer, 1968.

Lenz, J. M. R. *Werke und Briefe.* Ed. Sigrid Damm. 3 vols. Munich: Hanser, 1987.

——. *Philosophische Vorlesungen für empfindsame Seelen.* Ed. Christoph Weiß. Mörlenbach: Röhrig, 1994.

Lessing, Gotthold Ephraim. *Werke.* Vol. 2. Ed. Gerd Hillen. Munich: Hanser, 1971.

Leuschner, Brigitte. "Freundschaft als Lebensgestaltung bei Therese Heyne: Schwärmen und gut handeln." In Mauser and Becker-Cantarino, 195–212.

Linck, Dirk. *Halbweib und Maskenbildner. Subjektivität und schwule Erfahrung im Werk Josef Winklers.* Berlin: Rosa Winkel, 1993.

Linnhoff, Ursula. "Das zweifache Stigma: Zu einer Kulturgeschichte lesbischen Sexualverhaltens." In *Der unterdrückte Sexus. Historische Texte und Kommentare zur Homosexualität,* ed. Joachim S. Hohmann. Fulda: Lollar, 1977. 113–27.

Littlejohns, Richard. "The 'Bekenntnisse eines Ungeschickten': A Reexamination of Emancipatory Ideas in Friedrich Schlegel's *Lucinde.*" *Modern Language Review* 72 (1977): 605–14.

Lorenz, Angelika. *Das deutsche Familienbild in der Malerei des 19. Jahrhunderts.* Darmstadt: Wissenschaftliche Buchgesellschaft, 1985.

Luhmann, Niklas. *Love as Passion: The Codification of Intimacy.* Cambridge, Mass.: Harvard University Press, 1986.

MacLeod, Catriona. "Pedagogy and Androgyny in *Wilhelm Meisters Lehrjahre.*" *Modern Language Notes* 108 (1993): 389–426.

Maggiore, Dolores J. "Lesbianism." In *Encyclopedia of Homosexuality*, ed. Wayne R. Dynes. New York: Garland, 1990. 1:708–21.

Martens, Wolfgang. *Die Botschaft der Tugend. Die Aufklärung im Spiegel der deutschen moralischen Wochenschriften.* Stuttgart: Metzler, 1971.

Martin, Bernhard. *Goethe und Charlotte von Stein. Gnade und Tragik in ihrer Freundschaft.* Kassel: Bärenreiter, 1949.

Mattenklott, Gert. Review of *Die Schande der heiligen Päderastie*, by Paul Derks. *Forum Homosexualität und Literatur* 10 (1990): 93–95.

Maurer, Doris. *Charlotte von Stein. Ein Frauenleben der Goethezeit.* Bonn: Keil, 1985.

Mauser, Wolfram. "Freundschaft und Verführung: Zur inneren Widersprüchlichkeit von Glücksphantasien im 18. Jahrhundert. Ein Versuch." In Mauser and Becker-Cantarino, 213–35.

Mauser, Wolfram, and Barbara Becker-Cantarino, eds. *Frauenfreundschaft—Männerfreundschaft. Literarische Diskurse im 18. Jahrhundert.* Tübingen: Niemeyer, 1991.

Mayer, Hans. *Outsiders: A Study in Life and Letters.* Trans. Denis Sweet. Cambridge, Mass.: MIT Press, 1982.

Menninghaus, Winfried, ed. *Friedrich Schlegel. Theorie der Weiblichkeit.* Frankfurt: Insel, 1982.

———. *Unendliche Verdopplung. Die frühromantische Grundlegung der Kunsttheorie im Begriff absoluter Selbstreflexion.* Frankfurt: Suhrkamp, 1987.

Meyer-Kalkus, Reinhart. "Werthers Krankheit zum Tode: Pathologie und Familie in der Empfindsamkeit." In *Urszenen. Literaturwissenschaft als Diskursanalyse und Diskurskritik*, ed. Friedrich A. Kittler and Horst Turk. Frankfurt: Suhrkamp, 1977. 76–138.

Meyer-Knees, Anke. *Verführung und sexuelle Gewalt. Untersuchung zum medizinischen und juristischen Diskurs im 18. Jahrhundert.* Tübingen: Stauffenburg, 1992.

Meyer-Krentler, Eckhardt. *Der Bürger als Freund. Ein sozial-ethisches Programm und seine Kritik in der neueren deutschen Erzählliteratur.* Munich: Fink, 1984.

Miller, Nancy K. *Getting Personal: Feminist Occasions and Other Autobiographical Acts.* New York: Routledge, 1991.

———. *Subject to Change: Reading Feminist Writing.* New York: Columbia University Press, 1988.

———, ed. *The Poetics of Gender.* New York: Columbia University Press, 1986.

Mittner, Ladislao. "Freundschaft und Liebe in der deutschen Dichtung des 18. Jahrhunderts." In *Stoffe, Formen, Strukturen. Studien zur deutschen*

Literatur, ed. Albert Fuchs and Helmut Motekat. Munich: Max Hueber, 1962. 97–138.

Mohr, Heinrich. "Freundschaftliche Briefe — Literatur oder Privatsache? Der Streit um Wilhelm Gleims Nachlaß." *Jahrbuch des Freien Deutschen Hochstifts* (1973): 14–75.

Moritz, Karl Philipp. "Aussichten zu einer Experimentalseelenlehre." In *Werke*, ed. Horst Günther. Frankfurt: Insel, 1981. 3:85–99.

———. *Magazin zur Erfahrungsseelenkunde als ein Lesebuch für Gelehrte und Ungelehrte*. Nördlingen: Greno, 1986.

Mosse, George. *Nationalism and Sexuality: Respectability and Abnormal Sexuality in Modern Europe*. New York: Howard Fertig, 1985.

Mücke, Dorothea E. von. *Virtue and the Veil of Illusion: Generic Innovation and the Pedagogical Project in Eighteenth-Century Literature*. Stanford: Stanford University Press, 1991.

Müller, Friedrich von. *Unterhaltungen mit Goethe*. Ed. Ernst Grumach. Weimar: Böhlau, 1956.

Müller, Johannes von. *Sämmtliche Werke*. 26 vols. Ed. Johann Georg Müller. Tübingen, 1810.

Müller, Klaus. *Aber in meinem Herzen sprach eine Stimme so laut. Homosexuelle Autobiographien und medizinische Pathographien im neunzehnten Jahrhundert*. Berlin: Rosa Winkel, 1991.

Müller-Sievers, Helmut. "Writing Off: Goethe and the Meantime of Erotic Poetry." *Modern Language Notes* 108 (1993): 427–45.

Nägele, Rainer. "Götz von Berlichingen." In *Goethes Dramen. Neue Interpretationen*, ed. Walter Hinderer. Stuttgart: Reclam, 1980. 65–77.

Naumann, Ursula, ed. *Lucinde: Ein Roman. Mit Friedrich Schleiermachers "Vertrauten Briefen über Friedrich Schlegels Lucinde."* Munich: Goldmann, 1985.

Niestroj, Brigitte H. E. "Die Mutter-Kind-Beziehung im Kontinuum von Neuzeit und Moderne." In Joachim Heinrich Campe, *Über die früheste Bildung junger Kinderseelen*, ed. B. H. E. Niestroj. Frankfurt: Ullstein, 1985. 7–52.

Niggl, Günther. *Geschichte der deutschen Autobiographie im 18. Jahrhundert*. Stuttgart: Metzler, 1977.

Novalis. *Werke, Tagebücher und Briefe Friedrich von Hardenbergs*. Ed. Hans-Joachim Mähl and Richard Samuel. 3 vols. Munich: Hanser, 1978–87.

Parker, Kevin. "Winckelmann, Historical Difference, and the Problem of the Boy." *Eighteenth-Century Studies* 25 (1992): 523–44.

Paulys Realencyclopädie der classischen Altertumswissenschaft. Repr. Munich: Druckenmüller, 1972.

Petersen, Julius. "Goethe und Charlotte v. Stein." In *Aus der Goethezeit*.

Gesammelte Aufsätze zur Literatur des klassischen Zeitalters. Leipzig: Quelle & Meyer, 1932. 19–48.

Petig, William E. "Forms of Satire in Antipietistic Dramas." *Colloquia Germanica* 18, no. 3 (1985): 257–63.

Pfeiffer, Joachim. *Die zerbrochenen Bilder. Gestörte Ordnungen im Werk Heinrich von Kleists.* Würzburg: Königshausen & Neumann, 1989.

Pfotenhauer, Helmut. *Literarische Anthropologie. Selbstbiographien und ihre Geschichte am Leitfaden des Leibes.* Stuttgart: Metzler, 1987.

Phelan, Shane. "(Be)Coming Out: Lesbian Identity and Politics." *Signs* 18 (1993): 765–90.

Physische Abhandlung von der mütterlichen Pflicht des Selbststillens und ihrem Einfluß auf das Wohl des Staates. Nach der Vorschrift des Herrn D. Tissot und anderer berühmten Aerzte. Augsburg: Eberhard Kletts Wittwe & Franck, 1788.

Pichler, Caroline. "Briefe von Caroline Pichler an Therese Huber." Ed. Karl Glossy. *Jahrbuch der Grillparzer-Gesellschaft* 3 (1893): 269–365.

——. *Denkwürdigkeiten aus meinem Leben.* 2 vols. Munich: Müller, 1914.

——. "Kindererziehung." In *Zerstreute Blätter aus meinem Schreibtische.* Vienna: A. Pichler, 1836. 51–68.

——. "Louise Brachmann." In *Zerstreute Blätter,* 179–90.

——. *Sämtliche Werke.* 60 vols. Vienna: A. Pichler, 1828–45.

——. "Therese von Artner." In *Zerstreute Blätter,* 191–208.

Plato. *Symposium.* Trans. Alexander Nehemas and Paul Woodruff. Indianapolis: Hackett, 1989.

Ploetz, H. A. "Ein Lebensbild: Adelgunde Gottsched, geb. Culmus (1713–1762)." *Geistige Arbeit: Zeitung aus der wissenschaftlichen Welt* 2, no. 15 (1935): 12.

Pockels, Carl Friedrich. *Versuch einer Charakteristik des weiblichen Geschlechts. Ein Sittengemählde des Menschen, des Zeitalters und des geselligen Lebens.* 5 vols. Hannover: Christian Ritscher, 1797–1802.

Politzer, Heinz. "Auf der Suche nach Identität: Zu Heinrich von Kleists Würzburger Reise." *Euphorion* 61 (1967): 383–99.

Pomezny, Franz. *Grazie und Grazien in der deutschen Dichtung des 18. Jahrhunderts.* Hamburg and Leipzig: Leopold Voss, 1900.

Popp, Wolfgang. *Männerliebe. Homosexualität und Literatur.* Stuttgart: Metzler, 1992.

Poster, Mark. *Critical Theory of the Family.* New York: Continuum, 1986.

Prandi, Julie D. *Spirited Women Heroes: Major Female Characters in the Dramas of Goethe, Schiller, and Kleist.* Frankfurt: Lang, 1983.

Rasch, Wolfdietrich. *Freundschaftskult und Freundschaftsdichtung im deutschen Schrifttum des 18. Jahrhunderts vom Ausgang des Barock bis zu Klopstock.* Halle: Max Niemeyer, 1936.

Reed, Terence James. "Iphigenies Unmündigkeit: Zur weiblichen Aufklärung." In *Germanistik. Forschungsstand und Perspektiven. Vorträge des Deutschen Germanistentages 1984*, ed. Georg Stötzel. Vol. 2: *Ältere Deutsche Literatur. Neuere Deutsche Literatur*. Berlin: Walter de Gruyter, 1985. 505–24.

Rehm, Walther, ed. *Winckelmann Briefe*. 4 vols. Berlin: Walter de Gruyter, 1952–57.

Richel, Veronica C. "Luise Gottsched: A Reconsideration." Ph.D. diss., Yale University, 1968.

Richter, Simon. "Ästhetischer und medizinischer Diskurs im 18. Jahrhundert: Herder und Haller über Reiz." *Lessing Yearbook* 27 (1993): 83–95.

———. *Laocoon's Body and the Aesthetics of Pain: Winckelmann, Lessing, Herder, Moritz, Goethe*. Detroit: Wayne State University Press, 1992.

Richter, Simon, and Patrick McGrath. "Representing Homosexuality: Winckelmann and the Aesthetics of Friendship." *Monatshefte* 86 (1994): 45–58.

Rickels, Laurence. *Aberrations of Mourning: Writing on German Crypts*. Detroit: Wayne State University Press, 1988.

———. "Camp." *Modern Language Notes* 108 (1993): 484–99.

———. *The Case of California*. Baltimore: Johns Hopkins University Press, 1991.

Rihm, Werner. *Das Bildungserlebnis der Antike bei Johannes von Müller*. Basel and Stuttgart: Helbing & Lichtenhahn, 1959.

[Robinson, Therese]. *Deutschlands Schriftstellerinnen bis vor hundert Jahren. Von Talvj* [pseud.]. *Historisches Tagebuch* 32 (1861): 1–141.

Ronell, Avital. *Crack Wars: Literature, Addiction, Mania*. Lincoln: University of Nebraska Press, 1992.

Rousseau, G. S. *Perilous Enlightenment: Pre- and Post-modern Discourses, Sexual, Historical*. Manchester: Manchester University Press, 1990.

———. "The Pursuit of Homosexuality in the Eighteenth Century: 'Utterly Confused Category' and/or Rich Repository?" In *'Tis Nature's Fault: Unauthorized Sexuality During the Enlightenment*, ed. Robert Purks MacCubbin. Cambridge: Cambridge University Press, 1987. 132–68.

Rousseau, G. S., and Roy Porter, eds. *Sexual Underworlds of the Enlightenment*. Manchester: Manchester University Press, 1987.

Rousseau, Jean-Jacques. *Emile*. Trans. Barbara Foxley. London: J. M. Dent, 1993.

Rubin, Gayle. "The Traffic in Women: Notes on the Political Economy of Sex." In *Toward an Anthropology of Women*, ed. Rayna Reiter. New York: Monthly Review Press, 1975. 157–210.

Rudolf, Ottomar. *Jacob Reinhold Michael Lenz. Moralist und Aufklärer*. Bad Homburg: Gehlen, 1970.

Ryder, Frank. "Toward a Revaluation of Goethe's Götz: Features of Recurrence." *PMLA* 79 (1964): 58–66.

Sachs, Hanns. "The Delay of the Machine Age." Trans. Margaret J. Powers. *Psychoanalytic Quarterly* 11, nos. 3–4 (1933): 404–24.

Sadger, Isidor. *Heinrich von Kleist. Eine pathographisch-psychologische Studie*. Wiesbaden: Bergmann, 1910.

Salomon, Albert. "Die Freundschaftskultur des 18. Jahrhunderts in Deutschland." *Zeitschrift für Soziologie* 8 (1979): 280–308.

Sanders, Ruth Hetmanski. " 'Ein kleiner Umweg': Das literarische Schaffen der Luise Gottsched." In *Die Frau von der Reformation zur Romantik. Die Situation der Frau vor dem Hintergrund der Literatur- und Sozialgeschichte*, ed. Barbara Becker-Cantarino. Bonn: Bouvier, 1980. 170–94.

———. "The Virtuous Woman in the Comedies of the Early Enlightenment." Ph.D. diss., SUNY/Stonybrook, 1975.

Sanna, Simonetta. "Schlegels *Lucinde*, oder der ästhetische Roman." *Deutsche Vierteljahrsschrift* 61 (1987): 457–79.

Sauer, A. *Goethe und Österreich*. 2 vols. Weimar: Goethe-Gesellschaft, 1902–4.

Schaefer, Margret. "Kleist's 'About the Puppet Theatre' and the Narcissism of the Artist." *American Imago* 32 (1975): 366–88.

Schenck, Ernst von, ed. *Briefe der Freunde. Das Zeitalter Goethes im Spiegel der Freundschaft*. Berlin: Die Runde, 1937.

Schenzinger, Karl Aloys. *Hitlerjunge Quex*. Berlin: Zeitgeschichte, 1932.

Schiller, Friedrich. *Sämtliche Werke*. Ed. Gerhard Fricke and Herbert G. Göpfert. 5 vols. Munich: Hanser, 1973–74.

Schindel, Carl Wilhelm Otto August von. *Die deutschen Schriftstellerinnen des neunzehnten Jahrhunderts*. 3 vols. Leipzig: F. A. Brockhaus, 1823–25.

Schings, Hans-Jürgen. *Melancholie und Aufklärung*. Stuttgart: Metzler, 1977.

Schlegel, Friedrich. *Kritische Ausgabe*. Ed. Ernst Behler and Hans Eichner. 35 vols. to date. Munich: Schöningh, 1958–. Cited as *KA*.

———. *Literary Notebooks, 1797–1801*. Ed. Hans Eichner. Toronto: University of Toronto Press, 1957.

Schleiermacher, Friedrich Daniel Ernst. *Kritische Gesamtausgabe*. Sec. 5, vol. 2. Berlin: Walter de Gruyter, 1988.

Schlenther, Paul. *Frau Gottsched und die bürgerliche Komödie. Ein Kulturbild aus der Zopfzeit*. Berlin: Wilhelm Hertz, 1886.

Schmidt-Linsenhoff, Viktoria, ed. *Sklavin oder Bürgerin? Französische Revolution und Neue Weiblichkeit, 1760–1830*. Frankfurt: Historisches Museum, 1989.

Schneider, Helmut. "Bürgerliche Idylle. Studien zu einer literarischen Gat-

tung des 18. Jahrhunderts am Beispiel von Johann Heinrich Voss."
Ph.D. diss., Rheinische Friedrich-Wilhelms-Universität, Bonn, 1975.

Schöffler, Herbert. "Die Leiden des jungen Werther" (1938). In *Deutscher Geist im 18. Jahrhundert.* Göttingen: Vandenhoek & Ruprecht, 1956. 155–81.

Scholtz-Novak, Sigrid Gerda. "Images of Womanhood in the Works of German Female Dramatists, 1892–1918." Ph.D. diss., University of Michigan, 1973.

Schreiber, Sara Etta. *The German Woman in the Age of Enlightenment: A Study in the Drama from Gottsched to Lessing.* New York: King's Crown Press, 1948.

Schwarz, Gudrun. " 'Mannweiber' in Männertheorien." In *Frauen suchen ihre Geschichte. Historische Studien zum 19. und 20. Jahrhundert,* ed. Karin Hausen. Munich: C. H. Beck, 1987. 64–82.

Sedgwick, Eve Kosofsky. *Between Men: English Literature and Male Homosocial Desire.* New York: Columbia University Press, 1985.

———. *Epistemology of the Closet.* Berkeley: University of California Press, 1990.

Seiffert, Hans Werner, ed. *Wielands Briefwechsel.* 5 vols. Berlin: Akademie, 1983.

Sengle, Friedrich. *Wieland.* Stuttgart: Metzler, 1949.

Sill, Bernhard. *Androgynie und Geschlechtsdifferenz nach Franz von Baader. Eine anthropologisch-ethische Studie.* Regensburg: Friedrich Pustet, 1986.

Silverman, Kaja. *Male Subjectivity at the Margins.* New York: Routledge, 1992.

Sørensen, Bengt Algot. *Herrschaft und Zärtlichkeit. Der Patriarchalismus und das Drama im 18. Jahrhundert.* Munich: Beck, 1984.

Spickernagel, Ellen. " 'Helden wie zarte Knaben oder verkleidete Mädchen': Zum Begriff der Androgynität bei Johann Joachim Winckelmann und Angelika Kauffmann." In *Frauen. Weiblichkeit. Schrift,* ed. Renate Berger et al. Special issue of *Argument,* no. 134 (1985). 99–118.

Spuler, Richard. "*Lucinde*: Roman des Romans." *Colloquia Germanica* 16 (1983): 166–76.

Stafford, Barbara Maria. *Body Criticism: Imaging the Unseen in Enlightenment Art and Medicine.* Cambridge, Mass.: MIT Press, 1992.

Stahl, John Daniel. "Literature and Propaganda: The Structure of Conversion in Schenzinger's *Hitlerjunge Quex.*" *Studies in 20th Century Literature* 12, no. 2 (1988): 129–47.

Steakley, James D. "Sodomy in Enlightenment Prussia: From Execution to Suicide." In Gerard and Hekma, 163–75.

Stephan, Inge. " 'Daß ich Eins und doppelt bin . . .': Geschlechtertausch als literarisches Thema." In Stephan and Weigel, *Die verborgene Frau*, 153–75.

——. " 'Da werden Weiber zu Hyänen . . .': Amazonen und Amazonenmythen bei Schiller und Kleist." In *Feministische Literaturwissenschaft*, ed. Inge Stephan and Sigrid Weigel. Special issue of *Argument*, no. 120 (1984). 22–42.

——. " 'So ist die Tugend ein Gespenst': Frauenbild und Tugendbegriff im bürgerlichen Trauerspiel bei Lessing und Schiller." *Lessing Yearbook* 17 (1985): 1–20.

Stephan, Inge, and Sigrid Weigel. *Die verborgene Frau. Sechs Beiträge zu einer feministischen Literaturwissenschaft*. Berlin: Argument, 1983.

——, eds. *Die Marseillaise der Weiber. Frauen, die Französische Revolution und ihre Rezeption*. Literatur im historischen Prozeß, n.s., 26. Hamburg: Argument, 1989.

Stimpson, Catherine R. "The Androgyne and the Homosexual." *Women's Studies* 2 (1974): 237–48.

Stone, Lawrence. *The Family, Sex, and Marriage in England, 1500–1800*. New York: Harper & Row, 1979.

Straub, Kristina. "The Guilty Pleasures of Female Theatrical Cross-Dressing and the Autobiography of Charlotte Charke." In *Body Guards: The Cultural Politics of Gender Ambiguity*, ed. Julia Epstein and Kristina Straub. New York: Routledge, 1991. 142–66.

Streller, Siegfried, ed. *Heinrich von Kleist. Werke und Briefe in vier Bänden*. Berlin: Aufbau, 1978.

Susmann, Margarethe. *Deutung einer großen Liebe. Goethe und Charlotte von Stein*. Zürich: Artemis, 1957.

Sweet, Denis M. "The Personal, the Political, and the Aesthetic: Johann Joachim Winckelmann's German Enlightenment Life." In Gerard and Hekma, 147–62.

Szondi, Peter. *Poetik und Geschichtsphilosophie*. Vol. 1. Frankfurt: Suhrkamp, 1974.

Tabes dorsalis; or, The Cause of Consumption in Young Men and Women. London: M. Copper, W. Reeve & C. Sympson, 1752.

Taiminen, Tero, Tuuli Salmenpera, and Klaus Lehtinen. "A Suicide Epidemic in a Psychiatric Hospital." *Suicide and Life-threatening Behavior* 22, no. 3 (1992): 350–63.

Tellenbach, H. "The Suicide of the 'Young Werther' and the Consequences for the Circumstances of Suicide and Endogenic Melancholics." *Israel Annals of Psychiatry and Related Disciplines* 15, no. 1 (1977): 16–21.

Tenbruck, Friedrich H. "Freundschaft: Ein Beitrag zu einer Soziologie der persönlichen Beziehungen." *Kölner Zeitschrift für Soziologie und Sozialpsychologie* 16 (1964): 431–56.

Theweleit, Klaus. *Male Fantasies*. Volume 1: *Women, Floods, Bodies, History*. Trans. Stephen Conway. Minneapolis: University of Minnesota Press, 1987.

——. *Male Fantasies*. Volume 2: *Male Bodies—Psychoanalyzing the White Terror*. Trans. Erica Carter and Chris Turner. Minneapolis: University of Minnesota Press, 1989.

Thürmer-Rohr, Christina. *Vagabundinnen. Feministische Essays*. Berlin: Orlanda Frauenverlag, 1987.

Thürmer-Rohr, Christina, et al., eds. *Mittäterschaft und Entdeckungslust*. Berlin: Orlanda Frauenverlag, 1990.

Tobin, Robert. "Faust's Membership in Male Society: Prometheus and Ganymede as Models." In *Interpreting Goethe's Faust Today*, ed. Thomas Saine. Columbia, S.C.: Camden House, 1994. 17–28.

——. "Healthy Families: Medicine, Patriarchy, and Heterosexuality in Eighteenth-Century German Novels." In *Impure Reason: Dialectic of Enlightenment in Germany*, ed. W. Daniel Wilson and Robert C. Holub. Detroit: Wayne State University Press, 1993. 242–59.

Todd, Janet. *Women's Friendships in Literature*. New York: Columbia University Press, 1980.

Trumbach, Randolph. "London's Sapphists: From Three Sexes to Four Genders in the Making of Modern Culture." In *Body Guards: The Cultural Politics of Gender Ambiguity*, ed. Julia Epstein and Kristina Straub. New York: Routledge, 1991. 112–41.

——. "Sodomitical Subcultures, Sodomitical Roles, and the Gender Revolution of the Eighteenth Century: The Recent Historiography." In *'Tis Nature's Fault: Unauthorized Sexuality During the Enlightenment*, ed. Robert Purks MacCubbin. Cambridge, Eng.: Cambridge University Press, 1987. 109–21.

——. "Sodomy Transformed: Aristocratic Libertinage, Public Reputation, and the Gender Revolution of the 18th Century." *Journal of Homosexuality* 19, no. 2 (1990): 105–24.

Trung, Erich. "Seelische Kultur: Eine Betrachtung über Freundschaft, Liebe und Familiengefühl im Schrifttum der Goethezeit." *Deutsche Vierteljahrsschrift* 24 (1950): 214–42.

Tubach, Sally Patterson. "Female Homoeroticism in German Literature and Culture." Ph.D. diss., University of California, Berkeley, 1980.

Vaget, Hans Rudolf. *Goethe—Der Mann von 60 Jahren. Mit einem Anhang über Thomas Mann*. Königstein: Athenäum, 1982.

Varnhagen, Rahel. *Briefwechsel*. Munich: Winkler, 1979. Vol. 3.

Vicinus, Martha. "'They Wonder to Which Sex I Belong': The Historical Roots of the Modern Lesbian Identity." In *The Lesbian and Gay Studies Reader*, ed. Henry Abelove, Michèle Aina Barale, and David M. Halperin. New York: Routledge, 1993. 432–52.

Villaume, Peter. *Ueber die Unzuchtsünden in der Jugend*. Wolfenbüttel: In der Schulbuchhandlung, 1787.

Vollhaber, Tomas. *Das Nichts. Die Angst. Die Erfahrung: Untersuchungen zur zeitgenössischen schwulen Literatur*. Berlin: Rosa Winkel, 1987.

Voß, Lena. *Goethes unsterbliche Freundin (Charlotte von Stein). Eine psychologische Studie an der Hand der Quellen*. Leipzig: Klinkhardt & Biermann, 1922.

Wagener, Hans, ed. *Erläuterungen und Dokumente. Johann Wolfgang Goethe, "Egmont."* Stuttgart: Reclam, 1974.

Wagner, Irmgard. "Vom Mythos zum Fetisch: Die Frau als Erlöserin in Goethes klassischen Dramen." In *Weiblichkeit in geschichtlicher Perspektive. Fallstudien und Reflexionen zu Grundproblemen der historischen Frauenforschung*, ed. Ursula A. J. Becher and Jörn Rüsen. Frankfurt: Suhrkamp, 1988. 234–58.

Waldeck, Marie-Luise. "Klärchen: An Examination of Her Role in Goethe's *Egmont*." *Publications of the English Goethe Society*, n.s., 35 (1965): 68–91.

Walker, Barbara G. *The Woman's Encyclopedia of Myths and Secrets*. San Francisco: Harper, 1983.

Walter, Eva. *Schrieb oft, von Mägde Arbeit müde: Lebenszusammenhänge deutscher Schriftstellerinnen um 1800 — Schritte zur bürgerlichen Weiblichkeit. Mit einer Bibliographie zur Sozialgeschichte von Frauen 1800–1914 von Ute Daniel*. Ed. Annette Kuhn. Düsseldorf: Schwann, 1985.

Waters, Michael. "Frau Gottsched's 'Die Pietisterey im Fischbein-Rocke': Original, Adaptation, or Translation?" *Forum for Modern Language Studies* 2 (1975): 252–67.

Weber, Marianne. *Die Frauen und die Liebe*. Königstein: Karl Robert Langewiesche, 1935.

Weber, Samuel. "Introduction to the 1988 Edition." Trans. Benjamin Gregg. In Daniel Paul Schreber, *Memoirs of My Nervous Illness*, trans. and ed. Ida Macalpine and Richard A. Hunter. Cambridge, Mass.: Harvard University Press, 1988. vii–liv.

Weeks, Jeffrey. "Inverts, Perverts, and Mary-Annes: Male Prostitution and the Regulation of Homosexuality in England in the Nineteenth and Early Twentieth Centuries." *Journal of Homosexuality* 6 (1980–81): 113–34.

———. *Sex, Politics, and Society: The Regulation of Sexuality Since 1800*. London: Longman, 1981.

Weigel, Sigrid. "Der schielende Blick: Thesen zur Geschichte weiblicher Schreibpraxis." In Stephan and Weigel, *Die verborgene Frau*, 83–137.

———. "Wider die romantische Mode: Zur ästhetischen Funktion des Weiblichen in Friedrich Schlegels *Lucinde*." In Stephan and Weigel, *Die verborgene Frau*, 67–82.

Weil, Kari. *Androgyny and the Denial of Difference*. Charlottesville: University Press of Virginia, 1992.

Weinholz, Gerhard. *Heinrich von Kleist. Deutsches Dichtergenie, kämpfender Humanist, preußisches Staatsopfer*. Essen: Blaue Eule, 1993.

Wells, G. A. "Götz von Berlichingen: History, Drama, and Dramatic Effectiveness." *Publications of the English Goethe Society* 56 (1985–86): 74–96.

Westphal, Carl. "Die conträre Sexualempfindung: Symptom eines neuropathischen (psychopathischen) Zustandes." *Archiv für Psychiatrie und Nervenkrankheiten* 2 (1869): 73–108.

Widdig, Bernd. *Männerbünde und Massen. Zur Krise männlicher Identität in der Literatur der Moderne*. Opladen: Westdeutscher Verlag, 1992.

Wieland, Christoph Martin. *Geschichte des Agathon*. 1st ver. Stuttgart: Reclam, 1981.

——. *Musarion, oder die Philosophie der Grazien*. Stuttgart: Reclam, 1979.

Wild, Reiner. *Die Vernunft der Väter. Zur Psychographie von Bürgerlichkeit und Aufklärung in Deutschland am Beispiel ihrer Literatur für Kinder*. Stuttgart: Metzler, 1987.

Wilkinson, Elizabeth M. "The Relation of Form and Meaning in Goethe's *Egmont*" (1949). In *Goethe: Poet and Thinker*. London: Arnold, 1962. 55–74.

Wilson, W. Daniel. "Dramen zum Thema der Französischen Revolution." In *Goethe-Handbuch*, vol. 1: *Lyrik und Dramen*, ed. Theo Buck, Regine Otto, and Bernd Witte. Stuttgart: Metzler, 1995.

——. "Hunger/Artist: Goethe's Revolutionary Agitators in *Götz, Stayros, Egmont*, and *Der Bürgergeneral*." *Monatshefte* 86 (1994): 80–94.

——. "Zwischen Kritik und Affirmation: Militärphantasien und Geschlechterdisziplinierung bei J. M. R. Lenz." In *"Unaufhörlich Lenz gelesen. . . ." Studien zum Leben und Werk von J. M. R. Lenz*, ed. Inge Stephan and Hans-Gerd Winter. Stuttgart: Metzler, 1994. 52–85.

Winckelmann, Johann Joachim. *Abhandlung von der Fähigkeit des Empfindung des Schönen in der Kunst. Kleine Schriften, Vorreden, Entwürfe*. Ed. Walther Rehm. Berlin: Walter de Gruyter, 1968.

——. *Briefe*. Ed. Walther Rehm. 4 vols. Berlin: Walter de Gruyter, 1952–57.

——. *Geschichte der Kunst des Alterthums*. Dresden: In der Waltherischen Hof-Buchhandlung, 1764.

——. *Kleine Schriften und Briefe*. Ed. Wilhelm Senff. Weimar: Böhlaus Nachfolger, 1960.

——. *Sämtliche Werke*. Ed. Joseph Eiselein. 12 vols. Donauöschingen: Verlag Deutscher Classiker, 1825–29. Cited as *SW*.

Wingertszahn, Christof. *Ambiguität und Ambivalenz im erzählerischen*

Werk Achims von Arnim. Mit einem Anhang unbekannter Texte aus Arnims Nachlaß. St. Ingbert: Röhrig, 1990.

Wittels, Fritz. "Heinrich von Kleist — Prussian Junker and Creative Genius." *American Imago* 11 (1954): 11–31.

Wolf, Ferdinand. "Nachwort" to *Denkwürdigkeiten aus meinem Leben*, by Caroline Pichler. Munich: Müller, 1914. 2:389–91.

Woodward, Carolyn. " 'My Heart So Wrapt': Lesbian Disruptions in Eighteenth-Century British Fiction." *Signs* 18 (1991): 838–65.

Wurst, Karin, ed. *Frauen und Drama im achtzehnten Jahrhundert, 1770–1800*. Cologne: Böhlau, 1991.

Zantop, Susanne. "Caroline Auguste Fischer (1764–1842)." In *Bitter Healing: German Women Writers, 1700–1830 — An Anthology*, ed. Jeannine Blackwell and Susanne Zantop. Lincoln: University of Nebraska Press, 1990. 351–53.

——. "Trivial Pursuits? An Introduction to German Women's Writing from the Middle Ages to 1830." In *Bitter Healing*, 9–50.

Zelle, Carsten. "Zur 'Quérelle du théâtre' in der Frühaufklärung: Eine englisch-französisch-deutsche Literaturbeziehung." *Arcadia: Zeitschrift für vergleichende Literaturwissenschaft* 19, no. 2 (1984): 165–69.

Zimmermann, Hans Dieter. *Kleist, die Liebe und der Tod*. Frankfurt: Athenäum, 1989.

Library of Congress Cataloging-in-Publication Data

Outing Goethe and his age / edited by Alice A. Kuzniar.
    p.   cm.
    Includes bibliographical references.
    ISBN 0-8047-2614-0 (alk. paper). — ISBN 0-8047-2615-9 (pbk. :
alk. paper)
    1. Goethe, Johann Wolfgang von, 1749–1832 — Criticism and
interpretation.   2. German literature — 19th century — History and
criticism.   3. Homosexuality in literature.   I. Kuzniar, Alice A.
PT2200.H65O98   1996
831'.6 — dc20   95-36492
                                               CIP

⊗ This book is printed on acid-free, recycled paper.

Original printing 1996
Last figure below indicates year of this printing:
05 04 03 02 01 00 99 98 97 96